Endorsements

"Father Paul Roberts' story resonates with the reader on a core level. It doesn't matter if you are Catholic, Buddhist, or atheist, his story will speak to you about the myriad joys and sorrows which weave through the fabric of our humanity in this shared experience we call life. It is the voice of one man speaking from the heart which has the power to touch and impact all of our hearts on a deeply personal level."
~ Stephen and Ondrea Levine, authors of
Becoming Kuan Yin: The Evolution of Compassion

"*Bless Me Father For They Have Sinned* is a must read for anyone who wants to catch a more intimate look at the infrastructure of the Catholic Church. With his memoir, Father Paul Roberts offers us a historically relevant, yet compassionate and humorous, account of the inner workings of the oldest corporation in the world.

"This memoir introduces us to a man's life journey, from childhood, through the preparations for the seminary, the pitfalls on the spiritual path, to his maturation and commitment to entering the ancient order of priests.

"*Bless Me Father For They Have Sinned* does not shy away from the day-to-day encounters with sensual temptations, boundary violations, and alcohol abuse. The reader has a ringside seat as these men and women grapple with mental health issues, struggle with questioning power structures, instigate changes to training and rehabilitation protocols, and try to bring their venerable church into alignment with a contemporary modus operandi."
~ Ralph Steele, M.A., author of
Tending the Fire: Through War and the Path of Meditation

"An exciting journey into life in the Roman Catholic Church, a remarkable account of details and events. A wonderful book full of insight into the inner workings of the church. The author obviously has a broad and deep understanding of what makes people (and organizations) work, or not, as the case may be."

~ L.R. Sheridan, author of
Eyes of a Sociopath

"Thank you for giving me this opportunity to write about a book which I believe is a gift to the world. I also left my religion with no bitterness, as Father Paul seems to have done and can relate to his story—I believe him. Instead of being judgmental—he is simply stating the facts. I am confident this will come across to Catholics and non-Catholics alike."

~ Mary Myers

Bless Me Father

For They Have Sinned

Father Paul Roberts

Bless Me Father

For They Have Sinned

Copyright © 2015 by Father Paul Roberts

All rights reserved. No part of this book may be used or reproduced by any means, graphic, electronic, or mechanical, including photocopying, recording, taping, or by any information storage retrieval system without the written permission of the publisher or author, except in the case of brief quotations embodied in critical articles and reviews.

ISBN: 978-0-9822331-7-7
ISBN: 0982233175
Library of Congress Control Number: 2015935606

Cover and Text Design by: Miko Radcliffe

Sacred Life Publishers™
SacredLife.com
Printed in the United States of America

Dedication

*For all of you young men and women of courage
who seek the Divine in all beings and experiences,
and who strive to serve that Presence
with idealism and a listening
heart full of Love,
this is for you.*

Introduction

This is the true story of my life as a Roman Catholic Priest. Names have been changed in order to preserve the privacy of the identities of those involved in my story.

For many people, the words "Roman Catholic Priest" evoke a sense of the unknown and of the mysterious. Most people can only imagine and wonder about what goes on behind the closed doors of the Catholic Church. I am going to open those doors for you. For those of you who have ever wondered about what happens in the seminary to turn a man into a priest, or how we really handle celibacy, or what we talk about when there are no parishioners to hear us . . . and what it all has to do with God.

Follow along with me on this journey and I will answer those questions for you. I am inviting you to walk with me down the hidden corridors of this institution, where the un-ordained are forbidden to tread. You will see what I saw in its rooms and halls and nooks and crannies–the unconditional love and the appalling indifference, the selfless sharing and the coldhearted selfishness, the ageless wisdom and the dreadful ignorance, the noble deeds and the petty acts. I will tell it to you exactly as it happened to me.

My journey starts out in the zeal and innocence of my youth, and as we travel my path into maturity I will share with you all that I have learned–about myself, about all of you as we share in this experience of life, about the Divine Presence, and about the Catholic Church. I will answer your questions, unravel the mysteries, bring the secrets to light, and the unknown will become known.

See the Church through the eyes of this priest . . . for the truth always sets us free.

Contents

Endorsements

Dedication v

Introduction vii

Chapter 1   I Want to Fly 1

Chapter 2   Dropping out of the Sky in Flames 9

Chapter 3   The Rigors of Seminary 15

Chapter 4   God Calling and St. Francis 23

Chapter 5   San Francisco Here I Come 41

Chapter 6   The Feast of St. Francis and
             The Miracle of the Bees 53

Chapter 7   Jesus Moments: Meeting the Saints 63

Chapter 8   Welcome to Diocesan Seminary: Hell Part 1 and
             and My First Exorcism 75

Chapter 9   Welcome to Diocesan Seminary:
             Hell Part 2.5 87

Chapter 10   Burning Coals and Losing My Fruit of the Looms 99

Chapter 11   Crossing Over into the Twilight Zone:
             Meeting The Devil, Again 109

Chapter 12   Anything Goes 127

Chapter 13   The Sign of the Beast:
             Welcome to My Screwed-Up Diocese 141

Chapter 14   "666": Maturing in Understanding
             The Sacred Scriptures 149

Chapter 15   "Know Thyself" or Else! 161

Chapter 16	Exorcism #2: The Devil Made Me Do It 171
Chapter 17	More Jesus Moments 183
Chapter 18	My Internship Begins: "Deke" a.k.a. Fr. Deacon 197
Chapter 19	Ordination to the Priesthood 211
Chapter 20	Signs and Wonders 223
Chapter 21	The Devil's Revenge: The Beast Returns and He Is Stark-Raving Mad! 241
Chapter 22	"Exhausted," Literally 255
Chapter 23	"It's Either Him or Me! Your Choice" 267
Chapter 24	A New Beginning at The End of the World 283
Chapter 25	Here We Go Again 299
Chapter 26	Parish Life, Okay, My Life Is Never Dull 309
Chapter 27	New Life Begins Yet Again: My Counseling Degree 319
Chapter 28	Saving the World One Soul at a Time 329
Chapter 29	The Shit Hits the Fan: The Day of Reckoning Begins for the Diocese 339
Chapter 30	God is Love and Service 349
Chapter 31	The Real Truth Will Set You Free 363
Chapter 32	I'm Free! 371
Chapter 33	"Bless Me Father, For They Have Sinned" 379
Acknowledgements	 381
About the Author	 383

Chapter 1

I Want to Fly

This is the story of my life as a priest, but honestly I have to tell you that ever since I was little, maybe even just popped out of the womb little, I knew that I wanted to be . . . a pilot. Not very similar career paths, but what can I say? According to my parents, my first words weren't "Mama" and "Dada," but "Airplanes! Take me to the airplanes." They definitely were not "Take me to the church to light the candles!"

Some of my earliest memories, at around the age of five or six, are of going into town with my dad on Saturday mornings to pay our utility bills. It was a treat to spend some time alone with my dad or some time away from my mom, depending on how you looked at it. After a day spent driving from one end of town to the other, my dad would head to his favorite bar for a cold beer before heading home, and we would stop on the way at the Five n' Dime for a treat for me, which was usually a plastic toy airplane. As a bribe it worked really well. I never did mention the bar or beers to my mom.

And oftentimes my parents would take me to the local airport where we would sit on the ground outside the fence, kick back and relax, and just watch the airplanes as they were taking off and landing. They'd even take me over to the smaller planes and lift me up and let me sit on the wing of the plane, usually with my little sister beside me. I was fascinated! I was mesmerized! I was in little-boy heaven! I knew, even way back then, that this was *it*. This is what I wanted.

Sunday afternoon flight with my sister

My love of all things airborne continued as I was growing up and I did everything that I could think of to foster that connection. When I was a junior in high school, I took private flying lessons and actually soloed in a little Cessna 150, achieving my life-long dream of flying an airplane. It was as fantastic an experience as I had dreamed it would be! I joined the Naval Jr. ROTC and became the operations officer. I also became a cadet commander of the Civil Air Patrol (a branch of the Air Force's Search and Rescue Team) all in preparation for the life of flight that I so coveted.

Best of all, I had applied for and received an appointment to the Air Force Academy—a full paid scholarship! This was a pretty big deal for me because my folks weren't rich and there was no way that I could have afforded the tuition at a non-military flight school. So during the summers of my high school years, I was a frequent visitor at the academy. I wished that I could have been there twenty-four seven! I liked to watch the cadets at work, getting an idea of what military life was like. So I personally got to know a lot of the cadets, the officers, and the administrators. And they got to know me too (since every time they turned around—there I was!) and they knew that I had received an appointment to the academy and were expecting me to join them after I graduated from high school.

My family was ecstatic with my career choice, especially my dad. He was proud that a son of his would be in the military, and as an officer to boot. My mom—well, she just wanted me to get married and give her lots of grandchildren whatever career I decided to pursue. I had never, not for one second, ever considered any life for myself other than being a pilot, and now with my appointment to the academy, I would become an Air Force pilot—a fighter pilot! The priesthood? Never gave it a second

Chapter 1

thought—never even gave it a first thought! Wasn't even a blip on my radar.

Sure, I went to Mass every Sunday and to confession every two weeks because my parents made me. They were very religious, and their children were going to do the right thing or get whacked on the side of the head! This was the 1950s and kids did as they were told, especially "good Catholic" kids. So going to church was something that I had to do. I never felt any kind of spiritual connection in church, no warm fuzzies in my soul, and certainly no premonition that someday I would be a Roman Catholic Priest.

Although I certainly didn't consider myself religious, religion shaped my life as it probably did for many Catholic kids growing up in the '50s and '60s. I was brought up in an extremely devout, religious household. Life was made up of an endless cycle of things "Catholic"— going to Mass and confession, celebrating the Holy Days of Obligation, family baptisms, first communions, confirmations, and attendance at community feast days. We had these Catholic traditions and it was like our whole world—our "ethos"—was all about this religious and cultural influence. It permeated everything we did, and I was fascinated by how it encompassed every facet of our lives. It was like you just couldn't get away from this "Catholic" stuff.

So, of course, me being me, I asked, "Why?" My parents were forever telling me that I was a pain in the ass because I was always questioning things—always, always asking why. My mom jokes that this is how I came out of the womb—took my first gasp of air, demanded to be taken to the airport, and before I could even take a second gasp asked, "Why can't I fly?" When I asked my parents about things like God or the church or anything else for that matter, they would say, "Because we're your parents and we said so, and that's the way it is." I think that was a pretty standard parental response in the fifties. This was back in the day before parents felt that they owed their kids any explanations for anything. They speak, you listen; end of conversation.

Well, that answer might have been fine for my brother and sister, my cousins and friends, but it didn't answer any questions for me. It just made me more curious and I ended up with more questions than I started with. Seeing them so caught up in this religious thing yet not being able to explain it made me wonder—what is this "it" that rules everyone's lives—my parents, my relatives, my friends, my community, and the surrounding communities? Basically, my world.

Not getting any real answers from my parents or my teachers, I turned to books.

Not just for religion—I mean, I didn't go around with my head bowed and my hands clasped in prayer. You'd be more likely to find me outside catching frogs and lizards and putting them in empty Diamond matchboxes—the ones that hold those big kitchen matches. I used to bring them home to my mom who was deathly afraid of all creeping, crawling, and jumping creatures. I'd open the box and the frog or whatever would jump out, and she'd start screaming and grab the broom and either whop me with it or the poor little critter I'd brought into the house. I definitely was not a little angel around the house!

When I wasn't outside making friends with the bugs and frogs or playing with my dog (I love animals and always had a dog or dogs), I was reading. My head was always stuck in a book, looking for answers. Always looking for answers. For a lot of things, religion being just one of them.

So I read. Constantly, voraciously, any book I could get my hands on, about anything and everything. (Science fiction was a favorite of mine and remains so to this day.) This was my mom's doing, as she taught me to read at a very young age even before I started kindergarten. She's always been very big on education.

In my quest to understand the hold that religion seemed to have on everybody, I decided to read the Bible. If this book was the source of all of this religious stuff that ruled my world, I wanted to know what it said, and I actually read it several times from beginning to end. The first time I read it in grade school it really didn't make any sense at all to me. It was confusing and seemed to jump around a lot—saying one thing in one place and then a totally different thing in another place (in my view, anyway).

The second time that I read it, it seemed to make a little more sense. Or maybe that was just wishful thinking on my part! But it still didn't answer any of the questions that I had. I didn't know it at the time, of course, but one day I would know that Bible inside out and it would make a lot of sense to me, and sometimes I would even use passages from it that would stop some of my seminary teachers dead in their tracks and get them really pissed at me.

All of this was happening in grade school as I was growing up. When I look back now, I can see that while my "outside" life was pretty typical—going to school, playing with my friends, riding my bike, whatever—on the inside there seemed to be a space that I needed to fill, a feeling, even back then that something was missing, and that somehow there should be more. More of what I couldn't really articulate at the time. It was something that I thought about but didn't talk about because I didn't quite know how. It didn't seem to be anything that any of my friends ever talked about. So I asked my questions that seemed to have no answers, or not the right answers, or maybe I was just asking the wrong questions.

Chapter 1

I really did drive my parents crazy with my inquisitiveness. I can remember my mom telling my grandmother that I would never shut up and she didn't know what to do with me. My brother and sister were both good, quiet kids. Why did I have to be such a loudmouth? And I can remember my grandmother taking me aside and telling me to try and tone it down a little with my parents, and then when I wasn't with my parents to just be myself. So I developed a way of being that was acceptable on the outside to my parents, while creating and living a different—yet more real—parallel life on the inside.

So childhood turned into young adulthood. By my junior year of high school, I was firmly moving along on my path to becoming a fighter pilot. I had my flying lessons, the ROTC, the Civil Air Patrol, my friends at the Air Force Academy, and finally, my appointment to the academy.

I worked hard in school as it didn't come easy for me, but I always loved learning and still do. I had a part-time job as a waiter that I really loved. It was more than just waiting tables—it was constantly getting to meet new people and interacting with them, which was definitely my thing. I am, was then, and always will be, an extrovert! God, I love to talk! (Just ask any of my friends.) And this job gave me the opportunity to talk to a lot of people, even some movie stars who would come into the restaurant where I worked. I even met John Wayne once and he actually bought me a beer (of course I had a fake ID).

I had a great group of friends, and like many a kid at that age, I liked to party. I wasn't at home much. If I wasn't at school or work, I was usually out with my friends drinking and generally raising hell. I actually had a bit of a reputation as a party boy, and one of my nicknames was "hot lips."

So life was pretty good. I was looking forward to my senior year when I could get my Air Force physical, graduate, sign on the dotted line, and start the military life—my road to becoming a fighter pilot.

One odd thing did happen around that time. It occurred during the summer after my junior year when all I had on my mind was graduating and getting into the military. It was a dream that I had—a really weird dream (looking back, I think it was an omen).

My uncle had come to visit from out of town. Since my parents didn't have an extra bedroom, I gave him my room and I slept on the sofa. My uncle was going through a divorce at the time, and I remember lying on the sofa trying to sleep but I couldn't because of all of the noise. He and my mom and dad were up all night talking and I could hear every word because the house wasn't that big and the conversation was pretty heated. Back then the words divorce and Catholic weren't uttered in the same breath.

So with all of the commotion going on, I didn't fall asleep until about five in the morning. I woke up about two hours later after having the strangest, most vivid dream I'd ever had—so vivid that I can still remember it clearly today, more than forty years later.

In my dream I was standing on the top of the hill that's right behind my house. I saw an image of a man in a red and white robe come flying out of the clouds towards me. He flew right up to me and looked at me with a very worried expression on his face. Up close I could see that he had wound marks on his forehead, hands, side, and feet, and he looked just like the pictures that I had seen hanging in the church and in prayer books of the Sacred Heart of Jesus.

He said something to me, but I can't remember what it was. (Looking back it was probably, "Don't be a priest!" But I guess I'll never know.) But then he spoke again and said that he had a message for me to deliver. He said, "Go tell my people that the end is near." Then he flew off and I woke up.

When I woke I remember thinking to myself—whoa—what the hell was that about? I had a dream about Jesus? That was weird. I mean why would Mr. Military-Man-Hot-Lips-Party-Boy have a dream like that? Why not a dream about me looking hot in my military uniform, and soaring through the sky with the sun glinting off the wing tips of my plane?

So I forgot about the strange dream, and time marched on and suddenly it was my senior year. Two more semesters of high school to get through and then I would graduate and enter the Air Force Academy. A lifetime of waiting and yearning and preparing would come to fruition, and I would start my training to become an Air Force fighter pilot. Each new sunrise brought the thought—I'm one day closer to becoming a fighter pilot. God, I was so excited!

So what happened to end my lifetime dream of becoming an Air Force fighter pilot? One word: Vietnam.

It was Christmas break during my senior year. The war in Vietnam was raging, but life in my little town went on much as usual. Everyone was getting ready for Christmas and New Years and all that goes on between the holidays. Grandma was doing the Christmas baking. My parents were sneaking into the house with packages bundled under their coats. My brother and sister were on Christmas break too and were always underfoot.

I think it was a Tuesday night and I was sitting in front of the television set with the news on. I was filling out the application for my physical for the Air Force Academy while Walter Cronkite was recapping the prior week's events in Vietnam. Of course I knew that there was a war going on, a very unjust war. I had been in many anti-war

Chapter 1

demonstrations, had even led some, and in the ROTC I wore a black armband on my uniform to protest the war. I was the only cadet who did, very much to the displeasure of my captain, who was a retired World War II Commodore.

And of course I knew that this war was being fought by the military. But up until then I think I knew it only in an intellectual way. Well, that night watching the news, I knew it in a visceral way. On the TV screen I saw a burst of napalm hitting a village, and people—Vietnamese people—men, women, and children were running, screaming, and some of them were on fire. Those images were seared into my mind and they seemed to click in a backward sequence: burning children—napalm—Air Force jet—Air Force pilot—pilot . . . .

Oh God, I thought. I can't do that. In that moment and in that second my future came crashing down on me. Looking beyond the dream of the distinguished uniform and the state-of-the-art aircraft and the pride of being able to navigate the skies into the reality of a screaming, burning human being . . . I thought—I can't do that. I-Cannot-Do-That. I-Cannot-Kill-Innocent-People. So then I thought to myself, what's left? And my next thought was—there's nothing left. I'll become a priest.

I've no idea where that thought came from. Outer space. Inner space. I don't know. But that's how it happened. In the blink of an eye and in a flash of fire on the TV screen.

And as quickly as that, my whole life changed.

Chapter 2

Dropping out of the Sky in Flames

I decided to become a priest.

I gave up any thought of the Air Force Academy and let my appointment there drop. I even dropped out of my flying lessons, so I never did get my pilot's license at that time—I just let all of that go.

So how does one become a priest? I certainly had no idea. It was something I had never, ever thought about—it was a totally blank slate. But I did know that there was a Catholic seminary (a college that trains men to be priests) in the city, and I lived in a small town just outside of the city. I thought that I should start there. So I just showed up on their doorstep one day and talked to the vocation director and asked him, "What do I do to apply here?"

I had no money with which to go to college. I had given up my scholarship to the Air Force Academy, and without that I was back to square one. I was in the last semester of my senior year of high school when all of my friends had already gotten their college acceptance letters. And here I was—no money, not sure how I was going to get into a college this late in the semester, and no idea of how to start this priest thing.

So I decided to do the same thing at the seminary that I had done at the Air Force Academy. I started hanging out there to get an idea of what this seminary life to become a priest was all about. Many seminaries have their own colleges attached to them, but this particular one didn't. The seminarians lived at the seminary and did their religious formation work there, but did the academic portion of their training at a Catholic college in the city.

To train for the priesthood one needs to minor in philosophy, but can major in any academic area. Interestingly, to graduate from any military academy, one can major or minor in any academic area except for philosophy and theology.

I found out that the seminarians would begin each day with morning Mass at 6:30 a.m., so I decided that I would do that too. Attend Mass with them, get to know them, see what it was really like.

During my senior year of high school, I was always late for school—and I mean always! (Some people might see this as a less than admirable trait, but as you'll read later on, it was a trait that one day actually saved my life in the priesthood.) Sometimes I'd have to take a taxi to school because I'd get up late and miss the bus (I didn't have a car yet). My tardiness got to be such a regular occurrence that my band teacher—band was my first period class—threatened to not let me go on any more band trips with the class.

Yet once I'd decided to become a priest and focused all of my energy on getting acquainted with the seminary, I was never late for school again. I'd get up before six o'clock every day, get ready, and have my dad drop me off at the seminary on his way to work. I'd attend Mass with the seminarians and afterward one of them would drop me off at my school on his way to the college. Sometimes my dad would stay for Mass and take me to school later. I finally bought a car later that semester and then drove myself. I was never late for Mass—not once.

What did my family and friends think about my change in careers? They thought I was nuts. My dad couldn't understand my decision. We never really had a sit down talk about it, but he was extremely disappointed in me. My mom was aghast! Devout she might have been, but the priesthood for me meant no grandchildren for her.

And as for my friends, at first none of them really believed me. How could this be? I wasn't religious—far from it! I was the big party boy and usually the life of the party. A few of them even asked me if some alien life form had suddenly taken me over, 'cause this was nuts. Me, in the seminary? Was I crazy? In fact, years later after I had become a priest, some of them would actually show up at my church to see if it was really me, to see if it was really true that I had gotten ordained. I think that even then they had a hard time believing it.

So I started attending daily Mass with the seminarians and got to know them. They were a great bunch of guys and they started inviting me to a lot of the different functions at the seminary, like special talks that were being given by the priests, get-togethers they had for special occasions—the kinds of things that non-seminarians weren't usually invited to. I would pray with them, eat with them, and spend a lot of time talking to them and to the priests.

But while I enjoyed their company, I found that I wasn't too impressed by what it was that priests seemed to do—saying Mass, hearing confessions, and presiding at weddings and funerals. I actually thought that all of that seemed pretty empty. It just didn't excite me in any way. I can actually remember thinking 'Well, shoot, I don't want to do just that with my life,' and for someone who wants to be a priest, that's probably not a good thing. It seemed to be all about function without much in the way of personal growth, and not much about what it means to "be" a priest. Or maybe I just didn't pick that up at the time. I just knew that it didn't spur my imagination in any direction.

As I was continuing to explore the idea of becoming a priest, I began reading books about the lives of the saints. And then I found something that excited me. I read about the life of St. Francis of Assisi, and it was as if a light bulb went off in my head. Here was this wealthy boy (a party boy) who gave up all of his material possessions and took vows of chastity, poverty, and obedience in his quest to become more like Jesus.

His story resonated within my heart, and I thought, 'Ah, so that's what it means to be a priest.' The idea of living, of growing into whatever Jesus Christ was really about, of living up to that kind of an example, of growing into the experience of what it means to be a priest as an identity rather than just a function—now that excited me! That spurred my imagination in a profound way, and I knew that was the kind of priest that I wanted to be—a Franciscan.

St. Francis of Assisi
My inspiration

Up until this point, I think it had been more of an intellectual decision on my part to become a priest; more of a career choice (butcher, baker, priest?) than anything else. But now it truly felt, on a visceral level, like the right thing to do. I had read about the life of St. Francis and it opened up something within me; it ignited something within me. People talk about a vocation to the priesthood or a calling to the priesthood, but at that moment I felt an overwhelming pull—like a moth to a flame—to an interior life of connection to Jesus through St. Francis.

Throughout my life, even as a little kid, I always had the idea that there's more to life and wondered how can we discover more, how can we grow more, how can we be more than who we are—and thus become exactly who we are and fulfil our calling by God? (Although this conclusion only came later in my life.)

In the life of St. Francis I finally found the path to the life that I had been searching for. When I was younger and driving everyone crazy with my incessant questions, I believe in hindsight that I was trying (even back then) to answer questions about life and growth, although I didn't yet understand what those concepts meant.

For instance, when I became a waiter I couldn't be just a waiter. Something within me compelled me to be the epitome of what a waiter was—the absolutely best waiter. When I was the operations officer for the naval ROTC in high school, I had to be more than just the operations officer—I had to be the ideal of what the operations officer was—someone the other cadets could rely on and look up to, to be the example of the ideal. So I decided I didn't want to be just a priest. I wanted to be a priest's priest. A Franciscan. Another Jesus. I had found my ideal.

So I decided to become a Franciscan Priest. I let the vocation director at the local diocesan seminary know about my decision. He was a little upset because by that time he had gotten to know me, knew that I was sincere, and he was willing to accept me into their training program. But he said, "Well, okay, you try it out and if it doesn't work you can always come back to us." (Prophetic words.)

For those of you not familiar with the structure of the Catholic Church, a man can become either a diocesan priest or a religious priest. A diocesan priest is associated with a diocese—a region—with a bishop as the head of the region. Usually you're assigned to a local church that can also be called your local parish, which just means the church and the area that it serves. You live in the rectory—a house for priests which is usually attached to or close to the church. You make a promise of celibacy and of obedience to your bishop. You do not take a vow of poverty like many people seem to think. And you have a certain amount of independence when it comes to deciding how you're going to apportion your time and your duties.

A religious priest is part of a self-contained community where all of the members live and worship together and often work together. You take vows of poverty, chastity, and obedience. You adhere to stricter guidelines when it comes to determining how you will spend your time and carry out your duties because you must live by the rules of your community.

So what is the difference between chastity and celibacy? Chastity is a state of sexual purity in which one does not engage in any type of sexual activity, alone or with others. Celibacy simply means that you will not marry. In the Roman Catholic Church any kind of sexual activity is only allowed within the confines of the Sacrament of Marriage.

Men in the Catholic Church can also become religious brothers or permanent deacons, which I'll explain more about later on. And, not to leave all of you ladies out of the church loop, women in the Catholic Church have two types of religious life open to them—becoming a nun or a sister. There actually is a difference between the two. Originally, the term "nun" meant a woman who belonged to a cloistered religious order, meaning shut off from the outside world. A "sister" belonged to a religious order that worked in the secular (non-religious) world. However, these days we use the terms synonymously, as I will when I talk about them. Nuns actually played a major role in my formation as a priest, but again that's for a later chapter.

So now I had to apply to the Franciscan (religious) seminary. Luckily for me, the vocation director for the Franciscan seminary, which was in a different state, would occasionally visit the Franciscan church in our city and I had had the opportunity to meet him. I also had met some of the Franciscan Priests as I was growing up, having attended Masses at the Franciscan church. In fact, my parents had been married by a Franciscan Priest.

So I started attending Mass regularly at the local Franciscan church and started to spend time with the Friars (a Latin derivative for the word "brother"). They had a certain simplicity to them, running around town in their brown robes. They really seemed to be living their faith in a way that I hadn't seen in the diocesan priests, and I came to admire them.

So I talked to the vocation director of the Franciscan seminary when he was visiting here, found out what I needed to do to apply there, sent in my application, and basically crossed my fingers hoping it wasn't too late to get into their program. Thankfully, I was accepted.

I spent the remainder of my senior year filling out applications for loans and grants to pay for school, which was a real pain in the you-know-what because it was so late in the year, as everyone needing assistance had already applied. But I was able to get enough money to get started. I then went around letting all my friends know that I had dropped my appointment to the Air Force Academy and was going to the Franciscan seminary instead. With this latest news they all rolled their eyes at me, shook their heads, and said, "Yeah, okay, whatever." They stopped short of actually calling me a crazy fool, but I could definitely see it in their faces!

I finally graduated from high school in May and spent the summer working and hanging out with my friends. It was a bittersweet time because we all knew that soon we would be going our separate ways, maybe never to meet again.

Of all of the things that I did that summer—and it was a pretty busy time getting ready to leave home for the first time—there's one afternoon that I have always remembered. It happened about a week or two before graduation. It was after class and I was sitting on the hood of my dad's 1950 Chevy truck with my friend Anton and some of our other friends. We were just kind of passing the time, kidding around, talking about all of the things that we had done together, and the fun that we had together over the years. And that fun usually consisted of getting together and drinking beer or getting a couple of bottles of wine from somewhere and partying.

And for the first time we seemed to realize while sitting there with each other that we had always used alcohol as the reason to get together. We never said, "Hey, let's go bowling." It was always, "Let's find some beer and go drinking and then maybe we can go bowling." It was like we couldn't be honest or open with each other and enjoy our relationships without the crutch of alcohol. And maybe because of this we had missed out on something with each other. Maybe we could have been better friends, formed stronger bonds, and been more real with each other.

Girls talked about stuff like this. Guys didn't talk about stuff like this, ever. But here we were, all of us talking about it. Maybe it was because of graduation, knowing that we were all going off into our own futures. And so maybe now we were able to see the past and our real love for one another a little better. I don't know. But it was the first time we ever had a conversation like this and, sadly, it was during some of our last times together. I know that as we left each other that afternoon, some of us going home, some of us off to band practice or whatever, we were all feeling a little sad, feeling as if we had let something slip by, and it was too late to get it back.

So we graduated and summer passed by in a whirl of activity. I had to be at the seminary by the first week of August, and August was almost here.

I was ready to start my journey into the priesthood.

Chapter 3

The Rigors of Seminary

August arrived and it was time for me to leave for the Franciscan seminary. My parents loaded my siblings and me ignominiously into their car, and we headed off to the airport where they helped me unload my luggage and said, "We'll see you in four months" and sped off.

So much for grand farewells!

So I boarded the plane that would take me halfway across the country to my new life. This was my first time on a commercial airline. I had a great flight and took a lot of pictures, some of which I still have. I remember that it was a really cloudy day, but when we were starting our descent for landing, the cloud cover broke and I was actually able to catch a glimpse of the extensive seminary grounds.

The plane landed and I arrived in my new state with a suitcase, a backpack, and a little bit of money. But what I lacked in material possessions, I more than made up for in excitement. I was eager to get started on this new path that I had chosen for myself.

I was met at the airport by one of the fourth year seminary students who drove me out to campus in one of the community's cars. Originally I was supposed to be one of three guys arriving that day from my home state but neither of the other two had shown up. I later learned that one of them had decided to take a year off before entering. He took off that year, got married, had the marriage annulled, and then entered the seminary.

He eventually did become a priest, and later on in his career caused a big scandal when he was the pastor at one of the churches back home. He was protesting something—I can't remember what it was—and he had barricaded himself in the rectory and wouldn't come out. The bishop had to get involved and threatened to excommunicate him. He eventually gave in, "went under obedience" to the bishop (as it's called), and salvaged his career. He's still a priest.

So about an hour after leaving the airport, we arrived at the Franciscan seminary. My first impression, besides being overwhelmed by the sheer size of the place, was that I had taken a step back in time. The buildings had a medieval, somewhat mystical aura about them.

I remember thinking that if it was night time and I threw in a little swirl of ground fog, I could easily imagine Count Dracula flinging open the huge wooden double doors to the main building and come floating down the massive stone steps, face half hidden by his black cape, welcoming me to his castle. (I had grown up watching Bela Lugosi as Count Dracula on Saturday night television along with the Mummy, the Wolfman, and Frankenstein—they were the stuff of my childhood nightmares!)

I found out later that the nickname for the main seminary building actually was "The Castle." Although it somewhat spoiled the quasi-Gothic effect, the student dorms that we lived in were a modern addition tucked behind, but attached to "The Castle."

The Castle

I was shown to my dorm room (no roommate) where I unpacked, was given a meal, bid goodnight with instructions for the following day, and went to bed to sleep my last night's sleep as an ordinary guy, a layperson. From the following morning on, I would be a seminarian.

I got up the next morning eager to meet my fellow classmates. The freshman class that I entered with had about sixty-five students from all over the United States and a few from Canada. We had arrived on campus a few days before the other students so that we could attend our freshman orientation, which consisted of a tour of the buildings and grounds, talks by the seminary president, meeting the staff, and getting our class schedules.

The seminary campus was huge! It was like a little city in itself. It had its own bookstore, barber shop, tailors, candy store—all run by student volunteers. It had all of the amenities so there was no need for the students to leave campus for basic necessities.

What impressed me the most (other than the size of the place) was the chapel, a massive stone building, looking like something right out of the twelfth century. It was reminiscent of the churches that you see in Europe dating from the Middle Ages that tourists flock to see.

The first thing that struck me when I entered through its doors—and I know I'm repeating myself here—was how large it was on the inside. Walking in and taking that first step was almost an assault on the senses as you were totally enveloped by an overwhelming smell of incense. At almost the same moment, your eye was caught by the flickering of dozens upon dozens of lighted votive candles that, combined with the minimal amount of natural light seeping in, threw a multitude of wavering shadows onto the walls, giving it a somber, somewhat otherworldly effect.

Row upon row of burnished wooden pews seemed to stretch down as far as the eye could see, finally ending at the altar. A huge wooden cross was attached to the ceiling above the altar so that it hung suspended several feet above, but precisely in the center of the altar. It was a replica of the famous San Damiano Cross, which is the cross that spoke to Saint Francis when he began his ministry.

To both sides of and a bit behind the altar was the choir for which individual wooden chairs were built into the wall. Each chair had a drawer attached on one side where prayer books would be kept, and this is where the choir sat. When we think of choirs in modern Catholic churches, we think of a group of lay people who sing the songs of the Mass. Some of them also play guitars and other instruments. But originally, choirs consisted only of religious—brothers and priests—who did the chanting and singing. The famous Gregorian chant originally was a collection of prayers that were put to music.

The whole of the altar area was separated from the rest of the chapel by a floor-to-ceiling metal grille that ran the entire length of the altar. The original purpose of the grille was to separate the religious from the lay people attending the Mass. These grilles were common in the old days, reflecting the Catholic Church's attitude that the religious were "above" the lay people and should be set apart from them, an attitude that I believe persists to this day, but that's just my opinion.

After the reforms of Vatican II, which was an Ecumenical Council of the clergy and laity to discuss the future direction of the Roman Catholic Church, most of the grilles in churches were removed and downsized to altar railings that my generation grew up with. Now even those are mostly a thing of the past, and the altar is open to the congregation.

The walls on both sides of the chapel—beginning near the front doors and extending down towards the altar—each had about four recessed alcoves built into them. These alcoves housed small, individual altars that were dedicated to various Franciscan saints. As a Franciscan Priest, you were required to say your own daily Mass. So at any time during the day or night, you could find a priest at one of these side altars saying Mass to fulfil this obligation. It would be just the priest—no altar boys and no congregation—just the priest saying Mass in Latin.

Also in the old days—pre-Vatican II—the superior of the community would check with each priest on a daily basis to make sure that they had fulfilled all of their daily obligations: saying Mass, attending Morning Prayer, noon prayer, etc. If a priest didn't attend Morning Prayer, for example, he would have to "make it up" by saying the Morning Prayer on his own some time during that day, even if it wasn't done until the evening. So the superior would monitor each priest. By the time I entered the seminary, that practice had stopped and had become the honor system. As a priest you knew what your obligations were, and it was assumed that you fulfilled them.

What I remember most about the chapel was the smell—a blend of real beeswax, wood polish, and incense permeating the air. It seemed to carry with it a sense of the chapel's history, a feeling of the timelessness of its rituals—the innumerable candles that had been lit there, the scores of hands clasped in prayer resting atop the wooden pews, and the thurible (incense holder) gently wafting incense time and time again.

Thurible with incense

I could imagine the hundreds of young men who had entered this sanctuary before me, the prayers they had offered here, their joy, and their angst. The very air seemed heavy with it. I felt a sense of communion with them knowing that I would be joining my prayers to theirs. To this day the smell of wax, polish, and incense takes me back to that time and to that chapel.

So we finished our freshman orientation and then found ourselves with a lot of time on our hands and very little to do. The rest of the students hadn't arrived yet, and we didn't have any means of transportation to go anywhere (students' personal cars weren't allowed), and we weren't quite sure if it would be appropriate to leave campus and go to town. It wasn't actually a town but a small city on whose outskirts the seminary was located. So a lot of us ended up sitting around playing card games and Ping-Pong to pass the time, waiting for the other students to arrive.

A friend of mine recently asked me, "What kind of courses did you take in the seminary—something like Priesthood 101?" No, not in the college seminary. You get into that kind of thing in the graduate seminary, which are your last four years of training for the priesthood. And for the record, there is no such course as Priesthood 101!

Academically, this seminary was very similar to any other four-year college—or at least an all-boys' college. But in addition to regular college courses—English, sociology, economics, etc.—we also took classes such as Introduction to the Scriptures and Introduction to the Old Testament. You would take a typical course load of about seventeen hours a semester. You could major and minor in pretty much anything you wanted. The only requirement was that you had to have at least twenty-four hours of philosophy to graduate because that was a prerequisite for getting into graduate theology school, which is the last step in training for the priesthood. When you graduated, it would be with either a Bachelor of Arts or a Bachelor of Science degree.

Academics aside, there are a number of differences between a secular (non-religious) college and a seminary (religious) college besides the absence of women. The major difference is that a seminary college has what is called a formation program. We weren't here just to go to college, get our degree, and head off into the workforce. We were here to see if the religious life was something that we would be suited for. Formation is an exposure to the lifestyle—the rules and regulations of living a religious life that would lead to becoming either a Franciscan Brother or Priest. Or not.

So what's the difference between a Franciscan Brother and a Franciscan Priest? Whichever one you chose to be, the basic training is the same for both. The same academic program was offered to all of the seminarians, and everyone went through the same formation program so you would follow the same steps in the process of becoming either a brother or a priest.

The seminary was a four-year program. The freshman year was sort of the "sink or swim" year. If you found out early on that the religious life really wasn't your thing, or that the program wasn't exactly what you were looking for, or if you found the studies too hard, you could just pack up and go. Although guys did drop out in the upper grades, the majority who left voluntarily was greatest during the freshman year. You'll notice I used the word "voluntarily." Later I'll tell you about the guys who got kicked out.

So if you stayed in the program at the seminary and made it through the first semester of your second year, you could apply to become what is called a postulant, meaning that you are taking the next step in affirming your serious intent to become a religious. At the end of your second year, you would typically leave the seminary for what's called your novitiate year. During your novitiate year, which is spent at a different Franciscan seminary, you don't do any actual academic studies, but you are immersed in the intense study and spiritual practices of the Franciscan way of life.

At the end of your novitiate year, you would return to your home seminary for your third academic year of school and would take what are called "temporary vows" of poverty, chastity, and obedience. At this time you would also be given the brown robe that the Franciscans wear.

After graduation at the end of your fourth academic year— if you were pursuing the priesthood track—you would go on to a Franciscan graduate theology school for your final four years of training.

If, instead of being a priest you wanted to be a brother, you would take your "final vows" after graduation and join the community as a full member. Graduate theology school isn't necessary for a brother unless you also wanted to be a theologian. (You don't have to be a priest to be a theologian.) As a brother, you can go on to any graduate school to pursue whatever educational goals that you want—to become a teacher or a lawyer, for example.

Or, if you didn't want to pursue further education, you could work at the seminary as a member of the formation team, become vocational director, or even be the cook if those were your talents. But whatever you decided to do, the seminary would be your home base. You would live the communal life and adhere to the rules of St. Francis.

In my freshman class, most of the guys wanted to be priests but a few of them wanted to be brothers. So here I was, one among many in a group of sixty-five guys from all over the map, most of us only eighteen or nineteen years old, and many of us away from home for the first time. All different sizes and shapes, temperaments and personalities, not knowing what to expect or what exactly was expected of us, but all of us

Chapter 3

bound together by a desire, a calling, to be a part of something bigger than ourselves.

Within a few days of our orientation, the rest of the student body arrived and school began.

Chapter 4

God Calling and St. Francis

School began in earnest, as did this next chapter in my life.

So what was a typical day at the seminary like? My alarm clock would usually go off about six o'clock in the morning, sometimes earlier. Then a quick shower before getting dressed in regular street clothes, since you didn't get to wear the habit (the brown Franciscan robe) until you were a novice, which means that you had completed your novitiate year. Once you had dressed, it was off to the chapel for Morning Prayer.

Prayer was a major part of our lives from the very first day. We were each given our own breviary, which is a book of all the prayers that were used and you took with you to all prayer sessions. You basically carried it with you all of the time. The prayer day officially started at five thirty in the morning with the first prayers of the day, which are called matins. All official prayers were communal and held in the chapel. You didn't have to attend matins but were encouraged to do so. I went fairly often, and on those days I got up at five o'clock in the morning.

Morning Prayer, or lauds, was held at 6:30 a.m. Next came the midday prayer, which was held at noon right before lunch. For this prayer bells would ring out across campus signaling the start of midday prayer.

I always liked hearing those bells. They reminded me of the movie *The Sound of Music*, where Julie Andrews plays Sister Maria. In the movie there's a scene where the convent bells ring for prayer and all of the nuns immediately stop whatever they're doing. And, with hands folded into the sleeves of their habits and eyes cast reverently downward, they silently stream into the chapel from all directions. I thought that that was a pretty cool visual!

Evening prayers, or vespers, were held at 5:00 p.m., right before dinner. Our official prayer day concluded with night prayer, or compline, which was held at 9:30 p.m. I use the term 'official' because besides these prayers, you would also pray or meditate on your own during the course of the day.

So prayer was the center of our lives, the framework upon which everything else was built. Prayer was discipline. Not just the exterior act of getting to the chapel at the assigned times, but the more important interior aspect—learning to remove from your mind the many distractions of your daily routine, clearing your mind of the minutiae of life, and opening your consciousness so that your heart and soul were completely available to listen to God.

At Morning Prayer you could open yourself up to all of the possibilities that this new day could bring. It was a clean slate, not yet written upon. How would God guide you to write this day's story? How would you be a reflection of Him this day?

Prayer at noon and dinner were times to stop and reflect on how the day was unfolding; at night prayer you could think back on the day on what you did or didn't do. Not in terms of tasks, but in acts. Was I kind? Was I patient? Did I walk with Christ today?

In getting back to the daily routine, you would go to breakfast after Morning Prayer. We freshman had our own small dining room where we ate breakfast and usually dinner. There was also a very large main dining room called the refectory, where all of the student body and the faculty got together every day for lunch after the midday prayer.

Breakfast was a semi-buffet type of meal which was mainly cereal, toast, and fruit. There was a cook available (one of the Franciscan Brothers with culinary skills) who would make eggs for you if you wanted, or you could make your own. Sometimes one of the guys would start making eggs for himself and then we'd talk him into frying or scrambling enough for everyone. The food was plain, simple but good, and there was always plenty of it with a lot of fresh fruit always available. I usually just had cereal because I was always trying to lose weight. I think once I ate nothing but Special K for two straight weeks trying to shed some pounds (it helped a little bit).

After breakfast you'd go back to your room to get your books and then head to class. Our classes were held in the same building that housed our dorms, so although the campus was extensive, we didn't have to traverse it to get to class. Our dorm building was quite large—two wings off the main building with either three or four floors each—I can't remember exactly. It housed all of the student dorm rooms and classrooms. Some of the floors were closed off and empty because there weren't enough bodies to fill them. After Vatican II, which is when I entered the seminary, the number of young men entering the seminary actually dwindled significantly. In the old days the seminary was bursting at the seams. Now it was half empty.

Classes started at 8:00 a.m. and were usually held until noon when you'd go to midday prayer and then lunch. (Our class schedules were fitted around our prayer schedules.) And although many of the academic courses that we took were the same ones that you'd find in a secular college, all of our teachers were priests.

Lunch was held in the refectory, the main dining room, with all of the students, brothers, and priests eating together. (Not exactly together, since there was definitely a pecking order, but at least in the same room.) It was a large room with long, heavy wooden tables set up in a "U" shape along three of the walls. The tables were anchored to the floor and all of the priests and brothers sat at the bottom of the "U" and the students sat at the sides. A huge buffet table was set up in the middle.

The cooks would bring out all of the food and place it on the buffet table, and you'd get your own food and take it back to your table. Again, the food was simple but good and plentiful (like the stuff your grandmother would make such as meat loaf, pork chops, spaghetti, and macaroni and cheese). And simple desserts such as fruit, cookies, and pudding. For some reason I especially remember the pudding—probably because I was trying so hard not to eat it!

You didn't find any fancy kinds of food because the Franciscan charism (the Greek word for gift) is simplicity and relating to the poor. (Remember that St. Francis gave up all of his worldly possessions and owned only the simple brown robe that he wore.) So if you're trying to relate to the poor, you're not going to be dining on lobster and prime rib.

After lunch you'd head back to class until four or five o'clock depending on your schedule. Then off to evening prayer at five o'clock with dinner afterward. We usually had dinner in our own smaller student dining room with the cooks providing the food for us.

After dinner there was recreation time when you'd basically be free to do whatever you wanted (when you weren't involved in other activities, which I'll get to in a minute). You could hang out with your friends, go to the recreation room and play cards or Ping-Pong, or watch television. I remember a bunch of us watched the World Series that year. Or you could just relax and have a beer, or a "near-beer" with a negligible alcohol content for those of us under twenty-one. So while you definitely couldn't grab a six-pack and go hang out in your friend's room getting loaded, you could have a near-beer or two in the recreation room. Or you could spend some time by yourself, meditating or studying or doing homework.

As I mentioned, there were also other activities that you would be involved in after dinner. There were a lot of clubs that you could join like the drama club, key club, chess club, etc., whatever your interests were, and they held their meetings in the evening. I was interested in the performing arts so I joined the drama club. As a freshman I didn't get to do any acting, but I was told that I had a real talent for helping the actors learn their lines, so I did a lot of that. Sometimes it seemed as if I knew their lines better than they did! I also helped with the sets, costumes, and artwork—those kinds of things.

When I was there, the drama club was really high-powered, very active, and well known in the secular community. At this time they were performing *Antigone*, one of the classic Greek plays by Sophocles. Their performances were open to the public and always drew a large audience. They would also travel to other colleges to perform. I was able to go with them on one of their trips and it was a great experience for me, even being a minor part of this very talented group.

Another activity that everyone was involved in was our work assignments. We were all given a work assignment that rotated monthly. You would be in a group of three or four guys, and your assignment for the month might be to clean the classrooms, dining room, recreation room, or any of the common areas. Or you could be asked to wash the lunch or dinner dishes, or wash the floors in the hallways, etc. So in the evening you would be involved in that.

We had what were called our cell group meetings in the evenings. The freshman students were divided into groups of ten to twelve guys with a faculty member as each group's moderator. We would meet once a week. I think my group met every Wednesday night. The purpose of the cell groups was to help us in our adjustment to the religious life. We would talk about how we were doing, voice our thoughts, our expectations, and struggles. It was basically a group support system, although they didn't use that term back then.

A large part of our discussions were about our interactions with each other. Sixty-five guys living together in close quarters required a degree of adjustment on everyone's part. And the thing that you have to understand about seminary life is that there is absolutely *no* privacy—everyone's life is an open book. It was like being in a group counseling session twenty-four hours a day, seven days a week, four weeks a month, twelve months a year. It was just constant scrutiny from everyone around you.

At these meetings there would be a lot of personality issues discussed, things like "I'm having trouble with this person because they're too standoffish," or "That person is too judgmental," or "So-and-so seems to be drinking too much," or whatever the issue might be. At times there would be a lot of complaining and personal criticisms being voiced, and sometimes the issues would be broader; things that perhaps many of us were having difficulty with.

This was the forum where we could air all of those concerns with our moderator there to help guide us. Each of us also had our own spiritual director, a member of the faculty with whom we met with on a regular basis and could also talk to about our adjustment to seminary life.

Another assignment that we had was apostolic work, although that was done primarily on the weekends. Once a week we would go out into the community to do various types of work such as visiting the sick in hospitals, the elderly in nursing homes, a half-way house for addicts, or working in a soup kitchen. We would usually get a different assignment every week. On weekends we would all pile into the seminary's van. One of the older students whose work assignment for the month would be driving the van for us, would take us to our assignments and then pick us up at a designated time for the drive home.

Whatever you were involved in during the evening, you had to be in the chapel by 9:30 p.m. for night prayer. Sometimes I would stay in the chapel for a while after prayer to meditate because I found that it helped me to relax and focus. After prayer you could go to visit your friends in their rooms or they could come to your room as long as you were quiet, as other students might be trying to study or sleep.

So what kind of things did we talk about when my friends and I got together? The usual stuff—how classes were going, what subjects we liked or didn't like, the rules we found hard to get used to, how our favorite sports teams were doing—usual guy stuff. Did we ever talk about girls? Yeah, some of the guys would bring up their old girlfriends and past relationships, and some of them would talk about their sexual experiences. I don't know if they were always telling the truth, but I know that I would listen to some of their stories and think—whoa! Compared to some of them, I felt like a babe in the woods.

But past sexual exploits weren't a usual topic. We were here—voluntarily—to become Franciscans, to dedicate our lives to the service of God, knowing what that entailed. And in the Catholic Church, that meant celibacy. It was a twenty-four seven life, not something that you shook off at five o'clock on a Friday night so that you could go out clubbing. That wasn't a part of our lives anymore by our own choice.

Did I ever think about giving up all of that—no more dating, no more romance, no sex or marriage in my future? Yeah, of course, we all did. For me it didn't seem like a big deal at the time. I had gone out a lot, dated, and had fun. But I had never met "the one," and had never had a relationship that made me think—this is it, this is the person that I want to spend the rest of my life with.

For me relationships were about a lot more than just sex. It was about connecting with the person on an inner level, about being in love, and not just in "lust." Not a typical attitude for a teenage boy, or at least not one that many teenagers would admit to, but that was how I always felt. So with my past experiences being what they were, it didn't seem to me that it was such a big sacrifice. I was also very young and idealistic, and the thought of living a life in the service of God made up for anything I was leaving behind.

So after night prayer, visiting with your friends, doing your homework, studying, or just going to bed, a typical day in the seminary comes to its end.

Although we had a very structured routine, we did have free time in the evenings after our work assignment if there were no meetings to attend, on the weekends after we finished our apostolic work, and during the holidays. If you lived close to the seminary, you could go home on weekends. I couldn't do that as I lived too far away, and no one ever invited me to their home. So I spent my free time like a lot of the other guys did in the dorm and on campus. You could go into the city with your friends if you could find a ride, and go to dinner or a movie (or a bar). Or you could just hang out around the dorm playing cards or Ping-Pong (Ping-Pong was big that year), or watching television.

So this was the external structure that we followed at the seminary. But formation—exposure to the lifestyle and rules and regulations of living a religious life—also addresses our inner structure, our spiritual selves.

We were in a community where the members, the Franciscan Brothers and Priests, were trying to live and teach the example of St. Francis and to show us what this meant.

In our classes we were taught about the life and ministry of St. Francis, and about spirituality and spiritual concepts. (Spiritual does not equal religious.) One basic concept that we were taught is that we each have a whole inner life, a very rich inner life that we need to develop and nourish through prayer, meditation, and contemplation.

Our teachers were committed to our personal growth. They gave us ample opportunity to pray, taught us how to meditate, and instilled in us the value of contemplation. Their goal was to have us develop a whole spiritual lifestyle—a spiritual attitude towards life that permeated everything that we did—a lifestyle of poverty, of sharing, of living in common. So we were exposed to the spiritual concepts that create the charism of St. Francis.

At first it was kind of like, what the hell are they talking about? We were just a bunch of young guys; what did we know about any of this stuff? But we were also a group of guys with a common goal—we wanted to be good, to do good things, to be like St. Francis, to be like Jesus, and to spend our lives in service as priests and brothers. You've probably heard that current popular saying "What would Jesus do?" When I think back to the way our class was in the very beginning, I have to laugh because if you had asked that question to us back then, many of us would have had a perplexed look on our faces as we stammered "Uh . . . uh . . . ."

But we learned, and most of us grew spiritually. Some more than others, and I think there were a few who never really got it. But for me these concepts proved to be a real awakening. I was just a kid from Nowhere-ville, USA, yet here I was being given this wealth of spiritual wisdom that originated with renowned Theologians and was passed down through the ages. I thought it was fantastic and soaked it up like a sponge. As these teachings became clearer to me, I was able to understand, to make the connection, and to "get it."

When our teachers talked about the concept of a person being "in balance" and about the inner versus outer experiences that affect this balance, I was able to make the connection between what I was feeling on the inside (inner experience) being expressed by how I acted on the outside (outer experience). It became real to me—it was no longer an abstract idea floating around "out there," but incorporated "in here," inside of me.

And when they explained the concept of hypocrisy as behavior on the outside that doesn't match what you're feeling on the inside—not being in balance—I got that too. I found that now I was beginning to see things from the inside out, and that was a profound awakening for me.

And then, as a result of all of these spiritual concepts finally "meshing" for me, I began to see things very differently. Jesus was no longer an outside abstract for me. Now I also began to see Jesus in my friend Peter. I saw Jesus in my teacher. I saw Jesus in the sunlight (not that we saw much sun that semester). Jesus was in the snowfall (that we did see a lot of). Talk about an awakening! It was like the proverbial light bulb turning on inside my head—not just turning on, but shining so brightly I'd have to put on sunglasses!

It seemed to me that all of the angst of my younger years—asking questions that had no answers, searching for that elusive something "more," feeling a certain (real) way on the inside, but acting on the outside the way my parents wanted me to (not real)—all of this brought me to these watershed moments. The concept that to be in balance as a human being—your inside has to match your outside—well, it looked like I was finally finding my answers. To me these concepts were life altering, and I couldn't learn this stuff fast enough!

When I think back to the priests in that seminary, to our teachers, and the examples they were to us, one person stands out in my mind. I had previously mentioned that each seminarian had a spiritual adviser. I'll call my adviser Father Gregory, and I was probably closer to him than to anyone else there. He was a good, holy man.

One evening I went to his room to talk to him about some things, and I found him washing his socks in the sink in his room. It was an extremely simple room—a bed, a chest of drawers, and a sink. He didn't even have his own bathroom. The room was dimly lit by a candle, and there was a picture of Jesus hanging on the wall.

And there he was, washing his socks in the sink with some slivers of soap. He wrung them out and laid them on top of the radiator to dry. I asked him why he didn't use the laundry service that was provided for us, and he said that doing this was a small act of humility on his part, and that the poor didn't have laundry service. And I thought that was kind of neat. Silly maybe, but neat because he was trying in his own little way to live humbly, to live like St. Francis. And that small but heartfelt gesture was more than you'd see from many of the other priests. But I'll get to more of that in a moment.

That evening, like so many other times that I had met with him, we had a great conversation about good and evil and growth and God. I remember his listening to me and telling me that yes, God is inside of us. And that yes, I was being given the grace to see Jesus in others, and to see Jesus in nature. And telling me that oh yes, there is evil in the world and you've got to use discernment to figure out which is which because sometimes it comes masked one as the other. Just fascinating stuff. He was a really great spiritual director. He passed away many years ago, and I wish I could say his real name here as a way of honoring him.

So as we were learning these spiritual concepts, sometimes some of my friends and I would sit around after class discussing what we had learned and try to find ways to put them into practice. Learning about spirituality is one thing, but making your life spiritual is quite another.

I remember one day when the prayer reading was about service to others—a hallmark of St. Francis' ministry. So we were talking about how we could be of service to others, and it just so happened that my work assignment starting that week was to clear the dirty dishes from the tables at lunchtime. Normally when you did this, you'd basically wait until people were done eating and then you'd grab the used dishes from the tables, rush into the kitchen to drop them off, then rush back out for more and keep doing this until the tables were cleared. (I'm talking a lot of dishes.)

Well, I decided that when I cleared those dishes I was going to perform the best service that I could. I was going to clear those dishes with love in my heart. If you help people but don't do it with love, you're not emulating St. Francis. So I believed anyway.

So when the time came, I approached the first table and instead of just grabbing the dirty dishes I said, "Excuse me, Father, may I take these dishes? May I take anything else for you? May I bring you anything else?" I focused my attention, however briefly, on the person that I was taking the dishes from, made eye contact, and didn't rush. I figured that was probably how St. Francis would've done it, or at least I hoped so. That was all that I did. But honest to God, you would've thought I'd just found the cure for cancer from the way people reacted. People talked about what I did for weeks afterward. They even made a comment about it in my student file!

It might seem strange to you that such a simple thing could cause such a stir, but if you look at it in the context of what was "normal" in the seminary, it makes more sense. Most men who entered the seminary, at least back then, were a pretty introverted bunch. On the whole they tended to be kind of shy, more introspective, a quieter group, going with the flow (so to speak), and not thinking "outside the box." Priests weren't taught or encouraged to "think outside the box," at least until Vatican II came along.

Then here I come, a loud-mouthed never-shuts-up extrovert. They never knew what to make of me, not in any of the seminaries that I attended, or in the priesthood. The fact that I always seemed to be a round piece trying to fit into a square hole should have set off some warning bells for me, but at that time it didn't.

For those of you who are not familiar with it, Vatican II was a time of major reform in the Catholic Church. It was initiated by Pope John XXIII to update the mission of the church in the modern world in terms of its day-to-day operations.

Pope John XXIII

The structure of the church up to that point had been uncompromisingly rigid. The church was steeped in ancient traditions and made no allowances for modern thought, and no attempt to incorporate the changes brought by a modern society. (Look at how many centuries it took for the church to acknowledge that Galileo was right—that the earth revolves around the sun, and not vice versa.)

The pope, through his bishops and priests, exerted strict control over every aspect of the lives of the laity (the people). Basically, the clergy (ordained ministers) was told what to think and when to think it, and this is how they guided their parishioners. Everyone had to toe the party line, and dissension—even discussion—about the party line wasn't tolerated.

Pope John XXIII changed all of that. He loosened the structure, made boundaries more fluid, invited much more participation by the people, and invited discussion (up to a point). One major change that most people remember from back then was the Catholic Mass. Before Vatican II, the Mass was celebrated in Latin with the priest standing with his back to the congregation. One of my teachers in graduate theology school called this the "Ass Mass" because all you ever saw of the priest was his backside. After Vatican II, the Mass was said in English with the priest facing the people.

So while the pope's intentions were honorable (visionary even), they caused a lot of problems for many people, both clergy and lay people. Many priests got lost in this change. Instead of constantly (and comfortingly) being told what to do, how to do it, when to do it, and how often to do it, they now had to figure out a lot of those things for themselves. The church was no longer a rigid external structure that could completely hold them. Now it had to come from them. They had to reinterpret what they were doing to fall in line with this new vision of the church. And since they had never been taught how to do this, many of them simply couldn't handle it.

Some of them were confused, some were angry, and many were upset. Some of them acted like little kids let loose in a candy store as they were trying to find their new boundaries. It took a toll on their mental health, and a lot of them were having all kinds of personal issues that spilled over into professional issues and abuses of the lifestyle that they were supposed to be living.

In one way or another, this affected everyone at the seminary. Priests left the church in great numbers after Vatican II, and seminary enrollment declined. Interestingly, some of our recent popes have steered the church back to a pre-Vatican II ethos, with the pope in rigid control and taking no prisoners, as they say.

So our school routine continued pretty much the same—classes, prayers, and apostolic work. It was just about mid-semester, with many of us thinking about our futures—would we be coming back after this semester—when something out of the ordinary happened to me.

Earlier I talked about the odd dream that I had in high school with that figure in a white robe flying towards me. Well, I had something similar happen to me that semester. It was October 31, Halloween. Or, as the church calls it, the eve of All Saints Day. I was in the recreation room with some of my friends. We were just hanging out for the evening, sitting around talking, and drinking Cokes.

Suddenly I felt within me—it was like a little voice—that said, "Come to the chapel. Come to the chapel." I just ignored it for most of the evening, but it was insistent and getting more urgent: *"Come to the chapel. Come to the chapel. Come to the chapel."* So I finally told my friends, "Hey, I don't know what's going on but I've got this really strong urge to go to the chapel, so I'm going."

My friends said, "Whatever, we're staying here, see you later."

So I got up and went to the chapel. I spent a lot of time in that chapel. I liked going there late at night, usually around midnight, to pray and meditate many evenings for an hour or so. I enjoyed being there without any distractions. I'd be kneeling for that hour and sometimes I would fall asleep because it was so quiet and so late.

So I get to the chapel and kneel down and suddenly this voice says, "Don't kneel. Stand up because you fall asleep when you kneel." So I stood up.

The voice I was hearing seemed to be coming from outside of me but I was hearing it in my head. And it actually seemed to be coming from the tabernacle (a cabinet on top of the altar containing consecrated communion hosts), which I thought was pretty weird. (The whole thing was pretty weird.) So I stood up and listened. Then the voice said, "You're going to go through a great trial. You're going to feel as if I'm not with you. But I will be more present to you than I am right now. Live every day as if it was your last, and I am with you always until the consummation of the world."

And like a light switch being flicked off, it was gone.

I remember yelling out loud, "But...but...but...wait...wait...." But it was completely gone from the tabernacle.

And in that moment I experienced a profound awareness. Earlier I had mentioned the conversation that I had with my spiritual adviser who told me that I was being given the grace to see Jesus in people and in nature. Now I felt as if that grace had carried me to a new place, a new level of understanding. When I say that the voice was gone from the tabernacle, I mean that literally. Jesus was gone. The tabernacle was completely empty—devoid of any Divine Presence.

At that moment I felt it in my heart as well as in my head that the Divine Presence isn't "contained" in just a tabernacle or atop an altar or in a building, but is in everything. Suddenly I felt the living presence of Jesus in everything around me—in the light of the chapel, in the air of the chapel, in the very silence of the chapel. He was as alive to me as were the friends I had just left in the recreation room. It was an illuminating moment in my life—a moment of pure connection.

Typical Tabernacle

Then I noticed someone sitting in the choir stall beyond the altar. It was one of my teachers. He was the priest who taught us "Introduction to Scripture" and he always taught class with his eyes closed. He would give us the whole lecture with both eyes closed, from the minute class started until it ended. We were always making fun of him—I mean, that was pretty strange. But you could get away with a lot of stuff in his class—you could pick your nose, throw spitballs, and pass notes because he never saw what we were doing.

So father opens one eye and gives me a quizzical look. He didn't say anything, but his look said what the hell are you doing babbling in church. I'm trying to meditate here.

So I said, "Oh, excuse me, Father," and I left.

So what was that all about? I had no idea at the time, but looking back on it perhaps it was simply an outward manifestation of what my unconscious mind was trying to tell me. You can fool yourself, but you can't fool your unconscious. It seems as if my unconscious mind was really, really trying to get my attention. Maybe to say—what are you doing here, in this seminary? Do you think you'll find what you're looking for here? Perhaps I should have packed my bags and high-tailed it out of there that very moment. But I didn't.

So the days passed and the end of the semester was approaching. At the end of each semester a decision had to be made as to whether or not you would be returning for the next semester. This decision was shared by both the school and the seminarian.

If you were serious about your vocation and felt that this was what you wanted to continue doing, you would make an application to return for the following semester. The school would then consider your request, taking into account not only your academic record but also your "behavioral" record.

As I said before, from the very moment that you entered the seminary you were always under constant scrutiny—from the rector, your teachers, your cell leaders, your spiritual adviser, and the members of the formation team. They constantly (and I emphasize *constantly*) scrutinized your behavior and your conduct to determine if you would "fit in" to the communal lifestyle. Your life was under the microscope day and night, in class and out. Did you leave campus frequently to go out at night? Did you have a reputation for drinking too much? How did you get along with your teachers? Your peers? People in the community? Did you show up at all of the communal prayers?

That seems like pretty standard stuff to evaluate. But it went way beyond that. How did you talk? How did you laugh? What did you laugh at? What kind of jokes did you tell? How did you dress? How did you wear your hair? What kind of friendships did you make? Everything was looked at, discussed, weighed, and evaluated. Everything.

It was okay to have friends, but having particular friends—that was the term they used—was frowned upon. Because of celibacy and sexuality issues, there was an admonition about getting too close to any single individual, whether it was a fellow seminarian or a woman you might have come into contact with in the community as you were doing your apostolic work.

If they felt that a particular friendship was becoming inappropriate (in their eyes), they would really intensify the scrutiny. They'd address the issue with you, wanting to know if any kind of "affection" was developing in this friendship. They would counsel you about your behavior and make a notation in your student file. (Everything in this file was used to evaluate you when it was time to make a decision about returning the next semester.)

Now it always happens in a group, any group, that there will always be one or two individuals who you get close to more so than the others. I made some good friends while I was at the Franciscan seminary, some of whom I'm still in contact with. And since my experience in the chapel on Halloween night, I made it a point from that moment on to tell my friends exactly how much they meant to me and how much I loved them. (And if you think that that went over like a lead balloon with certain seminary officials, you would be correct.) You had to be very careful of how your relationships were perceived because from the first moment you got to the seminary, you were always under the shadow of being asked to leave. Always.

During the semester when I was there, a few of my fellow seminarians actually did "disappear." They were there one day and gone the next—their dorm room stripped bare, their seat in class empty. If you were involved in some major infraction—stealing, drugs, sex—you were told to pack up and leave. No discussion and no recourse. And they always seemed to kick guys out in the dead of night so that no one knew what had happened. So when classmates went missing, we were never officially told anything about it. They were never again mentioned; it was as if they had never been there. This was a fear that we all lived with every moment that we were there—that at any time we could be told to leave.

For some reason, when one of my classmates "vanished," it made me think of that old movie *The Nun's Story* with Audrey Hepburn. In the movie she plays a nun who eventually decides to leave the convent. She doesn't get kicked out in the middle of the night, but the way that they portray her leaving is really interesting.

She's in the convent for the last time, changing out of her nun's habit and putting on her civilian clothing before she leaves. It's deathly quiet in the convent, dark and somber. She finishes dressing, grabs her suitcase, looks around one last time, then opens the door to the outside, through which she'll leave and never be allowed back in.

But it's the moment when she opens the door that I find so interesting. Again, the convent room that she's in is silent, somber, and bare. She opens the door to the outside world and looks out through the door down the shadowy passageway created by the convent walls. Where the walls end there's light, life, and the sound of birds singing. I think there's an important message there!

When classmates vanished, of course, we talked about it among ourselves—you bet we did, and usually came to the conclusion that the transgression was sexual in nature. Whether that was actually true, I don't know. But we were at that age, that stage in life, when hormones were raging and physically we were maturing into our adult sexuality. But we never had any classes or talks about sex or celibacy—that was never discussed. Basically we were told, "You are a seminarian - no sex. If you're having any trouble with that, just pray. Or leave."

We knew, intellectually, that the life we were choosing meant no sex or marriage. But no one ever talked to us about it or gave us any guidance about handling sexual feelings. And we never really talked about it much among ourselves. (Though at times there was probably some of that praying going on.)

Occasionally, when we'd be watching TV, one of the guys might blurt out something like, "God, look at her—she's got really big boobs!" But even comments like that were few and far between, because of where we were and what we were trying to become. We were all of the same mind-set, wanting to be Franciscans, and sex was not a part of that.

This was not the place to be if all you could think about was getting laid. And also, too many overheard comments like that might wind up being discussed at your cell group meetings. Not that we exactly "ratted out" each other, but if something you said or did pissed off a fellow classmate, this was the place where they would normally bring it up. And things like that would end up going into your student file, and you didn't want that to happen.

So sexual feelings had to be repressed; not dealt with in any constructive way. And the handling, or non-handling, of sexuality issues eventually reared up and bit the church in its backside, but that's a discussion for a later chapter.

So why did I decide to leave the Franciscan seminary after my first semester?

When I entered the seminary I was very young and very idealistic. Being a part of this group, having a shared goal of letting go of worldly things, and emulating St. Francis and his way of life was a powerful, heady feeling, and I was filled with youthful zeal to live this ideal.

What happened, for me, was that the reality didn't live up to the ideal.

There was so much about my experience there that was good. Great, even. Being away from home for the first time was exciting. Being a part, however small, of the history and traditions of St. Francis was humbling yet awe-inspiring. I loved the rituals of the Franciscans—the prayers, the chants, the incense. I really loved that part of it so much so that I embraced, incorporated, and blended them with and into my own unique style, and one day the people at one of my future parishes would call me the "ritual" priest. And I loved learning and just being a part of this great group of guys.

But it wasn't enough. I've always looked for the "more" in life, and while there was all of that which was good, I still hadn't found my "more." Yeah, okay, the guys are great, the rituals are great, I love my classes, and I'm learning some fantastic things. So big whoop-dee-doo . . . s*omething* is still missing here.

I've talked about how closely we seminarians were scrutinized by the Franciscans. Well, we scrutinized them too. They were supposed to be our examples of the lived Franciscan way of life, but I and many of my fellow seminarians felt that they fell short of the ideal, that they were not living up to their vows, especially the vow of poverty. As the semester wore on, what we saw in reality left many of us disillusioned with the institution.

The Franciscan charism is to identify with the poor. It's more a spiritual poverty, relying on God, on the Divine, to help you through the day, and to help get your needs met. And there was little of that that we could see.

The Franciscan Priests and Brothers, at least in that seminary, had everything they needed—food, shelter, clothing, medical care, and cars. Everything was taken care of for them and they didn't want for anything. They lived in a fairly insulated world and didn't have to go out into the world to struggle or sacrifice.

Yeah, they could say that they identified with the poor. But then they could get together and have cocktails and occasionally go out for that lobster or prime rib dinner, or fly off to Aspen to go skiing on their vacations. They had advantages and opportunities that the poor didn't have, and it just didn't seem to me that this lifestyle was what I called identifying with the poor. This wasn't it.

And when I talked to some of the priests about this, basically they agreed with me. One of them, the Formation Team Leader, even told me that it really wasn't possible to live the life of St. Francis in the modern world. And when I was told that, I thought—well then, what am I doing here?

I was pretty concrete in those days; everything was black and white. And I think that I was so idealistic that it was all or nothing for me. If it wasn't perfect, then I couldn't be a part of it. Maybe that was a shortcoming on my part, maybe not. And maybe they were right. Maybe in an institution you can't live the ideal. But I felt that it was something that I could do in my personal life, whether I became a priest or not.

And if I did decide to become a priest, I could do it just as well at home. If ultimately there was no difference between a Franciscan Priest and a diocesan priest, then what was I doing here? I could train for the priesthood at home where I'd be closer to my family and friends, it would be a lot less expensive, and the outcome would be the same.

So near the end of the semester I met with a priest on the formation team. I'll call him Father Augustus. He was a very stern man. He even looked stern and forbidding. Father Augustus was this big German guy with a moustache, but he had a good heart. He met with me and said, "Well, we've talked about it and we'd all like for you to come back next semester." And I told him that I was troubled about that and just poured out how I was feeling. I said, "You know, I'm just a nobody student, and all of you have been living this life for years, and who am I to judge, but I don't think you all are really identifying with the poor in this life that you are living. You all work for this institution that takes care of everything for you, and I don't think that this is what St. Francis had in mind. For me, it's not enough."

Chapter 4

Farther Augustus looked at me straight in the eye and he said, "Well, son," (actually he used my real name but I can't say that here), "you're right. We have fallen very short as an example in terms of what St. Francis would live. But if you join us, you'll end up the same way. You'll not go beyond the level of the institution in terms of how we live this life. If you stay, you'll become just like the rest of us."

And at that moment, I decided that I wasn't coming back. (It seems like I made a lot of snap decisions back then.) So I told him right then and there that I wouldn't be returning next semester. He said, "Well, okay, it's your decision." He was very nice about it and wished me luck in my future, and said that if I changed my mind to let him know.

Father Augustus himself actually left the priesthood after that semester and got married.

Chapter 5

San Francisco Here I Come

I was going to leave the Franciscan seminary at the end of the semester.

It turned out that the majority of my freshman class also left at that time. Our class had started out with sixty-five guys and approximately forty of us left at the end of that semester. Our disillusionment with the institution was the impetus for most of us.

So what was I going to do next? I knew that I wanted to finish college, but I didn't know if I still wanted to be a priest. I was leaving the seminary, but I was taking the Franciscan charism with me. I had found my spiritual side and would always have that. I just didn't know if I would continue to have it as a layperson or as a priest.

There was a lot of discussion and planning going on among the guys who were leaving as to what they were going to do next. One of my good friends at the seminary, who was actually from that area and lived in the nearby city, asked me if I wanted to stay out there and get an apartment with him in the city and attend a different local college. Other friends of mine had decided to continue their education at different colleges around the country, and I got some offers to join them. And some of the guys talked about looking at different seminaries or even a monastery, and asked if I was interested.

I kind of wondered why I got so many offers from so many different people, some of whom I didn't even know that well. Again, most of these guys were quiet and shy, and I was the total opposite—like an erupting Mt. Vesuvius in their midst! Still the life of the party, talking to anyone and everyone, always joking around and laughing, and trying to get them to laugh, trying to lighten them up, and draw them out of their shells. So I got along really well with most of these guys, even the ones that I didn't know all that well, and I think it was probably because they thought that I was a lot of fun to be with and they wanted to keep the friendship going.

At that point, I began to think that maybe I should take a little time off to get my head straight and decide what I wanted to do before I committed to anything else. It just so happened that another close friend of mine, I'll call him Karl, who was a year ahead of me in the seminary, was also leaving.

He was having a really hard time with his studies and wasn't doing well in his classes, and decided that it was time to leave. He was going to take a year off to explore his options and was going to start by going to San Francisco (which you probably know is Spanish for St. Francis) to visit his aunt and uncle whom he hadn't seen in years. He asked me if I wanted to join him there and stay in San Francisco for a bit while we each thought about our futures.

His plan was to live among the poor as one of them, perhaps staying in a hostel, and serving the poor in the streets. I didn't think that was a good idea, especially not by himself because it sounded too dangerous. I thought that if I joined him we could serve the poor in a more responsible way by having jobs and living in an apartment, but still serving the poor as one of the poor.

So that's what I decided to do. The semester ended and I packed my bags and flew back home. My parents picked me up at the airport. I believe it was December 23, and they were a little surprised when they saw me because I had lost some weight and had let my hair grow long. I had always worn it really short when I was in high school and the ROTC, not quite a buzz cut, but short. My dad hated my hair and kept calling me a "hippie."

At first they were really happy that I had left the seminary. My mom's hopes of grandchildren were rekindled, and my dad hoped that I had finally come to my senses and would go into the Air Force. He still had dreams of seeing all of those medals being pinned to my uniform as I made general.

When I told them my plan to take some time off, hitchhike to San Francisco, and live there for a while, they went ballistic. I thought they were going to kill me. They thought they were going to kill me. All we did the whole time that I was at home was argue.

Luckily, I was able to get a job over Christmas break bussing tables at a local restaurant so I was working a lot of the time. But when I wasn't working, we were arguing. My mom valued education very highly—no one in my family had a college degree except for one of my uncles—and she was afraid that I would decide not to go back to school. My dad kept harping about cutting my hair and going into the military. It was one of the worst Christmases I've ever had.

In the end I told them, "I'm over eighteen, I can do what I want, and I'm going to San Francisco." So they brought out their "ace" card—that they had given me money for the seminary which now had gone down the tubes and that I "owed" them. So I brought out my "ace" card and I

Chapter 5

said, "Remember my car?" I had left my car behind when I went off to the seminary, and had just finished paying it off. While I was gone, my mom drove it to the store and got into an accident and totalled it. "Well," I told them, "We're even."

So, in mid-January amidst the screaming and yelling and gnashing of teeth and without their blessing, I left for San Francisco. I decided not to hitchhike but to take the bus since I couldn't drive there thanks to my mom totalling my car. My friend Karl was already there, living with his aunt and uncle, and he was going to meet me at the bus station.

The trip to San Francisco was fine, but something horrific happened when we got there. As we were getting off the bus at the terminal—a big, crowded, chaotic place—a male passenger who was about two people in front of me in line was mugged as he was stepping out of the bus. He was actually stabbed in the heart and died on the spot.

That was my welcome to San Francisco.

Luckily I quickly found Karl amidst all of the ensuing commotion—the police converging on the area, the ambulance arriving with sirens blasting, and the crowd of gawkers jamming up the place. We hopped a local bus to his relative's house where I met his aunt and uncle. They were a nice older couple, real "salt of the earth" kind of people. They told us that we could rent their extra bedroom until we got jobs and got on our feet, which was lucky for me because I arrived in San Francisco with my suitcase, backpack, and fifty-seven cents in my pocket. Talk about identifying with the poor!

Thankfully, we were both able to find jobs quickly, and ended up staying with them for only about two months. The apartment that we found and moved into was owned by a company called the Good Shepherd, which we took as a hopeful sign that God would look after us, and I believe that He did. There was a lot of violence in the city back then, and although our apartment wasn't in the best part of town, neither of us ever ran into any trouble.

Karl got a job at a McDonald's and my first job was doing inventory at the I. Magnin department store, but that was only temporary. My next job was also at a McDonald's, the one on Market Street, as a counter person. I was a damn good shake and fry man, and I still have the McDonald's watch they gave me when I worked there since I never throw anything away.

Neither of these jobs was very well paying, so with my years of wait staff experience, I applied to become part of the union in the food service industry. (You had to be a union member to work in the food service industry in San Francisco.) With my union card I was able to get a job at the St. Francis Hotel (St. Francis again) as a waiter on the breakfast/lunch shift. I also went to union headquarters, put in my card, and let them know that I was looking for extra work because they were always hiring banquet waiters for special events around the city.

So I also waited tables and did special events and parties at some of the other hotels in the area like the Fairmont (which was featured in the movie *Hotel*), the Stanford Court, and the Hilton. I gave up my job at McDonald's—I had to because it wasn't union—but I had gotten a promotion at the St. Francis Hotel and had a regular full-time shift there.

Although I was having a lot of fun as a waiter and making pretty good money, I was still thinking about my future. That was always in the forefront of my thoughts because I knew that I wasn't going to be waiting tables for the rest of my life. (As I look back on it, I sometimes wish that I had just stuck with that!)

I wasn't sure if I still wanted to be a priest, but I did want to pursue the spirituality of St. Francis. I also wanted to pursue more biblical studies. The Introduction to the Old Testament class that I had taken in the seminary whet my appetite, so to speak, and I wanted to learn more. Biblical studies actually became a life-long interest of mine, and according to my graduate theology professors, was where my talent lay.

So Karl and I talked, and he was also interested in living the spirituality of St. Francis. The idea of poverty and the whole romantic notion of serving the poor were still very strong in our minds. So, as a goal that we set for ourselves, we decided to save our money and make a pilgrimage to Assisi, Italy, to attend the annual Feast of St. Francis which is held every October 3-4. We decided to go to the source, to where it all began. We had left the seminary, but St. Francis still held us firmly in his grip.

In the meantime, I was still grappling with this poverty thing. It was always on my mind because it was such a big thing with St. Francis, and I didn't have a handle on it. So, after having been told by that Franciscan Priest in the seminary that one could not live a life of poverty in the modern world, I decided that I had to try and find out for myself whether or not that was true.

I decided to do this because despite what I was told, I just didn't believe that the time that you lived in had anything to do with it. If relating to the poor was a spiritual concept, then it transcended time and place. I didn't think it was any easier in St. Francis' lifetime to live a life of poverty than it is today. St. Francis lived during the height of the feudal system, where you had the very wealthy merchant class (of which he was a member), no real middle class to speak of, and the serfs, who were dirt poor and served the merchant class. It was the back-breaking work of the serfs that kept the economy viable.

St. Francis railed against the amassing of goods and money by the upper class while the poor had nothing. It was of such importance to him that he radically altered his lifestyle and devoted his life to it. Translated into a modern example, it would be like someone well known and affluent in today's world, someone like JFK, Jr. (if he were alive), giving all of his money and possessions to the Salvation Army and preaching his anti-establishment message up and down Fifth Avenue in New York City dressed in a thrift store t-shirt, shorts, and flip-flops.

This is something that just isn't done, whether it's the Middle Ages or the twenty-first century. Living that far outside of the norms dictated by your society and your social status is almost impossible to imagine.

For the Roman Catholic Church, the feudal system is still alive and well today. In the Middle Ages the Catholic Church adopted the feudal system as a way in which to administer its organization, which had become too big and unwieldy. The pope, bishops, priests, and deacons were the merchant class, and the laity (the people), were the serfs; and that model remains to this day. If you think I'm being critical here, this fact is a matter of historical record. Later on I'll tell you some of the things that we priests (yes, I eventually did get ordained) were told about "the people" (those of you who are reading this who are Catholic), that reinforces this system and will probably make your hair stand on end.

So to identify more closely with the poor, one day I decided (another snap decision on my part) to give away all—or most—of my possessions, and Karl did the same thing. We donated most of our clothing and all but essential material possessions to a local homeless shelter. I took the concept of poverty very literally and thought that this was a necessary first step for me to take in my quest to understand it. Karl and I reaffirmed our own private vows of poverty, chastity, obedience, and living according to the gospels.

I prayed about it and I said to God, "I've been told by the Franciscans themselves that I can't live this way in the modern world." So I asked God, "Teach me. I'm giving away all of my stuff like St. Francis did and I'm leaving it up to you, God. Either teach me that yes, I can live like this, live the gospels today, or no, I can't."

When my mom got wind of this, she called me and was really upset. She told me that I was doing crazy stuff and that I was being led by the devil. She had been told by a local Franciscan Priest back home, after he learned that I had left the seminary to go to San Francisco, that I was being led by the devil. My mother, being as religious as she was, took this statement very seriously. She was also very upset that I had given away the new travelling iron that she had given me. (To this day she still talks about that iron.)

So I had nothing left but two pairs of black dress pants for work, two pairs of jeans, two white shirts for work, two blue t-shirts, a pair of black shoes, a pair of sandals, some black socks, and some underwear. Oh, and my backpack, cross, alarm clock, toothbrush, and a razor. That's it. Karl and I continued to work because without our jobs we'd be out on the streets, and we didn't think we'd be able to help others effectively that way.

Since we couldn't sleep at night under a canopy of leaves in the forest or pick berries for our meals as St. Francis did, we decided to live as poorly as we could while still providing basic food and shelter for ourselves. We needed to adapt the rules of St. Francis to the world that we lived in today. We also needed to save what money we made to get to Assisi, which was very important to us. We were novices at this and were just kind of feeling our way as we went.

So what Karl and I ended up doing was working our regular jobs and then going off to do our apostolic work. We would volunteer our time at St. Boniface, which was the local Franciscan Church (St. Francis again), or work at the local soup kitchen, help out at the thrift store, or visit the homeless and the sick. We found all kinds of things to do because the need was so great.

We also put ourselves on a program of living out the gospels. We each had our little blue New Testament book *Good News for Modern Man* that we always carried with us in our back pockets. We'd read the scriptures each night, starting with Matthew, then Mark, then Luke, and John. We'd read all the positive things that Jesus said to do, like go visit the poor. Okay. That would be what we would do the following day, either on our own or together, depending on our work schedules, or we would do it after work.

Then the following night we'd read another few pages and it would say to feed the hungry. Okay. So the next day we would do that, in addition to what we had done the day before. So it kept building upon itself and we stayed pretty busy.

By the end of the Gospel of Mark, we were steadily doing all sorts of apostolic work that Jesus said to do in the scriptures. After the gospels we went through the writings of St. Paul, which didn't seem much different from the gospels but did give us a different perspective on what the gospels were about. And then we went through the Book of Revelation—of course we didn't know what the hell that was all about, but it gave us yet another dimension about how to understand what this growth experience of Jesus was about. For those of you who are interested, in a later chapter I can tell you exactly what the Book of Revelation—and its infamous number "666"—is all about.

So, here we are in San Francisco, Karl and I, trying to live out the gospels, trying to put into practice all of the positive things that Jesus said to do, and interpreting Jesus' words and how they fit into our modern world. We were trying to read His words with discernment, which means trying to understand what *He* wants, and not what *we* want. (That is the most basic, pristine question that drives spirituality of every religion—is it God's will or my will? And how do we know the difference?) Being positive began as a challenge, at least for me—saying only positive things, not being negative, and not putting people down. I had a bit of a rocky start on that. What I found, however, was that suddenly it wasn't a struggle to do. It was not a struggle to live life positively. In fact, it was pretty joyous, and no one was more surprised by that than me.

I mentioned earlier that we kept busy "doing" apostolic work. But as we grew into this experience, it no longer was a matter of going out and "doing." I don't quite know how to explain it, other than to say that it subsumed us—it became us or maybe we became it, but every moment of our lives was lived out of our connection with Jesus through St. Francis. Whether we were at home or at work or on the streets, the charism of St. Francis was our life.

It doesn't matter whether you wear a brown robe or a three-piece suit, or whether you live in a monastery or a mansion. The charism of St. Francis is something that is within you. And I remember thinking, "Ah, this is what it means to be a Franciscan." This is the something "more" that I was searching for at the seminary. And that maybe, without this experience, I wouldn't have understood it.

Did we see ourselves as holy? God, no. We were just two young, not very worldly guys trying to do the best that we could, trying to live out of our connection with the Divine, and hoping that we were getting it right. Sometimes we did good; sometimes we fell short of the mark. Were we somber and praying all of the time? Again no, not at all. No one has ever, ever accused me of being somber! We also lived out of the joy and laughter of our youth. I mean, here we were, away from home, away from our parents, doing exactly what we wanted to do, on our own in San Francisco in the seventies— how cool was that!

Our experience was all of those things that the early seventies seemed to represent—peace, love, happiness, harmony, and understanding (words from the musical *Hair*), flower children and flower power, naivete, and innocence. Life was always a "Hallmark Card" kind of existence. We felt empowered and thought that we could change the world. It was a great time to be young and full of dreams. It really was a joyous experience for us—living the gospels, working hard, praying, meditating, and helping others. We were living like seminarians but without a seminary, and people seemed to see us as an example of an alternative type of religious life. Once we even overheard someone comment about us, "Oh, those two—they're in love with Jesus."

As all of this was going on, Karl and I were beginning to garner a reputation of sorts. We would frequently hear comments (usually second hand) from a number of different people about these two "holy" guys who were going around "celebrating" God, and helping others, and about how happy they were, and about how much fun it was to hang out with them. We didn't go around trying to convert anyone. We weren't preaching it—we were trying to live it.

So other young people started gravitating towards us—friends, friends of friends, strangers, and other ex-seminarians who were also living in San Francisco. They seemed to like what we were doing and wanted to join us. So at any given time we would have a couple of extra people staying with us in our little apartment, both guys and girls. They would join us in our apostolic work for however long they could, and when they left to go back to school or work or whatever, others would take their place.

So it got to be a quasi-religious community of sorts. Karl came up with the idea of modelling our group into more of a real religious order. So using the life of St. Francis as a guide, we created some basic rules for this brotherhood that we had become, and we called ourselves the Franciscan Brothers of Jesus. We were constantly being asked to make it a more permanent group, but we didn't have the resources to do that.

So with that in mind and knowing that our plan was to go to Assisi in the fall, I put together a letter to the pope—at that time it was Pope Paul VI—asking for his opinion as to whether or not we should start a new religious order. I thought that instead of mailing it to him, we would travel to Rome from Assisi and attend an audience with him where I would hand him the letter.

It sounded good in theory, and it did happen, but not without a little drama. Do you know what most people, especially the pope's bodyguards, think when you suddenly approach the pope with your hand extended? Even back in those days it was not good thoughts. But this was my plan, however innocent it might have been.

A few incidents from my time in San Francisco stand out in my memory. One day I was walking down the street and I saw this little old lady waiting at the light to cross a pretty busy intersection. She had a couple of grocery bags in her arms that looked like they weighed more than she did. Well, I said to myself, it looks like she could use some help. So I approached her and said, "Ma'am, can I help you carry these?" as I reached for one of her bags.

Well, I scared the crap out of her. She must have thought that I was trying to steal her groceries because she started screaming at the top of her lungs and hauled off and hit me (and kept hitting me) with her purse.

Chapter 5

Needless to say, I did not end up helping her with her groceries. Sometimes the best of intentions can go seriously wrong.

Another time it was Good Friday, which according to the gospels is the day on which Jesus died on the cross. Karl and I were helping out at St. Boniface. We were going to clean the church and get it ready for Easter services. Both Karl and I had come straight from work, so we hadn't had time to go grocery shopping and there was no food in our apartment, not a crumb.

So we cleaned the church, put out the new missalettes (prayer books), and generally did whatever Brother asked us to do to get the church ready. He had to leave early, so he asked us to lock the doors of the church after us when we left.

We were getting ready to leave when out of the corner of my eye I noticed a package in the last pew. It was a package of cold cuts and deli meats still in its original wrapper. The whole time that we had been in the church—several hours—no one had come back to reclaim it.

"Well," we said, "we're hungry and we needed food and here it is. God provided for us."

But . . . it was Good Friday. Catholics abstain from eating meat on Fridays during Lent (a solemn period of a few weeks of contemplating, fasting, and sacrificing before Easter), and most especially on this day, the most holy Friday in the church year. Well, we thought, it's got to be okay because it's a gift from God.

So as we debated whether or not it would be a sin to eat it, we thought back to the gospels to one particular instance when St. Peter and St. Paul were discussing admitting gentiles to the new Christian faith. Up to that time, all Christians had been Jews first and still considered themselves Jews—Jewish-Christians.

But now there were people who were not Jewish who wanted to become followers of Jesus, and the question was—did they have to become Jewish first? And did they have to follow Jewish dietary laws? So Peter and Paul were discussing the dietary laws and "clean" and "unclean" food. And Peter has a vision where he is told by Jesus that he can eat unclean food, and Peter says, "Lord, I can't because the law says it's unclean." And Jesus tells him to eat it, that all food is clean because it comes from God.

So we ate the deli meat.

Another thing that happened was that my mother changed her mind about my being "led by the devil." San Francisco is a big tourist town and by waiting tables, I got to meet a lot of people from all over the country, even a few from my hometown. Occasionally, customers would be in a talkative mood and ask me questions like—what's your name, where are you from, what are you doing in San Francisco, what do your parents think of you being here—those kinds of things.

And I, of course, would blurt out my whole life story to anyone willing to listen, and with the unbridled enthusiasm and zeal that is typical of the young, I would tell them all about our little group and about what we were doing. Some of the customers would look at me with that "why don't you just shut up and take our orders" look, but every now and then some of them would say, "Oh, you belong to that group of young people that we've heard about who are going around town doing good works."

Well, a few of these people actually ended up contacting my parents, calling them or stopping by to see them when they continued on their travels, and telling them that they had met me and that I was a "good" boy, and that I was doing good things. I could hear my mother thinking—thank God he hasn't gotten anybody pregnant, and at least he's not running around with those dope-smoking hippies. (You'd have to know my mom.)

Even all these years later, my mom is still in contact with a few of the people that she and my dad met that way. So based on those encounters, my mom decided that I was behaving myself, not running around San Francisco drinking, carousing, and bringing shame to the family name.

So what did I learn from my time in San Francisco? I learned that being poor in spirit and identifying with the poor doesn't mean that you have to give everything away. But for me, by first doing the "outside" stuff like giving my possessions away, I had nothing left to fall back on but my real self, my "inside" stuff. I had to get rid of the outer distractions and grapple with myself and my motivations and with my relationship with the Divine Presence. And as I was doing that, I felt a shift on the "inside." And I grew, or you could say I was grown, to deeper levels of spirituality. The idea planted by the Franciscans of the outside needing to match the inside really came together for me.

I learned that "poverty of spirit" means emptying your inner self of all distractions—be it preconceived notions, your station in life, or your possessions. This way the "me" in ourselves can allow in the deepest "we" of connection with others so that we can be totally open and totally available to the needs of others. It means being disposed to listen—one soul to another—to what a fellow human being is saying. In addition, this means being present to the person in their need, not *my* need but *their* need. Whether it's finding a place to sleep, a meal to eat, words of encouragement, or a shoulder to cry on.

"Blessed are those who are poor in spirit, for theirs is the Kingdom of God," as the Beatitude says.

Chapter 5

    I gained a deeper understanding of Franciscan spirituality and finally understood what it meant to identify with the poor. And I learned it not in the classrooms of the seminary, but on the streets of San Francisco.

    Summer was approaching and it was time to start planning for our trip to Assisi.

Chapter 6

The Feast of St. Francis and The Miracle of the Bees

The Feast of St. Francis of Assisi is celebrated each year on October third and fourth in Assisi, Italy, which is Francis' birthplace. We didn't need to be there until the last week of September, but Karl's parents wanted him to come home for a visit before we left for Italy.

With that in mind, we planned to leave San Francisco at the beginning of summer. When I gave my two weeks notice at my job, my boss said that he was really sorry to see me go. He gave me a letter of recommendation so that if I ever again wanted to work in any of that corporation's hotels, anywhere in the United States, I would be assured of a job. That was really nice of him. So we quit our jobs, said goodbye to our friends, and hit the road.

In keeping with the idea of relating to the poor, we had decided to either hitchhike or take the bus to our homes. Back in the seventies hitchhiking was a fairly safe and economical way of travelling—which it no longer is. But it usually took you a longer time to get to where you were going, so we opted to take the bus. I was going to go home for a short visit myself, then head to Karl's place and stay with him and his family until we left for Italy.

So we said our temporary goodbyes to each other and headed off to our homes. I got home and did all the usual stuff—visited with family and friends and caught up on all of the things that had happened in my absence. I made it home just in time to attend my sister's graduation from high school.

My visit home wasn't a great success, although it wasn't as bad as my last one. My parents and an uncle, who was visiting at the time, seemed upset with me because I had "changed." They brought up the fact that in high school I had always dressed very nicely in a sport coat and tie and had short hair.

Now I was longhaired and no longer even owned a sport coat and tie. That's because I had given them away in San Francisco, which was another sore spot with them. For my sister's graduation I wore my waiter's uniform—black pants and a white shirt—because that was the only "dressy" clothing that I had. My folks were not happy about that.

While in San Francisco Karl and I had donned a laid back sort of quasi-religious garb—blue T-shirts, blue jeans, sandals, and identical wooden crosses on a leather thong that we always wore around our necks. We also had grey sweatshirts for the cold weather. It was all very simple clothing as simplicity is part of the Franciscan charism, so that's what I wore at home.

My family wasn't impressed with the external changes that they saw. We didn't have the constant arguments that marred my last visit home, but they weren't happy with me. They couldn't understand why I had given everything away (it's not like you're some rich kid who can afford to do that), and why my hair was long (you always used to look so respectable before). My dad was muttering the "hippie "word again.

My argument that Jesus had long hair fell on deaf ears. It irked me that all they seemed to care about were the external changes. Trying to tell them about some of the awesome things that I experienced on the inside got them glassy eyed and yawning.

After a very brief visit home, I got on the bus yet again and headed to Karl's house, which was several states away. I stayed at his parents' home. Since we were going to be there for a while, we needed to get jobs to make some money to live on. I wanted to pay his parents room and board, and we also wanted to save more money for our trip.

We both got jobs at a local funeral home. Karl worked the day shift and I worked the graveyard shift (pun intended). I spent most of my time driving to different parts of the state—it was a very large rural area—picking up the bodies of the deceased and bringing them back to the funeral home for embalming. I wasn't really involved in anything more than that, but I did get to observe the actual embalming process, which I thought was fascinating. As for what exactly Karl did there, I don't think I ever asked! All in all it was an interesting experience.

Since I had some daytime hours free, I also got a second job. I got certified by the state as a food service technician. One of the things that I was hired to do was to go into local restaurants to train or retrain their staff on how to upgrade to more of a "fine dining" experience. Wines were my specialty. I remember that I had turned twenty that summer, so I wasn't even legally allowed to serve liquor to customers myself. But here I was, teaching the restaurant staff who were all older than me, all about the different types of wines—their characteristics, how to serve them with flair, and which kinds of wines went with which foods.

Being back in the food service industry was a lot of fun. Who knows, maybe if I had stuck with that I would have my own reality television show on cable, something with a catchy name like "Wine Woes for the Woozy." Move over, Gordon Ramsay!

Every day that we were at his parents' place Karl and I would go to morning Mass. After Mass one day after everyone else had left the church, Karl and I stood before the Blessed Sacrament (the consecrated bread, or hosts, contained in the tabernacle) at the altar and again took our own private vows of poverty, chastity, obedience, and to live according to Jesus in the gospels.

We wanted to reaffirm our commitment to Jesus and to the Franciscan charism. We wouldn't be involved in any type of formal ministry here, but we would still live our everyday lives according to the gospels. We would still continue to be examples of St. Francis and Jesus in the ordinary acts of our daily lives with one another and with everyone that we met.

So we worked, went to Mass, and spent time with Karl's parents and relatives. Summer waned, autumn began, and it was time to leave for Italy. We said our goodbyes to everyone and boarded a bus to La Guardia Airport in New York City.

We got to the airport a few hours before our flight was due to leave, so we had time to freshen up in the men's room (like you could only do back then), and we just sat and relaxed until it was time to leave. We boarded the plane, had a nice flight, and landed in Rome with the clothes on our backs and our backpacks, which turned out to be quite a bit more than we eventually left Italy with, but that's a story in itself!

We didn't have any hotel reservations and no itinerary planned as to what exactly we were going to do when we got there. It wasn't that we were being lazy or irresponsible, it was more an attitude fostered by our experience in San Francisco. We were here seeking to connect with St. Francis and Jesus, and we would put ourselves in God's hands. We would let Him guide each day and go where Spirit led us.

Upon arriving we did at least have a place to stay. Back home, we had an order of sisters who had their Motherhouse in Rome. I knew several of them really well, and had kept in contact with them while I was at the Franciscan seminary. They knew of our plans to visit Assisi and said that we could stay at their Motherhouse while we were there. They had given me the name of a sister to contact when we arrived.

After we landed at the airport, I wrote the name of the sister and the name of their convent on a piece of paper that I showed to one of the airport employees. Neither Karl nor I was exactly fluent in Italian, but we were both conversant in a few languages (some more so than others). So with my piece of paper and our Italian phrase book, we were able to communicate enough to learn how to get to the Motherhouse.

Another bus ride took us to the convent where the porter at the gate didn't speak any English at all and just grinned politely at us. Thankfully, I had been given an Italian phrase to memorize by the sisters. When I repeated that phrase to the porter, he gave us a big smile and finally did end up leading us to the sister. (Thank you, Sister!) Since the sister was an American, she welcomed us to Italy in perfect English, showed us to our room, gave us a meal, and said that we were welcome to stay with them for as long as we wanted.

Originally we thought that we might stay in Rome and go to the Feast of St. Francis from there. But we found Rome to be a bit overwhelming for two kids from the sticks. It's huge, crowded, bustling, and noisy. We definitely felt a little out of our element—Karl especially—being a quieter, shyer kind of guy. But I have to admit that it was even a little intimidating for me too. It was kind of too much all at once. So we decided instead to head for Assisi, thinking it might be a little easier to get an introduction to the country through a smaller city.

We spent a day or two with the sisters, resting up and getting over our jet lag, said goodbye, and then headed to the train station. What a place! Huge station for a huge city. A cacophony of noise, color, and movement. People everywhere you turned; organized chaos all around. It was giving Karl a headache, but I thought it was kind of a fascinating place, at least a little easier to take than a whole city like this! We managed to find our way to the ticket counter, which was no easy feat. In my best Italian, I pointed to Karl and myself and said, *"Turista's, Americani's,* Assisi." It worked and they gave us our tickets and pointed us in the right direction.

The train ride itself was worth the trip! I know that not everyone has a thing for planes and trains and things mechanical like I do, but this was something unlike anything you'd see in the States. You didn't just hop onto the train and then hop off at your destination. Oh no. This was Italy where everything seems to be done with passion. This was more like a beautifully choreographed, well-executed train ballet!

You had the train engine, of course, then the first several passenger cars that were attached to the engine. This is where it gets interesting, or confusing if you weren't born in Italy. These first couple of cars would be designated for, say Assisi. So anyone going to Assisi like us would sit in those compartments. Then the next several passenger cars would be for, say Orvieto. So anyone going to Orvieto had to sit in those compartments. And so on for each of the towns or cities where the train would stop along the way, again each town with its own designated cars.

The train left the station (no surprises there), but when it got to the first town on its route, there would be this sudden flurry of activity as the last passenger cars designated for that town would be detached from the body of the main train, moved to an adjacent track, and reattached to a new engine. The passengers for that town would disembark, new passengers would get on, and off it would go. The main body of the train that we were on might be detached from its current engine and reattached to another, or sometimes not. Sometimes it would be left on the same track and sometimes diverted to another track. Sometimes new cars would be added and sometimes not. Then off we would go.

Same thing at the next stop—detach the last cars and go through all of those maneuvers again at each and every station. I don't know who wrote the script about when you got a new engine or not, or when you were diverted to a new track or not. But it was so much more complicated than our train system, and yet it was done so quickly and so efficiently every time that you hardly noticed. It was just amazing to watch! Well, I thought it was amazing. Karl slept through most of it. I wonder if they still do it that way....

After about a three-hour trip (like it says in the song from the *Gilligan's Island* sitcom), we ended up in a city called Santa Maria degli Angeli (St. Mary of the Angels). It is located at the base of this very large mountain, and Assisi is located at the top. The train doesn't go up the mountain so you have to take a small crowded bus to get the rest of the way. I remember that the ride up was very picturesque, but steep at times and occasionally a little scary—but only if you looked out the window!

Again, no real plans as to where we were going to stay but we had somehow, somewhere, heard about a group of nuns (thank God for nuns!) who were called the Franciscan Sisters of the Atonement or the "Graymoor Nuns." They were an American order from New York and they ran a guesthouse in Assisi called St. Anthony's. Kind of like a precursor to a modern bed and breakfast place, only quite a bit larger.

Most of the buildings in Assisi dated from the Middle Ages and were really big by American standards. These buildings were all made out of varying sizes of a pink marble-like stone, which caused the city to look like it was shimmering when the sun rose and set. It was a breathtaking sight. I don't think they make buildings like that anymore.

Anyway, the nuns were an American group and thankfully spoke English. They ran the guesthouse basically for pilgrims, and provided short stays for people coming to visit the places associated with St. Francis. So we ended up going there, and luckily for us they had a room with two beds that we rented from them. They also served meals—Mediterranean style food—which was new to both Karl and me, and it was just delicious stuff.

We arrived about a week before the feast and spent that week being tourists—sightseeing, taking lots of pictures, and buying souvenirs for our families and friends. Assisi was commercialized even back then with just about every other shop selling souvenirs of St. Francis. And there were always lots of people in the streets at all hours of the day and night because it was such a popular tourist destination.

Karl and I met a lot of people on our daily excursions, which wasn't hard to do because I, of course, would say hello and start up a conversation with just about everybody we bumped into. Usually after a polite "Hello," Karl would kind of hang back, smile, and roll his eyes as I blabbed away. Lots of people got to know our life stories whether they wanted to or not!

Among the people that we met that way were two older American ladies, Betty and Dolores who were both from Oklahoma and were there on a pilgrimage to see the birthplace of St. Francis. Neither of them was Catholic, but they were both very devoted to St. Francis. For some reason we just really hit it off with them, and the four of us ended up doing a lot of our sightseeing together. We all went to Rome together to explore that city.

I kept in touch with both of them after we returned to the States and they became life-long friends. Although Dolores lived in a different state, she actually came to my ordination and did one of the readings at my ordination Mass, and we still keep in touch. Sadly, Betty has since passed away.

And, of course, Karl and I went to all of the sites associated with St. Francis. We visited where he was born, where he was baptized, the Church of San Damiano which he rebuilt, and all of the other places of historical and spiritual interest. We had our guidebooks, and sometimes we would go to these places on our own, sometimes with our friends, and occasionally we would take bus tours.

We had a somewhat unique experience when we visited a place called Eremo Delle Carceri, which is situated on the mountainside of Mt. Laverna. This is the site where St. Francis received the stigmata, the five wounds of Christ. When Jesus was nailed to the cross, he had iron spikes driven through the palms of his hands and through his feet. At one point while he was hanging on the cross, a Roman soldier pierced his side with a spear.

According to Catholic tradition, there have been a few people throughout history (very few) who have received the stigmata, and who have had these same wounds appear on their hands, feet, and side. These wounds also bleed from time to time. Basically, to receive the stigmata means that you have been blessed by God. That, as one has imitated so closely the values of Jesus, even his "spiritual wounds" manifest as real physical wounds. And now that you are living in such spiritual union with Jesus, you have also been joined to His physical sufferings.

On this visit we were on a tour bus with a large group of tourists from several different countries. The bus could only take you up to a certain point in this mountainous terrain. To reach our destination, which was an ancient convent nestled higher up on the mountainside, we had to walk the rest of the way up a dirt footpath.

There must have been a large beehive close to the footpath that we somehow disturbed. One minute we were all walking peacefully along, enjoying the blue skies and the beauty of our surroundings, talking amongst ourselves about this place that we were going to see, and the next minute we were totally enveloped by a swarm of buzzing bees. It was as if someone had thrown a blanket woven entirely of bees over us. You couldn't even see the sky anymore—just bees everywhere you turned. Flying around us and through us and under us, landing in droves on faces and eyes, in noses and ears, and on every exposed arm and leg. It was like suddenly being plopped into the middle of a cheap horror movie.

Everyone was panicking, yelling, shouting, stumbling, and flailing about. No one wanted to get stung, and a few of the people in the group were yelling that they were allergic to bees. (I also have a bee allergy.) One elderly American lady was crying and shouting, "Oh my God, we're going to die here!" She was so agitated that I was afraid that she was going to have a heart attack right then and there. Everyone was lost in their own panic, thrashing about, trying to get the bees off them.

I didn't know what to do, but I knew that someone needed to do something. So I just started going around to everyone though covered in bees myself saying, "It's okay, it's okay, don't panic. Calm down everyone, calm down. It's okay. St. Francis will watch over us." And as I said this to each person I also hugged them as best I could under the circumstances. So I just kept repeating myself over and over, trying to be heard through the cries and shouts, and trying to keep my voice as soothing and calming as I could. I kept telling everyone to calm down, that it would be okay, that we were here at this holy place on a journey for St. Francis, and that he would protect us.

And people actually started listening to my voice, listening to those words over and over, and they did start to calm down. The flailing and thrashing were lessening. I'm sure that part of it was just the fact that someone was giving them some direction in the midst of the chaos, and part of it was the repetitive, soothing cadence of my voice. And most everyone likes a hug. But it worked and the panic was ebbing.

And just as suddenly as they had appeared, the bees were gone. Suddenly you could see the blue of the sky again and feel the gentle breeze and hear birds singing in the trees around us. And then this sensation, this feeling of being almost physically embraced in a peaceful swathe, descended on us. It wasn't just the absence of the bees, our relief that they were gone. It was a feeling of profound peace. It felt to me as if the spirit of St. Francis enveloped us. And by the way everyone reacted, glancing wide eyed at each other and breaking into smiles, I knew that they felt it too.

Although we were here in this holy place hundreds of years after his death, it felt as if the spirit of St. Francis was there with us, present to us, and cradling us in his love. It was a tangible feeling of contentment and connection that we shared for those few moments, and miraculously not one person was stung. People were murmuring that St. Francis had indeed watched over us. Some murmured that it was a miracle—the miracle of the bees of St. Francis.

I don't know exactly what happened there, but I know what I felt. Maybe it was our own attitudes that we brought to this place with us. A diverse group of people joined together on this day, in this place, in our need to walk the path that St. Francis had walked, and to share in his experience. A purity of purpose from each of us perhaps, that together was strong enough to be transformed into a perceptible joy. But whatever it was, we were able to turn a terror-filled experience into one of peace and connection to each other. That is what Spirit can do, and I believe that is what we experienced that day—our own small miracle on Mt. Laverna.

The purpose of our visit to Assisi was to attend the Feast of St. Francis, which we finally were able to do. The celebration started on the evening of October 3 in St. Mary of the Angels, the city at the base of the mountain. The focal point of the celebration was the massive outdoor courtyard of their church from which the services were being conducted. There were prayers and scripture readings interspersed with the singing of the Psalms and the telling of the story of the life of St. Francis.

It seemed as if there were thousands of people there—locals, tourists, pilgrims, and religious. I think that every religious order in the world associated with St. Francis was represented. People were massed in the courtyard, most holding a lighted candle and, as the sun began to set, the courtyard was aglow with shimmering waves of light. The effect was quite beautiful to see. It was a cool evening with a light breeze; just a perfect night. The crowd spilled out from the courtyard into the piazza, streets, and the hillsides of the city.

It was a celebration so there was a festive air, but there was no doubt that this night was dedicated to their beloved St. Francis. You felt surrounded by a loving aura, a spiritual emanation weaving through the very air. The crowd's collective love for this man was the impetus that brought them together in ways far beyond their physical proximity. This night was all about individuals connecting to each other through St. Francis.

Chapter 6

People were everywhere you turned, everywhere you looked, and many in heartfelt prayer. Countless voices were joined together as one as they stood or sat or strolled the piazza murmuring their prayers. Everyone was connecting and sharing in some way—bestowing warm smiles, holding hands, hugging each other, and even an occasional kiss was seen. Food and drink, laughter and stories, and prayers and conversation bound everyone together in their devotion to their saint.

The night was alive with love, peace, and goodwill, and the spiritual energy of all of these people illumined the night far more brightly than the candles could. There were no strangers on this night. It was intoxicating for Karl and me to share in this night with each other and with all of the other individuals that were here to honor this man.

The next morning the celebration moved up the mountain to Assisi. The day began at sunrise with Mass at their church, the Basilica di Francesco. It is an ancient building dating from the thirteenth century, an enormous multi-storied structure with a very large courtyard, or portico. The Basilica also houses the tomb holding the sarcophagus containing the remains of St. Francis.

Masses were held continuously throughout the day to accommodate the scores of people that were there. A sea of people from every country and every walk of life—from cardinals of the church to poor local farmers—all of them were there to honor one man.

Karl and I attended one of the Masses. We sat in those venerable surroundings—exquisitely painted frescoes all about us—knowing that we were in the very city that gave birth to St. Francis, and in the church that contained his earthly remains. We felt as if we had come home.

After Mass we joined the throngs that were strolling the streets of the city, each avenue awhirl with activity. All types of entertainment were on offer throughout the day—bands playing, choirs singing, plays being performed, outdoor cafes bustling, vendors selling food, and a never ending variety of souvenirs. It was a carnival-like atmosphere overlaid with the same spiritual energy of the evening before. The only purpose of the city that day and of everyone in it, was to honor their beloved saint. We had made our pilgrimage to Assisi, and it surpassed anything that we could have ever hoped for.

After attending the Feast of St. Francis, we didn't want to leave Assisi. Walking the streets that St. Francis had walked, breathing the air that he had breathed, all of it had been such a life-enhancing experience that we were reluctant to leave it. After looking at our finances, we figured that we had enough money left to stretch out our visit for another week at the most, and that was disheartening.

And then several things began to happen.

Chapter 7

Jesus Moments: Meeting the Saints

The first thing that happened had to do with the Sisters of the Atonement, the sisters we were staying with. We had gotten to know them really well, had gone beyond the role of guests, and had become friends with them. I think we were a bit of a novelty to them—these two young boys from America in their blue jeans and sandals and crosses. We stood out as being different from the other tourists both in our dress and our behavior. Again, we weren't in any kind of formal ministry but we were living by our vows, living by the gospels, living Christ's love with one another and with everyone we met, and they noticed this. Many people actually assumed that we belonged to a religious order.

It so happened that while we were there, a few of their sisters had become ill and were being sent back to the States for medical care. So they found themselves shorthanded when it came to running their guesthouse. Mother Superior asked us if we would consider staying on with them for a while to help them out. We didn't have any other plans, so we accepted their offer. They needed some general help—cleaning, shopping, cooking, serving meals to the guests, and handy-man kind of stuff in exchange for room and board. Even if we had had to sleep on the floor, I would've said yes just for their food! (You know I've got to talk about the food!)

Karl and I had been sharing one of their guest rooms. In our exploration of the inn, we had discovered this tiny, out of the way room—more like a landing than a room—that didn't seem to have any particular use. You went up a few stone steps at the end of a long hallway on the second floor and came to a pair of wrought iron gates. These gates were not solid, you could see through them and they opened into this small area, maybe five feet by six feet in size. As you entered into this small area, there were two stone benches built into the walls on the right and left sides (opposite each other), and there was a door on the far end that opened up to the outside. The door would lead you out on to a flat portion of the roof. If you were careful, you could eventually make your way down to the street via the flat portions and balconies scattered about on that side of the building.

The room was otherwise empty and we had never seen anyone use it, so we asked Mother Superior if we could use that room to stay in, giving them our guest room back so that they could rent it out to someone else.

She agreed and we moved our few belongings there. We each took a stone bench to sleep on at night. We covered them with blankets, added a pillow, and they made pretty decent beds. Of course, we were young at the time with no aches or pains yet, so it worked for us.

So we actually ended up staying with the sisters for about two-and-a-half months. I would help Sister Marta with the daily food shopping. It wasn't like shopping back home where you'd make out your grocery list and go to the supermarket and buy a week's worth of food. There weren't any supermarkets. Instead, you had an open air market in the center of town. You would also find small shops that sold certain items only, like a bakery and a butcher.

Early every morning sister and I would go to the market and buy food for that day, everything fresh to use for that day's meals. Fruits from the local orchards, vegetables fresh from the local farmer's fields, women selling homemade cheeses, and cream and butter churned the old fashioned way. And then off to the baker's for some bread fresh from the oven. Sometimes a stop at the butcher's for locally grown, freshly-killed chickens, hanging in rows by their necks, or for some locally-raised beef, veal, or duck. I would help her with the shopping and then carry it all back to the guesthouse.

After we got back from the market we would have breakfast. I remember a large glass jar, sitting on one of the kitchen counters, full of cereal. It was some kind of homemade granola because I never saw any actual boxes of breakfast cereal. Typically, we might have cereal, cheese, bread and jelly, coffee, and occasionally some pastries.

It probably doesn't sound all that exciting, but again, when the bread is freshly baked, the cheese is from the farm down the road, the jellies and jams are homemade and not from a store shelf, and the cream for the coffee is churned and not from a plastic carton—believe me, it's like manna from heaven! And the coffee was the best I'd ever tasted.

Lunch was usually hand-made pasta tossed with a little olive oil and fresh sautéed vegetables, not the heavy sauces we typically used back home when we made so-called "Italian" food. More freshly baked bread, local cheeses, olives from the sisters' olive grove, and wine. We didn't drink the water as they were having some kind of problem with the water supply while we were there, so we ended up drinking wine and bottled sodas, but mostly sodas.

Chapter 7

Dinner was basically a repeat of lunch, but with homemade soup on the menu (with the leftover pasta from lunch since nothing was ever wasted) and occasionally chicken or some type of meat, usually veal. Because it was fresh veal, it had a somewhat stronger flavor than we were accustomed to, very different from what you get in the frozen meat department in US supermarkets. And usually there would be ice cream or gelato (Italian style ice cream) for dessert.

You might be able to tell from the way that I go on about food, that I've had a bit of a weight problem most of my life and I'm still working on that. But when I was in Assisi, it was one of the few times in my life when I was as skinny as a rail. I think that was the miracle of St. Francis and the Mediterranean diet!

So we helped out with all of the chores associated with running a guesthouse. The house and grounds were in need of some minor repairs, and since I had grown up helping my grandfather build fences and fix anything that was broken, the handy-man role fell to me. The sisters' olive grove had fences that were in need of repair, and in the house there were always closet doors, shelves, and various other items that benefited from a hammer and nails. Karl worked mainly in the kitchen with food prep and cooking, and we both helped with general cleaning, so we both stayed pretty busy from morning until night.

Everyone worked hard, but one of the great things about Italy was that everyone took a siesta (that sounds more grown up than saying a nap, but basically it's the same thing). The whole town would close down at about three in the afternoon until five or six o'clock, then all the stores would reopen and everyone would go back to work for a few hours. Dinner was eaten late, at about eight or nine in the evening, and after dinner most people would head outside to the piazza in the center of town for a walk.

You could sit at one of the outside cafes and have coffee and dessert—mainly gelato—or stroll around listening to the minstrels singing. Sometimes they had outdoor plays in the evening. This was something that Karl and I got used to pretty quickly because it seemed to be just about the perfect way to live. It was so different from the rat-race rush that makes up our lives in the States.

There was a young man, a tourist, who had been staying at the guesthouse while we were there. When it was time for him to leave, he found himself short of money and he couldn't pay his bill. He had a motorcycle—a two-seat Vespa—that he left with the sisters as collateral until he could come up with the money to pay his bill.

I think it must have proven to be a temptation to Mother Superior because she asked if either Karl or I knew how to ride a motorcycle, which I did because I'd had one in high school. After a bit of praying about it, she asked me if I would teach the sisters how to ride it. At first she thought that maybe it wouldn't be appropriate for nuns to be seen on a motorcycle, but what the heck, this was the seventies so her adventurous side won out.

I gladly agreed, and teaching them was a hoot! They all wore these long, heavy brown habits with thick, ugly woolen socks and sandals. At first, their hopping onto the motorcycle proved to be a little awkward. But they quickly got the hang of it and soon were riding like pros, having a lot of fun in the process. The citizens of Assisi might have been surprised at first, but they soon got used to seeing the Vespa speed by with a quick glimpse of laughing nuns with brown robes billowing in the wind behind them.

Sometimes they would let Karl and me use the motorcycle on the weekends when we had time off, so we used it to explore the countryside. The area was so hilly that frequently it was more about pushing the damn thing up the hills rather than riding it, but it was still a lot of fun.

They also let me use it to become a little bit of a tour guide myself. As I said before, there were a lot of tourists in town and many of them had seen Karl and me riding the Vespa. Some of them asked if I could take them sightseeing on it since it was a two-seater. So I would take them wherever they wanted to go. While I never charged them for the trip, they always insisted on paying me anyway, and usually it was with a lot of lira (Italian money). Most of them wanted to see the places associated with St. Francis, so I took them to these historical places and shared the details of his life and ministry with them, adding my own spiritual connections and things that had inspired me.

A fairly-large number of those who asked me for tours were US military men and their families who were stationed in Italy. They were trying to get in some last minute sightseeing before their tours were up and they had to leave Italy. After I had given them their tour, many of them would not only pay me for the excursion, but also gave me what was left of their Italian money (once they left for the States, they wouldn't be needing it any longer). I like to think they did that because they were so impressed with my service, and maybe that was part of it. I did give them a lot of history about the sites we visited. I mean a lot—probably more than they cared to hear, but once I get going, it can be hard to shut me up!

But I also gave them my own spiritual insights about the sites we visited, and I think the fact that I was a fellow American who looked and acted like a religious brother had more to do with it. I was very appreciative of the gesture and gave most of what I made to the sisters, as they needed every penny of it to keep St. Anthony's operating. I might have given the sisters money, but they gave us so much more in terms of our experience there—things whose worth can't be counted in currency.

I had mentioned earlier that several things happened to us after the Feast of St. Francis. Our audience with Pope Paul VI was one of them. If you'll remember when Karl and I were in San Francisco, we thought about starting our own religious order, which we called the Franciscan Brothers of Jesus. We had written that letter to the pope asking his permission to do that, along with a set of rules that would govern the order. And how, instead of mailing it, we had decided that we would give it to him in person when we got to Italy.

Pope Paul VI
Who granted us permission to
start a New Order of the Church

So we attended a general audience with the pope. At the end of the audience, as the pope was being carried out in his chair right in front of me, I moved towards him and reached out my hand to give him the envelope with our letter in it. The pope saw me, turned towards me, stretched out his hand and had just taken the letter when suddenly security guards swarmed towards me from every which way and surrounded me, cordoning me off from the pope. I was lucky that they didn't tackle me!

They then snatched the letter from his hand, and for a moment all movement ceased. Everyone seemed to be frozen in place and you could hear a pin drop in the silence. I guess they wanted to make sure that I hadn't handed him a letter bomb or something because at that time in Italy there was a lot of terrorist activity occurring. After a few moments the pope looked at me again, looked me in the eye, put both of his arms out and gave his shoulders a big shrug, as if saying—sorry, it's out of my hands. And with one hand he waved at me and with the other he gave me his blessing. So I waved back and said, "Thank you."

The silence was broken, activity resumed, and they finished carrying him out. The guards dispersed, thankfully without me in tow! A few months after that meeting, we actually received a letter back from the pope giving us his blessing to start the order. But by that time, our plans and our lives were taking a different direction.

Another thing that happened to us had to do with Padre Pio. Padre Pio was a man who was born in Italy in the late eighteen hundreds and became a Capuchin Franciscan Priest. He died in 1968. He was widely revered in Italy as an extremely holy man who had received the stigmata (physical wounds) of Christ.

I had read about him when I was in the Franciscan Seminary—about his ministry and the miracles that were attributed to him. I remember reading that it was said that he was known to be in two different places at the same time. He would be seen, for instance, praying at a monastery in one part of the countryside in full view of people. Yet at the same time in a different part of the countryside, he would be seen by many people attending a Saint's Feast Day celebration. There was also a mention of flowers—violets—associated with him, that an overwhelming scent of violets would precede his presence, which they called "the odor of sanctity." (He has since then been canonized by the Catholic Church as a saint.)

Karl and I were intrigued and wanted to learn more about him. I don't remember exactly how it happened, but during our stay we bumped into someone who knew a woman who had been a personal friend of Padre Pio's. She had known him for many years and he had been her spiritual advisor. So I got the woman's name and address and wrote to her, explaining that we were two American Seminarians who had come to Assisi for the Feast of St. Francis, that we were trying to live the Franciscan way of life, and that we would very much like to learn more about Padre Pio.

She actually wrote back to us, agreed to meet with us, and invited us to her home. She lived in a small village about three hours from Assisi. So Karl and I took the train to her village, and walked to her house from the train station. We got to her house, knocked on the door, introduced ourselves, and she invited us in. She was a middle-aged Italian woman, very petite, very pretty, and just a very nice lady.

She lived in a small simple house by herself; her husband had died and her children were grown and moved away. Her home was extremely neat and clean and had these beautiful white-washed walls. She led us into her living room, and it was obvious that she was a very religious woman. The walls were adorned with pictures of the pope and various saints, and she had a small personal altar sitting on a desk top in the living room. It had pictures of Jesus and Padre Pio, vases of flowers (not violets), and some candles on it.

We sat down and ended up talking to her for about three hours. She didn't speak very much English, but with our facility with languages and the fact that our Italian had greatly improved, we were able to communicate fairly well and all in all it went pretty smoothly.

We told her our story, about how we were on a spiritual search, how we were trying to live the gospels and the Franciscan charism. We asked her to tell us about Padre Pio, about what kind of a man he was, what his philosophy was, what drove him, and what he was like as a friend.

Padre Pio
Capuchin Franciscan now considered a Saint

She said that she was pleasantly surprised by our request because most people who asked her about him only wanted to hear about the miracles that were associated with him and nothing more. She seemed fascinated by the fact that although we were so young, we were obviously sincere and on a real spiritual quest, and that this was very rare.

So she told us all about Padre Pio, about his devotion to St. Francis, his love of God, and about how caring for and helping others was always the most important thing in his life. She gave us personal anecdotes about his life. The way she spoke of him gave us a very real sense of the man, making us feel as if we knew him through her. And all the while as she spoke of him, she was just glowing. I don't know how to explain it other than she had this very warm and loving aura about her. We felt as if we were in the presence of a woman who, herself, was very holy.

At one point during our conversation, she offered us tea and left the room to prepare it in her kitchen. At that very moment an overwhelming scent of violets enveloped us. If you've ever smelled a violet, multiply that a thousand fold. It was a strong, somewhat pungent smell, dizzying in its intensity, and was simply overwhelming. I remember that I was beginning to feel a little intoxicated and a little headachy from the smell.

Karl and I looked at each other, and thought—okay, maybe there's some logical explanation. So I started to look around to see if I could find any obvious source for the smell, even though it seemed to be coming from just about everywhere all at once. I looked under the furniture, at the walls, behind pictures on the walls, looked under the rug, and sniffed the candles on the altar. I even stood on a chair to get a closer look at the ceiling to see if there was some kind of a vent there, but I didn't find anything that could be pinpointed as the source. Karl and I kept darting glances at each other because the smell wasn't dissipating; it remained strong and steady.

Our hostess returned to the living room carrying a large tray with a teapot, cups and saucers, cream and sugar, and some homemade cookies, which were wonderful. Wisely, by that time I was sitting down again. She walked in and then stopped dead in her tracks. Obviously, she smelled the violets too. Her face, which already had been radiant, now became almost transcendent as a huge smile blossomed across her features. She said, "He's here. And he approves of you." She said it very simply, very matter-of-factly. She served the tea and cookies and we continued talking, awash in the scent of violets.

She asked us if we would pray with her, which we did. It was getting late by then, growing dark outside, and we told her that we needed to be getting home. She then asked us if we would like to spend the night in her guestroom and head home in the morning, but we didn't want to impose upon her.

We thanked her for sharing Padre Pio with us. Before we got up to leave, she asked us to wait for just a moment saying there was something that Padre Pio wanted us to have. She went over to the desk and opened one of the drawers and removed two items that she brought over to us. To Karl she handed one of the brown gloves that Padre Pio wore on his hand to cover the wound on his palm. To me she handed a bloodstained piece of cloth that had covered the wound on his chest. She told us that she used to help him wipe the blood from his wounds and wash them when they bled. She also gave each of us a picture of him. We thanked her very sincerely and bade her goodbye.

Karl and I left her house and walked through the fields back to the train station. I thought of that priest in the Franciscan seminary who told me that you could not live the life of St. Francis in the modern world. I then felt such exaltation as I thought oh, but you can because we had just experienced a man who did just that.

We came away from that encounter feeling as if we had been in the presence of holiness, and had been personally touched by Padre Pio. We felt the spirit of a man we had never met, but who had left his mark on the world and now on us. I still have that bloody cloth and his picture, which is framed and hanging on my wall at home.

One of the most wonderful things that happened to us while we were in Italy was meeting Mother Teresa. Neither Karl nor I had heard of her in the States, but she was very well known in Italy. Everyone was talking about her—about this very holy woman who founded an order of sisters called the Missionaries of Charity. Their motherhouse was in Calcutta where she and her group of sisters worked with the poorest of the poor on the streets and in the slums of India, helping this desperate group of people that the rest of the world ignored.

Mother Teresa was opening convents—she called them "houses"—in different countries all over the world, and helped the poor of those countries. She also had a "house" in Rome. We heard that people in Italy were calling her another St. Francis, and Karl and I really wanted to meet her.

We called the convent of the Missionaries of Charity in Rome and asked if we could come and meet Mother Teresa. They said of course we could, but that she wasn't there at the moment, but was expected to be there in a week. I remember that when I talked to the sister there, and she used the word "mother," I had to pause for a moment, thinking—mother? And then, I remembered, oh, yes, they call her mother, not sister. So, by damn, we jumped at that opportunity and set up a meeting with her.

We had read that at every new house that Mother Teresa opened, the first thing that she did was to buy a cross—usually a large, plain, wooden one. It would be hung outside the door of the convent, like to the right or left side of the front door, to identify it as a house of the Missionaries of Charity. So Karl and I went shopping and bought a San Damiano cross, a replica of the cross that spoke to St. Francis. It too was large, made of plain wood, but beautiful in its craftsmanship and simplicity. We wanted to give it to her as a gift when we went to meet her.

History tells us that that the cross hanging in the Church of San Damiano spoke to St. Francis and told him, "Go, Francis, repair my church, for as you see, it is falling into ruin." Francis took those words literally and started repairing and rebuilding the churches in the area. Only later on in his life did he come to the understanding that it wasn't the external, physical church building that he was supposed to repair, but the spiritual part of the church—the "inner" experience of church.

We waited with mounting excitement for the week to pass. We then traveled to Rome to the convent, which as I seem to remember, was located near the Coliseum. We knocked on the door and one of the sisters let us in. We were a little surprised by how she was dressed. She was wearing a white sari with a blue sash. We had never seen a sister dressed like that before. We later found out that the sisters dressed that way because that was the clothing of the very poor in Calcutta. The only item that designated them as being religious was a small brown wooden cross that they wore over their left shoulder—over their heart.

We also found out that there is a "brothers" order of the Missionaries of Charity. This was started by a Trappist monk in conjunction with Mother Teresa because there were a lot of men asking to be able to join in her work. They had their own "house" and wore simple cotton pants, shirts, sandals, and the cross over their left shoulders.

We were led inside to Mother Teresa where we introduced ourselves and gave her the cross. It was about two-and-a-half by three feet in size, and we had wrapped it in plain brown paper and tied it with string. She graciously thanked us for our gift. I believe that our cross eventually ended up in Yemen, in the first house that she opened there.

The first thing we noticed about Mother Teresa was how darn small she was! She was just this tiny thing, and up close kind of reminded you of everybody's grandmother. She was very open and warm with us. After spending just a little time with her, we realized that this woman was a little bundle of energy! Even when she was standing still, you could still sense energy radiating from her.

Mother Teresa sat down with us and asked us to tell her about ourselves, what we were doing in Italy, and what our plans were. She asked us those things not with mere politeness, but with genuine interest. We spoke for a time about those things, and then she told us about the work that she and her sisters were doing. I remember her sitting there with this intense look on her face as she leaned in and spoke to us, the fervor in her voice as she spoke of the poor and their needs.

It was very powerful, compelling, and mesmerizing sitting there with her, listening as the passion of her words poured over us. Here in the flesh, sitting right next to us, was the Franciscan charism. We had heard that the people of Italy called her another St. Francis, and we now believed that, too.

We ended up spending the whole day with Mother Teresa and the other sisters. She invited us to pray the liturgies with them, which we did. She then held us spellbound as she spoke about spirituality in today's world, and about the work of St. Francis and how each and every one of us can walk in his footsteps and continue his work. We were just fascinated by her and her obvious devotion to St. Francis and Jesus. It shone through every word that she spoke.

We shared their meals that day, and Mother Teresa took the time to speak to both Karl and me individually. Later in the day when he and I were again sitting alone with her, we told her about our plan to start a new religious order. But after spending the day with her, we felt that a new order wasn't necessary because she was already doing exactly what we had been thinking of doing. And now that she had a brothers order, we could just join that.

So Mother talked to us about that, about our plans, and surprisingly to us, she counseled us to wait. She said that we were so young, and while it was clear that we were on a spiritual path and that our desires were genuine, we should not make any hasty decisions. Mother Teresa said that we should go back to the States and think more about it, pray about it, and if God wanted us to join her, then He would lead us back to her. She said, "God has something in store for you, so let's see where it takes you."

On a more practical note, she told me that she didn't yet have the facilities to train or ordain a priest to her order, and that I should continue my studies back at home. At the time of my ordination if I still felt the same way, then I could be ordained for her order and come back to serve with her. Since I have a bit of a history of making snap decisions, I listened to what she told me and took her words to heart.

Mother Teresa gave Karl the same advice, telling him to wait and think it over, and if it was God's plan for him to become one of her brother's, then that's what would happen. It was good advice, and as you'll see, it didn't happen for me, but Karl did eventually join the brothers portion of her order.

We had a wonderful day with Mother Teresa, a day that neither Karl nor I will ever forget.

Mother Teresa
Saint of the Poor

Several years after our meeting with Mother Teresa, she was giving a speech and spoke about these two young boys from America who had come to Rome to meet her, and how they had given her a cross for one of her houses. Although these two boys were very young, they had an authentic commitment to living the gospels, living their faith, and following in the footsteps of St. Francis and Jesus. She spoke of how one of them had returned to join her brothers' order, and that the other was studying for the priesthood. Mother Teresa said that it was her hope that eventually he too would also join her if that was God's will.

I had the opportunity to read her speech in one of the religious periodicals that I came across in the seminary library, and felt honored to be remembered by her.

So that was our time in Italy. It's kind of funny to think that what actually sparked our original idea of going to Assisi was a movie. Karl and I had gone to the theater to see the movie *Brother Sun, Sister Moon* by Franco Zefferelli. It was about the life of St. Francis, and it moved us so much that we longed to experience for ourselves the places that St. Francis had walked, and to feel closer to him by walking those same paths. So this trip started with a Hollywood movie, yet ended up being one of the most precious experiences of our lives.

I had made the comment that when we got to Italy, we would put ourselves in God's hands and go where Spirit took us. It seems that God did take care of us from the moment that we got there, and we left with a gift that would stay with us for the rest of our lives.

Chapter 8

Welcome to Diocesan Seminary: Hell Part 1 and My First Exorcism

Leaving Italy proved to be a bit more dramatic than our arrival. When we got to Leonardo da Vinci Airport in Rome, we decided to check all of our belongings—our backpacks and an old small suitcase that we had received from the sisters to carry all of our souvenirs home. Since this was the first time that either of us had been outside of the US, Karl and I had bought a lot of souvenirs. Because my mom is so religious, most of the stuff that I had bought was for her.

When we boarded the plane, we each had our wallets, passports, and a small cloth bag (from the convent's pantry) that held some papers and documents. We were sitting in the plane waiting for takeoff when some airport security officials boarded the plane, walked up and down the aisles, and eventually asked Karl and I to get off the plane and to get on to a different one. I don't know why they did that—no one else was asked to leave that plane. They didn't give us any explanation. We were upset, but didn't think that protesting would be the right thing to do at that particular moment, so we complied.

We were put on a different plane, found two seats, and no sooner had we taken off when all hell broke loose at the airport. Part of the airport terminal exploded. As we looked out the windows, we could see black smoke billowing from the building. I had mentioned earlier that there was a lot of terrorist activity going on at that time in Italy. It seems that someone, or some group, had planted a bomb at the airport. That stopped all activity for quite a while. No further airplanes were allowed to take off, and incoming flights were diverted to other airports.

Our plane was ordered to circle the airport, and then it was diverted to Germany. We landed in Germany but not at the regular airport. We were at an airstrip situated next to what looked like a large abandoned airplane hangar, with a couple of trucks of military personnel parked near it. We were ordered by guards toting rifles to disembark and get in line.

Inside the hangar they had set up dozens of portable screens, the kind they used in hospitals. Every passenger—each man, woman, and child—was then taken, one by one, behind the screen, escorted by three guards with their rifles, and told to strip. Then we were all subjected to body cavity searches.

I think, although I don't know for sure, that the authorities felt that the terrorists might have been on one of the outgoing planes. When the searches were finished, we all reboarded the plane and took off again, first to England and then on to the United States. I have to say that that was a novel experience and one that I hope never to repeat.

We landed in New York City to the eventual realization that all of our luggage was lost. We never got any of it back—our backpacks containing our clothing and personal items, all of our souvenirs, pictures that we had taken, and some rocks that I had picked up from some of the holy sites in Assisi. After I got home, I wrote a letter to the airline company, and they sent us an apology and a decent chunk of money. They refunded all of the money that we had spent on our round-trip tickets, money to cover all of the items that we had lost, and some extra money on top of that for the inconvenience that we had been put through. (I used my share of the refund money to go back to college.)

Karl and I stayed in New York City for a couple of days and did some sightseeing. We visited all of the tourist-type places and ate coney dogs and roasted chestnuts (it was December) as we walked past the Ritz-Carlton and Waldorf-Astoria hotels. We talked about all of the experiences that we had been through together, but realized that our lives were now heading in different directions. Karl wanted to join Mother Teresa's group of brothers, and I wanted to go back to school. I was still struggling with the idea of being a priest, but I was now leaning towards it.

We said our goodbyes and we each headed home. As soon as Karl got home, he started the application process to become a Brother of the Missionaries of Charity, was accepted, and sent to a facility here in the States for their training program. He was then sent to Cambodia for his novitiate. This was during those terrible times when the Khmer Rouge was slaughtering the population. The movie *The Killing Fields* was based on those events. I actually saw Karl on the evening news one night. They were showing US helicopters in Phnom Penh airlifting refugees out as the Khmer Rouge was overtaking the city. And there was Karl, helping people into the helicopters. Brave guy. We have kept in touch over the years.

I returned home and was pleasantly surprised by my parents. They were actually relieved to see me. My mom told me that she and my dad had been a little worried about my safety in Italy. I think she was afraid that my outgoing personality (read, big mouth) might land me in trouble. She also had read about the terrorist activity going on there, and knew that Karl and I had done some hitchhiking while we were in Italy. Here at home there had been some recent incidents on the news of hitchhikers being kidnapped and murdered.

But then she told me that they had again been inundated by a steady stream of letters, calls, and visits from people who had run into Karl and me in Italy. They had assured my parents that we were safe, being careful, and—again—being good boys. Even some of the military families that I had taken sightseeing on the Vespa in Assisi had called or written letters to them, and a few of them had actually stopped by and visited my parents. Thankfully, that was enough to convince them that we were okay, and that they didn't need to worry so much.

After that Franciscan Priest at home had told my mom that I was being led by the devil because I had left the Franciscan seminary to go to San Francisco, I imagined her having visions of me running around possessed—with my head rotating sideways on my neck and spewing green froth from my mouth. If you knew my mom, these visions would not seem so far-fetched. Also, when you're religious and you're told something by a priest, you tend to believe it. But the truth won out, they were placated, and actually happy to have me home. That was definitely a first.

I got home around Christmas time and I told my parents that I was going to go back to college, and that I had decided to continue to study for the priesthood. They were happy about the college part; not so much about the priesthood part. Considering how religious my mom was, you would think that she would be proud to have a son as a priest. There were a few women she knew–contemporaries of hers–whose sons were priests, and they never failed to bring up that fact in every conversation they had with anyone about anything. Every conversation seemed to start with, "My son, the priest, said . . . ." Not my mom. She actually told me that she thought that I was making a mistake, that it wasn't for me, and that I would be wasting my life.

I find it ironic that when I was younger and looking for advice, I felt as if my parents never really gave me any. They'd hear me out and then they'd say, "Well, that sounds good," or, "That doesn't sound good, but it's your life; do what you want, you usually do, anyway." That was the one time that my mom actually gave me some sound advice and I didn't listen to it.

So I applied to the local Catholic college with the refund money that I had received as compensation from the airline, and was accepted to their school. I also applied to the diocesan seminary and again was accepted.

Thinking back on it now, when I had reapplied to his seminary, if the rector had told me, "No, I won't accept you this time," he probably would have been doing both of us a favor. Since I was still "on the fence" as to whether or not I wanted to be a priest, I think a refusal from him would have ended my clerical career right then and there. I would have seen it as a sign of God's will. I would have probably said okay, it's not meant to be. There are other avenues that I can explore, and other things that I can do while still keeping on my spiritual path.

I knew that I wouldn't go into the military, but I could get back to flying and maybe become a commercial pilot. I loved the theater and acting, so who knows—maybe the lights of Broadway would be where I ended up. I also thought that medicine was interesting; maybe start off by being an EMT. So there were other things that I could have done, and definitely other interests of mine that called out to me.

But the rector said yes. And I know for sure that he regretted it the entire time I was there.

So I lived at home for about two weeks until the new semester started, and then I moved into the seminary.

The seminary campus was fairly small. It was situated on a little hill so at night you could look out and see the lights of the city. The large main building was very old. It had once been a hotel and had gone through several different incarnations before it ended up as a seminary. (Long ago my grandmother had actually worked there.) When you entered the main building, there was a large lobby with a reception desk and a huge communal dining room off the lobby. The upstairs housed the student dorm rooms. There were a few single rooms with attached bathrooms, but most of the rooms were two- or four-bed rooms with attached bathrooms, and at the end of the hall there was a six-bed room with a double bathroom.

There were also several other newer buildings on campus, including a second dorm building for students and a separate building for the faculty. Some retired priests had offices there, lived there, or both. The rector, Father Fremon, who ran the seminary, lived in the main building with the seminarians so that he could keep a closer eye on us. We also had a very large chapel on the grounds. No matter the size—whether it seats a dozen people or a thousand—a church that is associated with a seminary or a college campus is always called a chapel.

There was also a cloistered (meaning shut off from the world) convent on the seminary grounds, as well as the convent section in the main building for the sisters who did the domestic work and cooking for the seminary complex. To implement some of the reforms brought about by Vatican II, we had several nuns on staff. One of them was in charge of our Spiritual Direction Program and a few others were spiritual advisors to the seminarians. It was a good change, allowing the feminine to work its way into a very masculine interpretation of commitment to God. It provided a little more balance, providing some female common sense amongst all of those raging, male adolescent hormones.

I entered college as a first year, second semester freshman. But I ended up attending full-time classes, like sixteen or seventeen credit hours during the summers of both my first and second years. I eventually caught up on the year that I had taken off, and ended up graduating at the same time I would have if I was still with my original class from the Franciscan seminary.

When I entered the seminary, we had a total population of about forty-five seminarians, with maybe about twelve in my freshman class. We all wore regular street clothes at the seminary, and more formal attire would be a sports coat and tie. I had to do some clothes shopping with my refund money since I had given away almost all of my clothing in San Francisco.

There were also times that we were required to wear the cassock and surplice. The cassock is a black, floor length robe that either zipped or buttoned up the front. Then you'd put the white, smock-like cover, called a surplice, on over that. It was kind of like a white serape with a hole for your head, and this is typical clerical wear for a diocesan priest. We would wear that to Mass or when attending special functions.

I started this next chapter in my life with some advantages and some disadvantages. I was a little older than the other freshman students, since most of these guys were entering right after high school and I had taken a year off. At the seminary these guys had been together for that first semester, so friendships had been formed and the pecking order established.

I brought with me experiences that the other guys didn't have. While some of them thought that was neat, others felt that I somehow kind of one-upped them. Not only had I hitchhiked around the country and worked at all different kinds of jobs, I had been to Europe, had an audience with the pope, and met Mother Teresa.

The overall setup here was a bit different from the Franciscan seminary. Here the academic portion of our training was at the Catholic college, while the priest formation portion was at the seminary. For me it became almost like living two separate lives.

Since I loved school and loved learning, the college portion of my life was great. I had some great teachers; others, not so much. But by this time I had developed my own style of learning, and I knew that what I got from my classes was what I put into them. I wasn't big on taking notes or memorizing facts. I tried to understand in the moment what the professor in front of me was trying to impart. I asked a lot of questions and engaged the professor in dialogue so that my fellow students and I could better understand and assimilate the information being given to us. I would draw upon similar information from my own experiences, other classes, and my personal readings and add it to what the professor was giving us, and tried to bring it all together. I had some fantastic life experiences and some real spiritual growth, and now I wanted a solid knowledge base to help me weave all of that into a solid foundation upon which to build my life.

I got good grades, really enjoyed my classes, and even had a few of my professors tell me that I was "scholarly." I put together a program for myself that would lead to a double major in philosophy and religious studies with minors in theater and outdoor education. I made a lot of friends among my fellow college classmates, a fact that was actually used against me by the rector of the seminary. And I don't think that anyone at the college ever considered me a "pain in the ass," which were the rector's words. So that part of my life was fantastic.

Interestingly, I never told anyone at the college that I was also a seminarian. When my classmates and teachers eventually found out, they couldn't believe it because they said that I didn't act like a seminarian. It seems that the seminarians had a bit of a reputation at the college, and it wasn't a good one. The buzz was that because they were going to be priests they felt entitled, felt that they didn't have to do the work, and could just kind of slide by. And that they mostly kept to themselves with their noses up in the air. If you want to know the exact words that were used to describe them, I'll tell you what I heard them called by everyone—arrogant assholes.

I remember when one of my professors found out later in the semester that I was a seminarian he said to me, "You're kidding, right? You've got to be kidding! You're not really one of those guys, are you?" That's a pretty sad commentary and it really bothered me. We, as seminarians, were supposed to be examples of Christ to others, and this is how we were perceived. Something here wasn't right, and it bothered me enough to bring it to the rector's attention at one of our community meetings. I'll tell you a little later about how well that went over with him.

So our days would be spent in classes at the college. We would come back to the seminary in the afternoons or evenings for meals, to do our homework and studying, and to participate in the formation program that was fitted around our academic schedule. If I remember correctly, those of us who lived close could go home on the one free weekend that we had each month. We had to be back in the seminary by about eight o'clock on Sunday night, and would have to sign in so that the rector could check and make sure that everyone was accounted for. I think that even the guys who stayed there on the weekends had to sign the register on Sunday evenings. A lot of these guys were young, underage, and the rector was responsible for them and took that part of his job very seriously. We all had to be present and accounted for by the time that the 9:00 p.m. evening prayer service started.

The formation program here was similar in some ways to what I had been exposed to in the Franciscan seminary, but also different in some key areas. In the Franciscan seminary, the focus was on personal growth, interior work, balance, and values—it was growth filled. In the diocesan seminary, the focus was on learning how to be a priest, a functionary of the church. The focus was mainly external—it was performance filled. And as you'll see, that's what got me into trouble.

We had a formation team similar to the one at the Franciscan seminary. We had the dean of men (who was supposed to be the disciplinarian), the rector (who was in charge of the whole program), and the spiritual director. We each had our own spiritual advisors who were mainly priests and nuns from outside the seminary.

The formation program consisted of daily Mass, scheduled prayer times, and Days of Recollection during which we would reflect and meditate on the lives of Jesus, or Mary, or of any of the saints. We had retreats, lectures, and workshops on different subjects like spirituality or agapic love (sacrificial love as opposed to erotic love). We had classes on the sacraments and on the history of the church, and we also had our apostolic work in the community.

I described the diocesan seminary as performance driven. The goal was to make you into a priest; again, a functionary of the church. They wanted you to look like a priest, walk like a priest, talk like a priest, be able to efficiently say Mass, hear confessions, preside over weddings and funerals, and eventually to be able to run your parish in the "black."

So our formation program was geared to that goal. In our classes, lectures, and workshops we would be presented with the kind of information that we had gotten at the Franciscan seminary. But unlike the Franciscan's, they wouldn't connect it to an interior level, and they wouldn't talk about values or meaning; they would just use the words. They would tell us, "You need to pray." Okay. Why? "Because that's what priests do." "You need to learn the prayers of the church." Okay. Why? "Because that's what priests do." "You need to meditate on the life of Jesus." Okay. Why? "Because that's what priests do."

They never explained why all of this stuff was important. I brought with me a spiritual foundation so that even though they didn't make the connection between what we were doing on an external level and its value on an internal level, I was able to make the connection for myself because I already had the tools to do so. But most of the other seminarians didn't have these tools. So for the majority of them it remained a very external experience because it was a very external experience. They were teaching guys how to be priests, but not teaching them how to grow their connection to the Divine Presence. To my way of thinking, that was the ultimate sin of this seminary.

A friend asked me, "What happens in the seminary that a young man can walk in through its doors, and four years later walk out those doors as a holy man?" And my answer to that was, "Nothing." This seminary wasn't about teaching you to be holy. It was about teaching you a role to play, the role of a priest, a man of the church. An actor, if you will, and not necessarily a man of God. A holy man does not need to be a priest, and a priest does not need to be a holy man. I believe that the majority of priests who came out of this seminary "holy" did it in spite of the seminary, not because of it.

To the rector of this seminary, it seemed that the ultimate sin was in being different. And he found me to be very different.

My problems with the rector of this seminary started from almost the first day. This was the man that I had talked to— actually showing up on his doorstep—when first exploring the idea of becoming a priest. We had gotten along really well when I was hanging out at the diocesan seminary back then. But he was also pretty upset with me when I told him that I had decided instead to go to the Franciscan seminary. He said that if it didn't work out, I could try to come back here. He also said, in a moment of pique, that this didn't mean that he had to accept me back. So I'm not sure if it was that, my choosing the Franciscan seminary over his, or if I just rubbed him the wrong way.

I had only been at the seminary for less than a week when a silly incident happened that really sealed my fate with the rector.

It was evening and I was walking down the hall in the dorm. As I passed one of the dorm rooms of some of the upperclassmen, I heard this very loud chanting coming from inside the room. Curious, I stopped and knocked on the door. One of the guys—there were four of them in the room—opened the door and let me in. He had a very worried and serious expression on his face. They all did. So I asked him what was going on. He told me that they were hearing noises coming from inside the walls, and that they thought that it was the devil trying to scare them.

I thought hmmm . . . noises in the wall. This was a very old building so it was most probably mice or rats. Of course, instead of saying that, I had to be a smart ass and say, "Oh, really? The devil? As in demonic possession? Wow. This is heavy stuff."

Well I love scary stuff, and exorcising demons is right up there on my list of spooky things. So I sat down and watched them go at it. They were throwing holy water at the wall and saying, "You, the devil, Angel of

Darkness, leave." They were saying that kind of stuff and throwing in bits and pieces of some of the old prayers of the church that are used for exorcisms.

But the noises continued and became even louder. You'd hear this scrambling and frantic scratching, and the louder the guys got and the more they shouted, the louder the noises in the wall seemed to get. It was a little unnerving watching them because they were so intent and so dead serious about what they were doing.

I'm sitting there for almost an hour watching them. It wasn't working, and they were finally starting to get discouraged. They were despondent that they weren't exorcising the demons because the Bible says that Jesus said that all you had to do was get together and call on Jesus' name and demons would be exorcised. In my opinion, this is a very literal, simplistic way of looking at faith . . . but hey, that's just me.

So they finally gave up, turned and looked at me sitting there, and asked what I thought. At which point I should have said, "Call an exterminator." Instead I said, "Well, maybe you're going about this the wrong way," and they asked me what I meant by that.

"Well," I told them, "I don't believe in hell as a place. So if it is the devil possessing the walls in this spiritual place (their words), and we know that it is already in that experience of hell, and that it is not bound by a place, then all of your praying and chanting isn't going to change its experience of hell. Whether it stays or leaves, it will still be in that experience of hell. So why should it bother to do anything?"

Looking a little perplexed, they again asked me what I meant by that. So I said, "Well, why don't we try this." So I got up, turned towards the wall while the noises were still going on, and I said, "If you are evil, go to the Light and let the Light embrace you." It wasn't any kind of formal prayer that I said, and I think I said it somewhat flippantly—I mean, I was talking to mice here. Again I said, "Go to the Light. Let the Divine Presence take care of you."

And wouldn't you just frickin' know it—the noise stopped. Abruptly.

My guess is that the mice were exhausted by this time and finally fell asleep.

Well these guys all looked at me like they didn't know what to make of me—like they didn't know if they should kneel before me or flee because I obviously had power over demons. And by the next morning half the student body thought that I could exorcise demons and were afraid of me. The other half probably thought I was nuts and were afraid of me anyway.

So, of course, the very next day the rector comes up to me, tells me to follow him to his office, and very sternly says, "I heard what you did last night." He looked at me like I was the demonic one because the evil spirits had "listened" to me. He said, "I'm going to be keeping my eye on you because I don't know who's leading you, whether it's God or the devil. But I *will* find out." It reminded me of the incident in the scriptures when Jesus is exorcising a demon, and they thought that Jesus was in league with the demons because they "listened" to Him. Did the rector maybe miss that scripture class or maybe not understand what he read?

I just looked at him like—are you crazy? Is he really saying this to me? Yes, he really is saying this to me. For a brief moment I thought about saying, "Well Father, if you actually look at the archetypes for evil and light, it does make theological sense. The archetype of evil is ignorance, and the archetype of light is knowledge. So if you're evil (ignorant), go to the Light (gain knowledge), then you get rid of your ignorance and become enlightened."

But I didn't think he was in the mood for a theological discussion, and I didn't want to dig myself in any deeper so I didn't say anything. For once I was speechless. As he walked away, I could hear him muttering about this "power" of mine and how I had to be watched closely, I guess so that I didn't wreak havoc on the world or bring about Armageddon or something.

At that point what I should have said was, "Okay, I'm outta here. This is not going to work. This is nuts." But I can be a stubborn kind of guy. I had made a commitment and I was going to stick to it.

Of course, the way my luck was going, something similar and equally silly, happened less than a week later. I was beginning to feel like I was in the *Twilight Zone*, but that incident actually happened later on. I can't remember exactly why, but we had gotten a few days off from school, and I had gone home like most of the other seminarians. There were still a few guys staying in the dorm; guys who lived too far away to be able to go home. So one of these guys called me at home and said that they were bored and wanted to go and see a movie, and asked if I would like to go with them. They told me that they had also invited the rector. I said sure, I'd drive over to the seminary and then we could all go together.

So I get to the seminary and as we're all piling into the seminary van, I said, "What movie are we going to see?" They said *The Exorcist*. Okay, I know now that I should not have gone and should have passed on that one. But I'm a scary movie junkie and that one had gotten a lot of good hype, so I said okay. So off we went with the rector at the wheel of a van full of seminarians, off to see *The Exorcist*.

On the way to the show, the guys prayed the rosary I guess in preparation for seeing a movie about the devil. (That should have been a hint that this was not going to end well for me.) Anyway, we get to the movie and from the first moment these guys were scared shitless; most people in the audience were too. I don't mean to offend any of you who saw this movie when it was originally released and sat through it with your hands over your eyes screaming like a little girl, but for me it just didn't do it.

When the part comes on where Linda Blair's head rotates full circle and she starts puking out the green slime, everyone starts screaming and clutching at each other. I, on the other hand, actually started laughing my butt off. I thought it was totally hokey. I had worked on a lot of stage productions behind the scenes because of my minor in theater, and had done my share of special effects. So I'm sitting there, kind of analyzing how they did it, and it just seemed kind of silly to me. It just didn't scare me at all.

That obviously did not go over well with the rector and the other seminarians. They were aghast that I was laughing. This was a serious film about the devil and I was laughing. It sealed my fate, part deux.

But it gets even better.

After the movie we headed back to the seminary. The guys were still scared silly and again prayed the rosary in the car, but this time it was a little harder for them to do because their teeth were chattering so loudly. Because it was so late, I decided to spend the night in the dorm instead of driving all the way back home. I wish now that I had just driven home, but who knew.

So we get back to the seminary. We get out of the car, the guys still quaking in fear from the movie as the silvery shadows cast by the full moon shiver all around us in the howling wind—a total recipe for disaster. The guys were so scared that nobody wanted to sleep alone even though we were all staying in the same room. So they all jumped into bed together. There were like three guys in one bed and two in another. Honest to God, that's how scared they were. In case you're wondering, I slept by myself.

We finally all fell asleep, and in the middle of the night we were awakened by a noise. My first thought was—Oh God, I hope it's not mice in the walls! But the noise was coming from one of the windows. The wind had really picked up. It was slamming the building and battering the old, rickety wooden windows in the room. It was rattling one of the windows like crazy, and on top of that it was making this eerie whistling noise. At that same moment, we heard this loud howl that sounded as if it was coming from right outside of the window (there were coyotes in the area).

So put all of those things together and it was like being in our own horror movie. I remember thinking that all we needed now was for Bela Lugosi to come slinking out of the shadows to bite everyone's neck, followed by the Wolfman, then Frankenstein, and then the Mummy could bring up the rear trailing his dirty linen bandages.

By this time all of the guys except one were wide awake, shivering and clutching at each other and moaning about how awful this was. The one guy that was still asleep was lying there on the edge of the bed with his face turned towards the window. He was sleeping with his mouth open, snoring up a storm, but both of his eyes were wide open and you could see the moonlight reflected off his eyes. It was pretty weird and, of course, that scared the guys even more because it was so freaky.

I looked around, took it all in, and just started laughing again. I said, "Hey guys—this is too cool! This is like being in our own scary movie! This is like a once in a lifetime experience! And who knows, maybe our friend over there is possessed and he'll start levitating and howling and spit green pea soup all over us!" I was having a great old time!

And the guys looked at me with something akin to horror, and they said, "Oh, no, this is terrible! This is about the movie we saw—this is evil that followed us home! We are being faced with evil here! Oh God, this is terrible!"

And I said, "Oh, come on. That's bullshit. What's wrong with you guys? You're just letting that silly movie scare you. There's nothing to be afraid of except for your imaginations. Just go back to sleep." Then I turned over and went back to sleep myself.

Come Sunday evening I'm signing back in at the seminary like we were all required to do, and the rector is waiting for me. He confronted me saying that he had heard what happened in the dorm room. He said that I didn't have any respect for the devil, for the power of the devil, had made a joke of it, that it was not something to be laughed at, and that the devil was not a joking matter. And that I had actually laughed at the seminarians who, very rightly, understood the gravity of the situation.

He reiterated that he didn't know who was leading me in my aberrant behavior, but he was going to find out, and that he was going to watch me like a hawk. And he did—every minute, every hour, and every day that I was in his seminary. From that moment on every word I uttered, every movement I made, every laugh, every look, and every choice all made their way back to the rector. I literally caught "hell" for that incident, for making fun of something that I didn't even believe in.

Chapter 9

Welcome to Diocesan Seminary: Hell Part 2.5

The next two-and-a-half years of my life were spent at the Catholic college and the diocesan seminary where I got a great education and was being molded into a Roman Catholic Priest. Sort of.

The changes brought about by Vatican II were meant to bring the church out of the Middle Ages, and to bring more of a balance in the operation of the church. But many of these changes were slow in their implementation. As a result of that, our seminary was still being run as if it was the thirteenth century instead of the twentieth.

The problem that I and the other seminarians ran into was that in this seminary all of the power and control was concentrated in one person, the rector. It wasn't just about becoming a priest, it was about becoming what the rector felt a priest should be—his idea of a priest, which might not coincide with anyone else's idea. To start with, he didn't have the right kind of temperament to be in this type of a position. And then to give him total control over all of our lives proved to be disastrous for most of us and eventually for him too.

Although he seemed to be more focused on me than on anyone else, he didn't treat many of the other seminarians much better. He constantly scrutinized us (with me he perfected it to an art form), belittled us, and yelled at us. Everyone had a hard time putting up with it, even the guys who were "toeing" the line and tried to look and act like his idea of a priest. The only exceptions were his "pets." These were the "golden boys"—guys who were handsome in face and physique—and who were, for lack of a better word, "ass kissers." "Oh yes, Father. Of course, Father. You're right, Father." You'd find a couple of these guys in every class. These were the guys who always did well and could usually do no wrong. Heck, they're probably all cardinals by now. But the majority of the seminarians were very unhappy. This statement is borne by the fact that of the twelve or so guys that were in my freshman class, only two of us actually ended up getting ordained.

And it wasn't because they weren't good guys or they lacked a vocation, or because of their relationship to God—it was because of the rector. The majority of them eventually said, "If this is what the church is like, if this is what it means to be a priest, then it's not for me." And most of them probably would have made damn good priests.

We were all constantly criticized by the rector, but never in constructive ways. It wasn't meant to make you look at what you were doing, assess it, and grow from it. Rather, every comment from him was a negative one. I think what I remember the most from my time there was the never-ending belittling comments that he peppered me with on a daily basis. "Why do you wear your hair long? Why do you walk like that? Why do you talk like that? You laugh funny—why do you laugh like that? Why did you tell that joke? Why is your cassock wrinkled? Why are you wearing sandals instead of shoes? Why are you wearing that blue tie today instead of the brown one? Why are you wearing black socks instead of brown? Why do you have so many secular friends?" Why, why, why....

When you look at it in the context of what he felt was important—that we all looked the same and acted the same—then on some level his actions must've made sense to him. But because I was so different, he didn't know what to do with me. He didn't celebrate each individual's unique talents or gifts. He wanted cookie cutter priests and, by God, he was going to get them.

In my past experiences I had met priests and brothers and nuns and lay people who were good people, holy people. People that I wouldn't hesitate to bow down before because I was in awe of their goodness and their holiness—it would just shine through them. So I think I knew what "good" looked like. I was growing in my relationship with the Divine Presence on a personal level. I had a spiritual foundation upon which I was trying to build, layer by layer, the rest of my life.

But most basically, I knew right from wrong. And what the rector was doing to us, the way he was treating us, was wrong. Because he was a priest, was whatever he did right? I don't think so. And, of course, me being me I would tell him that. The other seminarians, being shyer, more introverted guys, would be really intimidated by him. I was the one with the mouth, and someone had to stand up for us. So not only would I stand up to him, I would often use passages from the Bible to back me up because I did know my Bible—I had learned it on the streets of San Francisco. And that would really make him go ballistic.

I remember one of the first times that we butted heads. It was a day when he had been especially vitriolic to us, and I can't even remember what it was about, not that he needed a reason. We were all kind of huddled together in a group listening to his ranting and raving. I went up

Chapter 9

to him and said, "Father, I know you consider us less than the dirt under your shoes, but you know we're people too. We deserve at least a little respect and we deserve a little better from you. It says in the Bible that to whom much has been given, much is expected. So you need to be a better example to us."

And that was unheard of—that anyone would dare speak to him like that. You could hear this horrified, collective gasp coming from the rest of the guys. And I watched as that little vein on the rector's forehead above his left eye popped out and started throbbing. I thought it was going to burst right then and there and splatter me head to toe with his blood.

He spluttered, "How dare you? How dare you quote the Bible to me?"

And I said, "Well Father, the Bible was given to all of us for all of us to use. And we're seminarians, so aren't we supposed to be using the Bible?" For that I think he put me on house arrest for a couple of weeks.

Not that anything changed. He was such an angry man, and that kind of anger needed professional help (which the church didn't believe in at the time). You don't need that psychology crap; you just need to pray more.

I remember another incident when we were all gathered in the dining room and again, the rector was really angry at us about something or other. So he had one of his famous temper tantrums, and he kicked the wall and broke his big toe. Right after that he was supposed to say the daily Mass for us, which he did, but he rushed through it in about ten minutes so that he could go to the emergency room. I believe that the dent in the wall that he made that day can still be seen in the dining room behind the priests' table.

One of the things that seemed to irritate him the most was my hair. He asked me, "Why do you have long hair?" And I replied, "What does that have to do with my relationship to God? Why don't you ask me how my prayer life is? Why don't you ask me about my relationship to the Divine Presence? What does the length of my hair have to do with anything?" And he never could give me an answer because it had nothing to do with it, other than not being his idea of what a priest should look like. He would just glare at me, that vein throbbing again, and mutter his mantra, "I'll be watching you."

One day he came into my dorm room where I had this really neat poster hanging on the inside of the door. It was a picture of Jesus, in silhouette, and in it you could see his long hair. Underneath the picture it said, "You guys can wear your hair any length you want. Just tell them I said so." And under that it said, "Jesus Christ."

The rector pointed to it and said, "What's that?"

I said, "It's my poster of Jesus." He reached up, grabbed it, and ripped it off the door.

I told him, "Father, I don't think you should be tearing my things down."

He said, "*I* decide what I can and cannot do. You know I have the power to throw you out of this seminary because your hair is long."

I told him, "I know that you can do that. But you know what, Father? It says in the Bible that whatever power you have is that which is given to you from above, from God Himself. If you choose to exercise it in that direction, then that's your right. I guess it depends on what God wants."

Another glare, and another, "I'll be watching you," and he stormed off.

When the rector confronted me, calling me on the carpet for all of these things, it was usually a spur of the moment thing. He'd see me in the hallway or the dining room or on the seminary grounds, march up to me, stick his finger in my face, and start in on me. Being spur of the moment, I never quite knew what it was that he was going to go off on me about. I didn't have time to think about what he was saying, much less how to plan my defense.

But I always seemed to have a spontaneous answer. The words were just there for me. I'd open my mouth and out would come the Bible passage or whatever. Jesus says in the New Testament something along the lines of, "When you're called upon before the courts to explain yourself in My name, don't worry about what you will say. The words will be given to you by God on High."

And I found that to be true. I was trying to live the gospels. How successful I was, God only knows. I'm not perfect, I'm certainly no angel—far from it. But I tried. And then when I was called on the carpet by this official of the church, I could answer him. Not in anger (well, mostly not), but in Bible passages. And it amazed even me with what came out of my mouth and the passages that would burst forth when confronted with his nonsense. And I remember thinking that it's true. What Jesus says really is true—it really does work in a person's life, although it took me a few more hard lessons to really incorporate that understanding into my life.

So my first year at that seminary proved to be rather challenging. I had come from the Franciscan seminary, which, though far from perfect, was focused on our personal growth towards developing our relationship to God. The Divine Presence was the root and the basis upon which everything else was built. Their expectation was for that spiritual relationship to be expressed in our thoughts, words, and deeds, and everything in our lives would be fueled by that and would flow from that.

Chapter 9

Now I found myself in a seminary where they used the right words to talk about prayer and spirituality and God, but basically they were just words. The meaning behind the words didn't seem important and wasn't the focus. It was a totally different emphasis. It was about serving the church, representing the church, and carrying out the functions of the church. This seminary was to make you into a man of the church. God seemed to be secondary.

It was a bit of a culture shock to say the least. It was kind of like having a bucket of cold water dumped over your head and also over your beliefs and experiences. I found it to be very external and very superficial. But, like I did in my academic studies, I decided I would get from it what I put into it. (I was still pretty young and idealistic.) I considered it a learning experience even if it was basically a negative kind of learning. I wanted to be a priest. Okay. So I had to learn to do the functions of a priest. Okay. And to learn the functions of a priest I had to go through the seminary. Okay. I could do that. And since all experiences, both positive and negative, can help you grow, I would grow—just from a different perspective than I had been used to. So unknowingly and unwittingly, the rector was helping me to grow—up to a point.

An underlying theme in our formation program was that we were expected to be blindly obedient to the rules of the church. We had to learn these rules so that we could guide the laity (the people) in their faith because God didn't speak to them. Oh no. He spoke to us, and through us to them. We had to know exactly what the church expected so that we could unerringly tell our parishioners what was expected of them. Tell them exactly what to do, how to do it, and when to do it so that they could gain salvation.

And this was probably the most important function of a priest, because without us, they were doomed. We were told that the people are like sheep—they need to be led by us because they can't think for themselves, and that their faith was too important to be left in their own hands. And because we represented God, they had to do what we said. And that if they didn't do what we said, they could face excommunication or even the fires of hell.

An awesome responsibility, don't you think? Would be if it was true. If we keep people dependent on us for the salvation of their souls, we keep the power and control. Gives us job security. Ain't that a kick in the patootie for all of you Catholics reading this?

And that attitude—fostering people's dependence on an institution, telling them that they can't have a relationship with God without our guiding them, and not "growing" them in their own relationship to the Divine Presence because they might start relying more on God and less on us . . . that to me is the ultimate sin of the institution of the church. But that's just my opinion.

And do you know the basic reason why you people are like sheep? Why you all are "less than" us priests? Why we have to guide you and intercede for you on God's behalf? It's because you have sex. Yep. That's it. Let me tell you how the church felt about sex at that time—not good. Not good at all. They felt that it "sullied" people, that it made them less pure, and less acceptable to God.

We priests, on the other hand, can devote our pure, chaste lives to God because we don't have sex. (Well, we're not supposed to.) You people, the laity, cannot do that because you engage in basic carnal desires. The church framework is hierarchical, and to the priests the laity framework is too. Back then if you were married and having sex only to beget children, you were at least acceptable in the eyes of the church. I mean someone has to produce new generations of Catholics for the church, as distasteful as that process may be. So these couples were somewhere on the middle rung of that hierarchal ladder.

Married men who have sex are a rung above married women who have sex, but you're both still on those middle rungs. If you are a single man and not having sex, or a married man but not having sex, you can rise a rung or two. Single women and married women not having sex can also rise a rung, but not as high as their male counterparts. Gets confusing, doesn't it? I guess you have to be a priest to understand it. And for those of you who are not married and having sex, especially if you are enjoying it—well I don't even want to go there.

Yes, this is what we were told. No, I am not making it up. Truth, as they say, can be stranger than fiction.

Marriage only became a sacrament very late in the history of the church. Vatican II actually had to put it in writing in one of its documents or encyclicals that marriage (in the church) was actually equal to celibacy. They had to write it down so that priests would start believing it and would have to believe it. But as I've said, it took a long time for these changes to filter down to the seminary level. When I was in the seminary, that particular change hadn't made it yet.

This is just personal conjecture, but I think that back then one of the hardest things for many priests to swallow when it came to that concept was that a woman—any woman—could be considered equal to a celibate man. For many priests women were still paying for tempting Adam with that apple. The modern church has taken some steps forward when it comes to women, has given them more active roles in the church, but they are still not considered equal to men. As in, how many women priests are there in the Roman Catholic Church? (Rhetorical question.)

This might seem like a contradiction, but in the first couple of years in the diocesan seminary they did allow you to date. They didn't like it, they didn't encourage it, but they had their reasons. They needed to let you "get it out of your system," so that you could decide sooner rather than later if you would be able to handle celibacy.

The last thing that they wanted was to have your diocese foot the bill for your education (as many did) only to have you decide at the last minute that you were missing out on something because you hadn't dated or had any relationships with women. So they allowed it so that you could make up your mind before they invested too much time and money in you. A few of the guys I knew at the seminary did date a few times, but most of them had already decided that since they wanted to be priests, they could handle celibacy.

Of course, we never really had any classes or lectures on how to handle celibacy. They were united with the Franciscans on that one. All these young guys, hormones raging, were never given any guidance about how to handle these feelings about their sexuality. We were never told why being chaste was so important to God, why sex was so abhorrent to God, and what it all had to do with your spirituality and your relationship to God—other than, you're seminarians—no sex. Pray instead. Because a lot of these guys didn't get any direction in this area and didn't know how to handle these feelings, problems arose later on. We all know about the problems in the church with pedophilia, but there were many other ways that the non-handling of this issue impacted and disrupted the lives of priests. Again, for a later chapter.

During a school break of my first semester, the rector did something out of the ordinary—he invited us to a movie. (No, it wasn't *The Exorcist*). There were a few guys still at the seminary, the few who hadn't gone home for the break. So one evening the rector invited them and a few of us guys that lived in the area to go to a movie with him, and he even invited me. So we all piled into the big seminary van and headed out of town to a nearby city because the movie that he wanted to see wasn't playing here at home.

So we were all in the van driving down the interstate just talking about stuff, and a couple of the guys asked the rector about some of the workshops we'd be having the next semester. One of my pet peeves, as I've already mentioned, was that we hadn't been given any kind of help with sexuality issues. I knew these seminarians pretty well because as I've also said, there's not much privacy in the seminary. So I knew that a lot of these guys were sexually immature, and that we could all use some help when it came to handling these issues. Not just the physiological stuff that was going on in our bodies, but also the canonical aspect of it—

like how celibacy impacted your relationship to God or your role as a priest—the stuff they never explained to us.

And they probably never explained celibacy to us because it really doesn't have anything to do with your relationship to God. All of the apostles were married. Priests in the early church were married. Current theological discussion hints that maybe even Jesus was married. That all changed in the Middle Ages, and it changed not as a result of intense theological debate, but because of property. The church was a great landowner, and it used to give a parcel of land to each of its priests so that the priest and his wife and family could work the land and sustain themselves and not have to rely on Mother Church for daily sustenance.

And that worked pretty well until eventually the church ran out of land. What to do? Well, simple—require that priests not be married. That way the church didn't have to give them any more land, didn't have to support any more wives, kids, grandparents, aunts, or uncles. Problem solved and celibacy was born. I had read that when they first changed the rules, things could get a little rough. After a priest died, the church would go after his wife and children to try and get their land back. I don't know how that worked out, but eventually it became a moot point. Priests had to be celibate.

So we're all in the van talking about the coming semester and I say, "Hey, Father, what about some workshops on sexuality?"

He slammed on the brakes. I mean we're driving down the interstate at like seventy miles an hour, and he slams on the breaks. This was before cars had seatbelts in them, so all of us go flying, and tumbling over each other every which way.

And he yells out, "If I *ever* hear you mention anything like that again, you're *out!*"

And I said, "Excuse me? What, because I think that sexuality is a really big issue for us and that we should talk about it and get some guidance about it?" And then I quoted St. Thomas Aquinas to him. (You know, sometimes when I get going I just can't stop!) St. Thomas Aquinas is a Doctor of the Church (a title for a saint who has contributed significantly to the doctrines of the church through their writings), and everyone looks at him as being the ultimate authority in terms of doctrine in the Roman Catholic Church. I had read his great work, the *Summa Theologica*, on my own. So I told the rector, "St. Thomas Aquinas says that grace works on nature, and if nature, human nature, is not disposed, which means has not matured enough to handle the grace of God, then God's grace cannot work on the individual."

I didn't notice the ominous silence in the van. I was on a roll.

"So," I told the rector, "if the person isn't mature enough to be able to figure out sexuality issues (like most of the seminarians), how is he going to be able to then receive the grace, the presence of God, the strength, whatever you might call it, to adjust to a life of celibacy or a life of commitment in any direction?" I said, "It won't work. St. Thomas Aquinas says that grace cannot then work. God can't work with the individual because they're not in a place where they can accept it."

Silence. The other seminarians looked at me in horror that I would dare quote St. Thomas Aquinas to the rector. The rector looked at me in horror that I would dare quote St. Thomas Aquinas to him. And then he said, "How dare you!" (I knew he was going to say that.) "How dare you quote the church to us? We are the church."

And I said, "Well, yeah, but you're not St. Thomas Aquinas." Needless to say, we never had any sexuality workshops.

Another thing that they told us in the seminary, though not in these simple words, was that we as seminarians would take certain prescribed steps to become a priest, and if you got through these steps and were ordained—bingo. You got the prize—you became "holy." You learn the rules of the church, you unquestioningly obey the rules of the church, you look, think, and act like their idea of a priest, you get ordained, and then—voila—you are now a "holy man."

You are now above all other mere mortals because God now speaks through you. He doesn't speak through every Tom, Dick, or Harry out there. Uh uh. Only through you and your brother priests. So now you are no longer subject to the same human frailties and temptations that non-priests are subject to. Basically, you can do whatever you want and it's okay because you are right up there with God. And God can do whatever He wants, right?

And what happens when young men are taught this and actually believe it? Well, believe me, nothing good. It's a license to wreak havoc on people, on parishioners, and on themselves for that matter. When the bishop of my diocese was asked why he didn't do anything about the priests in his diocese who were pedophiles, his answer was that he didn't know that it was wrong. Now he did know that slapping a priest was considered a mortal sin, but he didn't know that molesting a child was wrong. That is what that kind of teaching results in.

And, of course, me being me, I would speak up and say, "Umm, excuse me Father, but saying that once we get ordained it means that we don't sin anymore—that's crazy." Again, that collective gasp of horror from my fellow seminarians. Because you didn't question the church, you didn't question the priest, and you didn't question anything you were told. You just nodded your head and said, "Yes, Father," which, of course, I didn't do.

If something is crazy, it's crazy, no matter who says it. Yeah, father might believe wholeheartedly in what he's saying, but that doesn't make it true. (Now, if I had said *that* out loud, I would have finally gotten kicked out of the seminary butt first.) But their answer was always the same. We are the church. We know what's right, not you. Basically, just shut up and nod your head.

As they say on *Star Trek* reruns, "Resistance is futile."

So I had to really think about my values, and had to dig deep inside of myself to figure out my relationship to this seminary experience. I needed to rely on myself to get whatever it was that I needed, to incorporate it, and to continue growing. I also needed to find some value in it and make it an "inner" experience. I can't deny that it was a struggle to do.

The constant scrutiny was wearying, but occasionally there were rare moments of levity. One day I was on my way to Mass and one of the nuns saw me, called my name, stopped me and asked, "What are you wearing under your cassock?" I said, "Excuse me, Sister?" Then she bent down and lifted up my cassock a little, took a peek, then looked back up at me, one eyebrow raised. She repeated, "What are you wearing under here besides your shoes and socks?"

I said, "Well sister, we're learning about poverty in our classes right now so I'm not wearing anything else." At her horrified expression, I started laughing and said, "Sister, I'm wearing cut-offs, shorts." Sometimes it would be hot out and instead of wearing pants under our cassocks, we would put on shorts instead to keep cool. Or we'd get up really late and be in such a rush to get dressed that we'd grab the first thing we saw and end up with shorts on. So I guess when sister saw shoes and socks and bare legs she got a little concerned.

That was a really funny incident but, of course, the next day the rector cornered me and said, "I heard that sister was looking up your cassock yesterday. Why was she doing that?"

I said, "I don't know, Father. You'll have to ask her." For the life of me, I couldn't think of any biblical passages to back me up on that one!

Another incident that I found funny but that the rector, of course, didn't was when we had an out-of-state bishop visit our seminary. It just so happened that I knew him, and had waited on him several times when he came into the restaurant where I worked during the summer. So he comes into the seminary, sees me, gives out a big whoop and calls my name, gives me a bear hug, and says, "Oh, make me my favorite drink, would ya?" I just laughed and said sure.

The rector, who's standing there, glares at me and says, under his breath, "No! You shouldn't be doing that!"

I smiled at him and said, "Sorry, but he's a bishop, so I have to do what he says!" The rector was fit to be tied, but he couldn't very well say no to the bishop who outranked him.

Chapter 9

So our days were filled with classes, formation activities, studying, and apostolic work. We still did parties and drinking on the weekends, as we were still typical American teenagers in many ways. I didn't party all that much as I was working on the weekends. I was in a work-study program during the school year and had two part-time jobs—a janitorial job at the seminary and an office job at the college.

The semester finally came to an end, and we were due for our evaluations from the rector to find out if we were going to be asked to return the following year. We weren't given actual grades at the seminary for our formation program; everything was pass/fail. At the end of the semester, the formation team would meet and discuss your performance during the previous semester. They would evaluate you on all kinds of things: how did you get along with the other students and with your teachers? Did you attend all of the formation activities? Were you at daily Mass and at the prayer sessions? Were you prompt? Did you wear your cassock when you were supposed to? Were you always neat and presentable? Did you do well in the community in your apostolic work?

I remember one of the priests on the formation team pulled me aside one day and told me, "Y'know, there's a file on you like I've never seen before. It's crammed full of notes and pieces of paper from the rector saying on this day he did this, on that day he said that, on this day I found him doing this . . . I've never before seen a file quite like yours."

"Well," I told him, "it seems like I'm definitely a person of interest around here."

So I met with the rector and got a pretty negative evaluation. It started out with, "You don't cut your hair. I've told you to cut your hair. You act differently than the other students. You confront us about the church . . ." and it kind of went downhill from there.

And at the end of it he told me that I could return next year.

That about knocked my socks off! I mean, he was forever telling me that he had the power to kick me out. I heard that from him at least a couple of times a week, and here was his chance—and he didn't do it. I don't know why not. My sense was that despite his never-ending irritation at my being different from the other seminarians, something about me must've rung true. If I was different from the kinds of students that he was used to, I think it's because I was a little more centered, more focused, more inquisitive, less malleable, and definitely more opinionated and vocal than the others. But he couldn't accuse me of doing anything wrong, just of being who I was.

So I said, "Okay, I'll come back." Don't ask me why. Even today as I look back on it, I can't really answer that. Perhaps a momentary mental lapse? Come back for another year of this? I did know that I wanted to continue in my exploration of becoming a priest. Was I going to be a priest? I didn't know. But I knew that if I wanted to keep my options open, which at that time I did, then I had to get through the seminary.

So I decided to stick it out and stay in the seminary. And I almost made it.

Chapter 10

Burning Coals and Losing My Fruit of the Looms

Our first year was over. The semester ended at both the college and the seminary, and we all packed our bags and headed home for the summer. Since I had decided that I wanted to catch up on the year that I had taken off, I started summer school at the college taking a full course load. My work-study jobs ended with the school year, so for the summer I got a job as dining room manager at one of our local resorts.

Even though we were at home, we were still seminarians and were expected to act like it. Before leaving for home, the rector asked all of us what our summer plans were. He wanted to make sure that whatever we had planned for the summer wouldn't "tarnish" our images as seminarians. He especially wanted to know if any of us would have secular jobs. Not all of the seminarians had to work. Quite a few came from well-to-do families and didn't have to worry about paying their own bills. A few were going to be working with their dads or other relatives in family businesses.

When I told him that I would be working at a resort, he had a fit. He said that it wasn't an appropriate job for a seminarian. When I asked him why he felt that way, he said that it could put me in a possibly immoral environment—that male guests at the resort would be asking me where they could find women, and that female guests would either hit on me or ask me where they could find available males. I looked at him in disbelief. I was stunned. Why does everything have to be about sex with these guys? I said, "Father, that's crazy. I've been working in restaurants and hotels since I was sixteen, and nothing like that has ever happened to me. I have to work to pay for school." He wasn't very happy about it, but ultimately there wasn't anything that he could do about it.

Also, throughout the summer he regularly contacted the pastors of the parishes that each of us belonged to asking if we were attending Mass every Sunday, whether we seemed happy, if we talked about our seminary experiences, and if we were doing any volunteer work at our church. He was still keeping an eye on us albeit from a distance.

I kept busy with my classes and my job, so again I was hardly at home during that summer. My parents weren't especially happy with me, but I think that they were finally resigning themselves to the fact that my dad's dream of a military career and my mom's dream of grandchildren were just that—dreams.

Summer flew by and it was time to move back into the seminary to begin my second year of formation. I met with my college advisors and set up my class schedule for the semester, having just finished my summer classes. I quit my summer job, during which I was not propositioned and no one had asked me to do anything immoral. I was hired back for both of the part-time jobs that I'd had last semester for my work-study program.

While school went well, nothing had really changed in regard to my seminary experience. I was kind of hoping that since the rector had asked me back, and since I was no longer a "lowly" freshman and the rector now had a new batch of seminarians to fry, that this year might go a little easier. Wishful thinking on my part. Rather than getting better, the scrutiny seemed to be at fever pitch. Maybe he felt that time was ticking by, and that each minute that passed was one less minute left in which he could change me into a decent imitation of a priest. I think the first thing he said to me when he saw me was, "Why haven't you cut your hair?" (Oh, Lordy, here we go again.) And so it went, unabated, for the rest of my time there.

Life resumed much as it had been during the last semester. Our days were spent in class and the rest of the time at the seminary with formation training, apostolic work, and the rector doing his best to whip us into shape.

The rector and all of the seminarians would have periodic meetings when we would get together and discuss various issues. I remember one meeting when I spoke up and said that there was an issue that I thought was important and that we needed to address. I told him that we seminarians as a group did not have a good reputation at the college. We were perceived as being arrogant and lazy (I did not repeat the actual words that I had heard them called), and that we set ourselves apart from the other students with a "holier than thou" attitude. This reflected poorly on all of us, and what could we do to change that?

Well, of course, the rector blew up at me. He said, "How dare you! How dare you bring this up! How dare you tell us what we should do! *We* tell *you* what you should do!" And once again that one vein on his forehead was throbbing.

It just seemed to me that we needed to be accountable for ourselves and for our actions. Obviously, he didn't share that belief. In every other area that I had ever worked people were held accountable for their

Chapter 10

actions. Not so in this seminary. I even told the rector, at a different confrontation at another time, that it seemed to me that priests, in general, weren't held accountable for their actions. That one went over as well with him as this one did.

So I thought it might be best if I just kept my nose to the grindstone, did my own thing, and quit stirring the pot. Let the rector do his thing, and let me just get through this in one piece. I mentioned before that despite the negativity, everything is a learning experience. Let me tell you about a learning experience that I had that changed my world.

I had a new roommate that semester. We were what you might call the odd couple. I'm not a slob, but I'm not exactly a neat freak either. I know that they say that cleanliness is next to godliness, but I don't think that I have that particular gene in my DNA. My roommate was Mr. Clean with hair. This guy wore a suit and tie every day to class. *His* cassock was never wrinkled, and there was never a hair out of place. His side of the room was pristine and always smelled good like fresh flowers or something. My side was, well, not quite so pristine and had more of a dirty sock smell.

I did try to clean my side of the room every once in a while—you know, get rid of the cobwebs and keep the flies at a minimum. He would clean his side of the room every day—*every* day. He would actually put on a little apron and get his feather duster out and dust every day. I remember watching him clean his bookshelf. He would take out all of the books, one by one, dust each shelf, then he would pick up each book, one at a time, dust it off, and then return it to the shelf. And you can bet that they were all replaced in alphabetical order. There was never a speck of dust to be seen on his side of the room except for whatever blew in from my side.

So we were always at odds with each other over this. I mean, this guy was forever spraying Lysol at me. He was driving me crazy so we weren't on the best of terms. I felt that I was in the right and he felt that he was. It got so bad that the rest of the seminarians noticed our strained relationship. This was around the time that he put a strip of masking tape down the middle of the floor, demarcating our spaces, apparently so that I wouldn't accidentally cross over into his part of the room and contaminate it.

One day I was praying and reading from the New Testament. And I read this obscure passage—I think it was in the letters of Paul—that was talking about revenge. It said something like 'if you want to get back at someone, love them. And it will be like heaping hot coals upon their head.'

Well that caught my imagination in a big way! Hot coals. Hmmm. Okay, that works for me. I'll be the first to admit that my intentions weren't all that great. I'm not perfect, obviously. But I was just so fed up with the arguing. It was like no matter what I tried it didn't work, and I was just tired of it. Looking back I think I was getting tired of a lot of things—the constant scrutiny, the emptiness of the seminary experience, and now my freaky neat roommate. It was just too much.

I was just trying to find a way to live in peace with this guy. So I reread that passage and reflected upon it. I thought, okay, I'm going to listen to Jesus' words, really listen to them. I've found them to be true in the past. I'm going to stop fighting with my roommate. I'm going to start agreeing with him. I'm going to love him—even if it kills me.

So the next time he complained about something, I said, "You know what? You're right. I definitely could be a better housekeeper."

At that he stopped short and looked at me blankly for a moment like he couldn't believe what he was hearing. And then he got suspicious. He said, "What are you trying to do? Are you trying to use some kind of reverse psychology on me?"

And I said, "No, no, no, I'm not. I'm just saying that you're right. I need to be a better housekeeper and a better roommate. I'm going to try."

And then instead of avoiding him at all costs like I used to do, I started inviting him to join me and my friends when we hung out and did stuff. My friends were a little skeptical about that (actually a lot skeptical) because this guy and I couldn't have been more unalike—like black and white, day and night.

But that's what I did. What's really funny is what ended up happening, which is a testament to the power of Jesus' words when we really listen to them. What happened is that *I* changed. He didn't change, but *I* did! Son of a bitch (sorry, but those are the exact words that I uttered at the time). Talk about a tailspin! I actually grew to love this guy like a brother. By opening myself up to him, by seeing the good in him, by not letting my pride and anger get in the way—it changed *me*. I had learned about "poverty of spirit" in San Francisco, but it took this experience to make me realize that maybe this time I could have lived the gospels a little better. I went back and reread that passage wondering what had happened. Those coals were supposed to be on *his* head, not mine!

That's when I began to understand that a lot of this biblical stuff was metaphorical and symbolic. Like that line about the burning coals. It wasn't my roommate who burned; it was my anger that burned away—because of love. Because I loved, my heart changed. Not his; he remained the same. But I changed because real change is about us—not about the *other* person. That is the power of Jesus' words on an interior level; the power to change a person. I found that to be amazing, to be life altering, and to be life opening.

The idea of the priesthood, whether or not I was going to be a priest, kind of faded into the background and became of minor significance. But the power of Jesus' words—that became a major significance in my life. Look what happened to me when I decided to love this guy and not hate him. I thought— just imagine what would happen if I lived my whole life like this, according to what Jesus said to do. Imagine if we all did! Imagine to what extent we could be transformed, and imagine to what extent we could transform our world. Now *that* is power, and it's power that is available to all of us.

My roommate was like a lynchpin, a turning point in my life when it came to living out the gospels. It was amazing to me that this one incident could change me so completely. What would life be like if I continued to love like this? So that concept, and not the priesthood, became my goal. Later on in the semester, my roommate decided that the priesthood wasn't for him and he left the seminary. I was totally upset and saddened by this because I felt as if I had lost a brother. I missed him every day thereafter that I was there.

If the rector thought that I was a pain in the ass before, after that experience I was like a ball of fire—on fire with the beauty and truth and power found in the words of Jesus. The rector continued to argue with me about every little thing, "Why did you part your hair that way today? Why were you late for dinner last night? Why aren't your shoes shined?" (Honest to God, I am not making this stuff up.) And he still constantly threatened to throw me out. And I would look at him, shrug my shoulders, and say, "Okay, whatever you want to do, you've got the power." And when he was done I would just walk away because he really didn't have any power over me. I had seen the other side of the River Jordan; I had seen the "Light". He wanted cookie-cutter priests, but I was never going to be one of them and didn't much care. I cared about Jesus' words.

And that would make the rector even angrier. He would shake that finger at me and say, "How can *you* know what the Bible means? How can *you* think that you understand what Jesus' words mean? Who do you think you are?"

And I would tell him, "Well, I'm not anyone special, but I have a relationship with God, a connection to the Divine Presence, and that's not out of the ordinary. It's something we can all have. The annals of the church are filled with the stories of people, from every walk of life and of any age, who had a connection to God that they lived by and sometimes even died for. I'm not saying that I'm a saint by any means. I'm just saying that God is there for all of us, and my connection to Him is as valid as anyone else's."

Even though I noticed his face turning redder by the minute, I went on saying, "I think that God's words are available to all of us, and I think I've been given an understanding of what they mean, and of what they mean to us in today's world. I believe that God has given me the grace to understand His words."

The rector's face was as red as a beet by now, but I plowed on and I finished by saying, "Well, Father, Jesus says in the Bible that you know a tree by its fruit, and that a bad tree doesn't produce good fruit. And I can only look to the results of my actions. And if I've changed, if I've become a better person instead of a worse one, then I have to believe it's of God." And, like a broken record, he'd just repeat that he would be watching me as he stormed off. You all are probably getting as tired of hearing that as I was.

So the first semester ended and my second year at the seminary was half over. I had lived through it, went home for the Christmas holidays, and then went back to the seminary for the second semester. It was more of the same—loving my classes and having a great time at the college with my secular friends. I did a lot of stuff with them—went out to eat and went to movies and parties. I just really enjoyed that part of my life.

Same old, same old at the seminary. Father yelling and seminarians cowering. It was getting old.

The only incident that stands out in my mind from that semester was something that happened at Easter. As seminarians, throughout the year we were sent to help out at different parishes on the weekends or during school breaks or holidays. Working with different priests in their parishes gave us some real life experiences of what priests did, which was more of that hands-on kind of learning.

One of our local parishes was in need of some help at Easter. Easter is a very busy time, liturgically, for the church. There are Masses and other activities spanning four days—Holy Thursday, Good Friday, Holy Saturday, and Easter Sunday. At this particular parish the pastor had just retired, and a priest from another diocese was brought in as a temporary pastor until a more permanent replacement was found. He had called the seminary and asked for help with the Easter services, so the rector asked me and two other seminarians to go and help him out.

So we packed our overnight bags and early on Holy Thursday morning we each drove our own cars to the Mass of the Chrism. This Mass marks the beginning of the Holy Week services. At this Mass they bless the oils, which will be used at all of the diocesan churches throughout the coming year. These oils are used for anointing for special ceremonies such as baptisms and priest ordinations.

Chapter 10

After Mass we headed to the parish where we'd be helping out and met the pastor, Father Rupert, at the rectory. He talked to us about what he wanted us to do, outlined our duties, and gave us our assignments for the next four days. We started that evening by helping out at Mass where they had the Washing of the Feet. This is a symbolic reenactment of the Last Supper when Jesus washed the feet of the Apostles as a way of showing that Christians are called to serve one another.

After Mass we went out to dinner with father, then headed back to the rectory where we sat around and relaxed, had a few drinks, and talked late into the night. He seemed like a nice guy, was very cordial to us, and we had a good time talking with him. We said goodnight then headed off to our bedrooms to get some sleep for the busy day ahead.

The next day was Good Friday and we again helped out at liturgy where we had the reading of The Passion, which is the gospel account of Jesus' arrest and the events leading to His crucifixion. Liturgy lasted from noon until about three o'clock. That evening we helped at the Stations of the Cross where the participants follow the priest or deacon to different "stations." These stations are pictures hanging at consecutive spots along the church walls that depict specific key events of Jesus' suffering through His arrest, trial, and death. You stop at each station to pray and to reflect upon each of these moments in His life, and that took several hours.

After that we again went out to dinner with father. He drank pretty heavily at dinner that night. When we got back to the rectory, he brought out the cognac which flowed freely, mostly in his direction. Again, we sat around in the living room talking and drinking. I had some cognac that I didn't much care for, and it was pretty strong stuff, but I was by no means drunk. But father was.

It was getting late so we all said goodnight and headed off to our rooms. I normally don't wear pajamas to bed, just my underwear because I always get too hot and uncomfortable in pajamas no matter the season or the weather. So I'm in my briefs in bed just starting to fall asleep when there's a knock on the bedroom door, and then father comes in. He comes in and sits on the edge of the bed and just starts talking about the day and how well it had gone and how much he appreciated our help. When he came in, I had kind of scooted up in the bed a little and propped myself up on the pillows. I didn't turn on the light, but there was a little light coming in from the hallway. Although it was dim, I could still see father and could smell him too. He was drunk as a skunk with the fumes to prove it.

I thought this was a little weird but I said, "Well thank you, Father, it was a nice day and we were glad to help out." He reached over and patted my shoulder, and then he said, "Gosh, your neck muscles look all tense, let me help you with that," and he starts kneading my neck. I remember thinking, huh, this is not good and I turned away from him a little so that I had my back to him, not knowing what else to do. It was a bit unsettling. Okay, it was a lot unsettling! I kept hoping that he would just say goodnight and leave, but he just kept talking and massaging my neck.

Then he's done with my neck and starts giving me a backrub. Oh Lord. At that point I turned completely away from him and was lying on my stomach thinking—I don't have a good feeling about this, what am I gonna do here? But before I could form another thought, he grabbed hold of my shorts and in one fell swoop pulled them down and off and threw them in the corner.

I reacted faster than a bolt of lightning and grabbed the bed covers pulling them up to my neck, totally panicked, and I think I shrieked like a little girl, *"What are you doing!!"* I must have shocked the shit out of him because he shot up from the bed and bolted from the room, slamming the door closed behind him.

So there I was, lying in bed naked as the day I was born, sheets pulled up to my neck, thinking—oh boy, that was not good. My next thought was—I'm getting out of here. I didn't dare turn on the light, so I searched around in the dark for my shorts and couldn't find them. (To this day I wonder whatever happened to my Fruit of the Looms.) So I found my pants and pulled them on, found my socks and stuffed them into my pant pockets, slipped into my shoes, put on my shirt and jacket, grabbed my toiletries, and stuffed them into my overnight bag—all in the dark.

I cracked open the bedroom door and peered out. I had a clear line of sight to the back door of the rectory. No one was in the hall and father's bedroom door was closed. So I crept down the hallway and out the door and ran to my car. The rectory was situated on a little hill, so without even starting the car (I didn't want to make any noise) I shifted it into drive and coasted out of the parking lot and down the little hill. When I got to the street I turned on the engine and lights and got out of there. I went back to my parents' house for what was left of the night.

The next morning I went back to the church and saw father there. I said good morning to him, he said good morning to me, and I went about my duties. I stayed to help out at the rest of the services on Saturday and Sunday, never saying another word to father and he never said another word to me. When the services were over, I went back home for the night. The two other guys stayed the whole weekend. I didn't say anything to them, and I certainly didn't tell them anything. They didn't ask me why I wasn't staying at the rectory. Everyone was so busy that I don't know if they even noticed that I wasn't spending the nights there. I didn't think father would try anything else after that fiasco, and figured that there were two of them and that they could take care of themselves if the need arose, but it didn't.

On Sunday when all of the services were over, I went back home and called the rector. I told him that I had something really serious that I needed to talk to him about and that it couldn't wait. On the phone with him I could imagine him rolling his eyes wondering what kind of trouble I had finally gotten myself into. So I went to the seminary to meet with him. We went to his office and I told him what had happened. I remember that as I talked to him, he didn't look at me. He had his head down and had a pained expression on his face. He looked despondent. He thanked me for telling him and said that he would take care of it. I left his office and we never spoke of it again.

The rector must have gotten hold of whoever he needed to, even on Easter Sunday because I heard that by the next day Father Rupert was gone from that parish. (The rector was a member of the personnel board at the Diocesan Office, so that might have helped him expedite the process.) Father Rupert had the early Mass on Monday morning and that's when he told the parishioners that he was being transferred, that he had enjoyed his time there, and said goodbye to everyone.

I don't know what ever happened to him. I do know that at that time the normal course of action for a "misbehaving priest" was to remove him from that spot and just put him somewhere else—into a different parish or a different diocese. I don't know where he was sent, but I never saw him again.

Years later when I was a priest, I was reading a newsletter that I used to get from a seminary in a different state. One of the pages in the newsletter was a kind of a bulletin board where parishes and priests posted openings that they had for temporary help or for volunteers for certain events. As I was reading it, I came across a request from a priest who was looking for seminarians to help out for the summer at his church. The first and last name of this priest was the same as Father Rupert's. I didn't know if it was him as it was certainly possible to have two priests with the same name.

I called that seminary and told them who I was, told them that there were issues about a priest with that same name, explained that I did not know if it was the same person, but urged them to be careful and to investigate this person thoroughly before allowing him to advertise with them. They thanked me for calling them and said that they would look into it. Was it him? I don't know. But I do know that when these openings are posted in seminary newsletters, they usually run for months at a time. The next month when I received their newsletter, I noticed that this particular posting was gone.

Despite the history between myself and the rector, he listened to me when I came to him, took it seriously, and took the appropriate action. It didn't change our relationship, but he did the right thing when he needed to and I was grateful to him for that.

So that semester ended and I was back home for the summer. I was able to get my job back at the resort. The rector voiced the same concerns about it and I gave him the same response. I was going to summer school again and was taking both sessions with a full course load for each session. At the end of the summer I would have made up for the year that I took off. When we started school again in the fall, I would be a senior.

This would be my last year at the seminary. Hallelujah.

Chapter 11

Crossing Over Into the Twilight Zone: Meeting the Devil, Again

I will always remember my last year at the diocesan seminary as the year that I crossed over into the *Twilight Zone*. Rod Serling himself couldn't have written it better.

It was one of the strangest things that has ever happened to me. I couldn't explain it at the time, had no idea what it meant, but now, looking back on it, I think that it all boiled down to the power of the human mind—especially a mind under duress. Most especially, my mind under duress.

It happened during my first semester around the time that the rector had decided to install new locks on all of the seminary buildings. We had a porter, a student, whose job it was every day to unlock all of the doors in the morning, all of the doors on all of the buildings on campus, and to lock them again at night. The current locks were ancient, and at times it was getting difficult to lock and unlock some of them.

I think that all of the doors got locked at around ten o'clock. The rector gave each of us a key so we could let ourselves in if we were late. The keys that he gave us didn't open the main front door of the seminary, but only the side door leading directly to the dorm rooms. To reach that door you had to go way down the side of the building and then up a flight of narrow stone steps. The rector's room was on the first floor with his window facing those steps so he could see anyone coming or going.

We had to have a good excuse if we came in late, like we had been out studying. A lot of the seminarians liked to study at the library at the college. If someone had been out drinking and came in falling down drunk (and some did), the rector would know it. Actually, everybody would know it because these guys would inevitably make a real ruckus trying to get up those stairs. You know how it is when someone is drunk—the quieter they try to be, the more noise they end up making. And those steps were made of stone, which totally amplified every little sound, so one guy banging up those steps could sound like a herd of rampaging elephants.

I had spent the evening visiting with some friends across campus at the other dorm building. It was really late, around midnight, when we finally started to say our goodbyes. Everyone but me, and the guy whose room we were in headed out. This guy was actually a personal friend of mine. We had known each other since we were little and our families were friends.

So it's just the two of us left in his room and I wanted to talk to him for a few more minutes before I left. He was having some issues of his own. He didn't want to be a priest, but wanted to be a doctor. But his mom was super religious and really wanted one of her sons to be a priest, whether he wanted to or not. So he told her that he would give the seminary a try, but it wasn't working out. He really wasn't happy, so we were talking about that and some other stuff.

On his wall beside us was a picture of our new bishop that he had cut out from the local newspaper and framed. Our previous bishop had retired and the new one had just been named, and was actually a distant relative of my friend. In this picture the new bishop is angled away from the camera so it was more of a profile of his face, and he had a very somber expression on it, befitting his new position I guess.

So my friend and I are sitting there and talking. The picture was on the wall beside us. Occasionally, as we talked I would glance around the room and glance at the picture. The next time I glanced at his picture it seemed as if the bishop had started making faces, like frowns and grimaces. No, I wasn't on any drugs. I never did drugs. My friends in high school used to tell me that I should stay away from drugs because I was crazy enough without them. And yes, it was kind of dim in the room and maybe the light was playing tricks on my eyes, which were pretty droopy by that time. But whatever the reason, I saw grimacing.

We kept talking and the picture kept making faces. I didn't say anything to my friend, but at one point he glanced at the picture himself, turned to me wide-eyed, glanced back at it, and said, "Look! The bishop's picture is making faces!" So he saw it too. I told him yeah, I had noticed that too at which point he got really scared and said, "Oh God, what's going on? What does it mean? I think it means that something bad is going to happen to us! I think it's the devil! Oh, this is bad!"

He really was scared out of his wits. Whenever something strange or unexplainable happened at the seminary, it always got blamed on the devil. If something is good, it's got to be from God. If something is bad, it's got to be the devil. This is a very basic and very immature way of looking at things. Since this seminary was all about externals, the seminarians weren't taught how to grow from that basic outlook to a more mature understanding of good and evil. If we can blame it on someone or something else, we don't have to take any responsibility for it. The archetype of the devil is ultimate ignorance. So if we don't understand something or are ignorant of its meaning, we can blame it on the devil. An easy out if you ask me, but that's just my opinion.

I got up and went over to him, gave him a hug, and made the sign of the cross over his forehead. That's something that I used to do at the time, especially when I was saying goodbye to people. I'm not sure why other than that it felt like the right thing to do. Where I come from it's something that Catholic parents would do at night when they put their children to bed. They would give them a blessing and make the sign of the cross on their foreheads so that God would keep them safe during the night. In many cultures the night is associated with evil and the devil. So when your parents did this, it made you feel safe and secure and then you could fall asleep.

So I made the sign of the cross over his forehead and I told him, "Hey, it's late, we're tired, and the light is probably playing tricks on our eyes." I told him that nothing bad was going to happen to him because he was a good person, committed to God, committed to helping others whether he was going to be a priest or not, and that he needed to believe me, and to believe that good is far stronger than evil. And that nothing, especially not a silly picture, would harm him. He seemed to be calming down and asked me if that was really true—did I really believe that? And I said, "Yes, of course, I do. Trust me."

Then I went over to the wall, took down the picture and shook it a few times. Showing it to him I said, "See, it's just a picture, just a piece of paper. It's not evil, it's just a piece of paper." So he reached over to take it, saying that he was going to put it away by putting it in one of the desk drawers. And I said, "Nah, you don't have to do that. You don't have to be afraid of it. Don't give it any power. Because the only power that it has over you is your fear, the power that you give it." That seemed to satisfy him and I put the picture back on the wall. "There," I said. "It's fine. It's just a picture. And not a very good one of your relative, but hey!" He laughed at that and seemed okay. "Well," I told him, "I think we both need to get some sleep."

To myself I was thinking, it is a little dark in here and yeah, my eyes are tired, but we both saw the grimacing. I guess it must've been the light . . . .

I said a final goodnight, gave him another hug, and left. I went downstairs to the lobby, opened the door to the outside, and walked through it. As soon as that door closed and locked behind me, I knew that I was in for it. I just knew that something was going to happen and it wasn't something good. At that very moment I experienced a sudden, overwhelming feeling of distress. My heartbeat quickened, my breath shortened, and if I'd had shorter hair it would've been standing straight up. It was just the oddest feeling as if the click of that door closing behind me was the signal that I had entered the *Twilight Zone*.

I looked out, and the best way that I can describe it is that the night just felt wrong. Everything just felt wrong. A mist had sprung up, and down near the ground it was thicker and kind of swirling around. It reminded me of those old black and white Dracula movies where he pops up out of the fog to claim his next victim. Great. The sky was pitch black, an impenetrable dark curtain without a single star shining and no moon glowing. That's funny, I thought. I'd seen the moon and the stars overhead when I'd walked here earlier tonight. Even on the cloudiest of nights you could always glimpse a star or two. Hmmm . . . .

Okay, I needed to get back to my room in the main building. So, very reluctantly, I started walking and taking that first step wasn't easy. But I headed out nonetheless, and as I walked I noticed a couple of strange things at almost the same moment. The first was the absolute silence of the night—not a whisper of sound from any direction. All I could hear were my footsteps echoing off the asphalt and the beating of my heart, which I think was the louder of the two. And I had glanced to my right and couldn't see the lights of the city. You could always see the lights of the city from here. But not tonight.

My grandmother used to tell us kids when we were little that if you were faced with something scary, all you had to do was make the sign of the cross and say, "Blessed be the sweetest names of Jesus, Mary, and Joseph." She said to do that three times and you wouldn't be afraid anymore, and that whatever was evil or scaring you would leave. Well grandma, I thought, I'm trying it and it's not working!

I remember thinking to myself, oh boy, this isn't looking good. But I kept walking and I noticed that my legs were stirring the mist into these little whorls, and it was so thick near the ground that I couldn't even see my feet. Then I looked at the tennis courts off to my right as I was passing them and I thought, huh, that's really odd. The tennis courts had these two outside lights set high up on poles on opposite sides of the court and they always came on automatically at dusk, or at least one of them did.

One of them was this big, industrial-type light that was always on at night and was so powerful that it lit up half the court. But it was off. I had never seen it off before. Huh. The other light was this small, regular-sized bulb housed in a kind of wire cage. It had never been on, so we figured that it had burnt out long ago and no one had bothered to climb up the pole to replace it. Yet that light was now on.

Chapter 11

Very odd, as if everything was suddenly opposite from the way it was supposed to be.

I thought, okay, let's just keep walking 'cause I'm almost home. And I remember thinking that I felt as if everything was somehow backwards, like I was in the *Twilight Zone*. My next thought was, Oh, God, please let the dorm building be where it's supposed to be and don't let it have been sucked into another dimension.... I finally passed the chapel on my left (thank you, Jesus, almost there) and then I finally get to the sidewalk. The sidewalk starts at the chapel, curves around it, and leads to the main building—my destination. Once you get to the front of the main building (the door that I didn't have a key to), you'd pass it and veer left through this little archway into a courtyard, then through the courtyard, down the side of the building, and finally to the outside stairwell. Usually a short walk; tonight it felt like a never-ending journey.

So I stepped onto the sidewalk that was bordered by a short hedge that's only about knee high. And as I step onto the sidewalk, I hear a rather loud rustling noise in the hedge. So I stopped for a moment. The rustling stopped. I took a few steps forward and the rustling sound moves forward with me. Perplexed, I stopped again. The noise stops. So I took a step backward and the noise moves backwards with me.

Okay. Any relief that I had been feeling because I was close to home evaporated. I started walking forward more quickly and the rustling sound kept up with me. Again, that thought—this isn't good. But my second thought was oh, it's probably the cat! The spiritual director had a cat that he let roam around outside. So I figured that the cat must be following me by following the noise that I was making since it couldn't see me in the fog.

So I keep walking, feeling a little better again. The sidewalk continues, but the hedge ends about four feet before you get to the archway that leads into the courtyard that I had to go through. I took a step beyond the hedge, stopped, and turned back towards the hedge and bent down a little and said, "Kitty, is that you?" in a voice that sounded a little squeaky to me... okay, a lot squeaky.

And what shot out of that hedge was not a cat. It was . . . I don't know what it was. It was this bright red, liquidy thing! It was about six feet wide, and it just suddenly shot straight up from the hedge, maybe twenty five feet into the air. Just shot up right in front of me, enveloping me yet not touching me. It was like instantaneously having a gigantic red liquid blanket spreading up and around me. Again, I didn't feel anything touch me, but I could see it going up all around me. And in that squeaky voice I just kind of yelled, "*Ahhghh!!!*"

I instinctively went into a protective stance, kind of leaned forward with my head down with one arm covering my head and one over my chest. Thinking—what the hell? So there's this bright red liquidy, plasticky thing that just keeps shooting up and over me but doesn't fall on me. Sounds crazy, I know. Well, you should've been there. It *was* crazy.

And then, just as suddenly as it had appeared—*Whoosh*—it was gone. Disappeared. Needless to say, it scared the hell out of me. My knees were knocking. And to add to the freakiness, once that red thing had disappeared in a whoosh, everything around me returned to normal. The mist was gone. Now I could see the stars overhead. I glimpsed the lights of the city below me. I could hear the wind buffeting the treetops.

So forget the walking, I ran through the archway, across the courtyard, and saw the side of the building. In that courtyard there's a full-sized statue. As I ran past it, I glanced at it out of the corner of my eye and thought, okay, I'm good there as it didn't come alive and start chasing after me.

I got to the stairwell, ran up the steps, and got out my key. My hands were shaking so badly (keeping time with my knocking knees) that it took several attempts before I could get the key in the lock. I finally got the door open, barged through it, slammed it shut behind me, and stood there leaning back against it panting like a woman in labor as I tried to catch my breath.

I must've been as white as a sheet, and it was then that my grandmother popped into my thoughts again. Her first language wasn't English, and she could never till the day she died pronounce the word "sheet" correctly. She'd always say, "Strip your beds because I'm going to wash the shits today." And, of course, my brother, sister, and I would giggle like crazy until my mom slapped us and told us to knock it off. Whatever the word, I must've looked like it because as I had come in through the door, two of my fellow seminarians saw me and stopped in their tracks. They came over to me and asked what was wrong because I looked as white as a sheet, like I'd just seen a ghost or something.

So I stood there, teeth chattering, hands shaking, knees knocking, and I said, "I saw *something*." I told them what had happened and how scared I had been, and was still scared. I guess my story frightened them a bit because they looked at each other, turned tail, and ran back to their rooms probably hoping that whatever it was hadn't followed me back to the dorm.

I got to my room that I had to myself since my roommate had left by that time. I'm not big on communal living, but I really wished that I'd had someone there to talk to that night. I got ready for bed, crawled in, and pulled the covers over my head and tried to go to sleep. That didn't work too well. Every time I closed my eyes, I saw the faces of gargoyles—gargoyles with bloody gashes on their faces. Why gargoyles, I have no idea. So that made it a little hard to fall asleep, but eventually exhaustion overcame my terror, and the next thing I knew it was morning. (Oddly, a few months later, I saw the movie *Sorcerer* and there were these images of gargoyles on a sarcophagus that come to life, and they were the exact replica of what I had seen.)

I got up, still trying to figure out exactly what it was that had happened, and went down to breakfast. Standing at the door to the dining room was the rector, waiting for me with a rather pissed off expression on his face. He hadn't yet said a word but that vein was already bulging. "You," he spit out. "I need to talk to you *right now*," and he grabbed my arm and dragged me down to his office. He said, "What you saw last night," but I cut him off.

I said, "Oh yeah, let me tell you about it!"

But he put up his hand and shouts, "No! I don't want to hear about it! And I forbid you to tell any of the seminarians about it!"

I told him that I had already told a couple of the guys about it last night. And obviously it had already spread like wildfire throughout the seminary, that I had seen *something*.

I again said, "Let me tell you what happened," and again, that, "*No!*" He said, "I know what you saw. I have felt the devil's presence around here. Because I'm a priest, I can feel when the devil is around. And he has been hanging around for the last few days." (Those were the exact words that he used, "hanging around," like the devil was waiting for one of the guys to notice him and take him out for a beer or something.) "And he has appeared to you, and I forbid you to share that story with anyone else from this moment on."

Well, I guess it's not always just about sex with these guys. If it's not about sex, it's about the devil.

It would've been nice if he had sat me down and talked to me about it and given me some guidance. I was young, obviously conflicted about my life here, and some advice—heck, even just some plain common sense—would've been appreciated. Sit me down and said, "This is what I think is going on with you." Maybe that would have helped me figure out why this stuff was happening and what was going on in my head. Maybe we could all have learned something from this. But instead, we were just not supposed to talk about it.

Of course, all the guys did talk about it, and of course, I told all of them what had happened, just not within earshot of the rector. A lot of the guys were scared by it and believed, along with the rector, that I'd had an experience of the devil. And I told them, "C'mon guys, get real. If it was the devil, that was a pretty piss-poor performance (excuse my French). He must be pretty ineffectual because nothing bad happened to me. I'm still here and in one piece. And I never saw any devil." I didn't for one second believe that it had anything to do with the devil, probably because I didn't believe in the devil, at least not in the way that the rest of the guys did. Ignorance yes; devil no.

I did briefly throw around the idea that it was a practical joke that someone had played on me. At that time something called a space blanket had come on to the market. It was a blanket made of this shiny nylon material that was silver on one side and red on the other. It could withstand extremely cold temperatures, like for people who were out camping in the wilderness. You could keep one in your car in case you ever get stranded in a snowstorm so you wouldn't freeze to death— that kind of thing. I had seen one recently at a local sporting goods store, and it kind of had the same consistency as the shiny red thing that I had seen. But space blankets weren't big enough to shoot twenty-five feet into the air, so I nixed that idea.

So I never could explain what it was that I had experienced. I shoved it to the back of my mind, and after the initial interest wore off, never talked about it again. But looking back on it now, I think that the only explanation that makes sense is that it was just me. My unconscious mind was trying to give me a sign.

I had spent the last couple of years feeling as if I was leading a double life—my school life and my seminary life. There was constant conflict in my life. While your conscious mind might ignore the conflict, your unconscious mind will not. And with someone like me—loud, extroverted, always pushing that envelope—when the unconscious tries to make you take notice, it doesn't do it with a whisper but with a roar. Actually, I think that it had already tried whispering, but that hadn't worked.

My unconscious mind was processing everything that was going on in my life; everything that I thought I had a handle on and saying, "Oh, no you don't." It was trying to make me understand that in a big way. It was also trying to tell me that my experiences with the rector, the new bishop, and with the institution of the church, were not good ones for me. No matter that I was trying to put a positive spin on them, no matter that I tried to grow from them, it was just not working for me and would never work for me. I felt that my days were numbered, and that emotionally I was reaching the end of my rope.

I didn't fit in at the seminary and it was obvious to everyone but me. My unconscious mind knew that I didn't belong here and tried like hell to get through to me, even went to great lengths to do that—hence my bizarre experience. How did I describe it—as if everything just felt wrong? Duh. That's because everything *was* wrong. I guess I just wasn't ready to see it. I refused on a conscious level to see it. But your mind, as they say, is a very powerful thing. Ignore it all you want, but it will still get you in the end as I found out.

I don't know if I was being stubborn or blind or just stupid. Probably all three. I had said that I wasn't going to stir the pot anymore. What I didn't realize at the time was that I didn't need to say anything or do anything to stir that pot. All I had to do was be there. But again, I didn't see that. I kept trying to fit in. So I plodded on for a little while longer until I couldn't do it anymore.

The rest of the semester was more of the usual. The only new thing after the incident that I'd had was in being the only seminarian in the history of the diocese who had seen the devil. I hadn't, of course, but it was no use trying to convince them of that. This seminary was so external, so literal, so limited, and so medieval in its thinking that I gave up trying to tell them anything.

The semester ended, I went home for the holidays, and returned to the seminary in January for my last semester. I was almost done.

We had only been back from Christmas break for a few days when I made an appointment to meet with the rector. I know that I've been telling you all along about his crazy behavior and the way that he treated all of us, but he seemed to be getting worse. His temper tantrums were becoming a daily occurrence and his tirades more hateful. When he was assigned to say Mass for us, he would rush through it so quickly that he was basically making a mockery of the sacrament.

Everyone was talking about him, and a lot of the seminarians came to me to talk about it and express their concern. Why me? I know that I've mentioned how well I got along with my secular friends outside of the seminary, but I also got along really well with most of my fellow seminarians. They might not have understood me, couldn't really figure me out, but most of them liked and respected me. The qualities that made me different from everyone else—qualities that the rector hated—actually worked in my favor when it came to the seminarians. Again, most of these guys were pretty introverted, quiet, shy, and coloring inside the lines so to speak. I, on the other hand, was extroverted, loud, not afraid to speak up, and yes, sometimes a pain in the ass.

But I was also trying to live the gospels, trying to be honest and caring and loving. And something was working in all of that because a lot of the guys came to me for advice, and came to me when they needed to talk about stuff that they didn't feel that they could talk to anyone else about. So I helped them however I could, kept their confidences and, in a nutshell, loved them like Jesus said to do.

I think that I had kind of set the tone of my relationship with them during my very first days here. I had joined them during their second semester and had only been here for a few days when they asked me if I would become the chairman of their Student Spirituality Committee. This position was kind of a big deal and it entailed quite a bit of responsibility. As chairman, you could wield some power and be in a position of some power. But I told them no, and that it would be more fair for them to ask someone else, someone among them who had been here longer than I and deserved it more than I did.

So they knew from the get-go that I wasn't out to promote myself at everyone else's expense, wasn't out to compete with them, and wasn't trying to try to win any popularity contests. I knew that my behavior often baffled them because they told me so. I was always doing things that they didn't understand like volunteering to do stuff that most everyone else was trying to get out of doing, helping with stuff that I didn't have to help with, and standing up to the rector risking life and limb.

So a bunch of them came to talk to me about the rector. We were all concerned about him, concerned that maybe something major was really wrong with him. I took our concerns to some of the other priests that worked at the seminary saying that maybe one of them could talk to him and help him. They all thanked me for telling them, but we didn't get the impression that anything was done about it.

So I got appointed as the student spokesman, and I asked to meet with the rector. At the appointed time I went to his office and knocked on his door. He didn't answer. I waited for a few moments and knocked again. Still no answer, so I just went in. He was sitting in his chair looking down at his desk. He didn't look at me when I came in, didn't say anything, and didn't ask me to sit down. I just stood there not sure how to begin. So I said, "Father, I need to talk to you. I think we should start with a prayer." He still didn't look at me, but I said a short prayer and then just started talking.

I told him that the seminarians were all worried about him and that his behavior was worrying us. I mentioned some of the things that had been brought up like how he wouldn't talk to any of us, would just yell at us constantly, and how he was always rushing through Mass. I told him that everyone was upset, morale was really low, and that we were concerned that he was having some personal problems or that maybe he was sick or something. I asked him if he had anyone that he could talk to, like a friend or a therapist, or if any of us could do anything for him. I finished talking. Silence. The whole time that I had been speaking, he never once looked at me, never once acknowledged me, or said anything to me. I stood there for a moment longer, thanked him for meeting with me, and left. That was it. All in all, a very awkward and very strange encounter.

Chapter 11

He never brought it up and never mentioned this meeting. His behavior didn't change.

During the weekend of that first week back from our break we also had one of our parties. It would be the last seminary party that I would ever attend, and it proved to be a memorable one.

Once a month or so the seminary would host a party, a get-together in which all of the seminarians, the seminary staff, local priests, and any priests visiting our diocese would be invited. It was a chance for all of us to socialize, share soft drinks, a meal, and conversation. Sometimes we would watch a movie together. But its purpose wasn't just to provide an occasion for everyone to kick back and have a good time. It was an opportunity for social networking, although that term hadn't yet come into use.

The priesthood is very competitive, and the competition starts on the first day that you walk into the seminary. For most seminarians the goal is to get noticed by the people above you on the food chain—the people in power. And the earlier this starts in your career, the better. Being ordained a priest is only the first step on the road to that power. If you do well as a priest, and more importantly, if you impress the bishop, the sky could be the limit for you. You would want to have your name on that short list of candidates when it comes to appointing a priest to head an important committee or to fill a prestigious position such as Vicar General.

Once your name was on that list and you kept up the good work, maybe your name would be on the short list when it came time to appoint a new bishop or archbishop. And archbishops can be appointed cardinals. And a cardinal can become a pope. See where I'm going with this? It's basically about manipulating your way to the top, and it all starts in the seminary.

Every so often the bishop would send a letter out to all of the priests in the diocese asking them to submit the names of any priests that they knew who were doing a really good job, were looked up to by other priests, had a glowing reputation, and were popular with the people. I remember getting these letters when I was a priest working in my parish. The bishop was collecting names for his short list.

So these parties were an opportunity for people to impress and to be impressed. It wasn't mandatory, but the seminarians were strongly encouraged to attend. If you wanted to get on that road to power, you made sure that you attended these parties along with any other event where you could be seen and noticed, to get your name out there. I usually dropped in for a little while, and (you know me) enjoyed talking to anybody and everybody there. I don't know if I ever impressed anyone, but I didn't especially care. I didn't think I'd ever be on anybody's good list, short, long, or in-between.

So I'm at the party, and most everyone had congregated in this large main room. So I started off there, mingling and talking to people, and just sort of making the rounds. There were several smaller rooms off the hallway and people were ambling about with their drinks in hand, just little clusters of people here and there.

During the course of the evening, I left the main room and walked down the hallway a little ways and went into an adjoining room. Sitting there in this big armchair was one of the local parish priests—really drunk—and on his lap were squeezed two seminarians (who were actually brothers). One brother was on the priest's right lap and the other on his left. He had each of his hands down the front of each of their pants. I came to an abrupt stop and looked at them. I'm not sure what kind of an expression that I had on my face (disbelief? horror?), but when they saw me one of the seminarians was quick to say, "Hey, it's okay, he's our cousin."

Well, I thought to myself, isn't that special, a close-knit family. I told them—cousin or not—that what they were doing was really inappropriate, and that if this is what they were all choosing to do they needed to take it elsewhere or to get a room or something. I told them that playing with each other in public wasn't something that any of us wanted to see. Then I turned around and walked out, shutting the door behind me.

Both of those brothers eventually ended up leaving the seminary and neither of them became priests. About twenty years after that incident, one of those brothers actually sued his cousin, that priest, for sexual misconduct and he was subsequently kicked out of the priesthood for pedophilia issues. I remember that when the incident became public all those years later, my bishop remarked that it only happened because father was so drunk that he didn't know what he was doing. So he really couldn't be held accountable for it, could he? (Yeah, right.)

When I had described this party, I said that we got together for "soft drinks." That's because liquor was officially no longer allowed at our get-togethers. When the new bishop took office, one of the very first things that he did was to send a letter to all priests in the diocese banning liquor at any priest-sponsored functions. Before that, the liquor had flowed quite freely from what I was told.

We were told by some of the older priests about an incident that had happened a few years earlier. Some of the priests in the diocese were together for a meeting and there was a lot of drinking going on. Two of the priests had gotten pretty drunk. After the meeting they were supposed to be concelebrating a Mass at one of the local churches. They both got to the church in one piece, which was nothing short of a miracle considering the condition they were in.

Before the Mass started, the two priests were in the sacristy (a room off the altar where supplies for the Mass and the vestments—clothing—that the priests wear for the Mass are kept, and also where the priests dress), and they got into an argument. The argument turned into a physical fight, and soon they were brawling with each other and rolling around on the ground throwing punches. They then rolled out of the sacristy and onto the altar section of the church where the parishioners were treated to the sight of these two men of God, reeking to high heaven of alcohol, hurling four letter words at each other while they beat the crap out of each other.

The new bishop didn't drink, and apparently he didn't like other people to drink either. No one knew exactly why, but the talk at the time was that when the bishop was a young priest just starting out, he had an alcoholic pastor who had caused him a lot of grief. Whether or not that was true, I really don't know. Oftentimes, some priests would sneak in their own booze, which is what happened at that party.

Seminary life went on and we were approaching mid-term. I had been doing a lot of thinking about my future and about what I would be doing next. To continue on the priest path, I would need to go on to graduate theology school. There were several theology schools with excellent reputations, but they were also very expensive. Since your diocese helps to pay for your schooling, you have to take into consideration the fact that a really expensive school might be beyond their financial resources, and our diocese was not a rich one. I had spent last semester applying to about a dozen different theology schools, even the expensive ones. I thought what the heck and why not, you never know what the future could bring.

I had also kept in touch with Mother Teresa while in the seminary, and she and I had discussed several options. One of them was her original proposal that she had talked to me about back in Rome when Karl and I had met with her. She proposed that I attend theology school here in the States, and then go to Rome for my ordination to her Brothers' order. She also proposed another option—that her order would pay for me to go to theology school wherever I chose, and then again to Rome for my ordination to her order. She said that she was still watching to see if God's plan for my life would lead me back to her. But I honestly didn't think that it would.

At this point in my life, I was still growing into the idea of being a priest, but still wasn't convinced that it was going to happen. I found the idea of theology school to be very exciting, whether I ended up as a priest or not. But I couldn't let her pay for theology school and then end up deciding that I wasn't going to be a priest after all. That wouldn't be fair to her. I also knew that I wasn't suited to the communal lifestyle, and being a priest in her order would've meant communal living. I was too independent, too much of a free thinker and, as some of my teachers had told me, too much of a radical to fit comfortably into any group.

Living the Franciscan charism and serving the poor— those things were a given. That was a part of my life and always would be. If I could have done those things side by side with Mother Teresa, it would have been a dream come true. But it was only a dream, the reality of it being very different from what the actuality would have been.

I would've needed to first do the training to become a Missionary of Charity Brother because that was how they had set up their program. Even though I was a priest, I would still have to do the training to become a brother, which I certainly could have done, but again that would have meant communal living which just didn't seem to work for me. And I would not have been permitted to actually work with Mother Teresa because in religious orders the sexes are segregated. The sisters worked with the sisters, and the brothers with the brothers. Yeah, we would get to meet occasionally, but our actual work wouldn't be shared on a daily basis.

Now if I could have become a nun—that would've solved the problem! Later on in my life when I was a new priest, one of the sisters whom I worked with actually said to me, "Father, I think that you would have made a better nun than a priest!" She never really explained that one to me.

While working with the poor in other countries is a noble undertaking—one that I had given serious consideration to—in the end my calling seemed to be here, in my own country. Although in America we didn't have the appalling depth of poverty that is seen in third world countries, Mother Teresa told me that we did have what she called the "spiritually impoverished." You might not see hordes of people in this country scrambling on a daily basis for food to fill their empty bellies, but you did see them scrambling to fill empty lives, lives with a connection to things but without a connection to God. And of the two, she felt that ours was the more serious impoverishment. She told me that because of its materialism, she felt that the US had the greater need.

And that's what ultimately moved me—to help people to find and nourish and grow their connection to the Divine Presence. I felt that if I did end up becoming a priest—a diocesan priest—I could probably do the most good because I would have more independence and flexibility.

I was also considering more education even beyond graduate school. I found theology and biblical studies to be a real love of mine—one that I might want to pursue even further—and maybe get a doctorate in one of

Chapter 11

those fields. So there was a lot to think and pray about—decisions that would have to be made on top of still attending classes, living at the seminary, and being harassed by the rector on a daily basis.

And then it finally happened. It was about two weeks before midterm. One minute I was walking down the hallway, and the next minute I was walking into the rector's office to tell him that I was leaving the seminary. It happened that fast, between one footstep and the next. *I was done!* He was sitting at his desk and I walked up to him and I told him, "I'm leaving the seminary. I'm giving you my two weeks' notice." (I'm not quite sure why I gave him two weeks' notice other than it seemed like the right thing to do.) I definitely caught him by surprise. (I caught myself by surprise as well.) I half expected him to say, "How dare you leave?" He didn't, but he did look at me with astonishment on his face that quickly turned to anger, and angrily he asked me why I was leaving.

So I told him that I didn't fit in here, that I didn't believe that you had to go through hell to become a priest, that it didn't have to be a negative experience, that it had become an obstacle to my spiritual growth, that I was fed up with all of the bullshit, that I was tired of it, and that I was done.

He was livid. He told me that if I left now, he would never let me back, and that I would never become a priest. I told him that I wasn't going to come back, and that whether or not I became a priest was up to God, and not up to him. And that becoming a priest wasn't the most important thing to me, but growing in terms of spirituality and in terms of Jesus—this is what was important.

He said that if I left now, he could keep me from going to theology school, and that he had the power to do that. I told him that whatever power he had came from God, and that he was accountable to God for how he used that power. That got him even angrier because not only did I question what he told me, but then asked him to question himself about how he interpreted God's will. And no, he couldn't keep me from going to theology school—I was going. Then he said that he could keep me from getting into a graduate seminary. I told him to do whatever he had to do, and that I would do whatever I had to do in following the path of Jesus.

Then he asked me why I was leaving now when there was less than a semester left before I was finished. I told him that I simply did not want to do this anymore and would not do this anymore. I was done. He said, "You can't leave."

I said, "Watch me."

I knew what he was thinking. He could give a crap that I was leaving. In his heart he was most probably rejoicing and singing his happy song. However, for a seminarian to leave just a few months before the end of the program would definitely leave a black mark on the rector's book. It already didn't look good on his record that so many seminarians had left his program, and now here was another one. And to leave at a time like this, the people in authority would wonder what was going on here. And he knew that the administration might even want to ask me why and why now, and they did.

"Well," he told me, spit flying out of his mouth along with his angry words, "I will allow you to leave." (*Allow* me to leave as if I needed his permission, which I didn't.) "I will allow you to leave, but first you have to speak to each seminarian and tell them that you're leaving." I thought that this was a rather odd request, and asked him why he thought I needed to do that. He said that it was because I was upsetting the community by doing this and destroying the spirituality of the other seminarians.

I was tempted to ask him about all of the other guys who have left—and there had been plenty of them—the ones who just took off without more than a quick goodbye, if even that. (Most of these guys left without much fanfare. They'd tell the rest of us, "I'm not taking this shit anymore," and they were gone.) They didn't have to tell everybody that they were leaving; they just left. They didn't destroy our spirituality, so why do you think that my leaving would do that? I didn't say that, however, because I respected the position that the rector held, even though I didn't respect the rector as a man. So I told him that I would speak to each seminarian.

He then asked me exactly when I would be leaving. I told him in two weeks at the end of mid-term. He asked me where I was going to go, and I told him that I was moving into the college dorm. He asked me what I was going to do after that, and I said, "I'm going to be in a play." That's the first thing that popped into my head. Here we are having this tense, serious conversation, and that's the first thing that I think of! I had a minor in theater and the rector had told me that I could work on the sets, build props, and help the actors to learn their lines, but I was *never* to do any acting myself because that that was too "secular," not befitting a seminarian. So I told him, by damn, that I was going to do some acting! I finished talking with him, exit interview over, and left his office.

Over the next two weeks I did talk to each seminarian to let them know that I was leaving. None of them seemed very surprised, and a few thought that it was sad that I was leaving the "good ship lollipop." Let me explain that one! A lot of the seminarians were very frank about what they were doing in the seminary. They were here, they would put up with the shit (their words), they would do whatever they had to do, then they would get ordained, be given a parish, and live the good life from then on. They would have their housing provided for, wouldn't have to pay a mortgage or utility bills, be given a car, and have someone cook their meals. All they had to do in exchange for all of that was to say Mass, do baptisms, weddings, and funerals. In other words, live the good life.

So they jokingly referred to the seminary as the "good ship lollipop." A few of them asked if I really wanted to jump ship and give that up. And I told them—no offense—but what they considered to be the "good life" sounded totally boring to me. Maybe these guys weren't in the seminary for the best of reasons, but at least they were honest about it. And sadly, I would find this attitude to be just as prevalent in the graduate seminary.

I spent the next two weeks talking to the seminarians like the rector had asked, and I also told the rest of the staff that I was leaving and why. The "people in charge" did call me to ask why I was leaving and I told them. I found out later that shortly after I left, the rector was called in front of the bishop and the personnel board to explain why so many seminarians had left in the past few years. He was then removed from this position and a new rector was installed for the following year. After losing this position, the rector took a lengthy leave of absence and then, from what I've heard, returned a changed man, a better man.

Mid-term came, I packed my bags, said goodbye to everyone, and moved into the college dorm. My days at the diocesan seminary were over.

Chapter 12

Anything Goes

I moved into the dorm at the college to finish out my final semester of school. Since I already knew just about everybody there, it was almost like a homecoming. Everyone told me that they were glad that I was there, and it was like—okay, he's here, let the fun begin and let the good times roll!

When I had told the rector that I was going to be in a play, I had no idea if that was actually going to happen. But no sooner had I moved into the dorm, when the head of the Performing Arts Department approached me and said that he had just lost two actors from their upcoming production of *Anything Goes,* and asked if I could take over their parts. It was only two weeks until opening night, but he told me that he knew that I could do it. The poor guy was desperate. I said yes, so I finally did get to be in a play.

I developed a reputation as a "quick study" at both the college and at our community theaters as someone they could call on when they lost an actor close to opening night. I had minored in theater because I love acting and "hamming it up," which went hand in hand with my extroverted personality. I didn't know if I'd ever be another John Wayne (one of my idols), but maybe with a little practice, who knows? Well you have priests who used to be in the government (before the Vatican banned it), priests who are famous authors in the secular world (like Andrew Greeley), so why not an actor priest? What can I say–this was the seventies! But I had a blast doing it, and regretted that I hadn't stood up to the rector before this, and had let him bully me into not doing any acting during the last two years.

My friends and I also engaged in some childish but harmless college pranks. Streaking on college campuses was big that year, and we had to do our part! So a group of us, clad initially in our Fruit of the Looms, streaked across campus in broad daylight. As we ran through the sprinklers and got soaked, there went our Fruit of the Looms and we ended up wearing only our birthday suits! Waving into all of the classroom windows, laughing, and waving and yelling "hi" to everyone we passed, we had college security running after us like an episode right out of the *Keystone Kops*. Everyone knew who we were and everyone had a good laugh about it. The college was very tolerant of our silliness, and we didn't get into any trouble over it other than a stern warning not to do it again. Mooning was also popular at that time, but I'll plead the fifth on that one!

I had mentioned that last semester I had applied to a number of graduate theology schools—to Berkeley in California, the Theological Union in New York City, to Northeastern University in Chicago, and even to Levane in Belgium to name a few. Now I was getting acceptance letters back and was accepted to every school that I had applied to! I really wanted to go to Berkeley because in the seventies it was considered to be the most progressive and most radical theology school in the US I think that I would have fit in there just fine, and they had even accepted me. But I wasn't able to get a loan in California to cover the expenses, and believe me it was expensive.

So I decided on a school that was a little smaller but that had a good solid reputation, and it was located in a state that was willing to give me a loan. Since I didn't have the financial backing of my diocese, I was paying for everything myself.

Normally if you're going to attend a graduate theology school as a seminarian, you will also apply with the help of your rector to the seminary that is associated with that school. With the backing of your diocese your acceptance into the seminary is guaranteed, and they will help you out with the finances. Exactly how they do that depends on the diocese, but what it amounts to is that they will help to pay for your schooling, and in return you will work as a priest in their diocese once you are ordained.

However, since I was officially on a year's leave of absence from the seminary, which is what the official paperwork filed by my previous rector stated, I couldn't even apply to the graduate seminary here for another year. The rector couldn't necessarily stop me from eventually getting into a graduate seminary, but he could definitely continue to make it more difficult—that is, if he were around. But since he would be going on that leave of absence, he would now be out of the picture. (Mysterious how God works, isn't it?) I was just thankful that I was going to theology school because of the two—that's what was most important to me.

So the semester ended and I graduated from college magna cum laude. I moved back home for the summer and got a job at a local hotel. My parents asked me what I was going to do next. I told them I was going to graduate theology school and hopefully, at some point, into the graduate seminary. They both rolled their eyes, and in unison said, "Whatever."

Summer ended and I packed my car, which I would need at school, so I had to drive there. I also packed my parents who volunteered to go with me on the long drive. I had never been to this new city, didn't know a soul there, but my mom did. She had two friends whose daughters were both nuns in the same order and lived in a convent on the grounds of my new school. She suggested that we meet with them when we got there, and maybe they could help me get acquainted with the city, give me some advice on where to live—that kind of thing.

So that's what we did. Contacted the nuns and told them that we were coming, finished packing my Pontiac LeMans, hopped in, and headed out. I remember that we got there late on a Wednesday night and got motel rooms. The next day we met up with the nuns, had lunch together, and then we did some sightseeing. While I was running around doing school-related stuff, the nuns happily wined and dined my parents who stayed until the weekend. Then I took them to the airport so they could fly home. The nuns and I then did a little more sightseeing and a lot of apartment hunting. I managed to find a place that was only about four blocks from the school. The following day I signed the lease and moved in.

On Sunday that weekend there was an open house at the school for all of the new students. They put on a big bash and a barbeque, and the faculty and staff were there meeting and mingling with the students. I had a really great time at that gathering. I walked in, said hi to everybody, and just started talking up a storm to everyone. It was kind of weird, but a good weird because for some reason I just seemed to click with all of them–the professors and the staff. I found myself really comfortable with them, as if we were all old friends rather than new acquaintances.

They all made me feel so welcome, made me feel as if I belonged there. It was such a good fit that I felt as if I had come home. And if that was an omen, it was right on because theology school proved to be one of the best experiences of my life. At the party I also met my fellow students and a number of them were seminarians. These were the guys that I would have been at the seminary with, had I been allowed to attend.

School started the following day with an orientation where we formally met the faculty and staff and got a tour of the school and grounds. It was a mid-size campus with lots of old, mature trees, lots of greenery; a really pretty campus. We also finished the paperwork for the admissions process and were assigned our work-study jobs. I got assigned as the library assistant in the school's very big, very busy library. At the party the day before, I had met the two ladies who helped to run the library and had a great time talking with them. When they heard that I would be working there with them, they told me that they were "delighted." They were good people, and I told them that I felt the same way to be working with them.

The library ended up playing a very significant part in my life and I thanked my lucky stars that I was assigned there. The head librarian, Father Monti, was also our New Testament Professor. He was my boss and also became my mentor. He gave me my first "purse," which caused quite a stir in the school for us, but that happened a little later on.

So school started. In my freshman class we had about thirty students, with about sixty in the whole school. It wasn't a large number because theology is not a profession where you find hordes of people clamoring to get in. The freshman class usually starts out with a large number of students, but that number dwindles in the following years. Guys leave because they realize, belatedly, that this isn't what they want to do or if they're also seminarians, that the priesthood really isn't their calling. A few guys flunk out and a few are asked to leave. I think that back then for most of the guys who got kicked out, it was usually because of alcohol—or sometimes partying that was totally out of control.

As everyone knows, graduate school is serious business. There are no "fluff" classes in grad school, and you're required to get either an "A" or a "B" in all of your classes as any other grades were considered failing. Absolutely no outside jobs were allowed. You were here to learn theology, period. Classes started at eight in the morning for everyone, we all had lunch at the same time, and all classes ended for the day at five o'clock. You were required to have your Bible with you for every class.

Theology school was a dream come true for me. It was as if this was what I had been born to do; what I had been waiting for my entire life. I had finally discovered my "*It*."

So what kind of classes did we have that first year? All of the basic courses: the introductory courses such as Introduction to Sacred Scripture, Sacred Theology, the New Testament, the Old Testament, and Moral Theology, just to name a few. During the following years we would narrow the focus, get more specific topics, and study things like the Wisdom Literature, Pauline Theology, Johannine Theology, and the Synoptic Gospels. Basically, we covered every verse of scripture in the Bible and every type of theology that is available.

It was hard work—constant reading, constant studying, and ten to twenty page papers that had to be written at least twice a semester for each class. But the classes were exciting, stimulating, challenging, thought provoking, and growth filled. I felt like I had died and gone to heaven being presented with this plethora of knowledge. Our professors—every one of them—were wonderful, dedicated men, constantly challenging us to learn, to understand, and to grow.

Thinking back if I had to summarize that first year of school, I would say that it was the year that they tore apart everything that we thought we knew about our religion. We were being taught all of this up-to-date, cutting edge theology. It was so different from what we had learned growing up, learned in our religion classes, and learned from the pulpit of our churches. They plowed through all of the devotional stuff that we had been taught saying, yeah, you can look at it that way, we do look at it that way, but there is also another way of looking at it. It was a more mature way of looking at our faith, more in keeping with the reality of the experiences.

For instance, one of the areas that they addressed was the miracles that we associate with Jesus' ministry. Yes, there were miracles but we were going to interpret them in a more mature manner. Take, for example, the miracle of the loaves of bread and the fish. We are told that Jesus is on a hillside preaching to thousands of people, and that the crowd is getting hungry and all they had available were seven loaves of bread and a few fish. And to feed all of the people present, Jesus basically snaps his fingers and from the seven loaves and three fish he was able to provide enough food for everyone there.

According to Roman Catholic theology, the real miracle wasn't an abracadabra—let's magically multiply the food kind of thing. Rather, the real miracle was that Jesus got them to share the food they had so that no one would go hungry. Jesus got them to change what they were feeling on the inside, and change a hard-hearted inner attitude of selfishness to one of compassion and sharing. That's where the power of Jesus worked—on an interior level that wrought life-altering changes on the exterior level. We were told that this interpretation was more in keeping with what really happened.

I found it fascinating. Some of my classmates found it devastating—even called it blasphemous.

A number of the guys in my class had a hard time with these teachings. They felt that taking away the abracadabra aspect of it took away the magic of the experience and that it weakened their faith. (If He didn't do magic tricks, was He really God?) For me, on the other hand, it made my faith experience more real because Jesus *did* work miracles—in people's hearts. I had experienced the power of Jesus' words on an interior level and it was magical. So for me these concepts were more of an "aha" moment, and more of a "Yes this is what it's really all about" kind of thing. It made it more real, more meaningful, and more powerful. If you only have faith because of a few magic tricks, what kind of faith do you really have? Therein is one of the differences between myself, and many of the other students. Actually, one of many, but hey.

So that year was spent learning the differences between what Catholic Theologians espoused and what the church actually chose to teach to the laity. Again, it was a matter of believing that the people couldn't understand these concepts, and that their faith wasn't mature enough to handle them. So we had to interpret these teachings for them from the pulpit, giving them the "watered down" version because anything else would be too much for them to understand and would weaken their faith. We needed to keep our flock of sheep in place. That's much easier to do than teaching them these concepts, than growing them in their faith, and bringing them to the wonders of a God who works real miracles through the hearts of His people.

In my freshman class a few of the guys actually did leave because of this. They couldn't handle it or didn't want to handle it. A majority of the other guys said, "Why bother to learn this stuff? We'll never use it. We're not allowed to preach it. We'll go back to our dioceses and we'll be in the Dark Ages again when it comes to this stuff. So why bother?" And they wouldn't—they'd scrape by with the minimum effort needed. There were maybe three or four of us who thought that this stuff was mind boggling and life altering, and we talked about it—up, down, and sideways. We got from it everything that we could and wrung it dry.

And when it came to understanding what we were being taught, I had the keys to the kingdom, otherwise known as the keys to the library. What was extra special was the tiny little key that opened the room that housed the rare book section, which was located upstairs in a little back room. Its cabinets contained copies of the original manuscripts of the Bible in their original languages, most of which were written in Greek and some in Aramaic.

Also inside this cabinet was a dictionary of the ancient Greek language. When I saw that I felt like I had found the Holy Grail! Just imagine being able to read the Bible in its pure form. The thought alone gave me an orgasm! I didn't know Greek from Swahili, but I learned. I would spend hours poring over that dictionary, word by word, to find the meaning of the words as written by the original authors. There was no one else's translation between us, just me and the original writer's words. I think I felt the way that Carter must have felt when he unearthed Tutankhamun's tomb! Awed doesn't begin to describe it.

These books could not be removed from the library. So all during grad school if I wasn't in class or doing my apostolic work, or jogging the grounds trying to keep my weight in check, I was in the library. There was nowhere else on earth that I would rather have been. When the other guys went out drinking or partying, I had my own little party of three in the library—myself, the Greek dictionary, and the original scriptures.

When father mentioned a Greek word found in the original manuscripts in class, I would get so pumped! I would know what the original writer meant, which might not always be the translation that was eventually approved and used by the church. Using that dictionary was painstaking yet exhilarating work. It opened up the scriptures for me, brought me to a whole new level of understanding, and brought a whole new level of meaning to the classroom work. Comparing the theology that we were learning with how it was being lived by the church was mind boggling to me because this was life enhancing stuff, but the church wasn't using it. It seemed to me that the church believed more in the authority of its bishops' versions of theology than in the authority of Jesus' words.

As students we were encouraged to speak up, engage, dissect, and discuss what we were learning, and I needed no prompting to do any of that! In class I think I was always the first one to raise my hand, to open my mouth, to ask questions, and to challenge.

The professor would explain something, perhaps a concept that we had all been wrestling with, and sometimes I would have a sudden epiphany. I would "get" it and suddenly it all made sense to me, and I would get so excited that I thought that I would burst at the seams! I'd raise my hand, wave wildly at the professor, and engage him in a discussion. I would then go back and forth with him about these concepts, saying if that's how it's interpreted, then it follows that this means such-and-such and we should look at it this way instead of the other. The professor and I would be going on about it with me practically jumping up and down in my seat. Most of the other guys would be sitting there, sticking pencils in their ears or noses as they're yawning and scratching their butts.

The handful of us who were fascinated with our classes would get together after class or during our spare time and have these deep discussions about what we were being taught. Why was the interpretation this and not that? Were we one hundred percent sure that the original author meant a certain word to be used in this manner and not the other? Did God do this or did He intend to do that? What does all of this have to do with people's lives? With being a priest? How could we balance all of the conservative practices of the past with this open-ended, multidimensional way of doing things in the future? How could we narrow the gap between Catholic theology and Catholic practice? How could we get the church to grow? Just fantastic discussions!

The rest of the guys in class would say—and these are their exact words—"I just want to give the professor what he's asking for so I can get ordained and then I can live happily ever after in my rectory." The "good ship lollipop" guys, who, to my way of thinking, had completely missed the boat, so to speak.

I really did spend all of my time in the library. It wasn't only an opportunity for me to drown myself in theological concepts, but they also expected me to work! I ended up being the "copy" guy for the school. I would spend a lot of my time there making copies of articles or periodicals for the faculty and students. This was back in the day when copy machines (they were always called Xerox machines) were big, cumbersome, noisy things, and making copies was very labor intensive and time consuming. I'd make the requested copies and carry around one of those lined yellow paper tablets so I could keep a record of who was getting what and how many they were getting. They also taught me the art of book binding so I could rebind some of the older books that were falling apart, and that was kind of a neat thing to know how to do.

There weren't a whole lot of textbooks in theology at that time. As soon as one was published, it became outdated as new avenues of thought were constantly being formulated. Much of our knowledge came from periodicals that were regularly being published with the latest, most current information. When these periodicals were delivered to the library, I would usually be there to sign them in and disburse them where they needed to go. But first I would read them. Lordy, I was in hog heaven!

I would read the periodicals. If there was an article that had to do with, say, the most current interpretation of some aspect of Pauline theology, I would think maybe the professor who is teaching that class to the second or third year students would be interested in it. So I would make a copy of the article and put it in that professor's mailbox with a little note saying that I thought that he might find this interesting. I basically ended up doing this for all of the professors for whatever year or class they were teaching. There was a posted schedule of which professors were teaching which classes each semester, so I was able to direct the appropriate article to the appropriate professor.

It became my routine because it was a way for me to learn and to keep up with all of the latest theological developments, even in areas that I hadn't yet had classes in. It was also a small way that I could give back to the professors for all they were giving me. Maybe I could make life a little easier for them, and a little easier for them to access information. It just seemed like a natural thing to do because the professors were really good guys, hard-working and always busy, and I respected all of them and wanted to help in any way that I could. (Oddly enough, this got me into trouble with some of my classmates later on.)

Chapter 12

All of the professors were constantly using the library, looking up information for their classes, and striving to present the best information to their students. Yet in any given week, I might see only two or three students come into the library. There may have been more who came in when I wasn't working, but still that's a pretty pitiful number. The library, the periodicals, the rare book section—all of this was available to all of the students, but very few that I could see seemed to take advantage of it.

So I decided to do something to "stir the pot" a little bit. (As you know, I have some experience in that area.) We had a bulletin board in the library and we used it to list the new books and periodicals that came in during the month. It was just a list of the names of the books and articles—pretty dull—and hardly anyone bothered to even look at it. So I decided to spice it up a little. I took the bulletin board out of the library, placed it on an easel, and put it in the main hallway outside of the library where there was a lot of student traffic.

I then got a picture from a magazine of Farrah Fawcett-Majors, that famous picture where she's in a wet T-shirt. I think that at that time every guy in America had seen (and fantasized over) that picture! I put that up on the bulletin board, and I had a little paper rose that I taped over her mouth so that it looked like she was holding it with her teeth.

Then I found a picture of Pope Paul VI who was the pope at that time, and in the picture he was kneeling. So I adjusted his picture so that he was kneeling in front of her and it looked like he was kissing her hand. Above their pictures I put a bold headline that said, "Now That We've Got Your Attention, See How The Pope Views Women In The Church!!!" And then I'd list the name of the article or periodical that had come in dealing with the role of women in the church.

Another time I cut out a picture of the devil from a magazine. He had a shiny, bright red outfit complete with horns and a tail. I put that up on the board with the caption, "Burning Issues—Is Hell Still Relevant???" And then I listed the title of the theological journal discussing those questions.

After that, everybody started coming into the library to check out the articles including, I was told, some long-time staff members who up to then, had never before even stepped inside of it. The library staff told me that it caused a sharp spike in readership. It was a lot of fun to do, and I guess the professors were okay with it because all they did was shake their heads and roll their eyes at me! I found out much later on that the wet T-shirt poster actually caused quite a few behind the scenes discussions among my professors regarding my character and moral fiber.

As I said before, working in the library gave me the opportunity to get to know all of the professors in our school. Our library served as a resource for not only our theology school, but also for the faculty at the seminary and other schools in the area. I also got to meet all of those faculty members, and in particular, I got to know the rector of the seminary—the one that I was banned from attending for a year. I had actually met him before back in the diocesan seminary when he came to talk to us about his seminary. Kind of like career day in high school, the rectors or vocation directors of graduate seminaries around the country would visit diocesan seminaries to woo us, to promote their seminaries to us, and to encourage us to choose them when we were planning our futures.

There had been a bit of trouble at this particular seminary in the not-too-distant past. They had a bishop who was crazy, as in actually mentally ill, and his behavior was so bizarre that dioceses across the country that had sent their seminarians here became very concerned and started pulling their seminarians out of the program. So the number of students at this seminary dwindled dramatically, and there was even talk of closing the seminary. Instead, they got rid of that bishop, replaced him, and started to rebuild the seminary's reputation and enrollment.

Because of my job, the rector of this seminary and I got to know each other. He already knew my history as gossip is rife in church circles. He knew that my previous rector had labeled me as "unstable" because I had left the diocesan seminary early and said that I needed to be "watched." But he had also been hearing about me from his seminarians and a few of his professors who knew me, so I guess the things that they told him about me were all positive. After I told him that I did want to pursue becoming a priest, he told me that I didn't have to wait the whole year. And if I wanted, I could enter his seminary the next semester and that he was willing to accept me. So that's what I did. I formally applied for admittance, got accepted, and at the beginning of the second semester I moved out of my apartment and into the seminary.

While theology school taught us the academic portion of our training, the seminary was again the formation part of our training—where we would learn how to function as priests.

This seminary experience was a one hundred and eighty degrees change from my previous one—this was the real thing. By the time that you get to the graduate seminary, it's understood that you're serious about becoming a priest. No more dating, no more curfews, no more of that in-your-face scrutiny as if you were a little kid. There is still plenty of scrutiny, but it's all behind the scenes. You're still constantly watched and evaluated to see if you're "walking your talk." They watch how you conduct yourself, how you interact with others, what your moral fiber is, and if you're living it. If they notice what they consider to be a problem area, they talk to you about it, help you with it, help you to be a better person and a better priest.

Our rector was an outstanding guy. For him it was all about personal responsibility. Basically, he told the seminarians, "Do what you want, but know that there are implications in terms of outcome—in terms of consequences—for your behavior. Be able to justify your actions theologically or pastorally." The scrutiny was aimed at assessing whether or not we were connecting what we were learning and what we were studying with how we were living. Were we bringing all of these concepts together to develop an interior focus and a spiritual lifestyle? Were we learning to discern what we needed to do to make the right decisions so that we would ultimately make life better for the people we would be serving? Someday we would be running parishes, counseling people, and guiding them in their faith. Did we have what it took to do that?

Formation programs are all pretty similar and are based on the model of a diocesan parish. Most of us would end up being parish priests so our program was geared towards that. When you are at a parish, you live in the rectory with other priests who serve that parish. You have your own space and your own bedroom, although the other rooms are communal. You have your own car, your own bank account, and your own schedule. So at the seminary we too had our own rooms but shared a communal dining room and recreation room. As a priest living in a rectory, we would have a housekeeper take care of the cleaning, but our model didn't extend that far. We still had work assignments and were assigned rotating duties like cleaning the bathrooms or any of the communal rooms, washing the floors, and those kinds of things.

We participated in the typical formation activities—daily Mass, scheduled prayer times, workshops, Days of Recollection, and retreats. We had classes on the functions of a priest, guidelines on how to say Mass (I guess you could loosely call it Mass 101), and how to do the rituals. There's a book, sort of like a compendium, that comes out every year and covers all the rubrics—things like what color vestments the priest wears for the different liturgical seasons, what colors the altar cloths should be, and things like that.

We had classes where we had to practice giving sermons. They would assign us a scripture passage and we would have to pull our theology together and create a sermon that we would deliver to the class, and then they would critique it. We also got some counseling classes and a few psychology classes, which was unheard of pre-Vatican II. We had to do counseling practicums. I did mine mainly in hospitals and got to do another exorcism in a hospital emergency room, but that's a little later on.

During my first year there, Father Monti, the head librarian, went to Italy to participate in a theological symposium. I had mentioned earlier that he was my boss, but also my mentor. We had developed a very good relationship, and I greatly admired and respected him. When he was in Italy, it seems that the latest fashion trend was "purses" for men. According to him, they were a big hit there. Nowadays you see guys carrying all kinds of things—briefcases, fanny packs, backpacks, and shoulder bags. But back then, only women carried anything that could be construed as a purse. But here were all these macho Italian men carrying purses and they matter-of-factly called them purses.

Father thought that they were kind of neat and he brought one back for me from Italy. I thought it was cool, obviously it was fairly expensive, and made of this beautiful black leather. When he gave it to me, I asked him what it was. He said, "It's a purse. All the guys in Italy are carrying them."

I said, "Well, okay." So I started using it and I really liked it. Where's the written rule that says that only women can use these things to put their stuff in? I had a lot of stuff too! Well, that caused a lot of raised eyebrows.

Sometimes my classmates would stop me and ask, "What's that?" I'd answer them honestly and say, "It's a purse." If Italian men could call it a purse and get away with it, why couldn't I? These days you could call it a gender neutral personal possession device, but back then we didn't talk like that. Actually, these days you could call it whatever you wanted and no one would bat an eye, but back then, things were very different.

Well the school officials had a field day with that! It's hard to believe now that something so inane could cause such a stir, but it did. They couldn't understand why Father Monti would give one of the students a purse. Father wasn't effeminate, he was just a typical guy—what was he thinking? And what about the student who was using it? Could he have some psychological issues? Could he be a homosexual? And wasn't this the same student who had put up that wet T-shirt poster? I guess they just couldn't figure me out. (Welcome to the club.)

All of this speculation was going on behind the scenes, and I heard later on that they kind of kept an eye on me for a while after that to see if I exhibited any other kind of bizarre behavior—like if I started wearing lipstick and high heels. Well I didn't, and the drama died down. And I'm proud to say that I did my part, albeit a very small one, in breaking down that fashion barrier so that you guys out there today can carry whatever you want to!

So that first year was great. Loved theology school, loved my job in the library, and loved my seminary experience. Got all "As" in my classes, and was asked to return to the seminary the following year. Life could

Chapter 12

not have been better. Who needed drugs? I was high on life. I was in heaven.

And then summer arrived, and I crashed back down to earth.

Chapter 13

The Sign of the Beast:
Welcome to My Screwed-Up Diocese

During the summer after your first year in the graduate seminary, you're assigned to do pastoral work. (In the terminology of the Christian Churches, "pastoral" refers to having to do with the giving of spiritual guidance.) I was assigned to work in a parish back home, and my diocese would pay me a stipend to help cover my expenses for the summer. I would live in the rectory at the parish, assist the pastor in his duties, and help with the parishioners—all to get some real-life, "hands-on" experience. The purpose was to see what parish life as a priest is all about, start to "learn the ropes," and see how you do working with the pastor and ministering to the parishioners. It's an opportunity to start putting all of that neat theology that you've been learning into practice. At least that's what it's supposed to be about.

My bishop sent me to a parish in a different area of my state, far from my hometown. I was going to a parish that had a fairly new pastor, a younger man that I actually met before at some social functions. I'll call him Father Abdon. I knew that he had a reputation of being a really intelligent guy. I thought this should be good, as I was really into learning and kind of gravitated towards the intellectual types.

I figured that we'd have a lot to talk about, maybe have some deep theological discussions, and that I could learn some things from him. I was interested in seeing how a younger pastor—one who had been exposed to some of that new theology—was translating it on a pastoral level for his parishioners. I wanted to see if he was closing that divide between what the church's Theologians taught and what its priests actually preached.

So school ended, I drove home and spent a few days with my family, then headed out to my new assignment. I drove to the parish, got to the rectory, and met up with Father Abdon. He greeted me and first showed me my room and then showed me around the rectory. Then we sat and talked about my being there, and about my being his seminarian for the summer. I had a lot of questions—the kinds of things that you typically ask when you're trying to familiarize yourself with a new place, like how many families were in the parish, what the Mass schedule was, and that kind of thing.

I was a little surprised by father's response to me, or rather lack thereof. I mean, yeah, he answered my questions but it was just an altogether kind of strange encounter. He gave me the facts, but he didn't embellish his answers, didn't volunteer anything extra, and didn't give me any comments or insights. It was very cut and dried, like—you asked, I answered, we're done.

It didn't feel like an actual conversation between us; there wasn't a sharing of information. It was just a rather formal and concise question and answer session. It just felt odd and was a bit of a strained atmosphere—a strained atmosphere over a few questions. This wasn't starting out well, was my thought. And I didn't know it then, but this was not going to end well either.

Although I had met him before, I had never had a one-on-one conversation with him. During that very first meeting with him and talking with him, watching his behavior, it was obvious that he was an extremely introverted guy. He seemed awfully pessimistic and depressed and acted really "down." He didn't seem especially happy that I was there, but he didn't seem especially unhappy. He didn't seem especially anything, like he didn't care much one way or the other. Just kind of flat. Strange vibes.

I've had my share of experiences with introverted guys in the seminary. Usually, with my kind of personality, I could coax them to chill a bit and open up a little. But that didn't seem to be working with father. I didn't know much about psychology at that time, but it seemed obvious to me that all was not quite right in father's world. I couldn't really put my finger on it, but he seemed just a little "off," a little out of kilter, with some kind of an undercurrent that was a little unsettling.

We got to work, and my pastoral experience was basically tagging along after father (like an afterthought). He would take me with him when he did his priestly duties. One of the things we did was to go to the mission churches to say Mass. These were several smaller churches in the outlying areas that were too small to support their own full time priests, so father would head out there on rotating weekends to say Mass for them. We would also visit the sick, visit parishioners in the hospital or nursing homes, and take communion to shut-ins (parishioners who physically could not attend Mass). He would introduce me as his seminarian, but I never got the feeling that we were doing these things together or that we were a team. It felt more like he did his part, I did my part, and we just happened to be there together doing our separate parts.

Chapter 13

I spent a lot of time with him that summer, but we never really developed any kind of a personal relationship. It seemed that we never got past the point of being polite strangers. Yeah, he told me the stuff that I needed to know to be able to function, told me what I needed to do, but again, all of that was concise and to the point. Nothing more; nothing less. But he didn't seem to invest much of himself in it and didn't show much involvement in any of it.

And it didn't seem to be just me that he acted that way towards; it just seemed to be the way he was all of the time—just like with his parishioners. He was a busy guy and he took his duties seriously. He did all of the things for his parishioners that he was supposed to do, but to me it seemed like he did them because he had to because they were his duties, and he was going to do his duty. He didn't seem to get emotionally involved in it, and didn't seem to especially enjoy doing any of those things. It was more like it was just his job, and he was doing his job.

The only time that father seemed to show any real interest was when he was with the young people of the parish. Though he didn't seem to have much of a relationship with most of his adult parishioners, he was really good with the kids and they all seemed to like him. I wondered if that had to do with his self-esteem, of which he didn't seem to have much. Actually, I can remember the thought that popped into my mind at the time—that his self-esteem was in the toilet. Kids were less threatening than adults when it came to interactions. They didn't expect so much from you, so maybe that's why he felt more comfortable with them.

This parish was a fairly poor one, and I think that a number of the kids' parents worked much of the time to make ends meet. So the kids were left on their own a lot and maybe didn't get as much attention from their parents as they wanted. We were also in a rural area and there wasn't a whole lot of recreational stuff for the kids to do.

So father stepped in and filled that void for them. He loved talking with them, paying attention to them, and doing a lot of things with them. He took them swimming, went on picnics and to the movies, and went out for ice cream with them. For some of them, he seemed to be the one adult in their lives who was always there for them and who always had time for them. And, in return, he had their devotion. He was always surrounded by the kids.

Father and I never had any of those deep theological discussions that I had hoped for because we rarely talked in any meaningful way. The interaction between us was basically business-like. I never really felt all that comfortable with him because I just couldn't connect with him on an emotional level, and I think that that was a first for me. If the person that you're trying to interact with doesn't respond, there's not a whole lot that you can do, and I certainly tried. As the old saying goes, it takes two to tango. He was the pastor, he was calling the shots, and he obviously didn't care to tango . . . at least not with me.

Father was definitely odd, but a few times he did this thing that was beyond odd even for him. He would suddenly start talking to me about something out of the blue, and I would have absolutely no idea what he was talking about. It wasn't related to anything that was going on at the moment and wasn't related to anything that made sense to me. I would think—is he talking to me? And I'd realize that there was no one else around so yeah, he was talking to me.

It was like he was picking up and restarting a conversation at the point where we had stopped a previous conversation, only we had never had that previous conversation. It was kind of like tuning in to a soap opera for the first time when it's been on television for the last ten years. You don't know what the story line is and don't know what's going on. That's how it felt when he did this. I didn't know what the story in his head was, couldn't understand it, and I found that to be very disconcerting, even a bit scary.

When father was gone from the parish for a meeting or when he had his day off, I would often drive into town and just walk around and talk to everyone I ran into. (Yeah, that's me, you just can't shut me up!) I'd run into parishioners doing their errands, or I'd see them in the cafes or restaurants and stop in and have coffee or lunch with them. I made it a point to talk to them and get to know them, ask how things were going, and inquire about their families. I got to know most of them this way and got to be on a first name basis with them. Many of them actually became friends, and to this day I still keep in touch with some of them.

I remember that right after I had first gotten to this parish, one of the parishioners—a young man—had committed suicide. Father was gone that day so I went and saw the family. I spent a lot of time with them, counseling and consoling them as best as I could during this terrible time. I ended up becoming very close to the family, and we are still friends all these years later.

The days couldn't pass quickly enough for me because I felt like this assignment was basically a bust. If anyone had asked me to sum up my experience so far, I think I could've answered them in one word—blah. I really wasn't learning much except perhaps getting an idea of how *not* to run a parish! I felt like I was father's altar boy, not his seminarian. Because I assisted him with all of the Masses, I listened to all of his sermons. They were okay, no great shakes theologically, and really just very traditional.

Chapter 13

But occasionally his sermons too could be a little off. It wasn't really what he said, but how he said it. The word that comes to mind is "snide." Sometimes he would pepper his sermons with snide remarks. I would think, geez, this is just great, get up there on the pulpit as a representative of Christ to your parishioners, and be snide and snarky to them. I can remember thinking—what is it with him? What is this man's agenda? I just could not figure him out. And we didn't have the kind of relationship where I could just go up to him and say, "Yo, Abdon, what was up with that sermon today?"

But it was his sermons at the mission Masses that really made me wonder about him. Occasionally, at some of these Masses his sermons would go from being snide to being almost abusive. He would stand at the pulpit and start yelling at the congregation, berating them over this, that, and the other—kind of like fire and brimstone on speed. And you never knew when this was going to happen as there seemed to be no rhyme or reason to it. Sometimes it would be a normal sermon, sometimes it was the yelling ones. I had no idea as to what it was that would set him off. And I would think—where is this coming from? What happened? Did something happen with these people, or does he have some kind of an axe to grind with them that I don't know about? If it was unsettling for me sitting up there at the altar, how did the people in the pews feel, the people who were the target of his anger? It was just so bizarre. (Years later I finally did figure out what was going on at these Masses.)

And then, the oddest thing to happen so far. Father was giving another one of his fire and brimstone sermons at one of the mission churches. There he was yelling and shouting at everyone, but during the whole ten or fifteen minutes of his sermon, his eyes were locked on to this one young boy sitting in one of the pews. This kid looked like he was maybe fifteen or sixteen years old, and he was sitting there with his family. Father looked at this kid during the whole sermon and never once took his eyes off him. And people were noticing it. You'd see people look at father, turn and look at this kid, and then look back at father. People had frowns on their faces like they were wondering—what the hell is he doing? I wondered—*What the hell is he doing?* This was really, really, strange behavior.

Every three or four weeks during that summer the vocation director of my diocese (who had been a seminary classmate of Father Abdon's) would meet with me to check up on things. When I had my first meeting with him, he asked me how things were going. I said, "Mmm, well okay, I guess. Not great, though." I told him that father and I really didn't talk much, didn't communicate well, that he was doing some really odd things, and that he had these major bouts of depression. I told him that I really wasn't learning that much and was often uncomfortable with some of the things that father did.

I was pretty taken aback by what the vocation director told me. He said that Father Abdon was having a very hard time adjusting to his role as pastor and that he was really depressed. The bishop felt that he needed a "companion" because he was lonely and needed cheering up. And that's why I had been sent to him—to be his "companion." I said, "What? Aren't we given pastoral assignments so that we can learn about life in a parish and be guided in that learning by the pastor? You know, that 'hands-on' experience we were told that we needed to get?"

But the vocation director said, "Oh, don't worry about that. You would do well in any parish; you wouldn't have a problem. But this is a special circumstance. Father Abdon is majorly depressed and lonely and he needs some help. And you're a nice guy, upbeat and outgoing, and father said that he had met you before and liked you, so we thought that this would be a good match. So just be there for him, be a good example to him, be good company for him, and help cheer him up."

I was speechless, and that was getting to be a habit the more I learned about the workings of the church. Yes, father obviously needed help, but not from some wet-behind-the-ears seminarian. God, this was a mistake. They weren't doing right by any of us. Instead of assigning me to a parish so I could learn about being a priest, which I was told was the point of all of this since I was studying to be a priest (well duh), or even assigning me to a parish based on the pastoral needs of the parishioners, I was assigned to babysit a depressed priest. This wasn't meeting anyone's needs. My needs weren't a consideration, the needs of the people that we were supposed to be serving weren't a consideration, and father's needs weren't being addressed. He needed far more help than I could give him. He obviously needed a lot more than a "companion."

Welcome to my screwed up diocese. I was really angry, but there wasn't much I could do about it because as a seminarian, you don't really have a say in anything. You don't have any power, and you're on the lowest rung of that priest ladder. So I figured that I'd just have to get through it. It was just for the summer which was about half over anyway.

But the best was yet to come. A couple of weeks after that conversation with the vocation director, Father Abdon and I were both at home in the rectory. I was in my room reading, and father was sitting in the living room with one of the parish kids, a young boy. At one point I had come out of my room and was walking down the hallway and stopped to pick up a book that was lying on the floor. Where I stopped was right around the corner from the living room, and I could hear father talking to the boy and could hear him quite clearly. He was telling the

Chapter 13

boy, "You know that sermon that I gave the other day, the one where I was yelling at everyone?"

I heard the boy say, "Yeah, what was that about?"

And father said, "Well, remember last week when I asked you to go out for ice cream with me and you said no? When you didn't want to spend time with me?"

The kid said, "Yeah?"

Father then said, "Well, I yelled at everybody because of you. It's your fault. Because you wouldn't have ice cream with me, and because you didn't want to spend time with me, I had to take it out on them. That's what happens when you're not nice to me. That's what happens when you won't do what I want. I have to be awful and yell at everybody else."

And I heard the kid mumble, "Oh, I'm sorry."

Well, that stopped me dead in my tracks. I mean I was literally, physically stunned, frozen in place, blown away, aghast, and speechless. I could not believe what I'd just heard. Had I just been plopped down in the middle of an Alfred Hitchcock movie, maybe an Edgar Allan Poe movie? This was insane. I could not believe that father had actually said that. But he did.

Shortly after that I had my meeting with the vocation director. I told him, "You've got to do something about father." I repeated the conversation that I had heard. I told him, "This guy is nuts! He's blaming this kid for his own behavior! He's making this poor kid responsible for his own behavior! Is he doing this with all of the kids? That's crazy. You have to do something about him."

The vocation director said, "Well, maybe you misunderstood him."

I said, "I don't think so. I heard him plain as day. You can't misunderstand something like that." I said, "That is really screwed up. He is really screwing up that kid. To blame a young, impressionable kid like that, a kid who looks up to him, trusts him, and doesn't have the tools to defend himself. That is one sick dynamic. That's psychotic. You have to do something. This guy needs some kind of help!"

Then the Vocation Director said, "Well, yeah, father does have some problems."

I said, "Problems? He has some problems? His problems are off the scale. He's nuts! What are you going to do about him?" (I think I probably had spit flying out of my mouth by this time.)

His reply was, "Well, we'll have to think about this." Basically, he just brushed off my concerns. And I have to say that back then I never considered that there was anything more going on than father being nuts, maybe having some kind of a personality disorder, or playing mind games with the kids to boost his self-esteem. I never thought of it as being anything more than that, never thought that there was anything else, or anything sexual, going on. I had never seen or heard anything to suggest that. And honestly, it never crossed my mind. I was very naive back then. We all were.

Nothing was ever done. Father Abdon continued as the pastor. Again, welcome to my screwed up diocese.

Soon after that the summer ended and it was time for me to leave and go back to school. I was done with my pastoral assignment with Father Abdon but I wasn't quite done with Father Abdon. After I got ordained as a priest, he ended up being one of my pastors. And by that time his "odd" behavior, which had never been addressed, had escalated and was out of control.

Chapter 14

"666":
Maturing in Understanding The Sacred Scriptures

My summer pastoral experience was over. I packed my bags, left the parish, and headed home. I spent a few days at home, and then packed up again and headed back to school. It was really good to get back to the school and the seminary, and I was glad to put that whole bizarre summer experience behind me.

I started my second year of graduate school with quite a few less classmates than I had begun with the semester before. A couple of the guys were asked not to return for a combination of reasons. Some of them couldn't handle the academic portion and flunked out. Others had been asked to leave because of issues with drugs, alcohol, or sexual indiscretions. Some were told that they weren't appropriate candidates for the priesthood, and a few had quit on their own. A few more would leave during the coming year, and by the time that my third year of school rolled around, there were only about twelve of us left from our original class of thirty students.

The previous year I had caused a bit of a stir when I started using the "purse" that Father Monti had brought me from Italy. This semester I had everyone wondering if I was having an affair with one of the local nuns. It seemed as if life was never dull when I was around!

I had mentioned before that for most of our classes we had to do ten to twenty page reports. I worked my behind off doing those papers because they entailed a lot of reading, research, critical thinking, and writing. And then they had to be typed up, and I wasn't the world's best typist. I knew a lot of the sisters at the local convent and one of them, Sister Ann, was a friend of mine. She had been working abroad as a missionary but was now back in the States and between assignments. She was taking a little bit of a break, taking a few classes, doing some pastoral work, and had some extra time on her hands. And she was a killer typist!

So I asked her if she would type my reports for me and I would pay her for it, to which she agreed. But she also asked if we could go out to eat as part of my paying her back. The religious order that she belonged to was pretty conservative, and restaurant meals were not something they indulged in. But she loved going out to eat, so I said sure and would treat her to dinner as a way of thanking her for typing my reports.

It seems that word got around that one of the seminarians (me) was seen fairly regularly going out to dinner with a young pretty nun. (I had a lot of reports due.) Again, some raised eyebrows, and I later heard there was more of that behind the scenes speculation and discussion among the seminary officials as to whether there was also some hanky-panky going on. The rector, the other priests at the seminary, and my professors at the school could never quite fit me into the same molds as all of the other seminarians. I was extroverted, I was loud, I was outspoken, the life of the party, an "open book," and I talked to anybody and everybody. They never quite knew what to make of me. But I also had a reputation of being honest and truthful. After some scrutiny, they came to the conclusion that it was just me being me, and that sometimes dinner is just dinner.

So school started back at full throttle. We had gotten all of our introductory courses last year, so now we were building upon them and delving even more deeply into the mysteries of the Bible. That first year they tore apart everything that we thought we knew about our religion. The second year they helped us to replace all of it with a more mature understanding of scripture. We were told, "This is how it really happened, and this is how we are to understand it in terms of modern scripture scholarship."

We were taught the different forms of criticism, which means the different ways of interpreting the Bible. We were taught to know that it was not a book that came down from heaven already penned by God as he whispered into the ears of the evangelists. Rather, that it was written by the evangelists who were people just like us, writing out of their connection to whatever God was for them. They used the words of their day and the concepts of their culture to describe their experience of Jesus. Their stories were interpretations understood as such by the readers of that time—to teach a moral, and to help people grow in understanding of making their connection to the Divine Presence.

So while our stories of Adam and Eve and Noah's Ark may not be evolutionarily or historically accurate, behind these stories exists a moral and a truth that endure for all of us for all time—a truth that still has the power to speak to each of us more than two thousand years after being written. If most of you are yawning by now, let's talk about a book of the Bible that just about everyone is interested in—the Book of Revelation.

Chapter 14

The Book of Revelation is currently one of the most popular books of the Bible because it predicts the end of the world, right? Well no. You probably knew that I was going to say that.

It's really pretty simple. The Book of Revelation was written at a time in very early Christianity when Emperor Nero was demanding that his citizens offer sacrifices before his image because he considered himself a god. Well, that didn't go over too well with the early Jewish-Christians who were followers of Jesus. In fact, it was pretty abhorrent to them.

But what to do? If they didn't go along with it, they could lose their lives (think Coliseum and hungry lions). And actually many of them did lose their lives because of this. So to give them strength and support to stand together while living in this climate of fear and uncertainty, the Book of Revelation was written. That's what it's about—Christians standing firm in their beliefs in the face of adversity.

What did it say to them? Basically, it was a diatribe against the state religion of emperor worship. It exhorted them to be strong in their faith and in their relationship to God, and to know that He would not abandon them in the face of this adversity. The message of Revelation was meant to be understood by believing Christians, but not by the pagan Romans. So it was cleverly couched in veiled allusions to their current situation, using archetypal symbols understood by the Christians reading it, but not by the Romans who might come across it. It needed to be passed around and shared by the Christian community without fear of reprisals by the Romans. If the Romans had understood what was really being said, they would have seen it as sedition against the emperor—an act punishable by death.

This wasn't an era when the Christians could all go hang out in their local wine shop and complain about this appalling thing that the emperor was demanding. They couldn't hold rallies or public forums or even stand around on their street corners discussing it. They would have been killed for that. So the author of Revelation had to find a way to speak to all of the Christians without the Romans catching on—he had to "fly under the Roman radar," so to speak. The message had to be expressed in such a way that the Christians would understand its message of hope and comfort without the Romans understanding what was really being said.

For instance, when the author spoke of the "beast," the Christians knew that he referred to the despised Emperor Nero. They understood the allusions being made and were also able to "read between the lines" to understand the inferences being made about Nero. If the Romans came across a copy of it, which surely they must have, they probably wouldn't have given it a second glance—these were just nonsensical stories by those troublesome Christians. I think that if the author of the Book of Revelation knew that one day—thousands of years into the future—people would be using his words to predict the end of the world, he would've been dumbfounded.

Contrary to popular opinion, Revelation wasn't written to foretell the end of the world. But it was written to tell about the wonders of what was available to these Christians in their inner relationship with God, and to help sustain them during these perilous times. The author of Revelation interpreted what was happening to them—at that specific point in time—in light of what the prophets had said in the past to give them hope that their present difficulties would be overcome.

He wasn't predicting the future in the way that we have come to think of it, but was predicting that if they kept their faith with God, God would see them through this, and that He would keep His covenant with them as the prophets of old had promised. Thus, their *future* relationship with God would be intact.

What about that infamous number in Revelation, "666"? Well, back in antiquity, a number of the ancient languages assigned a numerical value to the letters of their alphabet. For the Hebrew language, this process was called gematria—kind of like numerology today. But a precise process it was not. Depending on how you spelled or pronounced someone's name, you would assign different numbers to each letter of that person's name, thus giving it a number value. So the numbers that made up Nero's name came out to be 666. But in some instances they also came out as 616. You can find both numbers in the ancient texts. Again, it was just another subtle way of identifying Nero to the Christians. Then the Hebrew texts were translated into Greek, and from Greek into Latin, and somewhere in all of that translating, the 616 got lost and the 666 got passed on. Maybe because it rolled off of the tongue more easily; no one really knows. I kind of think that if the number had been something a little more mundane—like maybe 1,083—we wouldn't even be having this conversation.

The early Jewish-Christians who grew up with these languages understood the allusions that were being made. They made perfect sense to them. But over time we have lost this understanding, so what we have ended up with is a story that is taken out of the context of the times in which it was written. We have lost the real inner meaning of Revelation's message, but have kept the outer symbols, which are used to make all kinds of dire predictions.

Revelation does have an enduring message for us today about our inner connection to God, and about how we can grow that connection in the face of our own adversities. To my way of thinking it's a timeless message. It spoke to people two thousand years ago, and it speaks to us

Chapter 14

today if only we take the time to understand its truth, which isn't the Hollywood version of the story.

The concept of the end of the world—Armageddon—is a popular moneymaking theme these days. There are lots of books and movies about the topic because it makes for great entertainment. We can all "ooh" and "ahh" over the exciting story lines and the dazzling special effects. This is easier and more exciting to do than to look inward where the real wonders manifest and where the real miracles occur.

As we were learning all of these modern theological interpretations, we also learned that while this may be the more mature way of interpreting Holy Scripture—as espoused by Catholic Theologians—to the Catholic Church it was only a very minor, secondary viewpoint. And that what the church teaches is the traditional view of scripture, the official church version, with abracadabra included.

So, of course, in class that hand of mine would shoot up into the air and wave wildly at the professor. I would challenge these concepts, the party line stuff. I wouldn't challenge the professor, just the concepts. I mean, our professors were the ones telling us all of this fantastic stuff—telling us that theology is a development, that it's always in process, that all knowledge is open-ended, and that one never comes to a final statement about anything. And then they would tell us, "But the church says that this is not what its priests will be teaching. As priests you'll teach the traditional, fundamentalist interpretation."

A few times the professor started class by saying, "Okay, today we're going to talk about how the church views . . . ." and here he would bring up whatever the topic was. Then he'd stop, look at me, say my name, and then he would say to me, "And you can just keep your mouth closed because we all know how you feel about this stuff, so you don't have to argue with me in class about it." He'd add, "We have to teach this to you because the church says we have to. That doesn't mean that it's theologically correct, it doesn't mean that we necessarily believe it, but this is where the church is at right now and it has to be included." And he'd cast me another pointed look and repeat, "So we need you to keep your mouth shut today so we can get through this." And wisely I would keep my mouth shut.

Sometimes the theology would be so exciting, so affecting, that I felt like jumping onto the top of my desk in joy, kind of like Tom Cruise jumping onto the sofa on *The Oprah Winfrey Show*, if you saw that episode. Being presented with this way of looking at scripture just opened up everything for me, especially because I came from such a traditional family and conservative diocese. It changed my outlook on everything–not just on scripture, but on the world around me.

I especially remember one class we had on systematic theology (in simple terms—a rigorous, disciplined approach to investigating Catholic doctrine using—philosophy, science, and ethics) that was taught to us by a visiting theologian from Canada. The whole class revolved around one sentence that he said to us. He said, "All of our studies should illumine our understanding of Holy Scripture." That really captured my imagination in a big way. That everything we learn—whether it's physics, literary classics, or astronomy—all of it should be used as a tool to understand scripture. I took that sentence to heart, dissected it, and wrestled with it. Then I thought—if we can use everything to understand scripture, then we can also use scripture to help us understand everything else. That was an "aha" moment for me.

I think that incorporating those concepts is what eventually helped me to become so successful in interpreting scripture. My professors actually wanted me to continue my studies and get a PhD in biblical studies and become a scripture scholar. At that time there were only two scripture scholars in the entire United States, and my professors felt that I had the ability to become the third one. However, as you'll read later, my bishop at the time didn't agree with that assessment.

The handful of us who were really into learning would get all stirred up in these classes, and we'd have these great back and forth rousing discussions between the professor and ourselves. Sometimes we'd carry these discussions over into our lunch breaks and free time. The professors thought it was great that we were so excited about this stuff. I heard that some of the stuff that I brought up in class was quoted by some of my classmates to their professors in their other classes. I think that there might have been a professor or two who thought that I was the devil incarnate for some of the things that they heard about me.

School was hard work but well worth it. Did I ever take a break or have fun? Well, school was fun, but the other kind of fun? Yeah, of course. I really wasn't a part of the drinking and partying crowd. There were still guys who would head out on Friday or Saturday nights to the bars, sometimes with a local priest or two in tow, and drink until they got shit-faced. Then they would spend the rest of the weekend hung over. I had done that a lot in high school and some in college, and didn't find it to be fun anymore.

My friends and I would go out to movies or dinner every few weeks. None of us had very much extra money, but I used to clip coupons from the paper for half-off meals or get those buy-one-get-one-free deals at the local restaurants. The city also sponsored free chamber music concerts that we would go to. I love music and singing—part of my wannabe-actor side. Sometimes I would get my friends together or just grab a bunch of guys, invite a few of the professors, find an empty room, and get everybody to sing John Denver songs. I really liked his music so I'd grab my records and my record player, find the words to his songs, copy them, and pass them around to everybody. Of course, none of us knew all of the words and we could really mangle some of those songs! We all had a lot of fun doing that, laughed a lot, and just had a good time.

Some of the guys thought that it was weird that I would invite our professors to do this with us, but I'd say, "Hey, we're all in this together, so why not?" And the professors seemed to appreciate being included. They told me that no other seminarian had ever invited them to do something like this. Yep, leave it to me.

I remember one day in particular during that semester. We got out of class early and had some time on our hands before a one o'clock meeting we all had with the rector. It was a nice day so I asked some of the guys if they wanted to go get an ice cream cone before the meeting. They said sure, so about five of us piled into my car and off we went.

On the way, I got a flat tire and didn't have a spare. It took a really long time to get the tire off and then find a place that would fix it. This was before cell phones, but I think I used the phone at the garage to call the seminary to leave a message for the rector saying we were going to be late for the meeting.

We finally got back to the seminary really late. The rector was fit to be tied because you don't keep rectors waiting for meetings. So I let the guys out, went and parked the car, and then went to find the rector. I told him that I was sorry, that I had invited the guys to go and get some ice cream, that I had a flat tire that took forever to get fixed, and that it was my fault that we were all late, that it was my fault that we had all missed the meeting, and I apologized again.

He said to me, "Well, son," (okay, he didn't say 'son,' he said my name), "I appreciate your telling me this because the other guys have already been here to see me and gave me all kinds of excuses about why they didn't make the meeting. Basically, they all lied about it."

And I said, "What? Really? Why would they lie? It wasn't their fault, it was mine. I invited them, I was driving, and it was my car that had the flat tire. So I'm the one responsible. I'm the one who should take the punishment for it, not them."

And he said, "You know what? That's what I like about you. You always tell me the truth; you always take responsibility for your actions. And that's why you have my respect. Whether you become a priest or not, you will always have success in your future in whatever you do. But those other guys couldn't tell me a straight story. They can't take responsibility for themselves. That's why they consider me such a hard ass."

He said it just like that, which kind of surprised me as I thought back to my experiences in the college seminary. If this had happened back then, that rector would have crucified me for it. But this guy used something as simple as going out for ice cream to assess our characters.

Again, we were scrutinized twenty-four seven, but it was a more subtle, behind the scenes kind of thing. They seemed to be aware of everything we did on campus or off. Yeah, guys could get away with stuff for a while. But whatever we did would eventually come out.

One of the things that we learned in the graduate seminary was how to perform the various functions of the priesthood, so we had classes on the different sacraments, on the Theology of the Mass, and all of their associated rituals. One of the most important functions of a Roman Catholic Priest is to celebrate Mass. For those of you who may not know this, the Mass is a commemoration of the Last Supper that Jesus had with his apostles. Later on I can tell you about what it means to Catholics, or what it should mean to them.

But for now, we all had to learn how to actually say the Mass correctly. So we had our classes and we had "practice" Masses where we would do the Mass with one another, practice when your hands were supposed to be up or down, or when you were supposed to kneel or genuflect during the ceremony. And we were all constantly helping out at Mass, basically learning by doing.

Each of us would be assigned to plan the liturgies for different weeks, which means planning either the morning or evening prayer services. If you were assigned to a particular Mass, it meant getting everything ready for the priest who would be celebrating it. This included making sure that everything was placed on the altar correctly, that the Bible on the altar was open to the correct passages that would be read during the service, that the correct vestments were laid out for father to put on, helping father to don the vestments, and then assisting father during the Mass. I would bend over backwards doing that stuff because I really loved the rituals, loved it in the Franciscan seminary, and loved doing it here. Being able to celebrate Mass had to become second nature to us, and eventually it did.

Another thing that a priest has to do is to hear confessions. Confession, before Vatican II, was a little different than it is now. When you went to confession, you would tell the priest your sins, receive "penance" (kind of like a minor punishment), and then be given absolution (forgiveness) of your sins. I remember going to weekly confession—almost always held on Saturday afternoons—with my "grocery list" of sins. Things like I punched my younger brother three times last week, I used a bad word five times last week, and I talked back to my mom twice last week.

Then the priest would give you your penance, usually something like having to say certain prayers like three "Hail Marys" and four "Our Fathers." Then he would absolve you of your sins and tell you to "go and sin no more," which usually lasted until your little brother started bugging you again or your mom got on your case about something.

The "confessional" itself, for those of you who may never have seen one, is this big wooden box set up against one of the walls inside of the church. You would find them in every church—sometimes just one, sometimes three or four— depending on the size of the church. It usually consisted of three connected compartments. The middle compartment was where the priest sat, and to each side of the priest was a compartment for the person confessing. The priest's compartment had a chair or bench for him to sit on, while the other two compartments had a padded cushion near the ground that you would kneel on. When you knelt on the cushion, you would be facing a smallish square opening that was composed of a tightly woven mesh grille that could be closed or opened by the priest on his side with a sliding wooden panel. You spoke to the priest through the grille, but you couldn't really see him other than as a shadowy form. Thankfully, he couldn't see you either. It was pretty dark inside as there weren't any lights in there, but a little light would seep in from the vents on the ceiling.

Traditional Confession Box

While you were waiting for your turn, the grille on your side would be closed so you couldn't really hear anything other than some indistinct murmuring. As a kid, I remember trying to listen really hard to see if I could make out what the other person was saying, but I never could. Then when father was finished hearing the confession of the other person, he would slide the cover of their grille closed and open the one on your side. The sound of that panel being opened by the priest was the signal that your time had come to "fess up." And everyone started their confession using the same words, "Bless me Father for I have sinned . . . ."

As a priest in the old days when you were ready to mete out the punishment to the person confessing, you had guidelines that you had to follow. There was a manual (a pretty thick one) that you used that would tell you the appropriate punishments for different levels of sin. The more severe the sin, the more prayers that you had to say as penance. When it came to someone confessing that they had an abortion, part of your penance actually included having to write a letter to your bishop about it because only he could forgive abortions.

Things changed for the better after Vatican II. The procedure is basically the same, but the "grocery list" of sins fell out of favor, and the approach became more pastoral and more personal. It wasn't so much looking at just the individual sin, but looking at it in the context of the person's life. The idea was to help them determine if there was a pattern to the things they were doing that were detrimental for them (sins), help them recognize this, and to find ways to help change their behavior. So it was more of a counseling session geared towards actually helping the person rather than the old grocery list of "sins/a couple of prayers for penance" formula.

As for penance, instead of using a rule book that was very impersonal, you'd use your common sense. Instead of having the person spout off a couple of prayers, you'd ask them to do things that would get them to look at their behavior, so it was more of a behavior modification type of response. You can still go to confession in the traditional way—in the confessional box—but now you can also do it by sitting down face to face with the priest. This way of doing it allows more of a conversation with the priest, more interaction, and it's more like an actual counseling session.

Activities that we all took part in were our pastoral assignments, which were being out in the community helping people. This was something that we would be doing as priests with and for our parishioners. That semester I was assigned to teach religion along with a priest at the local Air Force base. We did catechism classes for the kids who lived on base who were Catholic, and you'd think that this would've been a heaven-sent assignment for me. While I did enjoy being on the base watching those sleek F-105 Thunderchiefs taking off and landing, I didn't find the actual work especially fulfilling; not exactly my cup of tea.

During the next semester I was invited by a local bishop to work alongside him with inmates at the local jail, and would end up being on a Civil Rights Commission that reported to the government on the treatment of prisoners. Social justice issues were really big at that time.

Chapter 14

During my third year of school I would be working mainly in hospitals, and I found that to be challenging and more "real." When you're working with people facing major health issues—life and death issues—you really have to know your stuff. You can't just pat them on the hand and mouth off superficial platitudes because they'll either tell you that you're full of shit or kick you out of their room or both. You have to be real with them and connect with them on an inner level. I found this to be a real challenge of my skills and also very fulfilling. I thought that I was pretty good at it, but I still had a lot to learn. That learning would happen during the coming summer and it would be brutal.

You know that saying about how time flies when you're having fun? Well, that semester flew by. Hard, hard work, yes, but I felt this was what I had been born to do. And that semester ended with another nun incident. (I did tell you earlier that nuns played a big part in my formation as a priest, right?) We were in class and the bell rang for break. So we all head out into the hall, and a bunch of guys got in line to use the bathroom. In the old days there were never women in the school—it was exclusively a male domain. There were only two tiny restrooms, one on the first floor and one on the second floor, where we were. It was a small, boxy room with one toilet set against the back wall. Maybe three feet in front of the toilet there was a urinal up against the front wall, and a small sink to the side of it.

It was finally my turn to go into the bathroom, and I closed the door behind me but didn't lock it. So I'm standing at the urinal doing my business. In walks this very, very old nun who promptly lifts up her habit, pulls down her bloomers, sits on the toilet behind me and starts peeing. She said, "Good morning, Father, how are you?"

And without turning around I said, "Oh, fine, how are you?" I finished doing my business, washed my hands, and again without turning around said, "Have a good day, Sister," and left.

I walked out of the bathroom and there's this huge crowd of both students and faculty all crowded into the hallway, gawking at me, whistling and clapping, and yelling comments, mostly, "Hey, was it good for you, too?"

I yelled back at them, "Well, *I* was in there first!" Everyone was laughing their fool heads off! Right after that incident they put a sign up on the bathroom door that said "MEN'S ROOM."

So the semester ended, I was asked to return for the next semester, and everyone happily went home for Christmas.

Chapter 15

"Know Thyself" or Else!

The Christmas holidays were over and I came back to school for the second semester of my sophomore year. This semester I had some experiences that taught me some things about myself; mainly that I still had some things to learn.

In general, I think that I was pretty well liked by most people at the school and at the seminary—by both the students and the professors. I just seemed to get along really well with most everyone, and just had that kind of a personality. Of course, there were guys who didn't care for me one way or the other and probably a few who didn't care for me at all, but on the whole I think that I had more friends than not. I had a reputation of being open and honest and sometimes, as I was to find out, painfully so. Yeah, I was loud, outspoken, and pretty intense and didn't suffer fools very well. What I learned this semester and during the coming summer was that those were good qualities when they were kept in balance.

Let me tell you about the visiting bishops and myself. We would sometimes have bishops from different dioceses visit and stay with us at the seminary. I remember the first time I met one of these bishops. He had flown into town for the funeral of our archbishop. Another seminarian and I had been sent to the airport to pick him up as he would be staying with us at the seminary.

We were waiting for him at the luggage carousel. When we spotted him, I went up to him and introduced myself and told him that we were there to take him to the seminary. He looked at me without saying anything, tossed his bag on the ground at my feet, and started to walk off towards the exit. I didn't pick up his bag. I just started off after him, caught up with him, and continued walking at his side towards the exit. After a few moments, he glanced at me and noticed that I wasn't carrying his bag. He stopped abruptly, looked at me with a frown, gave a disgusted sigh and a shake of his head, and turned around and headed back to get his bag. I walked back with him. He picked up his bag and we headed out again. When we got to the approximate spot where he had first noticed that I wasn't carrying his bag, I turned to him and said, "Oh, Your Excellency, let me carry that for you," as I reached over and took his bag from him and carried it to the car.

Well, of course, one of the first things that he did when we reached the seminary was to find the rector to complain about my behavior. The rector stood up for me and told him that while I would bend over backwards to help in any way that I could, I expected to be treated with respect.

So why had I done that with the bishop? Because to me his behavior was a symptom of what I felt was wrong with the institution of the church, and when behavior is wrong it's wrong, no matter who is doing it. Jesus said, "Charity above all else." Yet here was a bishop of the church, a man who was supposed to be an example of Christ to us, a man who was supposed to be treating others with Christ's love, a man who was supposed to see *himself* as a servant to those in his care . . . a man who was treating other people like shit.

From his exalted position he could and did send out missives and directives telling other people how they should live, yet he wasn't living the gospels himself, and was totally out of touch with what Jesus says to us in the gospels. And I found that to be prevalent in the church, especially among those in power, so I felt that he needed to be reminded of that. I'm not a hypocrite and I don't do passive-aggressive. I guess I don't do luggage very well either! Did it mean anything to him? Probably not.

And he was just the first one. Another time another visiting bishop walks into the seminary's front door, and a few of us were gathered around when he arrived. He turns to me and says, "Pick up my luggage and take it to my room." (Some guys are a babe magnet; I must be a luggage magnet.) No smile, no hello, no introduction, just, "Pick up my luggage."

I said, "Excuse me? I would be glad to take your bags for you if you ask me nicely."

He looked at me like I had two heads and barked out, "What?" And I told him that I wasn't his servant to be ordered around, that I was a fellow human being who should be treated with respect, and that I would be glad to do anything for him if he asked me nicely. He glared at me and asked, "Do you talk to your bishop like this?" And I told him that I talked to everyone like this. Well, that didn't go over too well. He stormed off, bags forgotten, in search of the rector.

To be fair, the vast majority of bishops didn't act like this. There were many who were good men, Christ-like men, and they acted as such. A number of them were older guys who seemed to really enjoy talking with the seminarians. When they talked to me, they always remarked about my long hair, which they all seemed to get a kick out of. When these guys came to visit, they didn't even have to ask for any help. I would swoop in and grab their luggage and try to anticipate anything else they might need. They deserved our respect and they got it—in spades.

The next time that some visiting bishops were due to arrive, the rector and I were walking together down the hallway in the dorm, talking about how we had to be on our best behavior. He told me, "Listen, I know that some of these guys are assholes, and the way that they act is wrong. It is wrong, but try to pull back a little and exercise some impulse control. That's probably the proper thing to do with these guys. They have authority over us, and have an impact on the purse strings and on the way that our seminary functions. You don't have to compromise your principles, just try to hold it together a little better. If you can do that, you will be blessed. Greatly blessed." I agreed. He suddenly stopped and exclaimed, "Oh gosh, look at this! This is what I mean." He pointed at a poster of "Wonder Woman" hanging on a door. "We've got to take that down before the bishops see it."

"Oh yes, this is terrible, I fully agree, we must take it down!" I responded.

He asked, "Do you know whose room this is?"

I said, "Yes." I paused for a moment then continued, "It's mine."

After an incredulous silence, he then said, calmly, "Or if you want, you can take off for a few days and go visit some friends. You don't have to be here." And we continued our walk down the hallway.

He didn't yell at me, didn't talk down to me, didn't tell me that I was acting like a jerk, or tell me that what I was doing was wrong. He talked to me man to man, respecting the position that I was coming from. I sincerely admired and respected him, so I needed to respect the position that he was coming from.

I didn't take off. I stayed. I attended all of the functions that we had that weekend with the bishops and I didn't get in anybody's way or ruffle any feathers. Oh, and yes, I did take down the poster, and after that displayed it only on the inside of my room.

Afterwards, the rector came up to me and thanked me for being extraordinarily good that weekend. He actually said, "Bless you." And I told him that I appreciated his talking to me about it, letting me know that I needed to look at this, to see that there are different ways of going about things, and that I could change and do some things differently. I asked him to let me know when he felt that I needed to change something, to talk to me about it, guide me, and show me.

He shook his head and said, "You know, (here he said my name), you are really weird. Do you know what you are asking? Nobody ever asks me to tell them when they're doing something wrong. No one, not one other seminarian, has ever asked me to do that in all of the years I've been here."

Weird? Well, okay. I've been called all kinds of things, so what the heck. I told him, "I really doubt the fact that I may ever get ordained, and that you all are actually going to let me into the priesthood. So, that's not what I'm about here. I want to grow and I want to learn—that's what I'm about. So anything that you can do to help me in that process, I'm open to it. I may not always agree with you, I may balk at it, I may gnash my teeth, but I will look at what you tell me, and I will try to incorporate it. So just let me know."

The rector said, "This is just one of the things that's so different about you. We all know that you are one in a million. We've never had anyone like you here before, and I don't think that we'll ever have anyone like you here again."

I'm not exaggerating, embellishing, or bragging. That's what he said to me, and I have to tell the truth because—very possibly—he's out there reading this along with the rest of you! I did keep in touch with the rector after graduate school. Although we haven't talked in many years, the last time that we did talk he told me that back then they were right—that so far they hadn't gotten another character quite like me in their seminary.

I had mentioned before that my pastoral work this semester was working in a jail. One of the auxiliary bishops in the diocese asked if I could help him with liturgical duties at the local prison. (Liturgical duties are the official worship services including the prayers and songs of the service.) So I assisted the bishop with the liturgies and with visiting the prisoners. He was a part of a Civil Rights Commission that was collecting data on the treatment of prisoners. This was the era when we all were becoming more socially conscious, and the church was addressing many social justice issues.

We were looking at any overt or covert mistreatment of inmates; any kind of abuses in the prison system. The bishop would take the data we collected and present it to the commission, who would then make recommendations to the secular authorities. It was a pretty intense experience, and it was gratifying to know that perhaps our work would result in some positive changes occurring in our country's correctional system.

So again for me the semester seemed to fly by. I was busy learning theology at the school, busy learning to be a priest at the seminary, and all of it was going really well—just too quickly. I would've been happy to stay in theology school for the rest of my life!

Chapter 15

The only other event that stands out in my mind from that semester was something that happened with a classmate of mine, and it was a pretty big something.

We had a classmate who was in the same year that I was in, but was a couple of years older than the rest of us, and was actually from my home diocese. He also had a bad problem with alcohol that he kept well hidden, and none of us knew about it.

One evening at the seminary, a couple of my classmates rushed up to me and told me that this guy was in his room threatening to kill himself. Before we go any further, I just want to state here that at that time I didn't know a whole lot about psychology or counseling—so bear that in mind as I relate what happened. I have learned since then to temper myself.

So I go to this guy's room and he's sitting there on the bed. The first thing that I notice is that he's holding a knife. The next thing that I notice is the strong smell of alcohol in the room—the fumes were enough to knock you off your feet. The first thing that he said to me when I walked in was that he was going to cut his throat.

For whatever reason, the first thought that popped into my mind was that this guy just wanted attention, and that this was just an attention getting maneuver. (Not that I was anywhere near qualified to make that assessment, but that's what I thought and that's what I worked from.)

I said to him, "Well, okay if that's what you need to do, kill yourself. Go ahead, slit your throat." (I'm wincing as I write this, but yes, that's what I said.) "But don't be calling us and telling us that you're going to do it—just do it. Don't be scaring all of us and warning everybody that you're going to do it—just go ahead and do it. You know, everybody's concerned about you. What are you trying to accomplish here? What do you want us to do for you? Just ask us, ask us what you want us to do for you and we'll see if we can do it. We'll see if we can help you."

As I'm talking to him, I'm eyeing the knife that he's holding and trying to figure out a way to get it from him without either of us getting hurt. Nothing was coming to mind.

So I continued talking. I said, "But this stuff about killing yourself—if you're gonna kill yourself, kill yourself and be done with it. And we'll mourn your death and go on with life. Or, we could help you get whatever you need that you're not getting. So, if you really want to do it, do it right here in front of me. It's okay."

I had this vague plan that if I saw the knife coming up maybe I could try to grab it. But he just sat there looking at me and not saying anything. We were at a bit of a standoff. In my mind I was kind of arguing with myself over what was going on here. I was thinking that this guy needed to confront his issues, but that he didn't want to and was trying to manipulate the rest of us into getting his needs met without having to really address them. (No, I didn't have a degree in psychology.)

So as he's sitting there just looking at me, I said, "Okay, I'm leaving. And I'm not going to check up on you, and I'm gonna tell the other guys to leave you alone. So you decide what you need to do."

I left and went straight to the rector and told him what had just happened, telling him everything that I had said to the guy. The rector looked at me in what seemed to be some exasperation, rolled his eyes, said my name in his "Oh Lord, what am I going to do with you" voice, then thanked me for telling him. He said that they (he and the Spiritual Director) would handle it, which they did, but I didn't know that for sure at the time.

Of course, I stayed up half the night worried about the guy. The next morning I went to Morning Prayer and looked around, and he wasn't there. All I could think was—oh, shit—he killed himself. I should have realized that the seminary officials would have done an immediate intervention, but all I kept thinking was that if something bad had happened to him, *I'm* the one who had told him to do it. *I'm* the one who told him, "Yeah, go ahead, kill yourself." Oh God. I kept looking at my watch and watching the door. Oh shit. All the other guys were casting furtive glances my way. Oh shit. I'm thinking that maybe I should leave and go check on him; maybe clean up the blood. Oh God.

Then in he walks—head down, not looking at anyone, and very subdued. He sits down in one of the pews, grabs a prayer book, and finishes the service with us. Afterwards everyone, including me (especially me), went over to him and said that we were really, really glad to see him there and sincerely meant it. After everyone had left, I got down on my knees and thanked God that he was all right. And, I thought to myself that I needed to rethink how I sometimes talked to people, decided that I needed to rein in my intensity, and temper my bluntness. I started working on that more earnestly.

He was sent to therapy, and shortly afterwards he left the seminary.

So the semester ended and summer was here. Last summer was spent doing pastoral work; this summer we all had to participate in a Clinical Pastoral Education Program (CPE). This was a somewhat new and innovative program that was designed as a tool to help you determine how well you handled ministering to people who were in crisis. Since we would all be heading home for the summer, arrangements were made so we could each participate in the program in our home states.

Usually the clinical setting for this program is in a hospital because that's where you encounter life and death and crisis situations. I was assigned to a hospital about an hour away from my home. Ours was a twelve-week course, but you could also take a sixteen-week or even a six-month course. If you ask me, you would have to be a certified masochist to do that.

The program was interdenominational, meaning that people of all different Christian faiths were in the group. It was run by a religious—it could be a Protestant minister or a Catholic priest or nun. From a religious perspective, you would apply theological concepts from your own faith tradition and bring them to bear on your experience in the program.

The purpose of the program was to have you engage in critical reflection on your approach to ministering to people in crisis so that you could define that approach. It provided in-depth scrutiny in terms of your "helping" style; in terms of your interactions with others. The program would get you to look at yourself—really look at yourself—to see if you had what it takes to minister pastorally to people in life and death situations because this is something that you would be doing as a Catholic priest or as a Protestant minister. In reality, it was more akin to boot camp. It was constant, intense scrutiny of your behavior and interactions. It made the scrutiny that I had received in the diocesan seminary pale in comparison.

The group that I was in had five participants and was led by a Catholic Nun, Sister Veronica. I have to tell you that this woman made each of us break down and cry at some point during the program. Even us guys.

I remember the first day. In fact, I will never forget that first day. We were all sitting at a table in a small conference room in the hospital, going around the group introducing ourselves. When my turn came, I said, "Hi! My name is such-and-such, I'm a CPE student, and I like a challenge!"

Well. Sister Veronica tore right into me for that right off the bat. She said, "Oh, really, you like a challenge? You want a challenge? Well, we're going to give you a challenge." And she was true to her word.

We were each assigned to a floor in the hospital and we had to visit each patient on that floor every day. (On weekends we rotated working the night shift in the emergency room.) We would go into the patient's room, introduce ourselves as counseling interns, ask the patients how they were doing, and then proceed from there. We then had to write up a detailed report of each encounter for Sister Veronica and I mean detailed. It was more like a comprehensive case study of our interactions with the patient and their family members.

Sister wanted our report to reflect everything that we said and did. Everything. How we greeted the patient, if we smiled or if we didn't, if we laughed or if we didn't, if we sat down and how far from the patient we sat, if we moved closer to them or if we didn't, when we stood, where we stood, if we touched the patient in any way or if we didn't, and if the patient hugged us or if we hugged them. And the same reporting of our interactions with the patient's family members. Basically, we had to report anything and everything that we said and did—every nuance, every gesture, every move, and every word.

When the workday was over, we would then go home and type up our reports. This was wearying in itself, and was so time consuming that it usually took most of the evening to do. The next day we would give them to sister who would make copies of them and distribute them to all of us at our daily group meeting with her. At the meeting we would each go through one of our reports from the previous day's visits. Sounds pretty simple. It wasn't. It was excruciating.

Sister would scrutinize and challenge everything that we said and did at our patient visits. Let's say that in your report you said that you went into the patient's room, said hello, and sat down in the chair next to the patient. Sister would stop you and say, "Why did you say hello and not good morning? Why did you sit down? What kind of an attitude do you think that reflected?" (Attitude? Geez, it was just sitting down.) Or, if you said in your report that you stood next to the patient's bed, she would say, "Why did you stand? What kind of a message did that give to the patient?" And every time that she made a comment like that, we would have to stop and explain and defend what we had done and why we had done it that way. We had to give the reasons why we did what we did, and they had to be valid reasons or she would start picking those apart too.

When we were finally able to continue reading our report, within seconds she would stop you again and say, "You mention here that you said such-and-such to the patient—explain why you said it that way and not in a different way. How does that reconcile with your faith experience? And you said that you smiled when you said it—why did you smile? Did you think that that was appropriate in this circumstance? And in this next line you said that you sat down and crossed your legs— why did you cross your legs? Were you feeling uncomfortable? What kind of an attitude do you think that reflects? And here you said that you asked the patient this question—why did you ask him this at that specific moment? Did you think that was the right thing to ask him? Did you feel that it was the appropriate time to ask him that? Why do you think that?" And on, and on, and on . . . .

She would go through every word, every sentence, and tear it apart. Then she would invite the other members of the group to critique you. They might say things like, "Well, when you said that to the patient, you didn't sound very empathic," or, "That comment that you made sounds a little defensive," or, "That statement that you made sounded a little prejudiced against women."

By the time that they were done with you, you felt demoralized from the inside out. Just constant, intense scrutiny of everything that you thought or didn't think, said or didn't say, did or didn't do. Relentless, in-your-face scrutiny. You had to explain and defend everything. And we did this every day for twelve weeks.

This was the most exhausting experience that I have ever gone through. It was physically, mentally, and emotionally wrenching. But it did serve a purpose besides making you cry. This experience reflected every aspect of your personality back to you. It made you really look at yourself, really see yourself and your actions and motives in a way that you never had before. You learned what your capabilities were, where your boundaries were, where you began, and where you ended.

The supervisor was trained not to tell you how to be, but to help you discover how you were—how you interacted with others, and how you came across to people. And then she would make suggestions about how you could improve things. As a minister, how are you going to be able to recognize and then handle crisis situations with others if you haven't handled them within yourself?

By the end of this program you either knew that this was something that you could do, or you knew that it was time to cut your losses, get out, and become an accountant or a real estate agent or something. By the end of the program, I felt as if there was nothing left for me to discover about myself. I had been through the wash, been through the wringer, and it was all hanging out there on the clothes line, flapping in the breeze for me and everyone else to see.

Summer ended, the Clinical Pastoral Education program ended, and all I could say was, "Thank God."

Chapter 16

Exorcism #2:
The Devil Made Me Do It

Back to school for my third and final year of theology. Graduate theology school is a four-year program, but the actual academic portion is only for three years. At some point in our third year, most of us would get ordained as deacons, which is the last step before ordination to the priesthood. Our fourth year is spent doing an internship at a parish in our home state under the guidance of our pastor. At the end of that internship, you're either recommended for ordination into the priesthood or not.

Are there guys who get through their internship and then are told, "No, sorry, you can't become a priest?" Yeah, it's possible and has happened, but it's pretty rare. By the time you get to your internship, you've gone through a lot of levels of scrutiny and done a lot of self-examination and reflecting. Just about anyone who needed to be weeded out has already left. So you'd have to do something really off the wall during your internship to be told that they would not ordain you—like getting caught with drugs, getting caught in a compromising position with another man, or running off with the church secretary. It's all happened before. And the key words here are "getting caught."

This final year would be a really busy one for all of us. This first semester I would perform my second exorcism (or the first if you didn't count the incident back in the college seminary), and I would also have some of the seminary officials wondering if I were a closet communist. With me, if it wasn't one thing, it was another, but it was always something. And that in itself should have told me something, if I was listening.

Soon after we got back to school, our evaluations from the summer's Clinical Pastoral Education program were sent to us. In my evaluation, Sister Veronica said that I seemed comfortable in my role there, that I seemed to know myself pretty well, and that I had definite leadership ability.

She also said that I seemed to have an issue with authority, that I struggled with authority, and that I was too independent. She said that I would do what was asked of me, but that I always had to put my own "spin" on it, and had to do it my way—and she thought that was problematic. (In a church that values conformity, I can see how that would be considered a problem.) And she said I had trouble just "being," that I was too much of a "doer," and that also might be an issue.

I shared my evaluation with the rector, and told him that I could try to work on the areas that she had pointed out as being problematic. He read my evaluation and said, "Being? What the hell is that about? That's just psychological claptrap. Don't worry about it. That'll work itself out. They push too hard in terms of looking at yourself. As long as you do what the church tells you to do, you'll be fine. So don't worry about it."

I was a little surprised by the rector's attitude towards my evaluation, his dismissal of it. I remember thinking—God, I just went through the most gut-wrenching experience of my life, and he says not to worry about it. That's it? Well, okay . . . I think now that was most probably because it was psychology based, and the church has never given much credence to psychology.

Looking back, I wonder what would have happened had the rector taken the evaluation a little more seriously, and had said, "You know, looking at this, it seems to me as if you have some issues that might not make you a good fit for the church, that possibly it might not work for you, and that maybe we need to talk about this." That might have helped me to make some decisions that I should have made, and saved me some grief in the coming years. Who knows—maybe, maybe not. I could be really bullheaded.

On my own I did look at the issues that Sister Veronica had pointed out. I thought that maybe I could learn to deal with authority a little bit differently. I didn't think that it would ever not be an issue for me, but maybe I could find some kind of a balance there so that it wouldn't be so much of an issue. And I actually did some research into the concept of "being" as opposed to "doing," and what it means to just "be." This was important because I was definitely a "doer," always on the go, and always busy with something. Again, I needed to try to find the balance between the two in my life.

But I also looked at the positive things she said about my having leadership abilities—because there's leadership, and then there's good leadership. (I had this vision of myself standing in front of a horde of people, beckoning to them, and then everyone starting to follow me as I led all of us over the edge of a cliff!) Good leadership entails responsibility. It means taking everyone's needs into account, not just my own, and I wanted to make sure that was something that I was doing

Chapter 16

too. Although the rector didn't seem to think that it was a big deal, I did work on those things. To this day, I'm grateful to Sister Veronica for making me grow in those areas.

Years later as a priest, I ran into Sister Veronica again. I had been invited to preach at some religious conference, and she had also been invited by them to do a workshop. We had the chance to sit down and talk to each other, and she was just one of the nicest people you could ever hope to meet. Just the nicest woman—nothing at all like the mean, tough, hellish instructor that we had during that summer. And those were some of the nicer adjectives that we all used to describe her back then!

Now, about my being a communist....

Since our school had a fairly small enrollment, all of the students knew each other pretty well. There were a couple of guys in the incoming freshman class this year who were from my home state. Not only were they from my home state, but from the same diocese too. And one of them had actually been in the diocesan seminary at the same time I was there. Those of us in the upper grades would kind of take the new guys under our wings, and help them out in their adjustment to the seminary. So I noticed that these guys seemed to be struggling a bit financially. Work-study jobs were becoming scarcer due to ever increasing budget cuts and, within another month or two, all of these jobs would be eliminated except for mine, which caused some problems for me with some of the other students. I actually lost one of my friends because of it.

I wasn't rich by any means, but I had my job. Last year when I was teaching catechism at the Air Force base, they had given me a small salary for working there. My needs were few, and I was also pretty frugal and did a lot of coupon clipping. So I came up with an idea that I thought might make life a little easier for the freshman guys who were here from home. I figured that since we were all going through the seminary together, we would get ordained and then head back to our home states to work as priests. We would most likely spend the rest of our lives in some kind of proximity to each other in our dioceses back home, and probably end up as fellow priests for the long haul.

So I asked them if they would like to pool our resources, set up a "common fund" kind of thing amongst ourselves where we would all put money into the "pot" (or the bank), and then each of us could use it for the stuff that we really needed. For example, if one of us needed gas for our car but were broke until the next payday, we could take money out of the fund and then replace it when we were able to. That way, none of us would ever find ourselves totally broke. I figured that one of them could be the treasurer and keep tabs on things. I also figured that I would probably be the one putting the bulk of the money in, since I had more than they did right now, but that was okay with me.

I thought that it was a pretty neat idea—all of us looking out for each other. It's like watching one of those cop shows on TV, and one of the cops says something like, "I'm going in," and he tells his partner, "Cover me," and his partner says, "I've got your back." It was like that—we'd have each others' backs. I mean, here we were, coming from the same place, having the same roots, sharing our lives as seminarians, and possibly, some day, as priests.

So I approached them with that idea, which I thought was pretty cool. They didn't. They looked at me like I was from Mars or some far away galaxy. They said, "Why would we want to do that?"

I was stunned. I said, "Really? You really don't want to do that?"

They all said, "No." So I explained to them why I was suggesting it. I said that I had once been where they were now, struggling financially. By doing this they could ease some of their stress and not have to worry about money all of the time, and be able to concentrate better on their studies. And I reiterated that because of the bonds we shared that it would work for all of us. Again, they said no, they didn't want to do that, and didn't want to share.

I was shocked. I mean it shocked the shit out of me. But I just said, "Well, okay. If that's how you guys feel . . . ."

Somehow the seminary officials got wind of that conversation. Like I said, they always seemed to know everything that we did, and they called me in to talk about it. They said that they were concerned that I would do something like that, and asked me why I did it. I looked at them like I thought *they* were from Mars. So I explained my rationale to them, which I don't think convinced them because they said, "Well still, why would you want to share like that? You're not a religious, you're not in a religious community, you're diocesan, and you're going to be a diocesan priest."

I told them that this was true. But whether we were religious or diocesan, we were all in this together, and that we could help one another so that none of us would have to struggle. Wasn't that what it was supposed to be about— helping each other?

We kind of went around and around over it, and kept going over the same stuff. They really questioned me at length about it, and kept asking me about my motives because no one had ever proposed that kind of thing before at this seminary (surprise, surprise). To them, I think that it smacked a little of communism, and that's what they were concerned about.

You have to look at it in the context of the times. Back then the "Cold War" was still going on, and many people saw communism as a very real threat to everyone in America—an evil that could undermine our country's freedom. Seems kind of silly now, but it wasn't silly back then; it was dead serious stuff. I guess I finally convinced them that my motives were pure and that I was a good American, and that I even voted and everything.

Later on after I'd had time to think it over, I thought to myself, yeah, I'm going to be a diocesan priest (maybe), but still, as a priest, aren't we supposed to embody the concepts of Jesus—like sharing and taking care of each other? Is that or isn't that supposed to be what we do? Was I looking at all of this in the wrong way? Was I not understanding something basic here that both my classmates and the seminary officials thought what I had proposed was so off the wall? I just didn't get it. What was I missing?

I consider myself a fairly intelligent person, but I think that in some ways I could be really dumb. The fact that I was shocked by my classmates' response should have set off some warning bells for me (again). I didn't seem to think in the same way that everyone else thought and, in this institution, that wasn't necessarily a good thing. I saw things differently than everyone else did, and that maybe this wasn't such a good fit in some really important ways. But, I just *didn't*. What's that old saying, "There are none so blind as those who will not see."

Another example was when my classmates asked me why I bothered with all of the theology that we were learning. They said, many times, "Why bother? We can't use this stuff; the church won't let us. So why bother to get all excited about it?"

And I would tell them, "Well, we are then charged with the responsibility of bringing the church up to date—by teaching the people in our parishes, by our sharing of this knowledge with them, and by reflecting it in our actions and in our ministry." And if we did this, we could help bring the church out of the Dark Ages. *We* could change things.

I believed—and was very vocal in my belief—that if we didn't stand up and challenge the status quo with all of this scholarship behind us that the church would never move on, and would never grow to what it could be. Maintaining the status quo was why we were so backwards, why we made such dumb mistakes in history—like the Inquisition, like jailing Galileo, like denying the laws of physics—because they didn't jibe with church doctrine.

Instead of being a growth filled, life enhancing, dynamic force that brought people to consciousness and connection with the Divine Presence, we would hinder their quest for Spirit instead of growing them. We would eventually become ineffective in helping them at all in that quest because we were stagnant.

They would look at me like *I* was crazy. I was full of righteousness and zeal and fervor, and I would look at them like *they* were crazy. It took me quite a few years to realize that, in the context of the institution of the Catholic Church, they were not the crazy ones.

I had mentioned that work-study jobs had gotten scarcer due to budget cuts. Then federal and state subsidy monies were cut, and all of our jobs were eliminated. The majority of these jobs were either doing janitorial work (like cleaning jobs at the seminary and the school), working in the cafeteria (as cashiers or doing kitchen work), or doing some kind of office work (like the jobs I had at the diocesan seminary). Losing those jobs was a big blow to the students because off-campus jobs weren't allowed. To some of these seminarians, these jobs were what paid for all of their "extras," like putting gas in their cars or going out for an occasional meal.

I didn't lose my job—well I did and I didn't. My job was a work-study job, so yes, officially it was eliminated. What I didn't know at the time was that the school officials and the professors got together and decided that they didn't want to lose me in the library. In reality what I was doing was acting like a graduate research assistant for all of them, and they didn't want to lose that because it was so helpful and made life so much easier for them. So they decided to keep me in that position by finding a way to pay me out of a different fund. Again, I didn't know that at the time. I kept waiting for my pink slip to be delivered, gave a prayer of thanks each day that it didn't come, and just kept working.

After that I started noticing that some of the guys were acting a little cool towards me. I didn't give it a whole lot of thought mainly because I was so busy with other things. You all know by now how much I loved school, but that didn't mean that it came easy for me. It was constant hard work. I had to study my butt off especially at exam time. I'd read the material, jot down notes on the important stuff, read them out loud to myself, go over them in my mind, and then read through the material again. It took me forever to do. But that's what I had to do to learn. I don't have a photographic memory. I wish I did!

Every now and then I would wonder if I had done something to piss off some of the guys, but again it wasn't at the top of my to-do list. But then this guy who was a good friend of mine suddenly stopped talking to me and stopped hanging out with me. I tried asking him what was wrong and if I had done something to upset him, but he would never answer me. He'd barely look at me as he walked away from my questions.

Finally, one day I guess he got fed up with my asking him and he told me what was wrong. He said that he felt that I had "betrayed" him and the other seminarians because I hadn't quit my job when they had all lost theirs, and that I should have done that as a show of solidarity with them. I told him that I was really sorry about everyone's job getting cut, that it sucked, but that I couldn't afford to lose my job either. As sorry as I was for the other guys, I needed my job, and I wasn't going to quit and hoped that he could understand that. He couldn't, and I don't think that he ever spoke to me again after that.

This semester we started getting some real counseling classes. I believe they were called Introduction to Pastoral Counseling and Pastoral Counseling I and II. There is a difference between counseling in the secular (non-religious) world and pastoral (spiritual) counseling. Pastoral counseling is more of a watered down version of classic psychotherapy because everything that you do subserves the Bible, or your denomination's version of what biblical truth is. So unlike a secular therapist, you have to follow religious guidelines and stay within the denominational experience. Your counseling has to serve the denomination and thus serve the individual only within that belief system, which means you can't give any psychological advice that deviates from your denomination's belief system.

For instance, if a woman goes to see a secular therapist because she's thinking of having an abortion, that therapist would most likely talk to her about all of the options available to her—having the abortion, keeping the baby, or giving the baby up for adoption—and they would discuss the emotional impact that each option might have on her. There's a lot more to it than that, of course, but for explanation purposes, that's probably how they would start.

However, if the woman were Catholic and went for counseling to a Roman Catholic priest, he would tell her that no, she couldn't have an abortion because that's against church law, and that the church considers that to be a mortal sin. They would then talk about her other options—keeping the baby or giving it up for adoption—and they would discuss the emotional impact that those choices might have on her. Again, there's more to it than that, but these are just the bare bones facts to help explain this. So, because abortion is not allowed in the Catholic belief system, the priest cannot counsel her on having the actual abortion, other than telling her that she couldn't have one; that it was not an option for her.

Along with our classes, we also had to do a counseling internship where we would put our skills into practice. We would be assigned as a chaplain in either a nursing home, hospital, jail, or at an actual counseling center. I was assigned to work the night shift in the emergency room of a very large, very busy, city hospital.

The busiest time in the emergency room was on a Saturday night after the bars closed for the night and up until about seven in the morning. It was non-stop action—automobile accidents, gunshot wounds, stabbings, fights, with many of them being alcohol related. In the seventies there was also a lot of drug use, so drug overdoses weren't uncommon.

I had noticed that some of the ER staff tended to give anything drug related the lowest priority, and that they always seemed to take care of those types of patients last. I even asked one of the doctors about it, and he admitted that it was true. He told me that he took care of the patients who had legitimate problems before he took care of the "druggies," the ones who had brought their problems on themselves looking for a "high." He said that they could wait while he took care of the patients who had real problems.

So there I am on my shift on a Saturday night, dressed in clerical black, wearing my Roman collar and my ID badge that had my first name on it that identified me as the "Chaplain Intern." It was about three-thirty in the morning and the place was hopping—it was controlled chaos. The entire staff was hustling, and everyone seemed to be doing a hundred things at once, with patients packed into every nook and cranny. It wasn't quite bedlam, but close. Add to all of that the constant buzz of background noise—the ebb and flow of dozens of simultaneous conversations, doctors shouting orders, patients moaning or crying, monitors beeping, instruments clanging, and the loudspeaker paging this person or that every few minutes. It was a typical Saturday night in the emergency room.

I went up to one of the staff members and said, "I know you guys are really busy, but is there anything at all that I can do to help?" And they said, "Yeah, sure, would you go over there and watch that kid for us—he's a drug overdose. Just make sure that he keeps breathing."

In a lot of overdose cases, breathing is the first function to go. Sometimes you had to help the person become conscious of their breathing and encourage them to breathe. If you saw that they were really slowing down, you would pinch them on the stomach to get them to pay attention to what you were telling them to do—take a breath. If that didn't work, they might end up needing to be intubated and have a machine do their breathing for them.

So I go over to the kid on that stretcher who's young, looks to be about fifteen years old, and his arms and legs are strapped down with leather restraints because he was really agitated. I lean over him a little so that he can see me and I say, "Hi," tell him my name, and that I'm the Chaplain Intern. I ask him how he's doing and ask him to tell me what happened. I need to keep him awake, keep him engaged, and keep him breathing.

Suddenly, this ear-splitting growl comes out of him. He crosses his eyes and jerks them sideways towards me, and all I could think of at that moment was that he looked like a Picasso painting. He looks at me out of the corner of his eye and in this unearthly growl spits out, "What are *you* doing here? *My* power is greater than yours!" He had this deep, gravelly, commanding voice and it was a pretty intense loud growl. The whole emergency room instantly goes quiet. All you can hear now are the monitors going beep, beep, beep . . . Then you hear the doctors and nurses telling each other, in hushed tones, "Would ya' listen to that? God, I wonder what's wrong with him . . . ."

Then the kid lets out another growl, and in that big now silent room, it seems to echo off of the walls and bounce all over the room. He says, "*I am legion!*" and starts foaming at the mouth. (I'm thinking, whoa, this kid has definitely had one Alka Seltzer too many.) Now everyone is focused on this kid because, of course, he must be possessed by the devil to say something like that. The staff kept on doing their cutting and sewing or whatever, but they're glancing over at him every few seconds.

I'm still standing there next to him, and again I ask him what happened to him. And in this very soft, very scared little boy's voice he tells me that he was at a party and he thinks that someone put something into his drink. Suddenly, he starts yelling again, but in that deep, gravelly voice says, "Who are you? What is that on your neck? That collar will do you no good here. *My power is legion!*" And he's growling and roaring and foaming at the mouth.

William Peter Blatty couldn't have done a better job choreographing this kid. For those of you not familiar with the name, he's the guy who wrote the book that the movie *The Exorcist* is based on.

Everyone in the ER was deathly quiet, as everyone was listening to this kid. Someone dropped an instrument, maybe a forceps or something, and you could hear it go click, click, click, as it hit the floor, echoing in the silence. Then you heard a hushed, "Oh, sorry, doctor."

This kid was proving to be a real distraction to the doctors and nurses who were trying to do their jobs. It was like they were all holding their breath waiting for him to break through the leather straps that were holding him down, sit straight up like Dracula rising from his coffin, and in a puff of smoke, sprout horns and devour everyone in the ER.

Then the kid starts in again, really playing to his audience now. I think he was just warming up before. This time he's super obnoxious, yelling and growling to beat the band. He's distracting everyone so they can't focus on their work and care for the patients who really need their attention. I mean, we had some really sick people here—people having heart attacks, head injuries, broken bones and crushed limbs, and severe lacerations.

Again, the kid yells in that deep voice, "I'm going to tear that collar off your throat!" And I briefly thought in the moment just before I did it—ah, this is probably not a good thing to do—and I slapped him. I just reached over and slapped his face. *Smack*. (No, this is not a technique that they taught us in our counseling classes.) The second after I slapped him, all of this white, frothy foam goes flying straight up out of his mouth and straight up into the air. Everyone's eyes are fixed on the foam and everyone watches as it flies up, lingers for a moment in the air, then falls and splats on the floor.

And from everywhere in the room you could hear this collective *huh!* They were probably all thinking—Oh, God, the devil got into the Chaplain now!

I said to the kid very loudly, "Cut that out now! You're distracting everybody here who's trying to work."

And in that timid, little boy's voice he says, "Why did you slap me? That hurt!" And he starts crying. I told him that I was sorry about that, but that he needed to calm down. So I took his hand and held it, told him that I would stay there with him, but that he needed to calm down and focus on his breathing. I knew that he was breathing just fine, but I wanted to give him something else to focus on. He finally did calm down enough to talk to me. In between sniffles and hiccups and crying spells, he told me his story.

Thankfully, the spell was broken and the ER got back to its normal routine. I found that after that incident, though, the ER staff would part ways—kind of like Moses and the Red Sea—when they saw me coming. The talk was that I was an honest-to-God real exorcist, and that I had exorcised a demon from a patient.

And, of course, it got back to the seminary and the school. I get back to school on Monday morning, and everyone and their brother comes up to me and says, "Hey, we heard that you did an exorcism over the weekend, so how was it?"

And I told them, "I have faced the enemy and we have conquered." Everyone thought it was pretty funny. I saw the rector and he told me, "You might want to pull back a little on performing exorcisms out in public. The church doesn't look kindly on that kind of stuff."

And then he started laughing, and I told him, "Well, I tried, but the devil got the best of me that day!"

As for what happened with that kid, they finally got around to him and pumped his stomach, after which I don't think that he felt much like growling anymore. They kept him in the hospital overnight, and I checked up on him a couple of times for the remainder of my shift that night.

It seems that he and his friends had gone to see the movie *The Exorcist* earlier that week, as it was still a really popular movie. So that was in his mind when he overdosed. I believed his story about someone slipping something into his drink because back then some kids thought that it was a funny thing to do to other unsuspecting kids, not really considering the consequences of what could happen. It was seen by them as more of a prank than anything else. And when this kid had sobered up, he seemed like a very young, very naïve, fifteen-year-old, but basically a good kid.

He had told me that his parents were elderly, and were a lot older than all of his friends' parents. His dad was disabled and in a wheelchair, and his mom was always out working and cleaning other people's houses. His parents were simple people—very devout, very devotional, traditional Catholics, and that's what they passed on to their children. When you mixed together Sundays sermons about the devil and demonic possession with the movie that he saw, the psyche of this impressionable, vulnerable young kid came up with—the devil.

It seems to me that when you keep people focused on the devotional, keep them naive in terms of what the Bible really say's, then you can keep them vulnerable and more easily controlled. If you really look at it and really listen to how people around you talk about it, it seems like the devil actually has more power in people's psyches than God does. It's like no matter how good a person is, they know that the devil is lurking at every turn—hiding around every corner—just waiting to snatch up their souls, possess them, and wreak havoc. One would think that it would be the other way around, that with God in our lives and with us living out of our connection to the Divine Presence, that the devil would become less significant and less powerful in our lives. But that's just my opinion.

After this boy was discharged, I went to his home and met his parents who I found to be very nice people. They asked me if I could spend some time with their son because he needed a good role model. Because his dad was so much older and confined to a wheelchair, what he could do with his son was very limited.

So I ended up becoming like a big brother to him. After school sometimes we'd go and get a Coke and we'd talk about stuff, or we'd go to the basketball court to shoot some hoops. Sometimes we'd hang out at the community center with some of his friends. I became close to the whole family, and for the rest of my time there, I spent as much time with them and their son as I could. When it was getting close to graduation and I knew that I would be leaving, I enrolled the boy in the local Big Brother program so that someone could take over when I left. We still keep in touch, and I'm glad to say that now he's all grown up, doing well, and was never again possessed by the devil.

So the semester drew to a close. Since none of us had gotten any kind of vacation during the previous summer because of the CPE program, everyone was more than ready to go home for the Christmas holidays. The only sour note for me was that next semester would be our last one at theology school. I didn't want it to end, but the end was coming.

Chapter 17

More Jesus Moments

This was it—my last semester of graduate theology school. Just a few more months and then we would graduate. I think that most of my classmates were probably breathing a huge sigh of relief. They would now be one step closer to the "good ship lollipop."

I had mixed feelings. Sure, I felt some excitement about what the future would bring—new experiences and new challenges. But I'd had such a great experience here that I was sad to see it end. I loved school, loved learning, loved theology, and just loved everything about academia. Like the Energizer bunny, I could have kept on going. And, according to my professors, that's exactly what I should have done. Sadly, that was not to be.

The next step after graduation would be our internship at a parish back home. With that in mind, each of us was assigned this semester to do pastoral work at a local parish, help out the pastor and get more of that hands-on, real-life experience, helping to prepare us for our internship year. My assignment proved to be a good learning experience for me and I really enjoyed it. I found out later from my bishop back home, that he had gotten quite a few letters about me from the parishioners at the parish that I was assigned to. They wrote to him and told him that they sincerely hoped that I would get ordained and become a priest, and that I would be allowed to serve the people of God. They said that I came across as a truly good and caring person, that I strengthened their faith, and gave them a laugh at the same time. He told me that all of them always included that in their comments!

I thought that was pretty neat. I didn't ask anyone to write a letter on my behalf; they just did it on their own. It was gratifying for me to know that I'd had such a positive impact on them. Personally, I found it to be a really nice gesture on their part that I appreciated.

To my bishop, it didn't mean a whole lot. The church is not a two-way street, at least it definitely wasn't back then. It's a one-way highway—from the higher-ups on down—*that* is what is important.

When church officials speak, the people listen. When the people speak, the church officials make a show of listening. The wishes of the parishioners were never really much of a consideration in the scheme of things. It was all about the bishop, all about the priests, and all about what they wanted.

You might be thinking that I'm just being cynical here, a sour grapes kind of thing. But I'm honestly telling you what *I saw, what I heard, what I was told, and what I know to have happened. That's the way it was when I was there.*

My bishop also told me that no other seminarian had ever gotten so many letters of support from parishioners. Again, it was gratifying for me, whatever worth he gave it or didn't.

Our academic classes continued along with our seminary training. The focus of everything this semester was the pastoral aspect of the priesthood. Again, I got every last drop of knowledge from my studies that I could wring from them. Picture a man lost and wandering in a vast, barren desert—parched and thirsting, searching for that elusive drop of water, overturning each grain of sand in his quest—that was me. Knowing that this was my last semester was the impetus for me to leave no stone unturned in my quest for knowledge. My classmates might have been sighing in relief, but I was shouting for more!

I had mentioned before that by the time you get to your internship year, most everyone who wasn't suited to the priesthood had already been weeded out. Our seminary was traditional, conservative, and mirrored the church's attitude towards psychology—that mainly it was a bunch of woo-woo stuff. Yet at the same time, there seemed to be a growing sense in the church and in its seminaries that some of their students weren't quite stable. Some students saw the seminary as a place to hide from their problems, and those kinds of individuals had to be identified and kept from being ordained. You shouldn't ordain someone who was unstable because that could have dire implications in terms of both that individual and the people that he would be serving, and that they could wreak a lot of havoc and bring harm to the church's reputation.

The church was finally starting to recognize that this was a step in the right direction, for a lot of unstable men had been ordained and did wreak havoc (think of Father Abdon). And as conservative as this seminary was, it was still able to recognize that sometimes prayer wasn't enough, and that occasionally psychology had a place in the scheme of things. Sometimes there could be happy endings if the issues that some of these men had were taken care of instead of ignored.

As you already know, last semester I had suggested the resource pooling idea to some of the freshman from my home state, and how that

Chapter 17

didn't work out. Despite that rocky beginning, one of those freshman guys and I had become really good friends. I knew from talking with him that his home life hadn't been very good, and that he hadn't had a very stable family background. We all have our issues, whatever they might be, but he seemed to have risen above them and was okay, and really was a nice guy. Lately though, he had "discovered" meditation and spent a lot of his time meditating and praying. A *lot* of time.

One evening—I think it was about nine at night—I was in the dorm hallway at the seminary heading to my room. My friend had been in the chapel praying, but had returned and was also going back to his room. He sees me in the hallway and comes up to me with a frown and very somber expression on his face. Before I can say anything, he tells me that he had been praying and that he had a message for me from Jesus. I started to laugh and looked at him like yeah, right, thinking that he was kidding around with me, but no, he wasn't kidding around. He was dead serious. I'm thinking, this isn't sounding good. That one eye of mine opens up wide and the other eye goes to half mast, which as my friends can tell you, is not a good sign. I'm thinking to myself—what the hell?

He tells me again that he had been praying, and that Jesus spoke to him and that Jesus told him to tell me that I needed to get a haircut, that I didn't look like what I was studying to be, and that Jesus wanted me to cut my hair. He was very intense and very emphatic when he said this.

This guy was my friend and my buddy. We hung out and we did stuff together. And suddenly he's talking like a certifiable nut case. Whoa. Definitely rattled my cage.

I said to him, "*What the hell?*" It came out rather explosively, loud enough to wake the dead because I was pretty shocked, and my voice echoed down the long, empty corridor. A couple of the guys who had been in their rooms opened their doors and came out into the hallway to see what was going on.

I said to him, "Don't you think that Jesus has better things to do than to talk to you about my hair? Come on now. You need to take that brain of yours and use it a little bit, and figure out what the hell is going on here with you. Maybe this is your stuff? That maybe you wish that I was more of what *you* want me to be than what I am?"

I admit that by this time I was pretty riled up by what was going on, kind of thrown off balance by it. I told him, "This is crazy. You've got some problems here. And you'd better take care of them now because I don't think they're going to get better, not if you're covering them up with this Jesus thing." I could ream him out—he was my friend. And I was reaming him out but good.

By this time the rector and the spiritual director had also come out of their rooms and asked me what was going on. So I told them what the guy had said, told them that I thought they needed to intervene here. I said, "Tell me if I'm wrong, but something is wrong here; something is a little bit 'off' here."

They said okay, said that they would handle it, but that I needed to calm down, that it would be okay and that I didn't have to get so upset over it. And it really did upset me. Not that I was insulted about my hair. The seminary officials didn't care if I had short hair, long hair, or no hair, as long as the way I acted was appropriate to "what I was studying to be." And they didn't have any complaints about that.

But this guy was my friend, and right now here in front of me, he was wigging out. That really bothered me, coming out of nowhere as it had. I hadn't seen it coming and felt kind of blindsided, and I guess I got caught up in the heat of the moment. Tempering how I sometimes talked to people was something that I was still working on.

Again, this was another seminarian who got sent to therapy. As much as they may have dissed psychology, the seminary officials were wise enough to know that sometimes you had to do more than pray to take care of a problem.

Okay, you just heard about my reaction to this guy and his "Jesus moment." Some of you may be remembering that I had my own "Jesus moment" in the Franciscan seminary when I heard Him speaking to me from the tabernacle on Halloween night. So let's talk about these moments.

What are they? Basically, they are instances when your own unconscious psyche breaks through to your conscious mind to tell you something. Why do they happen? They can happen when you don't consciously want to face some significant issue in your life. Your psyche is screaming for you to pay attention, to handle the issue because it's not going to go away, and that you can't take care of the problem until you first recognize it. Basically, it means to stop being such a dumbass and pay attention.

In my case, it was trying to tell me that being a priest wasn't going to work for me, which is something that deep down I already knew. But consciously I wasn't ready to face that. If you fail to understand the message that your unconscious mind is trying to give you directly, it keeps trying and can break through into other areas of your mind indirectly.

So although my "Jesus moment" didn't exactly get through to me on the priest issue, it did get me to see other areas more clearly, and to grow in understanding in other areas that were important to my growth. Maybe I couldn't see the big picture all at once right now, but it was going to nudge me (and keep nudging me) into taking little steps until I could get to where I needed to go. It was of consequence to *my* experience. It was all about *me*—me trying to help myself—not trying to help anyone else. If the voice that you're hearing is talking about what other people need to do to make you feel better, then what's going on there is something entirely different, and you should probably seek professional help.

Let me tell you about my friend. He was actually in the diocesan seminary at the same time I was, though a few years behind me. Remember when I talked about the rector's "golden boys," the guys who could do no wrong? Well, he was one of them. We all knew that he had some pretty big issues going on at the time, but being one of the guys who could and did get away with anything, he didn't have to face his issues. He was coddled by everyone—by the seminary officials because he wowed them, and by his classmates who knew better than to piss off a "golden boy." So he always got his way, didn't have to attend to his issues, didn't have to be accountable for his actions, and basically didn't have to grow up.

But then he gets to the graduate seminary with a different rector, and he's no longer a "golden boy." Now he's just one of the guys. No one's coddling him, no one's giving him any special treatment, and everyone's expecting him to pull his own weight. Uh oh. He doesn't quite know how to do that, and those issues that he hasn't handled are now rearing their ugly head and demanding attention. But at least he's trying. He's meditating and praying about it and his psyche is telling him that he's not fitting in, that he's having problems with other people, and that those problems are keeping him from fitting in.

So what does he do with that insight? He decides that he needs to change those other people. Of course, this is not going to work because these "moments" are meant to help *you*, to change *you*, and not anyone else. Because of his response to his "Jesus moment" and because of what he said to me, he was put in a position where his issues were brought out into the open so he could get the help that he needed. It may have started off on the wrong foot, but it got him to where he needed to go.

So he was sent to therapy and he worked out his problems. We remained friends after that incident. Although his road was a bit of a rocky one after that, he eventually got ordained and became a priest. He's still a priest, and he's a good one.

If there's a moral here, I think it might be that ignoring your problems won't make them go away. I speak from experience.

All of the seminarians were looking forward to being ordained as deacons. Yes, it was the last step on your road to the priesthood but, in and of itself, it was a pretty big deal. As a deacon you would be able to do more—you'd participate more at Mass, be able to proclaim (read) the gospel, preach about the gospel, baptize people, and do the burial rites.

You'd have more responsibility and more standing in the church. You'd take a step up on that priest ladder.

We would be ordained as "transitional" deacons, meaning that it was a temporary appointment as we were transitioning towards the priesthood. The church also has "permanent" deacons who are laymen, both married and unmarried, who feel the need to serve the church in a greater capacity but don't want to become priests. They go through a training program, undergo ordination to the deaconate, and can then assist the priest with a lot of his duties. This is really helpful in today's world when the number of men becoming priests is at an all-time low. If a married man is a deacon and his wife dies, he cannot remarry. A single man who is a deacon can never marry. It's all tied in to that sex-is-bad stance of the church.

At some point during this semester, the rector would meet with you and tell you that you had been accepted as a candidate for orders to ordination to the deaconate. During your time in the seminary and the school, you had been watched, assessed, and evaluated. If they felt that you were definitely priest material, you would be allowed to advance to the next step.

You would have to sign a bunch of papers and then take—what I called it anyway—a loyalty oath. (They really hated it when I called it that!) Actually, you would put your hand on the Bible and say the Apostle's Creed, a prayer that says that you believe in God and in the Holy Roman Catholic Church, among other things. So you would say yes, that you believed in all of those tenets, and that you vowed to be faithful to them. Then you signed your name to it.

Once you signed those papers, it became an official contract between you and your diocese saying that you would finish the process of becoming a priest and then would serve your local diocese under your bishop. In return, they would take care of you—give you a job, pay you a salary, house you, pay your medical bills and your medical insurance, give you a pension to live on when you retired—those kinds of things. You'd be pretty well taken care of for the rest of your life.

In the old days before Vatican II, this was called the "Ceremony of Tonsure." Besides saying the Apostle's Creed and signing all of the papers, they would cut your hair. They would cut off a little circle of hair on the top of your head so you'd end up looking like Friar Tuck from the Robin Hood movie. It was a symbolic gesture because archetypically, hair means authority. So when they cut your hair, it meant that you were submitting your authority to theirs. You would become "incardinated" to them, which is a Latin word meaning that you would "give your heart" to them. This practice stopped sometime in the late sixties or early seventies, thank God. Otherwise I would've had to call in sick that day! I loved my long hair then and still love it now.

Many of us were ordained before graduation, and the rest during the summer. They held the ceremony back in your home diocese so that the parishioners of your parish could be involved and take part in this step with you. I was the only seminarian from my diocese who was being ordained that year, and they held the ordination Mass at one of the churches back home.

Usually it's a pretty small affair, a quiet, local celebration, especially with only one candidate for ordination as deacon. But my ordination turned out to be a pretty big bash with a cast of thousands! Normally, you invite everyone you know to come to your ordination. But when you're from out of town, it can be more difficult for people to accept the invitation. A few of the people I invited had to decline because they had to work or couldn't get the time off to travel. But the majority of them said, "Yeah! Road trip! Woo-Hoo! We'll be there!" And they were!

Of course my family and friends attended, but I had a ton of other people show up too—professors, priests, secretaries, and other staff members from both the seminary and the school. In addition, all of my fellow seminarians and a lot of parishioners—not only from my home parish and the parish where I was currently doing my pastoral work—but also from the parish where I had worked with Father Abdon that one summer. The church was packed! I couldn't believe how many people had actually shown up. It really blew me away. I was grateful to everyone who came, and felt honored to share this day with them. I remember my bishop scratching his head, a little frown on his face (like maybe I had given him indigestion or something) as he told me that he had never before seen so many people show up for a deacon ordination.

The ordination ceremony takes place during Mass, and I finagled it so that just about everyone who showed up had a part in the Mass. I had people carrying all kinds of things up to the altar, like the Ordination Book (containing the prayers and the rituals used in the ordination ceremony), the Lectionary (containing the Old and New Testament readings pertaining to the service), and the Bible. A lot of the others carried candles (I remember opening several boxes of candles), altar cloths, linens, and anything else that I could think of. I wanted to involve as many of them as I possibly could because most of them had traveled quite a ways to be there, and I wanted to show my appreciation.

I won't go into the kinds of things that you wear for your ordination—the different types of priestly vestments—but I will talk about it later because some of the history behind why priests wear what they wear is pretty interesting. One of the things that you do wear is called a stole, which is a piece of white material that goes around your neck and hangs down in front, kind of like a big scarf, and is considered a symbol of ordained Roman Catholic clergy. I had a special design, which I created myself, sewn onto my ordination stole by a nun that I knew. That was her ordination gift to me, and she was such a talented seamstress that my stole looks as good today as it did on that day.

You get to a certain point during the Mass and then you do the ordination. The candidate prostrates himself on the floor in front of the altar as the bishop says the prayers of ordination over you, then "lays hands" on your head and proclaims you a deacon. There's a little bit more to it than that, but if you really want to know more you can look up the ceremony on the Internet. So that's what I did—got down on the floor as a seminarian, and got up from the floor as a deacon.

After you've become a deacon, you will then assist the bishop with the rest of the Mass, and for the first time you will be allowed to proclaim the gospel and then preach about it. I was a little nervous about it. I mean, here were all these people that I knew sitting in the pews waiting to hear my first sermon as a deacon, and I didn't want to screw it up. But I think I did okay because no one fell asleep or walked out.

After the Mass they held a reception for me in the church hall that everybody attended. It was quite a crowd and we let the good times roll, with everyone eating and drinking and visiting with each other, and talking up a storm. We were a pretty boisterous bunch with lots of priest and lawyer jokes going around, lots of laughing going on, and we all had a lot of fun. Most everyone from the school and the seminary, including me, had to head back the next day.

I remember that shortly after I got back, we had a Day of Recollection at the seminary. I don't remember exactly what we were discussing, but I do remember that I made a comment about whatever it was, kind of mouthed off about it, and the rector turns and looks at everyone and says, "There he goes. You can tell he was ordained, 'cause there he goes. That's all he needed was ammunition behind him so he could mouth off about stuff. Now he has job security; now he really says it like it is—not that that's ever held him back before!" He had everyone laughing.

I could be pretty blunt back in the day, and from day one I did a lot of criticizing. My ongoing complaint, my "pet peeve" was—why couldn't we bring our theological learning down to the level of the parish and bring people up to that level? (The million dollar question.) I was a deacon, I was criticizing, and they didn't kick me out. That never failed to surprise me. And the short answer to that million dollar question—power and control. They were never going to relinquish it, and I was never going to stop asking them to—from my first day as a deacon to my last day as a priest.

Another thing that happened right after my deacon ordination was that I was chosen by the school faculty and recommended to be a part of a national council of Catholic clergy. This council was serving as an advisory board in the translation of traditional Catholic prayers into the language of the people who would be using them, and this was the first time in history that these prayers were being translated from English into another language. I received a substantial scholarship (one of two that I received that year) to help cover the expenses of the training program and the trip to Notre Dame to participate in liturgical conferences.

I was the only seminarian on this committee that otherwise was comprised of all of these renowned liturgical theologians from several different countries, and some of them world famous. Again, because of my facility with languages, I was able to converse with some of these theologians in their native tongue, and they seemed fascinated by the way I spoke. They said that many of the words and phrases that I used were old fashioned and not really spoken anymore. They were reminded of the way their grandparents had spoken, reminding them of home and of all the good memories that entailed. I used all of the old words that none of them had heard since their childhoods, and I think that it was because of this that I had such a good relationship with them—they all treated me like family—treated me like their little brother!

On the surface, what we were doing doesn't seem like such a big deal—you just translate from one language into another. But in the Roman Catholic Church, nothing is ever simple! Take, for instance, the word "is." In every instance where it was used, it had to convey a certain meaning, one that was not in conflict with the traditional, fundamentalist, and literal interpretation of the Bible that is taught by the church.

You had to have a whole council work on it, discuss it, debate it, create working papers, and then give your suggestions to the bishops, who would then decide if it was acceptable. If not, then it was back to the drawing board and you went through all of those steps again. And there are a lot of words in the prayers besides "is!" It was a lot of work, but I enjoyed the hell out of it. I got to hobnob, if only for a little while, with the movers and shakers of the theological world—my heroes!

One day, a few weeks before graduation, the rector called me into his office. Sitting there with him was the president of the theology school and one of my professors. The president told me that they all felt that I had a real knack for theology, a unique talent for interpreting scripture, and that they also felt strongly that I should pursue it. They said that there were many theologians in this country, but that there were only two biblical scholars, and they believed that I had the talent to become the third.

It was a very difficult and time-consuming program, and it would mean another eight to ten years of study (my insides were shouting *Yes!*). To begin with, I would have to attend Northwestern University in Chicago to learn the original languages of the Bible. It was an extremely expensive program, but if they could get my bishop to agree, then the theology school that I was now in would sponsor me and cover all of the expenses. He said that if I agreed to it, they would talk to my bishop about it. That was an unbelievably exciting moment for me—I felt honored, I felt humbled, but mostly just so excited! This would be a dream come true for me. Of course I said yes. Actually, I think I probably shouted it!

So the president, the rector, and a few of my other professors from the school went in person to talk to my bishop about their proposal. My bishop said - no. He said that he didn't need educated priests in his diocese. He needed priests who could bless the candles and the rosaries of the little old ladies at church. (I'm not kidding you, those were his exact words.) My rector told me that they were appalled by my bishop's stupidity (those were their exact words too). But that without my bishop's consent, there was nothing else they could do.

So my dream died shortly after its conception. Not just a miscarriage, but an abortion—ripped irrevocably from me. There was no way that I could afford to do this on my own. Because of the prohibitive expense, you had to have the backing of a diocese, which I had been denied.

I didn't have time to get angry. I got sick. The diagnosis was amoebic dysentery.

Physically, I was pretty exhausted. My schoolwork was catching up to me big-time, and taking a toll on me. I felt like the old, worn out mimeograph machine that we had at the school, constantly churning out paper after paper. I had kept up a 3.9 grade average all through school, and it was costing me. Between all of those papers and all of the late night studying, I think that my immune system was in the pits and that my resistance was down. And I was down emotionally too with leaving school and with my bishop's refusal to allow me to continue on in theology.

I started having all sorts of intestinal problems—the "trots," the "runs," barfing, even explosive vomiting, probably none of which you care to hear about! So the doctors tested me and said that I had amoebic dysentery. They weren't quite sure how I got it, maybe from the hospital work that I was doing. Although we were all assigned to do pastoral work in local parishes, we were still visiting the elderly in nursing homes and the sick in hospitals. Some of the patients I ministered to were quite ill, and I remember many a time sitting and holding the hands of the dying. They weren't quite sure if that's where I picked it up or not, and none of the other seminarians had gotten sick, so I guess it wasn't the seminary food.

This was during the last few weeks of school, so I was exempt from going on the end-of-the-year retreat. All of the students would have a retreat at the beginning and end of each school year, and they would rent part of a monastery or a large hall somewhere and we'd all travel there. They would hire a speaker—a priest or a bishop or a theologian—someone who was in good standing in the church. (Radicals need not apply!) Then they would give us a talk on some topic like "The Joys of Celibacy." No, only kidding! It would be something more serious, like "Maintaining Poverty as an Example of Witness to the People of God." Topics like that, which actually were usually pretty interesting and thought provoking.

When I first got sick, I was pretty much confined to my bed, feverish and weak. I really wasn't in shape for much company. One evening a few of my friends stopped by to express how worried they were about me being alone while they would be gone for the retreat. I knew they were genuinely concerned because after their visit, as they left, quietly without a word, they took my poster of "Wonder Woman" off the wall and repositioned it over my bed, on the ceiling right above my head so I could see it without any effort.

So most everyone in the seminary left for the retreat—seminarians, professors, and staff members. They left a token staff behind to keep an eye on things. I just stayed in my room and worked on finishing all of my essays and studied for final exams. So I'm in my room, surrounded by piles of books—stacks of them teetering every which way—and I remember one of the staff members coming in to my room to check on me to see how I was doing and if I needed anything.

This guy walked in and saw the stacks of books and rolled his eyes. He asked me why I was doing all of this, and said that I wasn't going to use any of it as a priest. He told me, basically, that I was just wasting my time, and that I didn't need to do all of this. And I told him that I really enjoyed this stuff, enjoyed learning it, and that I didn't know if I'd ever actually end up being a priest. And I remember him telling me, very matter-of-factly, "Well of course you're going to be a priest. You don't have to worry about that." It seemed like everyone was sure of that but me.

The dysentery finally ran its course and graduation was here. We had our graduate school ceremony with all of the pomp and circumstance that goes along with it. My parents weren't able to be there for it, but some of my friends from home were able to make it. They had a nice party afterwards for all of the graduates. It seemed like school was over in a flash. You don't really graduate from the seminary like you do from the school. Your deacon ordination is considered the climax of your seminary experience—your graduation—if you will.

I will always remember my last conversation with my rector, because it was a doozy. He came up to me and asked me to go for a walk with him. Over the course of my years in school, whenever exam time rolled around, my professors would ask me to go for a walk with them to take my tests. The other guys would sit in the classroom with pen and paper, which I occasionally did, but for the most part I would take my exams while walking with my teacher. As we were strolling, they would quiz me and ask me questions, and do the exams that way. I enjoyed doing it, and I never did ask them why they did it that way with me.

So the rector asked me to go for a walk with him. We started strolling around the seminary grounds, and he says to me, "Well, son (yeah, you know that he said my name), you've come to the end of your time here. I really liked having you here. But I do have to tell you that I'm really concerned about something."

I looked at him and said, "Oh really? About what? I've spent three years here and now you're telling me that you're concerned? I don't think I like the sound of this." I don't know why, but it made me think of a warden in a prison talking to a condemned prisoner in his cell.

He said, "No, it's not what you're thinking. But let me tell you, I do think that you're going to have a hell of a hard time in the priesthood because of the way you think, and the way you act. You really are totally responsible—that part's no problem. In terms of your being ordained—that's not a problem. But the way you do things—you're so responsible, you're so innovative, you're so creative, and you're so off the scale when it comes to these things that you're going to have a hard time. Because the church is not that way and your diocese, especially, is pretty backwards. To contain yourself is going to be the challenge. You've got all of this knowledge, you really applied yourself here, and you've made quite an impression on everyone here. We've never had a student like you here at the seminary before, and I doubt that we ever will again.

"And your school said the same thing. They said—where did this one show up from? You're very different in how you approach everything; you've made an impact on everybody here. You were like a little spark that got the other students involved to really question, to challenge, to think about themselves and their roles, their formation, the church, the future, in a critical way that would help the church to grow.

"You're a good kid, which doesn't translate well in terms of how you will feel personally in the priesthood. You're going to suffer a lot because

Chapter 17

the church is very backwards; it is so behind the times in terms of where you're at. It is not innovative and it does not look kindly on people who are innovative, who have creativity, who have the kind of faith that you have shown, the spirituality, and the inner focus. They just don't have that. And your bishop—he is way backwards. Conservative doesn't even cut it in terms of what you're going to face."

I said, "Well, thank you for telling me this now at the end. Couldn't you have told me this along the way?"

And he said, "Well, no because we wanted to see how you developed, and you've developed fine. You're fine in terms of— well, put it this way. If the church actually lived what it teaches, you would be at the top and the head of the class. I've never had to worry about you or think twice about you. Of course, everybody's eyebrows were always raised every week because of the stuff you said, and the way you did things. You were talked about, we met a lot about you, but it was because you were so outside the norm, but in a positive direction. You weren't negative in any way; it was just 'outside.' You were like a breath of fresh air."

I got pretty depressed listening to him. I told him that now I didn't know if I should pursue this.

He said, "Well, you've got some reflecting to do. So pray over this. What I worry about is your ability to handle the backwardness of the church and the diocese that you come from. And the personalities involved because it's not just your bishop, but your brother priests and those who are vying for power. There are very few spots of power in the church, and you have to spend your life sucking up, doing the right kinds of things, and making the right moves into those places of power. So, I just wanted to tell you that."

I found out later on that among the seminary officials, I was voted most likely to become the next bishop of my diocese, and that I was going to tear through the church hierarchy in terms of being promoted— if I could hold it together enough to survive the process.

I found this pretty interesting because I was so "not there" in terms of my thought processes. Most of the other students had a burning goal of becoming the next bishop of their dioceses—they made no bones about that. It was all about being promoted, and all about attaining those positions of power. And that wasn't even a thought in my head. I was focused on trying to change attitudes, to "grow" people, and to "grow" the church.

So we ended our talk. The rector said good luck, keep in contact, come by and visit, and told me that I would be remembered fondly. I packed my stuff into my car, and with a troubled mind and a heavier heart, headed back home.

Chapter 18

My Internship Begins:
"Deke" a.k.a. Fr. Deacon

I drove home in my new (well, new to me although it was a used car) little Volkswagen bug because my previous car had been totaled when I got hit by a drunk driver last summer. Since my route home took me right past my new parish, I stopped in unannounced to drop off some of my stuff. I met the pastor and the church secretary (I'm still friends with that secretary and her family). The pastor also introduced me to a young man, a "close" friend of his. I later found out that they had one of those "particular friendships," the kind that they had warned us against back in the Franciscan seminary. As it turned out, later on in the story I prevented this friend from being sexually assaulted by two of the parish handymen.

The pastor had me put my things in the guest bedroom, and said that he would give me all of the keys that I would need when I returned to officially start my internship. He also told me that if I wanted to extend my vacation and take off more time before starting, that that would be fine with him (I didn't). He invited me to stay for lunch, which I did, and our first encounter went just fine, which surprised me a little bit.

I had received notification of my parish assignment by mail a few weeks before graduation, and this pastor had called me at about the same time. I had heard from other people that he had a reputation as an "asshole," which is not exactly something encouraging to hear about your first boss. He had called me on the hallway phone at the seminary, and I remember that I was cleaning the bathroom when he called—and for some reason, that has always stuck in my mind! Anyway, he said, "Hey, son (yeah, he said my name), this is Father Tobias. I heard that you're going to be assigned to me. You've probably heard that I can be a real asshole." He laughed like crazy for a minute, and then he said, "So get yourself ready!" He sounded eerily similar to the Wicked Witch talking to Dorothy in the *Wizard of Oz*!

I told him, "Well, I don't know if you've heard about me because I'm pretty tough myself and I don't back down." Then I laughed right back at him.

Well, that stopped him cold. I must've caught him by surprise because after a few moments of silence, all he said was, "Oh, okay. Well, I'll see you in about six weeks," and then he hung up.

So our first meeting went well, and after lunch I got back on the road for the last leg of my journey home. I took about two weeks off, during which time I relaxed, caught up on family stuff, and took a few short, out of town trips to attend the deacon ordinations of a couple of my seminary classmates. Then I packed my car yet again, said good-bye to my family yet again, and headed back to my new parish to begin my internship year.

I arrived at the parish and went to the rectory where the secretary welcomed me and gave me my set of keys, as the pastor was taking a nap. Although I had let him know what time I would be arriving, he always took a long nap in the afternoons and it was sacrosanct—he was to be awakened only for catastrophic emergencies. Even his workday was scheduled around his naptime. Thankfully, I guess I wasn't considered an emergency. (Yet!) The secretary then introduced me to the four sisters who lived in the convent adjacent to the rectory who had come by to meet me.

They were from Ireland and belonged to an order called the Daughters of Mary and Joseph. After I got to know them a little better, I would joke around with them and call them the Daughters of Mary and Jesus. One of the sisters, Sister Clare, would always shake her finger at me and, in her lilting Irish brogue, say, "Oh no, Father. That would be incest. We can't have that. What are we going to do with you, Father?"

These sisters had recently been hired, by the pastor as teachers for the Catholic school that he was in the process of reopening. Many years ago a very famous, very wealthy gentleman who came from one of the small communities in this area had donated a significant amount of money to the parish to start a Catholic elementary school. The school had opened—but for some reason had eventually closed—and now the pastor wanted to reopen it. The original donor, who was now even richer than he had been back then, was again willing to foot the bill.

To me, the fact that the pastor wanted to reopen the school said good things about his character. Most priests don't really want to be in a parish that has a school because they consider it to be a pain in the ass. It takes up a huge portion of the pastor's time and most of them don't want to be bothered. Even though it can be considered a "feather in your cap" to be the pastor of a school (it looks good on your resume should you want to get on the bishop's "short list"), the fact that it's an enormous commitment doesn't hold much appeal for most priests. So I felt that his wanting the school spoke well of him.

So I met all of the sisters, my little welcoming committee, all very nice ladies, and Sister Eleanor volunteered to take me on a tour and showed me around the grounds. Just as we were finishing, we heard the secretary yelling out the rectory door that father was awake.

Father Tobias, the pastor, was a highly educated, extremely learned man. I mean this guy was *smart*. I found out that his reputation as an "asshole" came down from the top, from administration, because he didn't get along well with authority and tended to "buck" the system, so the top guns considered him an "asshole" for that.

Some people tended to be a little afraid of him and even a few of his fellow priests cowered around him. This was because he was very authoritative, a strict, stern guy with a gruff, abrupt manner, definitely not a touchy-feely kind of guy. He had a strong, in-your-face kind of personality and he expected you to know your stuff and to be honest with him. If you didn't do those things, it probably was wise to stay out of his way.

But he also had a wicked sense of humor and he could be—and often was—funnier than hell. He worked tirelessly for his parishioners, liked and respected them, and they felt the same way about him. He also hated the institutional aspect of the church, so on the whole, we got along really well and I came to admire and respect him.

Sadly, he also had a big problem with alcohol, but he never got falling down drunk when he was at the parish. He would take off for a few days at a time, sometimes for as long as a week, and either go to a friend's parish or head out of town to go on one of his "benders." I think that because he respected his parishioners, he didn't want them to see him in such an "unpriestly" state. He might have been an alcoholic, but when he was sober, he was a decent and caring man.

The problem I encountered was the longer that I was there, the shorter his periods of sobriety became. He also had a bad heart and he'd had several heart attacks already, and would have a few more while I was there with him. The last attack that he would have in this parish would be a major one, and they would finally order him to stop working and take time off to recuperate. When he left the parish because of that, life as we all knew it came to an abrupt end.

So father sat down with me and we talked about the schedule and my duties as a deacon. This was a big parish and it also had about eight mission churches that it ministered to, so we had a lot to discuss at our meeting. I don't remember all of the details of that meeting, but I do remember that he told me that he expected me to wear the black cassock for Mass and all official functions. When he said that, I rolled my eyes at him. I mean—how was that going to look? I already had long hair, and now he wanted me to wear a dress to church? But he just rolled his eyes back at me. He could be very traditional in some ways. I think I only owned one cassock (hated the things) so he had a few more made for me. I ended up wearing it whenever he was around, but whenever he was gone, I took the damn thing off. I figured he'd never know. I don't think anyone ever told on me because he never mentioned it to me again.

My first few days there were a whirlwind of activity. The first thing that father did was to take me to town—literally! He took me to every shop, store, restaurant, and even a lumberyard that was owned by one of our parishioners. He then took me to our local hospital where I met every nurse on every floor who was a parishioner. He introduced me to all of these people as his new assistant and, of course, he introduced me by name. But I think that was one of the last times that I ever heard him use my actual name. After that he only called me "Deke," short for deacon, which was okay with me because I thought it was pretty funny.

After lunch—at one of the parishioner's restaurants—he took me out to visit all of the mission churches scattered around the countryside, so I got to meet many of those parishioners as well. When we finally got back to the parish, it was time for evening Mass, which father celebrated with my help. He wanted me to help him give Communion to get used to being around and among the people of the parish.

As a deacon, I couldn't yet celebrate Mass by myself or consecrate the bread and wine, and I also couldn't hear confessions. When I did a service on my own, it wasn't called a Mass but a Communion Service, where I could basically do everything that the priest did except for the consecration. Any time that father would take off from the parish to go on one of his drinking binges, he would first consecrate tons of hosts for me to use. There would be hosts stuffed everywhere you looked (in containers and cabinets and drawers) because if I ran out, I couldn't make new ones.

Later on, when I was doing a Communion Service on my own, I would often see father ride his bicycle in through the back doors of the church, park it against one of the walls, and stand there and listen as I was preaching one of my sermons. Or he would take a seat in one of the back pews, sit with some of the parishioners, and before you knew it there'd be all this talking and laughing going on back there, with all of them having a merry old time.

After listening to some of my sermons, father told me that my preaching style reminded him of St. John Chrysostom who was an early father of the church (a bishop who was among the next generation of leaders in the church after the deaths of the original twelve apostles). I was more "eastern" than "western" in my philosophy and theology

Chapter 18

because I felt that it was more in keeping with the views of the early church—the purer version of the church—before all of the changes (some of them not so good) that occurred during the Middle Ages. The early church was more in tune with what Jesus was really all about, in my opinion, anyway.

But it was the nuns who really helped me to hone my preaching skills. I used to spend a lot of time preparing my sermons, and then I would write them out and read what I had written to the congregation. Well, the nuns didn't like that. So one day at one of my "Deacon Masses," which is what the pastor called my services, I had placed my written sermon on top of the podium as we were preparing the altar for the service.

As the service began, I'm walking up to the altar when I see Sister Clare quickly glide up to the podium, snatch my sermon, give me a little wave and quietly glide back to the first pew, with my sermon clutched in her hand. All of the nuns were sitting there with smug looks on their faces. When I got to the altar I gave her one of my meanest glares, but other than making a fuss and bringing unwanted attention to the matter, there was nothing I could do.

Sister Clare just smiled angelically back at me and mouthed the words, "You can do it!" Well, yeah, I guess that I would have to, but it would've been nice if she had talked to me about it first! I guess I just needed that little push because from that time on I gave my sermons to the parishioners without reading it from my notes. When I say that it was nuns who molded me into a priest, I really mean it!

After Mass that first evening we went back to the rectory and I was beat. It had been a really busy couple of days. Father wanted to go out for dinner although our fridge was well stocked. Parishioners were always bringing us goodies, and we also had a housekeeper/cook, a young woman who worked half days during the week. She did the cleaning and the laundry, but not mine though. I did my own laundry because it just didn't feel right to me to have someone else washing my dirty underwear! She also cooked every day, making enough food for a big lunch, which was our main meal, and then food for dinner.

Most times we went out for dinner, either at parishioner-owned restaurants or we'd be invited to eat at people's homes. After I'd been there for a few months, father decided that we needed to start eating "healthier," so he made arrangements with the local hospital's cafeteria to provide dinner for us every night that we wanted it. Nice, healthy, well-balanced meals. I think that lasted for all of about three weeks!

Our housekeeper had a child out of wedlock, which was a really big deal back in those days. She brought her little boy to work with her every day. She told me that she wanted children but didn't want to be burdened with a husband. No one would think twice about that in today's world, but back then it caused quite a few raised eyebrows in the parish because father would allow an unwed mother to work for the church. But father didn't care what people said, other than to say that it was none of their business.

It was sometimes funny watching the two of them interact because although father stood up for her when it came to employment, they really didn't get along all that well. Their personalities just didn't seem to mesh and she was also a little intimidated by his brusque manner. They had a bit of a fiery relationship with a fair amount of bickering and arguing going on. I can remember them getting into some heated shouting matches every now and then. She would have a second child while working for us, and after Father Tobias left, one of the things that the new pastor accused me of was of fathering her child, but we'll get into that later.

That first day came to an end, and I swear that it was one of the busiest days that I've ever spent in my life. That night when my head hit the pillow, I was out like a light in thirty seconds and slept like the dead! Little did I know that there were many more days like that to come.

So I plunged head first into my new assignment. Father Tobias was a good role model for me to follow when it came to pastoral work. And I was lucky in that respect because parishes are molded in the image and likeness of the pastor. It's not according to Jesus' image, it's not according to what the parishioners need or want, it's what the pastor wants—period. If you have a good pastor, someone who is psychologically stable, he does take into account the needs of the parishioners and balances that with the demands of the administration and with his own goals.

But if you have a pastor who is not stable, then the only thing that is important are his needs, and that can become a nightmare for the parishioners. It can also become a nightmare for the deacon or priest working with him. I've heard stories from other priests about how their rectory was run like a fiefdom straight from the Middle Ages, with the pastor being the "king" and the assistant priest being the indentured serf, lucky to get any leftover scraps of anything, while the parish was falling down around everyone's heads. And if you tried telling this to the bishop, he would clasp his hands, smile beatifically, and say that yes, the pastor was certainly a colorful character, God was in His heaven and all was right with the world. (Yeah, right.)

Father Tobias was used to working hard for his parishioners. He liked and respected them, and became a positive influence in their lives. He was forever being invited by them into their lives—having dinner with them, partying with them, going to their kids' baseball and basketball games, and sharing the good times and the bad. There was hardly ever an evening in the rectory without it being full of the conversation and laughter of people. He was always inviting people in—either the parishioners or fellow priests—to eat and drink (or just drink!), to play cards, or just engage in conversation.

There was a very strong fraternal bond among the priests in that area, feeling that they were brother priests out in the "wilderness," and they would frequently visit each other and spend time in each other's parishes. That rectory was a "happening" place!

Although the parish was a large one, the people in it were a very close-knit group. They obviously cared for each other, looked out for each other, shared their lives during the good times, and helped each other out in the bad times. If someone had a sudden unexpected crisis—like the death of a family member or the loss of a much-needed job—father and the parishioners would get together and plan bake sales and car washes and special collections at the Masses to raise money for them. In addition, they would bring them food, run errands for them, spend time with them, and help them in whatever way they could. They were always "there" for each other. They didn't have to be asked to do it, they just did it. It was a way of life for them.

I'm not saying that they were perfect, of course, because they weren't; no one is. They were just typical people with all of the ups and downs that life entails. But they were a true "community," woven together by empathy, respect, and love. It was a beautiful thing to see and to become a part of. This love, this caring, this sharing in the fullness of our imperfect lives—*this* is what "church" is. *This* is what Jesus was talking about. Or so I believe.

In my new role I kept busy from morning until night. Because father was the first to admit that he didn't have a lot of patience with kids, he gladly handed over that aspect of ministry to me. He said that since I was young, they could relate better to me. On the whole we had a good group of kids in the parish, and I was the first deacon that they had ever had there. They weren't comfortable calling me "Deke," like father always did, so they ended up calling me "Father Deacon."

So I started a youth group in the parish, and I think that I was pretty successful in getting these kids to connect to their "inside" stuff—to their feelings. As I've said before, to live your life in balance, the "inside" stuff has to match the "outside" stuff. But first you need to know how to access your inside stuff and to realize the value that it has.

When I told them at one of our first meetings that we were going to do some exercises that would help them to uncover their "heart" connection, they all looked at me like—what? I think they were expecting Bible readings and sermons about the cigarettes they were sneaking, the underage drinking that none of them admitted to, and the partying all night that their parents were always complaining about. Instead, we talked about their "inside" stuff, about their feelings, about warmth, empathy, love, and how to "feel" their connection to the world around them, to each other, and to God.

I remember telling them at that meeting, "Shh . . . quiet down, listen, do you hear the Spirit moving?" And, of course, most everyone would say, "Huh?" I told them that I wanted them to feel the experience of God that joins us all together. I didn't want them to tell me about what they had "learned" about their faith, but what they "felt" about it. Faith is a heart-based experience, and if they couldn't connect to their hearts, what kind of a connection did they have to their faith? To other people? To themselves?

It must've worked because a lot of those kids told the pastor that they weren't quite sure how I did it, but they came away from our sessions feeling as if they had "an experience of God." Well, that's because they had! Many of them were still at very basic levels of understanding, thinking that if you wanted to find God, you went to church. That's okay, but that's just a very tiny piece of it and not even the best piece.

I arranged for field trips to the city so that they could see that there was a big world out there that they were a part of. We rented a little bus and went to the youth program at the opera and visited museums and other places I thought they might be interested in. I wanted to open their eyes to all of the possibilities that existed beyond their little corner of the world. I would sprinkle a little spirituality into the mix, and they would all come back from one of our trips inevitably feeling pretty good about the world and about themselves, feeling "connected" to all of it, which was the ultimate point of those trips. They "got" it. God, I love working with young people!

I gave a somewhat unusual sermon one weekend when most of the parish kids were home from college, and I've heard that to this day it's still talked about. At the time, the song *Jeremiah Was a Bullfrog* (by Three Dog Night) had come out and was popular with the kids. So I got up to the pulpit and began my sermon by singing the first verse. (You can take the priest out of the theater, but you can't take the theater out of the priest!) Then I went on to talk about Jeremiah, the prophet, and how we were all supposed to be prophets because of our baptism, and how we should all "belt it out" like a bullfrog about living our connection to the Divine Presence.

And I know that some people still do remember it because not too long ago I was at a restaurant and had gone to the men's room. I'm standing at the urinal doing my business, and I feel this tap on my shoulder. I turn and this guy who's probably in his late thirties and whom I don't know, says to me, "Hey, hi, you were the priest who gave us that sermon about Jeremiah the bullfrog! That was so cool! I still remember that!" I thought that was great, but this wasn't exactly the best place to reminisce about it!

Another thing that father had me do was to become the chaplain for the extracurricular groups that were a part of the church ministry. He later on admitted to me that he did this as sort of a joke on me because he felt that these groups were way too conservative even for him, and he had no interest in them. So, stick the radical young deacon on them, and let him get bored to death at their meetings.

I think that there were three or four of these groups— like the Sacred Heart Men's Group and the Women's Altar Society. I think they each met once a month. I made it a point to attend all of their meetings, which made them really happy as no one in the clergy had ever done that before.

But I did have my own agenda. After I had been their chaplain for a little while, I asked them if they would do something for me. Because they were so happy to have my support for their groups, of course they said yes. (I knew they would.)

So I asked the men's group to sponsor a meeting for all of the boys in the parish. I would bring in a speaker to give them a talk on hygiene and the horrors of venereal disease. Basically, it was a sex education kind of talk, without calling it that (which was pretty unheard of in those days, especially among very conservative Catholics). They agreed and that's what we did.

I also approached one of the women's groups and asked that they do the same thing for the girls in the parish, which they also agreed to. When the pastor heard about it, he was speechless—he couldn't believe that I had pulled it off. He just could not believe that I gotten some of the most conservative Catholics in the parish not only to agree to a public talk about something having to do with S-E-X, but also to actually sponsor it. He said that he had never before seen that happen in any parish, and that I had "done good."

Another duty that father gave me–and by this time I was seriously beginning to wonder what duties he had left for himself–was as the assistant to Sister Clare. She was the religious education sister, and she was in charge of setting up the CCD (Congregation of Christian Doctrine) classes at the missions—basically, religion classes. So the two of us spent a couple of days each week going to the missions and organizing their CCD programs.

I would also give talks to the parishioners there and set up retreats for them. These were always busy, work-packed days, but spending time on the road with sister was a lot of fun, and it gave me a chance to get to know these people far better than if I only saw them every other weekend or so for Mass.

Sometimes at day's end we would be running a little late, and we'd have to rush back to the parish so I could do my evening Communion Service. When we got there, I'd jump out of the car, rush into the church while I was trying to put on my cassock (which had been lying crumpled in the back seat of the car all day), and sprint to the altar panting from the exertion with my hair flying every which way!

When the pastor was gone, which happened fairly regularly, things would go from busy to insane. The secretary would call me and tell me that the pastor had gone AWOL and that he wanted me to run the ship, which meant that I would be running my tail feathers off from the crack of dawn to sometimes way past midnight.

There was always so much to do—the morning weekday Mass at the main parish, visiting the sick in the hospital every day, visiting parishioners who were in nursing homes or homebound, office hours when people had made appointments to come in and talk about issues or problems, administrative meetings—some of which I would have to leave the parish to attend—and the regular office stuff that needed attention to keep the parish running. And those were just the daytime duties!

In the evenings we had the evening weekday Mass, the various group meetings, the sacramental preparation classes, CCD classes for the local Catholic kids who went to public schools, and occasionally more office hours. On top of that there were always emergencies popping up, like when we'd be called out to give someone the Anointing of the Sick, which is a special anointing for someone who is near death (it used to be called the Last Rites), or be called to the hospital or a parishioner's home, or to the scene of an accident.

And then there were the weekends to cover, which could be a logistical nightmare. I'd have to try to find another priest to come in to help me because I couldn't do the confessions on Saturday or cover all of the Masses. You'd have Masses at the missions to attend to, and then multiple Masses at the main parish. And when you went to the missions, the people didn't expect you to say Mass and then just rush off, which I actually had to do many a time. They wanted you to spend time with them, talk to them, and be guests in their homes.

I developed a reputation in that area as the priest with the lead foot on the gas pedal, and that got started because I was rushing from one mission church to another, trying to get to all of them before the next millennium dawned. I would also put the pedal to the metal on my bicycle because around town I would often bike instead of drive, and there I'd be—with my doggie tucked securely in the basket on my bike and cassock flapping in the wind—as I rushed from people's homes to the hospital and nursing homes, visiting the sick and the shut-ins.

I had talked before about the "good ship lollipop" seminarians who couldn't wait to get ordained so they could live the easy life. Looking at the schedule that I just mentioned, you might be asking yourself–what's so easy about that? Well, if you become the pastor, you don't have to do any of that, or at least not much of it. 'Don't want to bother with all of those Masses? Just change the schedule to one Mass a day and make your assistant do it. Delegate the bulk of the rest of it to your assistant priest or to the deacons. You're the pastor–what you say is the law of the land.' Your role as a priest can be as involving, or as barren, as you want it to be.

I was beginning to notice that the more that I learned to do and the more I did, the less the pastor was around. He seemed to be going AWOL more often. There were times when the secretary would pull me aside and tell me that a certain event was on the pastor's schedule—like a wedding or a baptism—but that she wasn't sure that the pastor would be around for it, so I should be available "just in case."

So one of the things that I did was to find all of the manuals and booklets that described all of the different rituals and prayers used in all of the ceremonies we performed, and I memorized all of them. Loving rituals as I did, I didn't find it too difficult to do. That knowledge came in handy when father didn't show up at the last minute and I had to do the service or the ceremony in his place. He wasn't there to show me how to do it, so I had to be prepared. I think that by the time I was ordained a priest, I had already done hundreds of marriages. (It felt more like thousands!)

I even got to be so good at it that the parishioners started calling me the "Ritual Priest." I could put together a ritual for any occasion. I would use the official prayers and guidelines we had, but I would always put my own spin on it to make it more personal and meaningful for everyone. Afterwards, I always had people come up to me to thank me, to tell me that the ceremony had been beautiful, and that it had really spoken to them, and had touched their hearts. (There is a method to my madness!)

When I needed advice or needed to "hash" something out with someone, I turned to the nuns. They were always there for me, always ready to help, and I felt like I was going through my "novitiate" with them. (Again, in religious communities, this is a year of introduction to the religious life for someone who desires to join the community but has not yet taken any vows.) Although, of course, I would never take any vows to become a nun, after the sisters were through with me, I think I would've aced that one and made a damn good nun!

The sisters were very protective of me, treating me like a beloved little brother. Sometimes Sister Eleanor would laugh and say, "Father, I just don't know what kind of a nun you're turning out to be!" Thinking back on it, I was being shaped into a priest, not by another priest, but mainly from the feminine perspective of the sisters, which I believe helped me to become a better man and a better priest.

One of the things that Father Tobias did do with me on occasion was to have some of those deep theological discussions that I had been hoping for. We would talk about all kinds of theological concepts. One of the discussions I remember having was about Incarnation Theology. This theology was a product of the very early church regarding salvation, saying that Jesus' birth, and not His death, was salvific. It says that the Divine Presence is all around us, and that at a specific point in time it became concentrated in an individual human being—Jesus. And that it was His birth and the example of His life that brings us salvation, rather than His death. Concentrating on His death as the point of salvation was a concept that was brought about much later in the church. I was pro-incarnation, Father was not, and we would sit and debate these concepts for hours on end.

Another theology that was being discussed back then was called Liberation Theology. This theology was promulgated by South American theologians, and it was based on the critical reflection of the spiritual practices of the poor in that region. It was a theology of justice, saying that the authoritarian governments (mainly dictatorships) of that region had no right to suppress people, especially the poor, for the government's profit.

The governments in question found this concept to be threatening, as anything that took power and control from those in authority and gave it to the people was not to be tolerated. So the Catholic Church, whose bishops were aligned with these governments when it came to issues of power and control, also found it threatening and condemned Liberation Theology. Around that time a few Catholic nuns, priests, and even a bishop who advocated for justice for the poor, were murdered.

Of course, I was pro-Liberation Theology, but Father Tobias and I never really got around to discussing this one. I think that because the church condemned it, he had never learned enough about it to be able to argue it one way or the other. Although in all other areas, he was very vocally on the side of the poor. Later on I'll tell you more about my own personal theology as a priest and some of the sermons that I would give based on that theology, and how it got me reported to the bishop on a fairly regular basis.

In some ways my internship was harder because father was away so often. I worked my butt off and often had to figure things out for myself, and who knows if I always figured them out correctly. I did have the nuns to turn to for a lot of things, and thankfully they all had a lot of good common sense, so I don't think I ever veered too far off course. But there was also an upside to father's management style. Some of my friends who were also doing internships, had told me that their pastors were constantly on their backs, looking over their shoulders and breathing down their necks. They were constantly being told do this, don't do that. They couldn't develop their own style of ministry because they had to emulate their pastor's style.

Thanks to father's frequent absences, I got to learn a lot about running a parish from the ground up. I was involved in just about every aspect of it, even things that aren't normally a deacon's responsibility because I had to be. When father wasn't there, I had to do it, including the financial stuff. Normally as a deacon, you have nothing at all to do with the financial aspect of the parish, but financial matters had to be taken care of whether father was there or not, and more and more often he wasn't.

So I got a crash course in business management from the secretary and the parish financial officer, and I even learned about "cooking the books!" Let me explain that one. A certain percentage of the money that all parishes in the diocese bring in from their Sunday collections goes to the diocesan office for operating costs. The central office uses it for all kinds of things—to fund different programs throughout the diocese or to pay the bishop's salary, to name just a few.

Each parish also had to have its own bank account, and whatever money didn't go to the central office was put there for the parish to use for its own operational costs. But sometimes, the bishop would "borrow" money from the parish's bank account—perhaps to help pay for something in a different parish that might be having a cash flow problem. Occasionally the bishop might neglect to pay it back, or might take a long time to pay it back, and that could leave your parish short of money. And you couldn't refuse the bishop when he wanted to use your parish's money for other purposes.

So what Father Tobias had done was to have a second parish bank account that the bishop didn't know about. He kept meticulous records and it was all very above-board, except for the fact that it was a secret from all but a very few. He didn't want his parish to be short of money when it was needed, so he found what he felt was a creative way to protect the interests of his parish.

I might have been crazy busy, but every cloud has its silver lining. With all of the running around that I was doing, with biking all over town instead of driving, with never having time to sit down and eat a real meal, I was again as skinny as a rail! It wouldn't last, but it was great not having to worry about this because I definitely didn't have time in my schedule to do the amount of jogging that I had done throughout my seminary years.

My internship was supposed to be for a year, but I was only in the parish as a deacon for about three months when my pastor told me to call the bishop. It was time to talk about my ordination to the priesthood.

Chapter 19

Ordination to the Priesthood

The pastor told me to make an appointment with the bishop to talk about my ordination. Father Tobias had already met with him to discuss how I was doing in my internship, and from his perspective, I was good to go; I was ready for ordination.

So I made the appointment and went to see the bishop. One of the first things he told me at our meeting was that he had been inundated with calls and letters from my parishioners, and that it looked like everybody and their brother wanted me to become their priest. He said that the people really loved me, and that obviously I must be doing some good there.

He actually showed me this big file stuffed with letters. Although he didn't let me read them, he did read portions from several of them to me. They said some really nice things about me—positive comments that had me smiling. He also told me that he had never gotten letters like this for any of the other seminarians.

Those letters just about knocked me off my feet. I had been hashing and rehashing that last conversation I'd had with my rector before I left school, wondering if I was doing the right thing. And now, with these letters, it seemed that the decision that I had to make just got a whole lot easier.

In the old days in the early church, a man who wanted to become a priest was only ordained by acclamation of the people. This meant that the people themselves, and not the bishop, would decide if a man could become their priest or not. They would present their candidate to the "Elders" of the church and let it be known that they wanted this man as their priest.

So no, the people of the village no longer gathered in the courtyard of the church to yell "yea" or "nay" as the bishop pointed to the candidate for priesthood. Instead in the modern world, they made phone calls and wrote letters. Since my philosophy was rooted in the early church, I thought of this as a sign from above. Because the will of the people was being made manifest in this way, the people themselves were speaking for me, the people themselves wanted me to be their priest—I felt like I was being shown that this was meant to be. This gesture on their part warmed my heart and, theologically, held a lot of meaning for me.

The bishop said that we needed to set the date for the ordination, which I wanted to have on the Feast Day of St. Francis. I thought that that would make things come full circle, as St. Francis had been the one to start me on this path. The bishop, however, felt that I should be ordained on the Feast Day of the Archangels, which was the Feast Day of the parish where I was at, and which fell just a few days before the Feast Day of St. Francis. Since that was actually more in keeping with how it was done in the early church, I said okay, that would be fine.

We set the date and I returned to the parish and gave Father Tobias the news. My next step would be going on a retreat. Every time that you took the next step on the priest path—from seminarian to deacon, from deacon to priest, from priest to bishop—you had to do a weeklong retreat. It could be a formal arrangement at a retreat house, a week off by yourself spent in solitude, or anything in between, as long as that time was used to pray and reflect upon the step that you were taking, on whether it was the right thing for you to do.

I contacted a parishioner, an older woman that I had gotten to know from one of the missions. She was a widow, a retired schoolteacher in her late eighties, and a real down to earth lady with a great sense of humor. I just loved this lady. She had a little guesthouse that she had told me about, and had said that I was welcome to use it if I ever needed to. So I asked her if I could use it for my retreat, just to spend the time there by myself. She said that she would be "tickled pink" to have me there. After I got there, she went around on an almost a daily basis, telling all of her friends and neighbors that she just loved having father there.

I packed a little bag, said goodbye to everyone at the parish, and headed off to her guesthouse. I didn't exactly spend the week in solitude as my hostess insisted on making breakfast for me every morning, and the two of us would eat together. And when the kids in the area heard that I was staying there, they would show up on my doorstep after school and just hang out, talking and visiting with me. But for the most part, I had a lot of time to myself and I was able to do some serious thinking and praying.

Again, I thought about all of the things that the rector had said to me, and all of the issues that he had pointed out. He had made some valid points. I knew that I didn't care for the institutional aspect of the church, that I didn't have any patience with its backwardness and its fear of growth and change, or for the politics, which should have no place in

Chapter 19

the spiritual realm. But the "people" part of the church—that was fantastic! That part of it made me feel like I was in heaven—to be able to serve them, be with them, and to share in life with them.

When you find yourself emotionally "nourished" by the people around you, celibacy becomes almost a non-issue; it just kind of fades into the background. Real connection is about relationships. When you have relationships—true relationships with people who love and nourish you—your emotional needs are taken care of. You don't have a driving need to go out and find a wife and get married or look for sex. At least I didn't. Your needs are being met in a fulfilling way. You become a part of these people's lives and a part of their family. It's comparable to having a family of your own because they become a family of your own. But instead of being limited in the number of relatives you have, it's more like having a global family network. And for me, that was just the neatest thing.

Because of these people, I wanted to become a priest. I wanted to minister to them, help them to grow, and help them to connect to the Divine Presence. That is the best gift I felt that I could give them. I believed that I could put the institutional aspect of the church to one side, and that it was a conflict that I could keep in balance. And for a long time I was able to do that. But in time my life became a balancing act—straddling two different worlds. And always, always, one of those worlds has to win. You can't straddle an emotional fence forever. It takes a toll on you, and eventually you're going to fall.

But for right now, I was sure that I could make it work. Maybe I could change the church—maybe I couldn't—but I could at least change my little corner of it. I made my decision. I would become a priest. I spent the rest of my time there designing the invitations to my ordination and the program; it was a little booklet that would be used during the Mass. I even did my own artwork and I thought it looked pretty darn good. (Even though, when a few of my smart-ass friends saw it, they complimented me on the "cartoons" that I had drawn.) I called my mom and my sister, and they helped me draw up the invitation list and the parish mailed the invitations for me. I also contacted the people who I wanted to participate in my Mass and had them save the date.

Decision made, I thanked my hostess and went back to the parish for a day, and then headed to my parent's house to spend a little time with them before the big event. They didn't say too much about my decision. I think they had resigned themselves to the fact that this was going to happen, and to say that they weren't overjoyed would be putting it mildly.

The night before my ordination we had the rehearsal, which is very similar to a wedding rehearsal. All of the key participants showed up (except for the bishop who didn't need to be there), and we went through the ceremony–where they'd each stand, when they were supposed to do their part, that kind of thing.

You usually have a "Master of Ceremony" in charge of the whole thing, and I had two of them sharing the responsibilities. One of them was my uncle from out of town who was a priest, and the other was a priest from my home diocese. They were trying to get everyone to cooperate and get through the dress rehearsal, but it was pretty much a losing battle.

Everyone there seemed to be in a party mood. There was more talking, laughing, and joking going on than rehearsing. This was especially so when a seminarian friend of mine decided to pretend that he was the bishop. He started doing the bishop's part in the ceremony, which for him consisted of swaggering all over the place and yelling out inane comments as he tried to imitate the bishop's voice and mannerisms. It kind of went downhill from there.

So we got through our poor imitation of a rehearsal and everyone headed out to dinner. After dinner I went home, but some of my friends—including my uncle, the priest—stayed out drinking until the wee hours of the morning.

My ordination day arrived and my brother drove me to the church. The ceremony was scheduled to start at ten o'clock. When I got there at about nine, the place was already filling up. Again, a huge crowd showed up and again, I tried to find a way to have as many of them as possible participate in the Mass. The rector of my graduate seminary, as well as the president of the theology school, the Director of Vocations, and my current pastor would all be co-celebrating the Mass with the bishop. I had friends who were deacons and priests from all three of my seminaries helping out. My friend, Dolores, who I had met in Assisi, would be doing one of the readings. My parents, brother, and sister would present gifts to me, the nuns from my parish would bring up the offertory gifts (the bread and wine to be consecrated), and everyone from candle bearer to usher were friends of mine.

For the music and singing portions of the Mass, I had a local church choir along with a children's choir from another city. A woman from a different church choir with a beautiful voice sang "The Ave Maria," and knocked it out of the park. It was like an extensive family reunion!

I headed to the dressing room to put on the garb that I would be wearing for the first part of the Mass. I had a brand new set of beautiful wheat-colored vestments that were given to me by a friend, an older woman who lived in the area. She was not only a local celebrity, but had a name that was nationally recognized, being the heiress to a nationally prominent business company. She was also an extremely religious woman and very involved in church affairs. Over the years she had donated large amounts of money not only to the church, but also to individual seminarians and priests. (Later on Pope Paul VI named her a "Princess of the Church" for her monetary donations.)

I had first met her when I was about sixteen and working in the restaurant of a local resort that she frequented. She would often come in with a good friend of hers who was a bishop from out of state. At dinner they would both invariably get quite drunk. I would have some great conversations with them while I was serving them, and when they were drunk they were quite an act.

The bishop would tell me to stop what I was doing and bow my head, which I would do, and amid peals of laughter, he would give me his "papal blessing"—several times in fact during each course of the meal! She would try to give me money, but I always said no. I thanked her for the gesture but never took her money. She later told me that I was the only seminarian who had ever refused to take money from her. Because of that, she said, she was proud of me, respected me, and told me that I had integrity.

When she first found out that I wanted to be a priest, she wanted me to go to the seminary in the city where her friend, the bishop lived. (It was actually her money that built the seminary and the theology school for that bishop's diocese.) She said that they had a place reserved for me, and that she would pay for all of my schooling. Again, I thanked her but declined the offer.

As an ordination gift, she gave me a beautiful set of vestments to wear. In her honor and during the part of the ceremony where I remove my deacon vestments and don my priestly vestments, I would use the chasuble (one of the vestments) that she gave me. And, of course, she was there for my ordination. I still have those vestments hanging in my closet.

So I'm in the dressing room, dressed all in black–shirt, pants, socks, and shoes. I put on the vestments provided by the church because during the ceremony I will exchange them for other ones–the chasuble from my friend and the stole from my deacon ordination.

The first thing that I put on is called the alb. It's a white cotton, neck-to-ankle covering with long sleeves that belts at the waist. In the very early days of the church, the priest would wear this as a covering to keep him clean. During the offertory portion of the Mass when the bread and wine to be consecrated are brought to the altar, people would also bring up gifts of food to the altar for the priest. This was a corporal offering of thanks to the priest for the spiritual "nourishment" that he was giving them. On a more practical note, they wanted to feed father, keep him alive and well, so that he could continue being their priest.

People would bring up all kinds of food, usual kinds of things like bread and cheese, but they also might bring unwashed vegetables straight from their fields, or freshly slaughtered animals—like chickens, dripping with blood. So father had to "cover up," so that he didn't get his clothing dirty and bloody. Thus, the alb was born.

After the alb I put on the stole, the white, scarf-like piece of clothing that goes around the neck. As a deacon, the stole is placed over the left shoulder and down the body to the right where it's pinned in place, and that is how I put it on to begin the ceremony. Once you're ordained a priest and given your priestly vestments, your new stole is placed squarely over the back of both shoulders and hangs down evenly in front, which is how I wore it to end the ceremony. The stole stands for "obedience" to the church. In the early church its function was for warmth. Those old stone cathedrals were cold and drafty places, so father stayed warm by putting a scarf around his neck. The stole has since become symbolic of ordained Roman Catholic priests.

After the stole comes the dalmatic, which is the deacon's smaller version of the priest's chasuble, which is a one piece affair with an opening for your head to slip through that hangs down to your ankles and is slit open on the sides. It symbolizes the "purity of Christ." Again, in the old days it was basically another layer of warmth for father to wear so that he didn't catch pneumonia in the cold church.

All of the clothing that a priest wears today had a very practical function in the old days. We no longer need to use the vestments to stay clean and warm, but we have kept them for the spiritual component attached to their use.

For those of you who are familiar with the Mass, you know that there is a point during the Mass when the priest "washes" his hands. In the old days, the priest did this to wash off the dirt and the blood that he got from handling the food gifts the people had brought him. He needed to continue with the Mass and consecrate the bread and the wine, and he couldn't do that with unclean hands. We have kept that act, but now it symbolizes the washing away of our sins—the cleansing of our iniquities.

Another thing that many of you may be familiar with is the use of incense during the Mass. Its function in the old days was twofold. Because the smoke from burning incense drifts upward, it was said that the smoke was carrying the prayers of the faithful up to heaven, up to God. Again, on a more practical note, it was a great way to mask the smell in the church. This was before the days of regular bathing and the use of deodorants, so a building with no air circulation that was packed with hundreds of dirty, sweaty bodies, could become a pretty rank smelling place. The incense helped to mitigate the smell, and the

Chapter 19

people's prayers were accompanied by an odor that they felt was more pleasing to God.

So I'm all dressed up and ready to go when I'm told that the bishop wants to see me. I go to his dressing room, knock on the door, and he tells me to come in. He's all dressed up in his finery, his bishop's ring shining and glinting in the light (later I'll have to tell you the ring story), and he's sitting in his bishop's chair. (This is a huge, really heavy piece of furniture, high backed with carved armrests and a red velvet cushion to sit on. It looks like a throne.) At the foot of his chair is a little matching footstool.

I go in and someone closes the door behind me. The bishop asks me to come in and sit down, and he uses my first name. I always know where I stand with him by how he addresses me. If all is well, he calls me by my first name. If all is less than well, he addresses me as "Father" and uses my last name. So far, so good. I sit down on the stool that he points to so that I'm sitting at his feet, much lower than he is so I have to crane my neck to look up at him. The feeling was akin to a little kid being called in to the principal's office.

The bishop says to me, "Well, son, (again, he uses my first name), you have a decision to make here." I look up at him and say, "Excuse me?" He repeats, "Yes, you have a decision. I need to ask you–do you want to get ordained?" I gave a little laugh and said, "Well, we're here, aren't we? A cast of thousands, people who've travelled from all over the world to be here." Then, on a more serious note I said, "If it is the will of the people that I be called to service, then I submit to that calling." That's how I answered him, which was in keeping with the early church, and was perfect theology, but imperfect in terms of our relationship because it went right over his head.

He said, "Well yes, but do you want to get ordained today?" So I repeated what I had already said, he again repeated what he had said, and we go on like that for about ten minutes, with him starting to get frustrated because we can't quite seem to connect on this issue. Then he said, "I have to tell you, those letters that I have received from people about you–I cannot even tell you how many–and because of them, I am happy to ordain you because people like you." He kind of chuckled and jokingly, or maybe not so jokingly said, "I don't know why!"

And then, more seriously, he said, "There's something about what you do for them. And it's interesting how they explain it. They all say, 'Oh, it's just him (here the bishop said my name), it's just his 'thing.' They talk about how you bring them closer to God, that you somehow connect with them in a way that makes them 'see' God, and that they become more spiritual and more faithful because of you. That's what has impressed me about ordaining you because they obviously love you, but it doesn't stop there. Their relationship with you makes them want to connect with God."

Again he asked, "So do you want to get ordained?"

I replied, "If it were just up to me, I would probably say no." (I think that was the voice of reason warring in my head making its last stand.) "But the people say that they want me to be their priest. And all I can say—and I'll quote St. Augustine, one of the founders of the church—'that it is my privilege to be a Christian alongside all of these people, and it is my burden that I accept the call to serve as their priest.' So yes, I will get ordained based on the call that I have received from the community."

At that, he said, "Oh, okay. Okay, let's do this."

We were running late. It was already about ten fifteen, and later I was told that quite a few of the people sitting in the church were wondering what the hell was going on between me and the bishop. They said, "Uh-oh, we don't know if he's going to go through with this thing. He got close, but we don't know if it's going to happen now." The bishop could have stopped it. He had the authority, and he could have said no, that he was not going to ordain me. He could have sent all of us packing, which is probably what he would have preferred to do. We already had a rocky relationship. But with all of the letters of support that I had gotten, there wasn't any way that he could justify not ordaining me—since personal dislike isn't considered a valid reason. But he didn't stop it, and I know that this was a decision that he eventually came to regret.

So I come out and everyone seems to breathe a huge sigh of relief (everyone except for my parents who still had a glimmer of hope in their eyes, which at that moment flickered out.) I could see some of my friends, looking a bit hung over, rolling their eyes at me as those of us who would be in the initial procession head to the back of the church, go outside, and line up in the proper order. They give the signal to ring the bells and Mass starts.

We process in following by the cross bearer, the candle bearers, the priest wafting the incense, the altar boys, the priests who will be concelebrating the Mass, and finally me and the bishop. Music is blaring, antiphons are being sung all to herald my "triumphant" entrance, and it was actually quite beautiful. When I get to the foot of the altar, I bow and then head to the front pew to sit with my family.

The bishop and everyone else take their places around the altar and begin the Mass, which for the first part of the ordination ceremony, is just a regular Mass. Then after the reading of the gospel by a deacon friend of mine, the bishop stands up to give his sermon, which is all about the ordination. The bishop then sits down and the ceremony connects from that point on to the actual ordination.

Chapter 19

At this point my uncle (the priest), who was looking pretty hung over himself and the other priest from the rehearsal, take the Ordination Book over to the bishop along with his mitre (bishop's hat) and his crozure (shepherd's staff). He had worn the mitre and carried the crozure when he processed in, but then took them off before starting the Mass. These, along with his ring, are symbols of his office as bishop. You remove the hat and staff for Mass so that you are at the altar as a priest—an "equal" to the people you are serving—not up there "lording" it over everyone. For the ordination part of the Mass he would be working from his role as bishop, so he needed to use the symbols of his office.

The bishop then stands up and says, "Let he who is a candidate to be called to Orders be called," and he calls my name.

I get up from my pew and go and stand at the foot of the altar, and I say, "I'm present." The bishop then asks the representative of the community that has called this man to service to come forward, and a parishioner from my current parish comes up and reads a letter from the parishioners about why they want me to be their priest. After reading this very nice letter, he gives some personal anecdotes about me—all very warm and thoughtful and funny—and he had the congregation smiling and laughing.

The bishop then takes over again, telling the congregation that I am being presented to the church for ordination into the "Order of Presbyters." Presbyter, a word meaning Elder, is a priest's official title in the church. I am becoming an Elder Prayer Leader. The consent of the people is required for the candidate to be ordained, so the bishop asks everyone present to express their agreement by applauding. This could be a tense moment because if all you get from the congregation is a polite, half-hearted round of applause, it could be a little embarrassing. But suddenly the church erupts with sound as everyone starts applauding and hooting and yelling. Boy, was I grinning! The bishop then continues with explaining to both myself and the people the responsibilities of the priesthood and all that it entails.

When he's done with that, he begins what is called the "examination" to see if the candidate is "worthy" of ordination. Basically, he asks three questions of me to which I'm supposed to respond, "I do" (like wedding vows). So he joins me at the front of the altar where I'm standing, and I kneel in front of him and he grasps both of my hands in his to begin the examination. This part of the ceremony has its roots in the Middle Ages and copies the loyalty oath that was required by a king of his princes and knights.

I remember that the first question was asking if I was ready to assume the responsibilities of priestly ministry, to which I gave the appropriate answer. I can't remember what the second question was, but

I answered that one appropriately also. But it was the third question that caused an unintentional problem. He said, "Do you promise me, as your bishop and my successors, obedience and respect?" Of course, everyone had been listening intently up to this point, and the church is so quiet that you could hear a pin drop.

Well, I was nervous and by this time my mouth had gotten really, really dry. What came out of my mouth when I attempted to answer him was this forlorn, excruciating noise. I said, "I do," but it sounded like the answer was being tortured out of me, more like the screeching of a wounded cat or something out of *The Pit and the Pendulum*, by Edgar Allen Poe. In the silence of the church, I hear these little snorts and snickers from all over the place. My friends thought that I was joking around, but I wasn't—mortified would be more like it.

The bishop kind of tugs on my hands and looks me in the eye like– are you serious? And in a really croaky whisper so that no one else can hear, I tell him that I'm sorry, that my mouth is really dry. (Looking back on it, that tortured response was almost prophetic in terms of the rest of my ministry.) But I do promise him my respect and obedience, and he then invites the congregation to join him in praying for me.

After that I prostrate myself on the floor (also based on the rite of loyalty from the Middle Ages). I lie flat on the floor, face down, with my arms out to my sides. (At this point the bishop might have been hoping that I would turn blue down there from lack of oxygen!) The "Litany of the Saints" is sung, invoking the presence and prayers of all of the saints, named and unnamed, and the chanting goes on for about fifteen minutes. This concludes with the bishop asking the Holy Spirit to bless the one to be ordained. I was then lifted up off the floor by a few of the priests who were present, and again went up to the front of the altar and again knelt down.

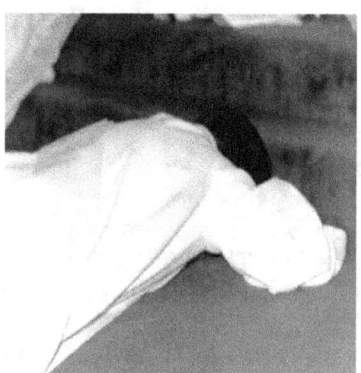

*Me Lying Prostrate
During Ordination Ritual*

In total silence so that the Holy Spirit can work through him, the bishop comes over to me and lays his hands upon my head, and that is the actual moment when ordination is conferred. The second before the laying on of hands, I was just a regular human being. The next second I am filled with grace and have become a priest, never again to go back to the "lay" state. I've been asked by people if I felt any differently at that moment. Truthfully, no. Still nervous, still really dry, but other than that, no.

After the bishop performs the "laying on of hands," all of the other priests present and only those who are ordained priests wearing the symbol of their priestly office (the stole), approach me and they too lay their hands upon my head which expresses their sharing in the priesthood with me. As the priests leave me, they all walk away with their left hands over their hearts and with their right hands extended upwards, pointing up to heaven. This symbolizes their part in ordaining me to the priesthood, that their actions—together with the bishop's—express our shared responsibility of being pastors unto the people.

While all of this was happening, the "Song of Propheta" (the Prophet) is being sung in the background by the children's choir in honor of my deceased grandparents. When this is finished, the bishop says the prayer of consecration and asks the congregation to affirm what has been done by saying "amen," which they do.

Then my mom, dad, sister, and brother bring up my stole and my new chasuble and present them to me. I removed my deacon's stole and dalmatic and they help me put on my priest's stole and chasuble. So I'm invested with the vestments of the priesthood. My family goes back to their seats, and I again kneel in front of the bishop for the anointing. He anoints my hands with chrism (holy oil), because now my hands will be used to perform the holy rite of consecration, changing the bread and wine into the body and blood of Christ.

After that comes the offertory gifts, and as part of that my parents bring up the paten (the platter which will hold the bread) and the chalice (which will hold the wine), both of which were bought by my parents as gifts for me. (Traditionally these are the gifts that the soon-to-be priest is given by his parents.) They give them to the bishop to present to me along with a Book of Gospels that he has for me. As he gives me the book, he says, "Receive this Book of Gospels. Believe what you read, preach what you believe, and practice what you preach." As he gives me the chalice and paten, he says, "Use these vessels to perform the holy rites of Jesus." I then hand everything to one of the deacons to place on the altar.

The next part of the Mass is the sign of peace. The bishop and all of the other priests and deacons share the sign of peace with me, and then I go and do the same with my family. It seemed like just about everybody in the church then came up to give me a big smile, a hug or a handshake and to say "Congratulations" along with their "Peace be with you."

The rest of the Mass happens. I go up to the altar to join the bishop and the other priests for the consecration, and for the first time, I share the consecratory words over the bread and wine with the bishop. When it's time for communion, there are lots of us there at the altar to give it to the throng of people lining up. But it seems that everyone wants to take communion from the "new priest," so my line is really long, but we finally get through it. The Mass winds down with a recessional song, and we all process out where I'm swarmed by people, again with hugs and kisses and congratulations.

Mass was over. I was now an ordained Roman Catholic priest.

Chapter 20

Signs of Wonders

After the ordination Mass they held a reception for me in the parish hall. Everyone showed up and the place was bursting at the seams with people eating and talking and just having a good time. A lot of people gave me gifts—mostly money—but also religious items like vestments that I could wear and chalices to use during the consecration at the Mass. As the reception wound down and my various friends left, they all said that they'd see me in the morning. The next day was Sunday, and I would be doing my first Mass as a Roman Catholic priest at my home parish church.

That evening my parents had a small gathering at their house for our relatives and some close friends. Nothing fancy, just drinks and finger foods. Everyone was tired out from the day's activities and just wanted to kick back and relax. I remember that my mom had the lights on the dimmer switch, lighted candles scattered around the rooms, and a fire going in the fireplace, so the mood was pretty mellow. Everyone was just kind of lounging around, sipping drinks, nibbling food, and talking quietly. As family and friends passed me (or stumbled over me in the dark!), they would give me a little pat on the arm or an affectionate punch and say things like "good job," or "you did good today," along with a lot of approving smiles and warm hugs and kisses.

But I will always remember that night because of an unsettling encounter that I had. An old friend of mine dropped in to visit and give me a gift. We had been in the diocesan seminary together and he had been one of the rector's "golden boys"—but in a good way because he was the only one of them who actually deserved the title. He was just the nicest guy, loved by everybody, and was the most popular guy in school. He had a charismatic personality and his warmth and goodness just drew people to him. He was funnier than hell and was always playing pranks and getting into mischief, but it was always the funny kind of stuff, stuff that made people laugh, and he never got into trouble over any it.

It was predicted that he would become the perfect priest and go far in terms of the church hierarchy, get to the top of that priest ladder in record time, and the sky would be the limit for him. Who knows—he might have even become the first American pope. That's how well thought of he was by everyone. He had always known that he wanted to be a priest and had entered the minor seminary when he was around twelve or thirteen years old. He had been in the Franciscan seminary, had gone through his postulancy, and had even taken his first set of vows. And then he left. This stunned everyone.

So he stops by and we find a little corner off by ourselves, and he turns to me and says, "Do you really realize what you've done? Do you really think that you can do this?" I looked at him in surprise because that wasn't what I had expected him to say. He was so profoundly serious when he said this and he looked so sad. It was surreal—the lights were dim, shadows were dancing all around us, and you could hear the soft tinkle of laughter in the background. And here he was, like the devil's advocate, asking me this. I said, "Um, I don't know. I think so. (Profound response on my part.) I think I'm just going to take it one step at a time, and I'm going to try to do this."

He shook his head and said, "It's funny, ya know? 'Cause I'm the one who was supposed to do this. I'm the one who was supposed to become a priest. I was the 'golden boy.' And you? Everybody said, 'Who, him? Are you kidding? He's always in trouble, with his long hair and always mouthing off, always challenging things, always getting yelled at.' Never in anybody's mind were you the kind of person who would do this. It just doesn't fit. Yet here you are. But me—I couldn't do it. That's why I left. I just couldn't do this anymore."

I didn't know what to say to him after that. It was just the oddest conversation. It almost felt like a portent of disaster. He handed me my gift; it was a little frame with a few lines written on it that he had done in calligraphy. It said "When a person discovers themselves it's as if mankind has discovered fire for the second time," a famous quote of Teilhard de Chardin. He was a Jesuit priest and one of my favorite scientists/ philosophers, and in the diocesan seminary I would often get into trouble for quoting him because the Catholic Church blacklisted him for his views. I thanked my friend for his gift, walked him out to his car in the darkness of the night, and he drove off.

A few years later he was living out on the west coast and jumped off of a bridge and killed himself. He had discovered that he had AIDS, and that, combined with having to admit to everyone that he was gay, was too much for him to bear. No one had any idea that he was gay, he never acted any differently than anyone else, wasn't effeminate in any way, and was just a regular guy. But he couldn't face people knowing this about him.

So this funny, loving, and talented man killed himself so that he wouldn't have to face the contempt in people's eyes or the ravages of this awful disease. I still mourn his death, and I will never forget the words he said to me that night, "Are you really sure that you can do this?" It was as if he gave voice to a question resounding from the depths of my identity, a question that he could hear but that I, as yet, could not.

I would say my first Mass as a priest tomorrow, stay at my parents' place for another day or two, and then head off on a vacation. Nothing extravagant, just visiting some relatives who lived in warmer climes. I would also attend a few priest ordinations of some of my classmates. After that I would head back to the same parish where I had been doing my internship, as that was the parish I was now assigned to as a priest. The bishop had made the announcement at the ordination Mass—and it didn't come as any big surprise because that's how it's usually done—that your first assignment would be in the same place where you had been doing your diaconate internship.

My first Mass went off without a hitch. Just about everyone who had been at my ordination showed up. Since my home parish church is a small one, it was standing room only. Again, I involved all of my friends in it and thankfully was less nervous than I had been the day before. My voice remained strong and steady, and this time I didn't elicit any snickers! There was another reception for me after that, and my mom, my relatives, and many of the parish ladies graciously did all of the cooking for it. Again, we all had a good time. I got to say goodbye to everyone since most of them had to head back home the next day either to work, or for the seminarians, to get back to school.

I took a month off for my vacation and then headed back to the parish. When I got there, the secretary told me that Father Tobias was AWOL. Again. She said that he had called and asked if "Deke" was there, and she said that she answered him by saying "Who?" And he told her, "You know, 'Deke,' my assistant." She then told him yes, "Father" had just arrived, but that I was now a priest, which of course he already knew. So he told her to take care of me, show me the ropes (as if I didn't already know them inside and out), and that he'd try to be back by the weekend. She was rolling her eyes as she was relaying this to me.

So I hit the ground running. I resumed all of the activities that I had been doing before, but now as a priest, I could do even more. Yikes! Back to my usual routine—up at dawn, busy every moment of the day, crawling into bed well past midnight, and feeling totally exhausted. But really, this was my own doing. Remember that summer pastoral program that I went through where they told me that I was too much of a "doer" and had to learn to just "be?" Well, screw that—I had things to do! I was going to bring these parishioners an experience of God heretofore unknown in the history of humankind!

I showed up with my Superman cape on over my cassock, the ordination oil still wet on the palms of my hands, and was ready to turn the world on its head and take no prisoners in the process! That really is the attitude that I started out with. One could look at that and say—wow, that's a positive attitude, or whoa, this guy's either really full of himself, or maybe, full of God? I think it was probably a combination of all of those things.

The pastor eventually found his way back to us, and I think it was around this time that he had another one of his heart attacks. He'd had them before, had already had a bunch of tests done, and was on heart medication. This seemed to be a minor one, and he didn't take it very seriously. I think he only took off for a few days to rest and then was back at work.

One of the first things that he did after I got back from my ordination was to finally reopen the Catholic elementary school. The sisters who were running the school asked me to teach the physical education and health classes. I wasn't a certified teacher so officially I was called their "assistant." Of course, I told them that I would do it, so I ended up teaching both of those classes. In the kids' health classes I was able to talk to the older kids about their sexuality, and to all of the kids about ways to keep themselves safe, and about things like "good" touch and "bad" touch.

Around that time we had started hearing rumblings about incidents of pedophilia and priests that occurred in different parts of the country. It seemed to be just a few instances that had happened, and as yet there wasn't much being said about it in the mainstream news. But I was keeping my ears open, and I used the health classes to make the kids more aware of what was acceptable behavior and of what was unacceptable. I also addressed it in my sermons, which was unheard of back then (and I think even less so today), especially by one of their own priests.

As a priest, I felt that one of the most important things that I could do was to share with my parishioners all of the exciting theology that I had learned, to "grow" them in their faith and in their relationship to the Divine, and to talk to them like the adults that they were, not like children or sheep. The church here hadn't even made it to the Middle Ages yet; it was still in the Dark Ages. The mindset was—I'm the priest, I tell you what to do, you do it, and you'll get to heaven. That's all you need to know. (I was still trying to figure out where in the Bible Jesus said that.)

Chapter 20

Honestly, knowing that Jesus didn't say that, and knowing that it was just power and control bullshit, I would tell my parishioners, "Question everything that's being told to you. Research it. Masticate it. Chew on it. Digest it. If it fits—good! If it doesn't fit—find a new way. *You* are the church. The church as an institution needs to take guidance from *your* experience because your experience is valid." Of course, this was the complete opposite of anything they had ever heard in the past. It got me reported to the bishop more than a few times, but he could never point to anything I said as being wrong theologically. It was just—different. I was just—different.

I tried to preach whenever possible–a sermon for any occasion and then some! When I said the weekday Masses, I would read the gospel and then give a sermon about it. I remember Father Tobias asking me why I was doing that because normally you don't preach at the weekday services. These are typically shorter services because in the morning people need to get to work, and in the evening they want to get home and eat dinner. Because there's no collection plate passed around during the weekday Masses, most priests don't want to spend much time on them because it's not going to make them any money. And no, I'm not being sarcastic here; I'm just telling you what the priests say to each other behind closed doors.

I told father that coming to Mass just to "eat" Jesus and run wasn't good theology. I said that we needed to show people how to incorporate the life that Jesus led, to make it real for them, and make it alive for them. Father would just roll his eyes at me and say, "Okay, St. John Chrysostom."

Sometimes, in my boundless enthusiasm, I would get to the church early for my services and I would greet people as they were coming in. I would say good morning, shake their hands, ask them how their morning was going, and welcome them in. I remember Father Tobias coming up to me one day and telling me that he had heard that I was doing this, that I was even kissing babies, and he asked me what the hell I thought I was doing–running for office or something? I told him no, I wasn't running for office and I wasn't kissing the babies, I was blessing them. And for me, this was a way to show people that I was "of" them and not "above" them. These people were the church, and I was their servant. Again, this was early church theology that was no longer being practiced.

Humorously enough, my parishioners actually did ask me to run for office! When I preached, I brought up a lot of social issues—not just global issues—but things that hit closer to home. If there were things in the community that needed attention, anything from local roads needing repairs to social services not being effective, I would bring them up and ask what was being done to address these issues. I had a captive audience, and I did take advantage of that because more often than not, I would have the mayor sitting in one pew, the Transportation Department manager in another, a legislator in yet another. I would look them in the eye and ask them what they were going to do to fix the problems and to get people—the people they were supposed to be serving—the help that they needed.

I also spent a lot of time helping people get the medical care they needed. We were in a rural area and didn't have the specialists and sophisticated medical equipment found in the bigger cities. Even routine medical care was sometimes not the best. There were some good doctors here and we did have a good hospital, but we had a few medical practitioners who had gotten kicked out of the bigger cities due to medical mistakes that slunk to our part of the state and wreaked their havoc on us. Some of my parishioners, especially the elderly, were overwhelmed by the medical system so I helped out by calling the medical specialists for them, setting up the appointments, and coordinating as much of the process as I could.

I would also get local dentists to provide dental care and braces for some of the poorer kids for free. I would have the church donate a third of the cost to the dentist's favorite charity, and I would raise another third for charity with the dentist covering the rest of it.

Because of my involvement in those areas, some of the parishioners approached me and said that an opening in the city council was coming up, and that they wanted to put my name on the ballot as a candidate. They said that if I agreed to run for office, they would take care of campaigning for me. They felt that I had a good chance of being elected, as I had become pretty popular among both the Catholics and non-Catholics in town. I told them, well, the Roman Catholic Church did write the book on political intrigue!

I gave it some serious thought, and found it appealing because I would then be in a position where I could help people with secular problems, influencing social institutions, as well as with spiritual problems. And campaigning sounded like it could be fun—talking to people, shaking hands, and actually kissing the babies! In the seventies there were a lot of socially active clergy and quite a few of them actually were in politics—some even being members of Congress. The parishioners said, "Hey Father, the city council today, and the House of Representatives tomorrow!"

So I decided that I would do it, and wouldn't you just know it, right at that time the pope—I believe it was John Paul II—sent out a letter saying that the clergy could no longer be involved in politics or hold political offices. This caused a bit of an uproar across the land, and I remember hearing about a number of priests and nuns who defied his edict and eventually were kicked out of the church. So regretfully, I declined, as I was still just beginning to learn how to be a priest.

I had mentioned before that in many parishes the pastor acted like the king with his assistant, be he deacon or priest, not having any authority, and being treated like crap. That wasn't Father Tobias's style, and I was grateful to him for treating me like an equal. We might not always agree on things, but we respected each other and found ways to work out our differences so that we always presented a united front to the parishioners. Because I was younger and less experienced, some of the parishioners thought that I would be a "pushover" and that they could circumvent Father Tobias through me.

I remember a few times when parishioners would come to the parish office to talk about problems. After father welcomed them in, they would tell him that they didn't want to talk to him, they wanted to talk to the "nice" priest. From my office I would hear father yell, "Hey, Deke, someone here to see you," and I would take the person to my office, sit down with them, and after a few minutes when they realized that they weren't going to circumvent anything with me, they'd abruptly stand up and say that they changed their minds and would rather talk to Father Tobias.

Then it would be my turn to yell, "Hey, Father Tobias, they've changed their minds; now they want to talk to you instead." Sometimes it was hard to keep a straight face when this happened!

Father thanked me for not making it a popularity contest between the two of us, and for not letting the parishioners divide us. He cared for each and every person in his parish and treated everyone with respect. For him the goal was to always do what was best for the parish. It was kind of funny because he was very conservative and I was a radical, yet we were always able to meet in the middle, to collaborate, and make the best decisions for the parishioners.

Some of you might remember the Charismatic Movement that sprang up in the Catholic Church in the seventies, which I think was also called the Holy Spirit Pentecostal Movement. I think that every Catholic parish in the country suddenly found itself being invaded by this group of religious fanatics who were being "slain" in the Spirit. They would be "visited" by the Holy Spirit, talk in "tongues," and preach that everyone needed a second baptism. When the movement started in our parish, I remember father pulling me aside one day and saying, "Oh God, you're not one of those crazy Pentecostals, are you?"

I said, "Are you kidding?" and assured him that I was not a Charismaniac and he breathed a sigh of relief. As it turned out, we had quite a run in with them.

From the pulpit we both preached against the excesses and abuses that this movement was generating. This group of people were hearing the Holy Spirit "talk" to them, which in reality for most of them, was nothing more than their own dysfunction, their own voices that were being projected onto others and telling others how they should live their lives. For the most part, they seemed kind of off the wall but harmless until it was all brought to a head when a tragic accident happened in the parish.

We didn't get much rain in this part of the state, but one weekend we had terrible thunderstorms with days of non-stop rain. There was an old wooden bridge right outside of town, and it was late on a Sunday evening when one of our parishioners, a young high school girl, crossed the bridge in her car and the bridge, weakened by the rain, collapsed and killed her. The Pentecostal parishioners went to the girl's home to comfort her mother, but they also told her mom that the "Spirit" had spoken to them, telling them that her daughter had been having premarital sex with a local boy and that's why she died.

When father and I heard about this, we both went through the roof. We knew that we needed to talk to this group, so we asked them to come to the parish office to meet with the two of us. I asked father if I could handle it and he said that I could. Of the two of us, I became the more vehement in reigning in the tendencies of these people whom I saw as using this as their own personal emotional escape from the hardships of day-to-day living.

So they came to our meeting, and I was so upset, and so angry that my words were singeing the hair right off their heads. (I've heard that the people in this parish still talk about the confrontation that father and I had with them at that meeting.) Basically, I told them that they were not only acting crazy, but that they *were* crazy. I said that this bullshit wasn't Jesus, it wasn't the Spirit, it wasn't even the devil—it was their own mental illness that was coming out. (Though I hardly knew real mental illness from ordinary dysfunction, I recognized that it seemed to fit.) And that they needed to take care of their own emotional problems that they were projecting onto others, instead of covering it up with this "pious" crap they were spouting.

I told them that this was not what our faith was all about, that it never had been, that it was not about to become that now, and that we would not have their craziness in our church. And that if they couldn't get their act together, we didn't want them in our church—period. We had been letting them use one of the parish meeting rooms in which to hold their "prayer" meetings, and I told them that from now on, either Father Tobias or I would be at every one of their meetings. I remember turning to father at that point and saying, "Right, Father?" And he replied, "Yes, sir!" which I think must have been a first for him because no one ever, ever spoke for father like I just had. But we were both committed to making sure that this insanity stopped here.

What I found amazing, and slightly disturbing, was that they accepted my chastising because they said that the Holy Spirit had spoken to them and had told them that I too was a born-again Christian, and because of that they recognized me as an authentic authority. (Uh-huh). Whatever . . . as long as they listened and did as we asked.

So that's what we did, and from then on one of us was always present at their meetings. I don't know about Father Tobias, but when I was at one of their meetings and heard something that I thought was nuts, I would stand up and tell them that—point blank. What ended up happening was that a number of them actually left our church because they were upset about the way they were being held accountable for what they were doing. That was fine with us since we didn't want them there anyway. I made it a point to contact the pastors of neighboring parishes, both Catholic and Protestant, letting them know what had happened with this group. I told the pastors that if these people showed up looking for new venues from which to operate, to be very careful and very discerning when they interacted with them.

Something else that sprang from that incident was that a few of these upset members reported me to the bishop and complained to him about what had transpired at our meeting. The bishop forwarded their complaint to the priest at the diocesan office who headed the Office of the Pentecostals. This priest, who was himself Pentecostal, called me to tell me that a complaint had been filed against me by some of the parishioners, and he wanted to know what was going on.

Being young, brash at times (I was still working on that), and still angry, told him that if he supported this crazy, judgmental stuff in the name of Jesus, then he wasn't welcome here either—and he could quote me to the bishop on that. But once we started talking, he sounded like a reasonable guy and our phone call went well. He did end up coming to the parish to speak to the parishioners. He turned out to be fairly level-headed, a good guy, not too crazy, full of the "Spirit" in a sound, spiritual way, and he told the parishioners that he fully agreed with me and Father Tobias. He told them that they had to be very careful in discerning the "Spirit" to make sure that it really was "of God," and not just "of themselves." I think the Charismatic movement ran its course and then kind of fizzled out.

And somehow—don't ask me how—after that encounter I ended up with the reputation of being the local "Discerner of Spirits," a "real authority" in that area for not only the parish but also in advising the diocese in these kinds of matters, which amazingly, they did ask me to do on several occasions. All I had done was to yell at this crazy group of people, and now I was an authority on the matter. Oh well. All that ended up doing was bringing me more work.

I had said that I started out in this job with my Superman cape on. Well, my cape was starting to get frayed around the edges. I was so busy doing things that I was always exhausted, and I was beginning to wonder what good all of my "doing" was actually doing. I would look out at the parish and wonder—is anyone changing? I mean, really changing? I was a whirlwind of activity, busy from morning until night, trying to bring people an experience of God—but is that what they were getting? Were they getting an experience of God—or an experience of me? My attitude at that time was that it was my responsibility to get my parishioners to heaven. That I, and I alone, was charged with this sacred duty, and at day's end, Jesus would pat me on the back and say, "Well done, good and faithful servant." Talk about pride . . . .

The model that we were taught in the seminary was that as priests, we knew what was best for everyone, we had to tell everyone what to do in order to attain heaven, and that they couldn't do it without us. While I certainly didn't believe that or agree with that model, I still felt that it was my responsibility to do the work, and still used that model in a modified way. I was constantly presenting all of the stuff I had learned to my parishioners, exposing them to the theology that I found so inspiring, wanting them to be inspired too, and hoping that they would eventually "get it."

But in reality, I realized that I had set it up so that I did everything. They didn't have to do anything on their own, they just had to do what I told them, and by golly they'd get to heaven. They could just ride there on my vestments, so to speak. I wasn't allowing them to develop their own connection, and didn't give them the chance to do it their way. And that was a disservice to all of us. I realized that I had to change my attitude and my approach because I wasn't responsible for getting them to heaven—they were.

And then I had a dream. I went to bed one night, exhausted as usual, and dreamt that I was wrestling with someone and we wrestled all night long. I was so exhausted from it—just totally worn out—because this went on all night. I finally was able to get a good hold on the other person, and I remember saying "gotcha!" and as soon as I said that, the person that I was wrestling with disappeared. I was suddenly alone, and at that moment I heard a voice say to me, "I don't need you to *do* anything for me. I need you to *be* someone for me."

Then I woke up. It was daybreak and I was still exhausted physically. But mentally and emotionally, I felt as if I had one of those "aha" moments (interestingly) in my sleep. It was pretty clear to me that

Chapter 20

I had been wrestling with myself all night long, wrestling with my attitude that wasn't working. I felt that it was the voice of Jesus talking to me, telling me to leave his people alone, and to back off because I was driving them and myself nuts! And that it was time to stop "doing" and start "being." If you don't learn your lesson the first time around, God—or the universe or your unconscious—keeps at you until you do by presenting the same issues over and over again in different ways and circumstances.

So that's what I did. I backed off. I still did all of my priestly duties but stopped running from thing to thing to thing, thinking that if I didn't attend this meeting or that one, it would all fall apart. It didn't. I had to stop thinking that if I wasn't there twenty-four seven to shepherd my parishioners that they would stray from the path. They didn't. I had to let people take responsibility for their own growth, to let them "become" in their own way, not in mine. I needed to let go. I decided to stop telling people what to do unless they specifically asked me. When they needed me, I was still there for them. But now I was going to "be" for them, not "do" for them.

For each of us on our journey towards the Divine, the most important thing is just being ourselves—our unique, one-of-a-kind—selves. Being authentic, walking our path with love, honesty, and integrity; doing no harm to anyone. This is where greatness lies for each of us, whether you're a priest or a homeless person or the President of the United States. Not in how many meetings you've gone to, but in the example that you are for others.

Basically, I was learning to stop and "smell the roses." Because of my personality, that's not easy for me to do and it's something that I still work on to this day. But it brought me a peace that I didn't have before, and I'm sure it brought some peace to my parishioners by not having me in their faces all of the time! I was still busy but the exhaustion was gone. You can be a witness to Jesus in the simple act of having a cup of coffee with a parishioner, not by lecturing them while you're drinking your java together, but just by being there with them and for them—of which I now had time to do.

I still loved my preaching. That was something I'd never stop doing, and probably would've preached twenty-four seven if they had let me, which wisely they did not! I was told that when I got up to the podium and started speaking, even the babies would stop fussing. (A friend of mine insists that it's because my voice could put anyone to sleep!) I remember the church secretary commenting about it once to me. She said that when I started preaching, it got downright spooky! She said that it got so quiet in the church that you could hear a pin drop, that I had everyone mesmerized and eating out of the palm of my hand, and that it was a good thing that I was on the side of "good" because otherwise I could have wreaked a lot of havoc!

Although she was kidding with me about it, I remember a meeting I had with the bishop when he had called me in on the carpet about something or another. I can't remember exactly what it was about, but during our conversation the bishop made a comment to me about the power that priests had over their parishioners. I put in my two cents worth, and ended up in the doghouse with him yet again because I told him that I felt that most priests abused that power. Whatever power they had should be used as a positive force in people's lives, to help them grow and to empower them, rather than using it as a way to "lord" it over them, manipulate them and keep them in line, which is what I believed that most priests did—used this power not for God but for themselves. The bishop didn't like that comment, but then he and I didn't see eye to eye on very many things.

With my new attitude of "being" rather than "doing," I think I actually ended up spending more time than ever with my parishioners, sharing more in their everyday lives, and felt even closer to them than I had before. The comment that I remember most from that time was the parishioners constantly telling me that I was "one of them." They liked and respected Father Tobias, they included him in their lives, but there was still a feeling on their part that his priesthood kept him in a place that was just a bit out of their reach.

They had no such qualms with me, maybe because in my sermons I talked about how we had to end that divide between "us" and "them," between the laity and the clergy, and that as priests we needed not to be above them, but as one with them on this journey towards the Divine. And that as priests we were no more special than they were, but all equally special in the eyes of God.

And not only did I preach it, I also lived it. They hardly ever saw me wearing clerical garb. They usually called me by my first name rather than "Father," but saw me as their priest, as one of their own. They gave me respect, but they also gave me their friendship and their love. I felt that they gave me far more than I ever gave them.

I remember one day when the sisters told me that they were concerned that Father Tobias suddenly seemed to be taking off from the parish more and more often, leaving me on my own. What they didn't know was the reason for that. Father and I had a decent working relationship and a decent personal one, but it was a tenuous thing. There is so much dysfunction in the church and so much dysfunction in its relationships that nothing can be taken at face value. Intrigue is the name of the game, and when father dabbled in it, it backfired on all of us.

Chapter 20

Father Tobias had a good friend, a fellow priest, who had been on a leave of absence but now wanted to re-enter ministry. Because they were such close friends, father wanted him to come and work with him in this parish. The problem was . . . me. I was already there as father's assistant and father couldn't justify having three full-time priests. So the obvious solution was to get rid of me, which is what he set out to do.

What Father Tobias told me was that my talents were being wasted in parish work, that I was "too intellectual" for this kind of work, and that he was going to call the personnel board and recommend me for the diplomatic corps, which currently had advertised an opening.

The Diplomatic Corps trains you as a diplomat and then you are sent to a foreign country as an Ambassador of the Vatican. You first have to be a bishop to be a diplomat. If you pass the training in Rome, you are then ordained a bishop before assuming your position. I thought—wow—sure, that sounds pretty exciting. Who wouldn't love a chance to do something so exciting?

What Father Tobias told the bishop, however, was a little different. He did tell him that I was wasting my time in parish work, that I was too intellectual to be stuck in a parish, and that my talents lay elsewhere. But, since he really wanted me out of there and wanted to cover all of his bases, he also told the bishop that I wasn't very good at parish work, so get me out of there and put in his friend, who was good at parish work and whom he could help in his readjustment to ministry.

Well, we all know that the bishop works in mysterious ways. I think he must have only heard the part where Father Tobias said that I wasn't any good at parish work, and if I wasn't good at something as simple as parish work, how could I handle something as complex as being a diplomat? And if I screwed up, it would be a black mark against the bishop. So he said no; I was staying where I was.

Father Tobias's friend was sent elsewhere, I had a black mark on my record saying that I wasn't any good at parish work, and Father Tobias became very angry and bitter that his plan didn't work out. So he started drinking more than ever and leaving the parish so often that weeks could go by before we saw his face again. He ended up having more and more severe heart problems resulting in another heart attack, and our relationship was never quite the same after that.

So, you might be asking, why didn't Father Tobias just be honest and upfront with the bishop about what he wanted? Tell him that he really wanted his good friend here with him, that he thought that he could really help him to ease back into ministry, that maybe they could find something else for me to do, and that among all of us we could find a way to work things out?

Because priests in this diocese couldn't be honest; it was too dangerous; if you were honest, you were vulnerable. If you told the bishop your real feelings, he could hold them against you and it would give him even more power over you. And there was no such thing as confidentiality around here. Anything that you told the bishop would be blabbed to his friends, so that all of a sudden everyone knows your innermost thoughts and feelings. It could (and would) come back to haunt you, and probably hinder your future prospects in moving up that ladder. That's the kind of atmosphere that surrounded priests in this diocese. So as a defense, they would lie and scheme and engage in intrigue, and get angry and bitter. Did all priests act like this? No. Did most priests? Yes.

As I said, father had a second heart attack around this time, which didn't slow down his hard living one bit. When he wasn't around, there wasn't anything that we could do other than run the parish as best we could. I became extremely close to the parish secretary, as most of the time it was usually she and I running the place. She was a hard worker, and every now and then, as a way of thanking her for all that she did, I would tell her right before her lunch break to take the rest of the afternoon off. She'd protest, say that she couldn't, that she had too much work to do, but I'd tell her that I would stick around, answer the phones, and take care of anything that popped up, and that she should just go and enjoy herself and take a little break from everything.

Sometimes when things were really crazy around the office and no one could leave, I'd go and get ice cream cones for everyone—myself, the secretary, the finance officer, and the sisters—and we'd all take a short breather during the busy day. Sometimes that's all we needed to do to recharge our batteries. Whatever we did, we always ended up having a lot of fun together.

I had mentioned that when I first stopped in at the parish on my way home from grad school that I had met a young man who was the pastor's "particular" friend. I didn't know that at the time; it was something that I found out later through the grapevine. The pastor was very discreet, and there was never anything untoward happening that I was aware of, but gossip among priests is an art form. Nothing is secret or sacred. Anyway, this young man, who seemed to be a nice guy, was one of the professional staff who worked at the parish. Father also had several men help with keeping the physical aspect of the church and offices and rectory running. It was a big complex and there was certainly enough work to go around.

One day I came back to the rectory early because a meeting had been cancelled. When I walked into the living room, I saw this young man pinned down on the floor with two of the handymen wrestling with him. Initially I thought that they had just been horsing around, but it looked to me as if they had been trying to pull the guy's pants down. He had a panicky look in his eyes and when he saw me he said, "Help me." So I stepped in, told the two guys to break it up and get back to work, which they did, albeit with smirks on their faces. Father's friend got up and thanked me, didn't say anything else, and then left.

I don't know what was going on, whether it was horseplay that got out of hand or something else, but the vibe that I picked up was definitely a sexual one. The guy never said anything to me about it after that, but I did mention it to father when he came back from one of his jaunts. He listened when I recounted the incident and thanked me for telling him, but we never spoke of it again.

I remember one unexplainable thing that happened around that time. Father Tobias had been gone for about two weeks—out drinking and gallivanting with his friends—when he called me at the rectory and told me to cover the weekend Masses for a friend of his who was the pastor at a church in a different city. I told him okay, I could do that, but then someone else would have to cover the weekend Masses at our parish. Father said that he would find someone to take care of our parish, and to just make sure that I was at his friend's parish in time for the evening Mass on Saturday as well as for all the Masses there on Sunday.

Okay, if that's what he wanted me to do, he was calling the shots. So I headed down to that parish, got there and did the Saturday Mass. Late that night, I got a call from one of the local hospitals saying that they had a family that belonged to this parish and that they were asking for a priest. Their son had taken a turn for the worse and was dying, and being Catholic, they wanted a priest to come.

I went to the hospital and met with the family who told me that the doctors had told them to say their goodbyes to their son, and to call their minister or priest. Their son was a young boy, maybe about ten years old, and I don't think that I asked what was wrong with him. I really can't remember now, though I think I might have heard that it was some type of cancer, maybe a brain tumor, but I'm not really sure. But he did look very ill, was unresponsive, and had slipped into a coma. It just broke my heart seeing this young, innocent boy lying there so sick, with his devastated family surrounding him.

So I sat with the family and I explained to them that this sacrament that I was going to give their son, the Sacrament of the Anointing of the Sick (which replaced the old Sacrament of the Last Rites), wasn't about dying but about healing, no matter what was to happen. I spent hours with them that night, talking with them, praying with them and over their son, anointing the boy, praying again, keeping vigil with them. I remember that at one point we held hands as we all prayed together over their son, and I encouraged them to touch him and hold him and talk to him, so that the love that connected them all would give him the strength that he needed to face whatever was before him. During my prayers, I thought of the story in scripture of Jesus at the tomb of Lazarus. I felt a bond with their son, and I remember pleading with God, over the hours that I shared with them, to spare his life. I was there for quite a while with them and their son, and in the early hours of the morning, after a final blessing for all of them and heartfelt hugs for his family, I left and went back to the rectory.

I did the Sunday Masses the next day and just hung around the rectory, but no one else needed me for anything so I left for home the next morning.

The following week Father Tobias was back at the parish, and about mid-week he got a call from the pastor of that church that I had helped out at the previous weekend. The pastor told Father Tobias, kind of tongue in cheek, that the parents of the boy that I had anointed were looking for me but didn't know my name, didn't know who I was, or where I was from. They said that they wanted to thank me because a little while after I had left them, their son opened his eyes and woke up. The doctors told them that they now couldn't find any sign of what had been making him sick, and he seemed to be on the mend.

Father Tobias relayed that to me in a teasing manner. Then he kind of snickered and said, "So now you're performing miracles?" He gave a little laugh and shook his head. I told him that whatever it was that had happened, I was really, really happy to hear that the boy had gotten better.

I told him, "Well, he received the Anointing of the Sick, which is a sacrament of healing. Isn't that what the sacrament is supposed to do, Father? Heal people?" He just rolled his eyes at me.

I don't know whatever happened to that boy, whether he stayed well or whether he went on to have a good life, but I hope so.

On the exact day that I was ordained a priest, a litter of mongrel puppies was born in my hometown. As my dad told the story, they were born of an illicit union between a horny male Chihuahua and a pedigreed Pekinese female who was in heat. There were two neighboring households out in the countryside, not next door to each other but not that far apart, and the Chihuahua was out in his fenced yard when he picked up the scent of love in the air.

Being a resourceful fellow, the little guy dug a hole under the fence, crawled through a drainage ditch to his lady-love's backyard, dug another hole, and enticed the female doggie into the ditch. As her owners enter their backyard, what do they see but this little rat-like thing atop their prized Pekinese, humping away like there's no tomorrow. They scream in horror, but alas, it's too late and the damage has been done. She got pregnant and her owners gave away those puppies quicker than you could blink.

So my dad called me and asked if I wanted a puppy and if I could have a dog in the rectory. I didn't even ask father; I just said yes. Father Tobias had a dog, a little, extremely fat bulldog that did nothing but eat, sleep, and fart all day. Father never walked him or took him anywhere. The only exercise he got was going through his doggie door out to the backyard to pee. And although he was a male dog, he peed like a female! And his diet was as bad as father's.

Exactly a month after my ordination, my dad brought me my new puppy—a tiny little jet-black male that did sort of resemble a rat. My mom named him, and started calling herself his godmother. She said that since I wasn't going to give her any grandchildren, she might as well have a grand-doggy. My mother can be a "hoot" when she's feeling well and in a good mood.

I introduced father to my puppy and told him that we had a new member in the parish—another assistant—and he rolled his eyes at me. My puppy would follow father's dog around and started picking up some bad habits from him. Father's dog was so fat that he couldn't lift his leg to pee, so he would squat down like a female dog to do his business. My puppy would follow him out to the backyard, start to lift his leg, look at father's dog squatting down, then squat down himself. I didn't know if I should laugh or worry about him having an identity crisis!

My Bambino

I didn't want my puppy ending up fat like father's, so not only did I walk him, but I ended up taking him with me whenever I feasibly could when I went out. He became my buddy and constant companion, even riding in my bicycle basket with me as I biked around the parish on my rounds.

So this was my life as a newly ordained priest, and I relished every minute of it. I was beginning to think that maybe the concerns that my graduate seminary rector had talked to me about on that last day had been magnified out of proportion because I was doing what I loved, and I loved what I was doing. This was great stuff even with all the twists and turns and sometimes not-so-smooth sailing. This was my life at the parish with Father Tobias for about a year and a half, and then everything changed and it all went to hell in that proverbial hand basket.

Chapter 21

The Devil's Revenge:
The Beast Returns and He Is Stark-Raving Mad!

Father Tobias had another heart attack, a more serious one this time, and administration decided that it was time for them to intervene. They told him that his parish work was over, that he had to take medical leave, and that he had to rest and recuperate. He was more than upset about it, but he had to do what the bishop said. Back then you didn't say no to the bishop—unless you were a friend of his—then you could do just about whatever you wanted. You had pledged obedience to him at your ordination, and defiance could get you demoted or kicked out of the church, and no priest wants to lose their pension. So father said his reluctant goodbyes to us, and it was quite an emotional farewell, with everyone saddened by his leaving. If I had known what was coming, I would've grabbed on to his cassock tails and made him take me with him!

We got word that our new pastor would be—Father Abdon, the priest who I had spent that summer with. When I heard that, I remember rolling my eyes and thinking, oh God, I hope he's worked out his crazy shit and has gotten better. As it turned out, he hadn't, and boy, did we start off on the wrong foot.

What happened was that we threw him a surprise "Welcome to the Parish" party. Getting a new pastor is a big deal for the parishioners. Of course, everyone wants to meet the new priest, welcome him, get a chance to talk to him, and see what he's like. So I helped them to organize a nice get-together for him, which many of the parishioners were involved in, and even invited Father Abdon's mom and sister to it.

Father arrives at the parish and the next day he's going to say his first Mass. I'm with him at the Mass, and before it starts I get up there and welcome him to the parish. Everyone claps, we get through the Mass, and at the end of it I make a short announcement inviting everyone to the parish hall for cookies and coffee and punch to welcome father. He looks at me and says, "Well, okay," and off we go.

So I walk him over to the parish hall. When we open the doors to go in, this huge crowd of parishioners yells, "Surprise! Welcome, Father Abdon!" Everyone's smiling, they start clapping and cheering, the church choir starts singing, and his mom and sister come up to congratulate him—at which point he has a temper tantrum! There in front of everyone, he turns to me, furious, and rather loudly spits out, "Why did you do this? I know you're the one who did this! You should have asked me first!" Oh, he was livid. And of course, the people nearest to us heard him, the smiles were fading, and they were exchanging curious looks with each other.

Very quietly, out of the corner of my mouth and with a smile still plastered on my face, I said, "Well, of course I did. This is what they wanted to do for you. This is a party for you from them. We're in public right now, and I think you need to cool down and act appropriately." At that moment I knew—I just knew—that our relationship was not going to be a good one, and that it was going to be downhill from here. And it was.

He at least seemed to cool down a bit and in a slightly less petulant tone of voice told me, "Well, I don't like surprises."

I told him, "Well I'm sorry, but this is what parishioners do. They welcome their pastor. And they all went to a lot of trouble for you, so damn it, just act like you're enjoying it. Besides, you should know this already and expect it—this isn't your first assignment."

It was a disaster.

The parishioners were welcoming and friendly and they showered him with all kinds of gifts. We had a few parishioners who were talented artists and craftsmen, and they gave him things they had made. I remember that someone had given him a wood carving that they had done of the Catholic saint that father was named after; a beautiful piece of work. He just gave it a cursory glance, and I don't even think he said thank you. Someone else presented him with this huge box of chocolates, and his reply was, "I don't eat that stuff." (Nyah nyah nyah . . . .) At that point I turned to him and very quietly said, "What's wrong with you? Just take it and act thankful. Sheesh, I'll eat it!"

He got money, paintings, statues, crosses, food items, and flowers— they just inundated him with gifts. But none of it seemed worth his interest. After my comment he seemed a little sheepish and turned his attitude down a notch, but on the whole his demeanor was cool and standoffish, and his interactions bordered on rude. Even his mom and sister didn't get any better treatment from him.

The parishioners, however, treated his mom like royalty. To be the mother of a priest—to them it was like having the Virgin Mary there! They clasped her to their bosoms and were very solicitous of her. They

Chapter 21

treated his mom with the utmost deference, doted on both her and father's sister while father barely acknowledged them. Both of these nice ladies treated everyone very graciously, and I think they were as embarrassed by father's behavior as the rest of us were.

A couple of the parishioners sidled up to me and made comments like, "What's wrong with him?" or, "He's kind of different, isn't he?" With my smile still in place, I told them that he was just tired or other excuses along those lines. I don't generally apologize for other people, but these parishioners, especially after all the work they had done to put this party together, didn't need to have this crap flung in their faces like he was doing.

Thankfully, the party finally ended and on behalf of father and myself, I thanked everyone for coming and thanked them for all of their hard work then shook hands and said personal goodbyes to everyone there. I asked the secretary if she would send out thank you notes to everyone on father's behalf.

Father Abdon and I then headed back to the rectory. As soon as we were inside, I turned to him and asked him what was wrong. He said that he was tired, didn't like surprises, and that I shouldn't have asked his family to come because he didn't get along with them. I told him that the family stuff was his issue, not ours, and that they didn't have to come but they did. I explained that this is what parishioners expected and this is how they acted when they got a new pastor, that he had been a priest a lot longer than I had, and that he should know that this is how parishes operated. That whoever the new pastor had been, we would have done the same thing, so why make such an issue of it? He didn't really say anything else after that, just walked away from me and went to his room.

Father had been a priest a lot longer than I, yet I had to tell him that he wasn't acting appropriately in that situation. Something was more than a little wrong with that picture.

Most pastors make changes when they come to a new parish. All new bosses do. They have their own way of doing things and will change things around to reflect their style. Usually they get settled in, get the lay of the land (so to speak), see how things are run, and then little by little, they'll implement their changes. Well Father Abdon didn't even wait for the dust to settle. The changes started coming fast and furious. It almost seemed like he wanted to erase every last vestige of Father Tobias's time there.

It started the morning after the party. It was early and father and I were still in the rectory when the housekeeper and a couple of the handymen came in. Father asked me how they had gotten in and I told him that they had keys. He then asked why they had keys to the rectory, and I told him that it was because they had work to do here and had to be able to get in. Well, he didn't like that at all. He didn't say anything else about the keys, but he did tell the housekeeper that he didn't want her going into his side of the rectory for anything—not even to clean—and that he would clean it himself. After he walked away, she looked at me and said, "What's wrong with him?" I blurted out the first thing that popped into my mind. I said, "He's sick." Little did we know just how true that statement was.

The next day was business as usual. I had been working at the parish office and around lunchtime I went back to the rectory. But I couldn't get in because my key didn't work. So I went back to the office and told the secretary that I couldn't get into the rectory. She winked at me and whispered, "He changed the locks everywhere." And I said, "Well, okay, but he didn't tell me that he was going to do that." Again, she whispered, "I know. He didn't tell anybody. I think we're going to have a problem with this one." Then she gave me a big smile. Scary. It kind of reminded me of Jack Nicholson in *The Shining*.

I went to his office and knocked on his door, went in, and told him that I couldn't get into the rectory and asked him what was going on. He said that too many people had keys to all of the buildings, that it was out of control, and that he had all of the locks changed. Well that's fine, he's the pastor, and he had the right to do that. But to do it on the sly, not to tell anybody about it–that was just downright weird. I told him well, okay, but I needed keys to all of the buildings, and that I needed to get into all of these places. For a second there I kind of held my breath, wondering–what if he says no? But he gave me a set.

A few days after his arrival, father came up to me and asked me what I did here at the parish. I thought okay, he'll want to talk about my duties, about what his plans are, maybe see how we can share some of the responsibilities, and let me know what he expects of me. So I told him what I had been doing, told him the things that Father Tobias had done, and what our routine had been. He said, "Okay," and walked away. That was it. That was the extent of our conversation about it.

So we settled into the day-to-day work of running the parish, and it was a very different experience from the one that I'd had with Father Tobias. I had made the comment that during that summer that I worked with Father Abdon that we didn't work as a team. It was exactly the same this time around. I just kept doing my thing and he did his thing—whatever that was—because he didn't talk to me about it or discuss anything with me. I knew that we were not going to be friends on any level, but I also knew that I had to respect the position that he held and would do my best to work with him for the good of the parish. That was the goal to keep sight of, whatever the differences in our personalities.

My opinions weren't asked for, my attempts at friendliness were rebuffed, so basically I led my life and he led his.

All in all it was a strange situation, but it was what it was and I needed to make the best of it. I had left him that summer feeling that he had some very definite psychological problems, and my opinion hadn't changed. I could tell that he hadn't been to therapy, but if he had, it had been a dismal failure–he hadn't been placed in a straightjacket and put away. Did I just say that? Yes, I did. That's how severely his problems came across to me. This was more than "funny" or odd stuff going on. This was deadly serious, although I seemed to be the only one who thought so.

Next came his war on liquor. I was heading back to the rectory one day when I noticed that the outside trash cans were all overflowing with liquor and wine bottles. I asked him what he was doing, and he said that there was too much liquor in the rectory, that he didn't drink, and was throwing it all out. He said that from now on at our communion services we would serve grape juice instead of wine. I asked him if he had a problem with alcohol—was he an alcoholic and wanted to remove the temptation—and he said no, but that it could happen because it ran in his family. Okaaay. I was tempted to ask him if we should change the consecratory words during communion from "take this wine and drink of it," to "take this grape juice and drink of it," but I didn't think that would go over too well, so I didn't. No one could ever accuse father of having anything even closely resembling a sense of humor.

Usually when you saw me around, you saw my dog with me because I would take him with me whenever I could. Now that he no longer had the previous pastor's dog to pal around with, it could get a little lonely for him when he was shut up by himself in the rectory. He was still just a puppy, full of boundless energy and inquisitiveness, and I didn't want him tearing the place up out of boredom.

When Father Abdon showed up, one of the first things he told me was that he didn't like having a dog in the rectory. I told him sorry, but my puppy was here first and that he was staying. One evening Father Abdon said the strangest thing to me. Out of the blue he said, "You love your dog more than you love me." That stopped me in my tracks.

I said, "Excuse me?"

He repeated himself. "You love your dog more than you love me."

Okaaay. With my one eyebrow raised and one eye at half mast, I asked him, "What exactly does that mean, Father?"

He said, "Oh, I just want you to know that I noticed." Good grief, how do you respond to something like that?

So I said, "Well, yeah, that's true. My puppy is like my child, dependent on me and I do love him more than anything, including you.

He's my responsibility and I feed him, take care of him, and protect him. I don't believe that you need me to do any of those things for you, Father, and I don't think that loving my dog has anything to do with my relationship with you."

That comment of his just blew me away—that he would come up with something like that. I remember thinking—what the hell is going on with this guy? How weird can you get? Well, he wasn't done with weird yet. A few days after that on a Saturday afternoon, I was at the church doing Reconciliation Services. I had left my puppy in the backyard of the rectory while I was at the church. Out of the corner of my eye I see Sister Eleanor come hurrying into the church. She comes over and quietly waits until I'm finished, and then she leans down and whispers into my ear, "Father, Sister Clare was looking out the kitchen window of the convent and she saw the pastor open up the back gate of the rectory and push your dog out."

I said, "What? Okay, thank you for telling me."

So I hopped into my car, and started driving around looking for my dog. Thankfully, he hadn't gotten too far because after just a few minutes of searching I spotted him cruising down the sidewalk, just happily trotting along without a care in the world. I stopped the car, called him over and picked him up. He was just fine except for a few smears of dog poop over his face. I guess he had been investigating a pile left by another dog, and now it was matted in his fur. I was just so relieved that he was okay and hadn't been hit by a car or worse. I drove back to the rectory, cleaned him up, and then went looking for Father Abdon.

I found him in the rectory and asked him, "Father, why did you let my dog out?"

He said, "I didn't do that."

I snorted and told him, "You were seen doing it by the nuns. So c'mon, what the hell is going on here?"

He said, "Oh that, well, I noticed that there was a crack in the gate and I was trying to close it and your dog ran out."

I told him, "That's not the way I heard it. But let me tell you something—if you have a problem with me, talk to me about it. Confront me about it. Just leave my dog alone. If anything happens to my dog. . . I'm just warning you. So watch it." God, I could not believe that I was having this conversation with my pastor, of all people. This was just so "out there;" talk about the *Twilight Zone*. I felt like I had stumbled into it again.

After that incident, I made sure that my dog was never alone with Father Abdon because I honestly was afraid that he would try to harm him. So the sister's convent became his new sanctuary when I wasn't around, and the sisters and the secretary became his nannies. (And I think he loved all of that attention from the ladies!) Parishioners would see me out and about, always with my dog, and they would say things like, "Oh, father never goes anywhere without his doggie, isn't that sweet?" Oh, if they only knew!

A few days after that incident, father told me that he was separating his part of the rectory from mine. Okaaay. Our bedrooms were already on opposite sides of the rectory with a common living and dining room in between. Off the dining room was a hallway that led to his rooms, and at that junction, he had a wall put up with a door in it, and a lock on that door that only he had a key to.

When I asked him why he was doing that, he said that he needed his privacy. I told him that he already had privacy, that I had never gone to his area of the rectory or to his bedroom, that I had never bothered him when he was in his room, and what in God's name was he thinking? He just kept saying that he needed his privacy. After that, if we were both in the rectory and I needed him for something, I would have to use the intercom system that we had to get a hold of him. Something was seriously out of kilter with father.

And then I started noticing more odd goings-on. From my bedroom window I could see a portion of the backyard, and although I couldn't see father's back door, I could see anyone who went in or came out of it. And I was starting to see young boys coming out of father's door at one or two o'clock in the morning. They were parish kids that I knew, and they all seemed to be between the ages of about twelve to fifteen years old. I didn't have a good feeling about it, so I confronted father, told him what I had seen, and asked him what was going on. He told me that they were just coming over to play darts and listen to music with him. I told him that I didn't think that it was appropriate for young boys to be at the rectory with him so late at night. At that moment, I saw this tidal wave of rage well up in his eyes. I have to tell you, it scared me enough that the hairs on the back of my neck stood up. The look that he gave me was so hate-filled that my first thought was that I needed to put a second lock on *my* bedroom door. I knew that I would have to watch myself with this guy.

So I did something a little sneaky, or okay, maybe it was a lot sneaky. The next day off that father had when I knew he was going to be out of town, I searched high and low and finally found a key that opened his door and went into his quarters. In his bedroom I noticed that he had a large bulls-eye drawn on one of his walls with a couple of darts sticking out of the wall, so I guessed that part of his story at least was true—that he was playing darts with the kids. It was weird that he didn't use an actual dartboard but instead was using the wall, which was riddled with holes. And he had gotten rid of his bed, at least the frame and box springs, and just had a single mattress on the floor, which I thought was odd. With the holes in the wall and the mattress on the floor, it looked more like a room in a flop house rather than a rectory. I didn't find anything else that was suspicious, but I still felt that I needed to pursue this further.

I knew most of the kids that I had seen leaving the rectory via father's back door, so one day I saw a few of them together and told them that I wanted to talk to them. I asked them to tell me what they were doing at the rectory with father so late at night. I told them that I had seen them leaving at all hours of the night, and I wanted to know what was going on. They said that they were just "playing" with father, so I asked them what they meant by "playing." They said that they were just hanging out with him, playing darts, listening to music, that it was fun, and that he was "really cool." I asked them if there was anything else going on, but they said no.

I talked to them for a while, but they stuck to their story, and said that's all they were doing. I asked them if their parents knew where they were that late at night, and they all said, um, not really. So I told them that when they came to the rectory, they had to tell their parents where they were going and that they had to leave at a decent hour. I told them that I didn't want to see them here that late anymore or I would call their parents myself. Rather sheepishly, they all said okay and I let them go. I definitely didn't have a good feeling about this.

Despite the crazy stuff that I and the other staff were witnessing, life in the parish still went on much as usual. The parishioners weren't as yet too affected by all of this, but that would soon change. For now, my routine was about the same, and a couple of things happened around this time that started out as good things but brought me grief in the end.

I had gotten a couple of calls from some of my graduate school professors saying that they had some vacation time and wanted to come and visit me. I still kept in touch with them and thought it would be great to see them again. Then those wheels started turning, and I thought, hmmm, my theology teachers here, my parishioners here—why don't I get them together? Since my priority was to teach my parishioners, I thought that this would be a great opportunity to expose them to more of that cutting edge theology.

So before the first professor came, I called and asked him if he would consider spending one of his evenings here having an informal get-together with the parishioners to talk about some aspect of theology. I think I called it a "fireside chat." (Not that we had a fire, like President Roosevelt did at his famous chats, but I wanted people to feel welcome and relaxed.) I told him that I could pay him a small stipend for his time, and that way he could not only have his vacation but also make a little money in the process. He thought it was a great idea so that's what I did with every professor who came to visit me. I also did it with a couple of bishop friends of mine who visited. Yes, I actually had friends who were bishops—who would have thought that?

The parishioners loved it, especially when the bishops came! To think that a bishop would deign to sit down with them on an informal basis, like a friend, and talk to them about their faith—that was unheard of! They just thought it was the greatest thing and those sessions were always packed. People came away from our meetings feeling pretty good about their faith, and I know that they all learned some things, and all grew in some way. I was feeling pretty good about those meetings myself. But I soon found out that, once again, I had stirred the pot.

I started hearing rumors about me from my fellow priests; innuendos about my behavior. I heard through the ever vigilant church grapevine that I was doing this because I wanted to get "noticed," that I wanted to "one-up" them, zoom past them all on that priest ladder, and become the next bishop. Why else would I bring in theologians and bishops? Who did I think I was? (I think—and I could be wrong—that maybe the real question that they were asking themselves was damn, why didn't we think of that first?)

I thought back to that conversation with my rector when he said that the church didn't look kindly on innovation from its priests. Okay, so maybe he hadn't magnified it out of proportion. All I know is that this put a nail in my coffin, so to speak, because from that point on my reputation took a hit. I again became the "malcontent," the guy who didn't follow the rules, and the guy causing trouble for the rest of them.

The other thing that happened pounded yet another nail in my coffin with my pastor and my fellow priests. Following the guidelines issued by Vatican II, our diocese had been divided into eight geographical sections called "deaneries." All of the priests in each deanery met monthly to discuss various issues, and they were presided over by the "dean," the priest that they elected from amongst themselves as their leader.

It was election time for our deanery, so the bishop asked us to meet and elect a priest to become our new dean. The dean would represent all of the priests in that deanery when he attended diocesan meetings, and would be the conduit for not only getting information to the bishop, but also for implementing policies and procedures from the central office to each parish. The priest who is elected dean is given the title of "Vicar Forane" for as long as he holds that office, which is for however long he remains in that particular deanery. He is no longer simply addressed as "father" but as "very reverend." You address a priest as "father," or as "reverend," or as "very reverend," depending on their position in the church. It has nothing to do with piety, but rather to where you stand on the hierarchical ladder.

Usually for a position like this, you elect someone a little older, a little wiser, someone with more experience, and someone you might want to reward for their hard work. You probably know where I'm going with this.

As priests, we all had to attend these meetings together to discuss different policies and procedures, talk about how things were going in our parishes, maybe bring up issues that some of us were having, and discuss various solutions. In reality, these meetings were a chance to eat a fancy lunch, surreptitiously imbibe in alcohol (since it wasn't allowed to be served at these meetings, it was sneak in your own bottle), and engage in a gripe session. Mainly everyone talked about how crazy the bishop was, how crazy some of the policies were, how the policies didn't work—yada, yada, yada.

So we're at our meeting where we need to elect a new dean, and yes, you guessed it—they elected me. I thought it was a real hoot, and I actually believed that they did it more as a joke than anything else. I said, "Hey guys, I don't think this is going to work, I haven't even been a priest for two years yet, and we're supposed to elect somebody with more experience than that." There's an attitude in the priesthood that says that you have to be a priest for at least five years before you're considered worthy of the title. Until you attain those number of years, you're considered pretty much worthless—or as I've heard it said among my brother priests—you're considered a piece of shit.

But the group said, "We voted, the majority rules, and you're it. We'll let the bishop know."

All I could think was boy, the bishop's going to go through the roof over this. He and I didn't have a good relationship. I'm not sure what that initially stemmed from, but I think that it might have been the ring incident, which had occurred years before when I was a new seminarian. The current bishop, as I've mentioned, was named when I was in the diocesan seminary. One of the symbols of his office is a ruby ring, and of course, he was wearing it the first time that I met him when I was a young seminarian.

Upon being introduced to him, I shook his hand, and in my enthusiasm I guess I squeezed his hand a little too hard because he yelled and grimaced and looked down at the blood on his finger where his ring had cut into it due to my overenthusiastic squeeze. He got really pissed off at me over that even though I apologized profusely. I don't know if he thought that I did it on purpose or something, which I hadn't. I was just excited and happy for him, and I guess I got carried away. After that whenever I ran into him, he either ignored me or was cool to me. I really can't think of any other reason why he would have disliked me so much from the get-go.

So we get back to the parish after the meeting, and the pastor went through the roof over my election. He was really angry and told me, "I've done more work in this diocese than you ever will! I should be the Vicar Forane! I should have this honor!" I told him that I didn't think of it as an honor, more as a joke played on me by the other priests, and that any honor was in name only, and that the bishop just needed a flunky to carry out his orders.

But I did remind him that now—although he was my pastor and my boss—in matters of implementing policies and procedures, I was his boss. He looked at me kind of strangely but agreed that, procedurally, that was true. I then told him, "Since we're talking about policies, I think we need to implement a new one right now. I think that from now on, none of the parish kids should be at the rectory late at night; not at our parish or at any other parish." He just walked away from me.

My pastor wasn't the only one upset by my election as dean. I also made a number of enemies among my fellow priests because of it. They felt that not only was I was too young and inexperienced to hold such a position, but that (according to them) I had a reputation of being a loud mouth and a hot head, so how could this have happened? They wondered what strings I had pulled to get the position, because, obviously, many of them deserved it more than I did. To think that they would have to call someone younger than they "very reverend" was galling to them.

Again, I thought of the things that my graduate seminary rector had talked to me about, how there were too few positions of power in the church, how everyone was vying for those positions, and that the competition was cut throat. I realized, belatedly, that my rector was a very wise man. This rift with my fellow priests would never heal, and in time would only worsen.

I then get a call from the bishop's office asking me to meet with him about my new position. I get to his office and he greets me as Father and uses my last name. Not good. I knew that he wasn't particularly happy about this turn of events, and wondered if he was going to tell me that he was going to veto my appointment and call for a new election. I had heard that this had been done a time or two before in other deaneries. But he didn't. Instead, he starts off by saying, "Well Father, it looks as if you've developed quite a reputation for yourself."

I laughed and said, "Really? I hope it's a good one."

He just ignored that and said, "Your brother priests, whom I have contacted and spoken with, feel that you have the leadership potential to do this." He went on to tell me that although the younger priests weren't in agreement with it, the older priests felt that I was ideal for the position, and that it was they who had swung the election.

I told him that I thought it was a little silly myself, and that I hadn't been ordained long enough to do something like this. But he told me, "Let's go ahead and do this. This is an honor and you should take it as such. This title hasn't been bestowed on someone as young as you since probably the Middle Ages."

I said, "Really? Well, okay. But what exactly does it entail?" He went on to outline some of the duties, which he seemed to downplay, saying that I would have to attend a few meetings, and not much more than that. Well, that part of it didn't sound too bad. But me, representing the bishop? Me, representing him—the guy who didn't like me? But yes, he names me to the position. How insane is that? Ah, welcome to the church in our diocese.

I eventually found out that it was indeed a bit more than he had told me. For one thing, I would have to periodically visit each parish in my deanery in the bishop's stead, and go over all of their records—things like baptismal records—to make sure that everything was done properly and was being recorded properly. Back then, a baptismal certificate could be used in place of a birth certificate, so they were considered not only church documents but could also be used as legal documents. And I also had to review certain financial records to make sure that no one was "cooking the books" or absconding with church money, both of which had been known to have happened in the past. So in my naivete, I said, "Just attend a few meetings? Okay, I guess I can do that." So I added another load of work to my already overflowing workload. The upside of that was that I got to meet a lot of new people and I made a lot of good friends throughout the deanery.

The whole situation was kind of ironic. I had brother priests who were scheming and plotting to get noticed, to get ahead, to climb that ladder, and get to the top. Their whole lives revolved around it. I, on the other hand, didn't give a crap about any of that, despised the politics, and was trying to get my foot off that damned ladder. For me, I had already attained the only goal of any importance–being with my parishioners, "growing" them and growing with them, and giving them an experience of Jesus. For me, that—and only that—was what being a priest was all about. The rest of it was just bullshit. I wanted nothing more and did nothing to promote myself with the administration. Yet here I was, acting for the bishop, getting my name known by one and all. And all I did was attend a meeting. Go figure.

After that election meeting, a couple of the older priests, ones that the bishop had spoken with, called me and said that they knew that I was right for the job, but that there was a lot of jealousy towards me from the

Chapter 21

younger guys. The younger priests said that I didn't look like a priest, hardly ever dressed like a priest, and didn't act like any priests they knew. And that they were all getting sick and tired of hearing about how much my parishioners loved me, and how everyone else in the other parishes loved me too. Uh oh. (Parishioners aren't supposed to love you; they're only supposed to respect and obey you. And if they're a little in awe of you, all the better. They should know their place.)

When the older priests told me that, at first I thought— c'mon, you have got to be kidding. Jealous of me? That's a good one. My second thought was—oh God, everything my rector said to me is actually happening. It's like I'm on a different planet from everyone else, which shouldn't have surprised me that much, but it did. I guess I'm a slow learner.

So I'm still sitting there with the bishop and we're winding down our meeting. I know that he's not particularly pleased about any of this, and I know that what I'm about to say next will probably be yet another nail— or more like another dozen— in that coffin.

"Well," I said to the bishop, "as my first official act in my new position, I would like to talk to you about my pastor."

"Oh," he says, "how is that going? How is Father Abdon?"

I took a deep breath, girded my loins, and proceeded to tell him. I told him that I had some real concerns about the pastor's behavior. I told him that he was doing some really odd things, like putting up walls and dividing the rectory in half so that he could have his "privacy." But worse, I had seen something that I felt was very inappropriate, that I had seen young boys, parishioners, coming out of father's back door very late at night. He was entertaining young boys in his room behind locked doors late at night. I didn't know of anything more specific than that, I hadn't seen anything more than that, but that it was inappropriate for this to be happening. This wasn't a good thing to be going on, and I had an uneasy feeling about it, and I thought that the bishop needed to investigate and to talk to father about it.

The bishop's reply was, "Oh, we do have some colorful personalities in this diocese!" (What? Did you hear what I just told you?)

But I said, "I don't think that this is about colorful personalities. I think there's some stuff going on here that needs to be looked into. I want to bring this to your attention because I don't know what exactly is going on, I don't understand it, but I really think that it needs to be looked into and you're the bishop so I'm bringing it to you."

He said, "Oh, I think it's just a personality issue between the two of you." Okaaay.

I told him, "Well, I think it's his own particular personality that's having issues, though I'm no psychologist. But I don't think that's the problem. I think it's a little bit more than that."

He then told me, "I'll look into it," and our meeting was over.

That was it. That was his response to the concerns that I brought him. I had thought long and hard about what I told him because you can't go around accusing people without proof. You could ruin their reputation as well as your own, so you'd better have your facts straight. No, I hadn't really seen anything glaringly nefarious, but in my gut I knew that what was happening wasn't good. I didn't think that the bishop would necessarily take my word for it, our relationship being what it was, but I had thought that he would take it more seriously than he had. Despite the fact that I hadn't seen more than I had, what I had seen was still suspicious.

The church rigorously maintained its veneer of respectability, and usually anything that threatened that—any hint of impropriety— was swiftly dealt with. It was that Old World "boys club" mentality that says that what you do in private is your business, and no matter how awful, it's fine as long as you're a model of virtue in public. Keep the public image untarnished, be discreet, and all's right with the world.

And to be fair, in our society in the seventies that attitude was prevalent and shared by everyone in power—judges, police, and elected officials. And since what I had seen would look improper to anyone else who saw it, I thought that for that reason alone the bishop would intervene and keep any hints of impropriety from tarnishing his administration. But as far as I know, at that time nothing was ever done. Well, nothing was ever done to father. I, however, paid a price.

Chapter 22

"Exhausted," Literally

I returned to the parish after that meeting with the bishop feeling frustrated. Either I hadn't gotten through to him, or I had, and he didn't believe me or he didn't care. One never knew with him. One of the complaints about him that you would hear at some of our meetings was that he didn't hold any strong opinions of his own, was wishy-washy, and was easily swayed by other people. The priests stated that the opinion of the last person that he talked with would end up being the bishop's opinion. So, if you were at a group meeting discussing something with him and you were hoping that he would vote your way, just make sure that you had the last word! But I decided that I would keep my eyes and ears open, and maybe talk to a few more of the kids.

Not long after this, it was my weekend to say the Masses at the mission churches. After I got back, a couple of the parishioners approached me and asked if I'd heard about the sermons that Father Abdon gave at the Masses that weekend. I told them no, and asked them what he had said. They told me that at every Mass he told the parishioners that we couldn't afford to have two priests at this parish anymore. He said that his fellow priest (me) was spending too much of the parish's money on food and utilities, and that he couldn't afford to keep me there any longer. He also said that he didn't really need a helper, and that he could do it by himself with the help of the parishioners. (What—all of a sudden these parishioners, on whom he looked down his nose, he now considered his co-workers?)

And then it came to me. I thought, ahh, he wants to get rid of me. I think I touched a nerve somewhere.

I didn't know what our financial status was because Father Abdon had taken over every aspect of our finances. He didn't let anyone help him with it, not the secretary nor the finance council members. He kept all of the books to himself and he kept them close. But I really didn't think that we were suddenly having financial difficulties. So I just came out and asked him why he was going around telling people that we couldn't afford to have two priests here when just about every weekend we had to bring in a couple of priests to help us out because we were so busy. He never really answered me, but then he never really talked to me about anything anyway. He only repeated that we didn't have the money. Another weird encounter. I tried my best to just ignore his nonsense.

Another simmering bone of contention between us was over something that he had done previously—shutting off the heat in the rectory. He told me that I was using too much heat so he shut it off. We had quite a few arguments over that. I would tell him that it was freezing in the rectory and that icicles were hanging off the kitchen faucet, but he wouldn't turn the heat back on. I tried to engage him in conversation, get him to talk to me, to tell me what the real issue was, but he wouldn't. With mounting frustration I cornered him one day and blurted out, "What the hell is wrong with you? You won't put the heat on and you're walking around the rectory with a parka on. That's just nuts!" He'd just repeat that I was using too much heat. So I told him, "Okay, let's try to compromise. We'll turn it on but keep it really low, just high enough so that the pipes don't freeze."

He said, "No."

After all my common sense pleas had failed, I told him, "I'm sorry, Father, but I'm putting the heat on. It's freezing in here, and my dog (whom I love more than you, which I didn't say) and I are not going to freeze to death (because of your crazy stuff, which I also didn't say). I did say to him, "C'mon, Father, talk to me. What's going on with you? Are you okay?"

He looked at me quizzically, like he couldn't understand my concern, and said, "Yes. Why do you ask?" His response sent a shiver down my spine.

So I defied my pastor and turned on the heat, and his response to that was to close up the heating ducts all over the house except for my bedroom. He boarded them over with cardboard and duct tape so that even though the heat was on, it didn't get into the other rooms. It was only warm in my bedroom. The rest of the house was still freezing and he was still wearing his parka in the rectory. That was really, really weird. (God, how many times have I used the word "weird" already?)

I had talked about our housekeeper before and how she had a child out of wedlock. Back when she'd had her first child, Father Tobias would tease her and say that we had our very own "virgin birth," because she would say that her baby didn't have a father. Well, we had another "virgin birth." She had gotten pregnant again, and again there was no father in the picture. She didn't work much during her pregnancy because Father Abdon thought it was scandalous that she was an unmarried mother and that she was working for us. I don't know why he didn't just fire her because he was so upset by it, but he didn't; he just cut her hours. This time her "virgin birth" produced a little girl.

So I spent another one of my weekends at the missions. Again I come back, and within minutes of my arrival the parish secretary finds me and tells me that I won't believe what the pastor said at the Masses this weekend. I remember thinking, Oh my God, now what? She told me that at all of the Masses Father Abdon had told the parishioners that I had fathered our housekeeper's child! He said that from the pulpit! I said, "Really? He said that? I don't believe it! Really?" I was completely blown away. I just could not believe that anyone would be crazy enough to say something like that from the pulpit. To get up there and say, well folks, today instead of talking about Jesus, let's talk about that other priest who works here—the one who got our housekeeper pregnant and is the father of her child. Oh, I believed it all right. I was beginning to believe that Father Abdon was crazy like a fox. If he couldn't get rid of me, maybe he could get the parishioners to throw me out.

Then the secretary said, "You know what was neat about it? At every Mass when he said that, the parishioners started talking back at him from their pews, saying things like, 'No, that's not true,' or, 'No, we don't believe that,' or, 'Why are you saying that about him, that's a lie!" With a big smile she told me that they just about booed him off the altar, and that absolutely no one believed the crap that he was saying. I knew that Catholics have to be pretty riled up to talk back from their pews because normally they're a quiet, well-behaved bunch. At least that made me feel a little better—that they all knew the kind of person I was and that I would not do something like that. I wondered what would happen the next time I went to the missions. I shuddered to think of it.

So here we go again. I confronted father about it and he flat out denied it. He said that he had never said that, and that they misunderstood him. He gave me some kind of a bullshit story, saying that he was talking about us as priests and how I was good friends with her, so it must be hard for me that she'd had another child. (Huh?) I told him that I didn't know who to believe because I'd heard it from a number of different people. Was I supposed to think that everyone else was lying? I didn't tell him that I had also heard it from the parish staff because I didn't want to get them in trouble with him. It was obvious that his vendetta was against me, and I didn't want them getting caught in the crossfire.

So I asked him to tell me what was going on with him, what was the problem that he had with me, did he want me out of here—did he want me to leave? I told him to just tell me what it was that he wanted. He didn't say anything. I asked him to just talk to me about it. Again, not a word; he just walked away from me.

And here I was again, feeling like I was living two different lives. My parish life—being with the parishioners—was everything I could have hoped for. I found it life affirming and fulfilling. The parishioners gave me their love, and oftentimes that's what kept me going when the going got rough. I can't tell you how many times they took me under their wing and cared for me when I most needed it. I'd be walking down the street in town, heading back to the parish office after making hospital rounds, and I'd hear someone call my name and it would be one of the parishioners wanting to say hello. So I'd stop and the person would say something like, "You know what, Father? You look really down; I think you need a break. Come with me," and then they'd take my arm and say, "I'm going to call the secretary and tell her that you've got an emergency and won't be back for a couple of hours." Then they'd take me to the local coffee shop, or we'd go for a drive, or they'd even take me back to their house where we'd kick back and drink some sodas and listen to music. Men did this with me, women did this with me, even the kids did this with me! God, they were such good people.

But eventually, the day would end and I'd have to go back to the rectory and Father Abdon. I knew how Alice felt when she landed in Wonderland. Nothing was the way it should have been, and everything was the way it shouldn't be. Father and I really had no relationship other than what was required for us to work together, and we were nothing more than two strangers living in the same house. He didn't talk to me if he didn't have to, yet was often quick to yell at me over the most inane things. His relationship with the parishioners on the whole was equally superficial.

To me he was the worst example of a priest that you could find, but in the good old boys club called the church, it seems that wasn't an issue. As far as I knew, no one had ever talked to him about his behavior, nor had ever questioned any of the inappropriate things he had done. He wasn't held accountable for his actions, but worse—to my way of thinking—the people in charge, those who were responsible for him, weren't held accountable, either. They never bothered to find out what was wrong, and never offered him the help that he needed. No one was held accountable for anything, and he went on to wreak havoc in parish after parish, but I'm getting ahead of myself here.

Not long after my election as dean, I had to attend a meeting at the diocesan office that the bishop held for just the deans. I think there were about eight of us present, including the bishop. He wanted to talk to us about some new policy that he was presenting, but the conversation turned to some item that had been in the local news—about some politician who wanted to implement something—I can't even remember now what it was. But I do remember the bishop bringing it up and getting all riled about it, and the consensus was that we should all write letters to that politician telling him that we did not agree with what he wanted to do. So I raised my hand and told them that this was fine, but I thought that perhaps before we started telling other people what to do that maybe we should look to ourselves first and fix some of the things that we were responsible for.

They asked me what I meant, so I told them that I felt that one of the things we needed to look at was the way that we treated our secretaries, especially the secretaries at the diocesan office. I told them that the secretaries were upset about a few things, like not getting good benefits and health care, and being treated like second-class citizens. I knew this because some of the secretaries had called me, saying that they were uncomfortable talking to their bosses about it, but felt comfortable talking to me and maybe I could advocate for them.

Well, that went over like a lead balloon. It actually got quite ugly. One of the deans yelled out that they didn't have to listen to me, and said that I wasn't even wearing my collar, I wasn't even dressed like a priest, but like a businessman. (I was wearing a sport coat and tie.) He even cast aspersions on my ordination, saying that I probably wasn't even a real priest. While the bishop—the man who had ordained me—sat there with a little half smile on his face, hands clasped as if in prayer, and didn't say a word. He just watched us all pick each other apart, and enjoyed every moment of it. Just keep us all angry and at odds with each other so that the focus didn't land on him.

So, never claiming to be a saint myself, I yelled right back at him. In fact, I believe I told him that he was full of crap. I said, "If we're going to talk about problems, aren't you having some in your parish that perhaps we can help you take care of here?" Not long before this meeting, the priest who was yelling at me had been punched in the face by one of his parishioners for making a pass at the parishioner's wife. I told the group that we needed to clean our own house first before we started telling other people how to clean theirs, and that we needed to clean up our act because we were supposed to be a model for others. I told them that people were starting to scrutinize us, and if we didn't do something to take care of our own problems, we were going to be in big trouble. It wasn't a matter of "if" but a matter of "when" that would happen because this wasn't the old days anymore when we could keep things hidden.

They booed me down and conducted the rest of the meeting as if I weren't there. Of course, none of our problems or the secretaries' concerns was discussed, but they sure had a lot to say about that politician and all of the things that he was doing wrong. Of the eight of us there that day, five of that group eventually faced legal charges. They were either charged for sexual misconduct (including pedophilia), or for financial misappropriation (stealing), and four of them were kicked out of the priesthood.

Around that time, I heard from some of the parishioners that a number of parents in the parish had called the diocesan office to complain about Father Abdon, saying that they were concerned about his relationship with their children, and that they felt that something inappropriate was going on. I wondered if that meant that father would finally be receiving a call from the bishop, but as far as I know that call never came. I had taken my concerns to the bishop, had talked to him about this very thing, and . . . nothing. Now parents were calling the bishop and complaining about the same thing, and . . . nothing. I couldn't believe it. Why was the bishop ignoring this?

I knew in my gut—having worked with Father Abdon before—that he had been doing the same thing in that parish that he was doing here, and that this wasn't new behavior for him. He wasn't giving those awful screaming sermons here like he had back at that other parish, but I figured that only meant that he had learned to be more discreet. I didn't have any proof that the bishop already knew what was going on with him, but I knew that he'd have to have been deaf, dumb, and blind not to. And last I'd heard, the bishop was not suffering from any of those afflictions.

So I decided to talk to some of the boys that I was still seeing coming out of father's back door late at night. This time I talked to some different kids than I had talked to before. I cornered a few of them one day and bluntly asked them to tell me what they were doing late at night with father in the rectory. It was the same story—the darts and the music—and about how "cool" father was.

I hadn't been able to get the other kids to tell me any more than that, and I didn't know how to get these kids to open up to me. I didn't know what to say to get them to trust me, so finally I told them—perhaps foolishly—that if they told me the whole truth I promised that I wouldn't tell anyone else. And I hoped it wasn't a promise that I might have to break. I asked them point blank, "Is anything sexual going on?" They sort of hemmed and hawed for a little bit but then said, "Yeah, sometimes." Oh, Lord. I decided that this was going to stop here and it was going to stop now.

I told them that what was going on wasn't healthy, it wasn't good for them, and that I didn't want to see any of them at the rectory ever again. I told them to tell all of their friends that too. I also told them that they should only be around father in public and never again to be alone with him. I told them that if they didn't do what I said—starting right now—I would break my promise and call their parents. As one voice they said, "Oh, no, please don't do that." Oh, Lord.

Chapter 22

I had never encountered anything like this before—it was beyond my experience. I needed to think about how to handle this and what to do next. I was going to make sure that no kids came to the rectory, even if it meant standing guard all night long, which should take care of the immediate problem. But this was a long-term problem. I knew that I had to talk to the bishop again, even though he hadn't listened to me before and he wasn't listening to the parents now. I needed to find a way to present this to him, and to get beyond his attitude that I was just misunderstanding things. I didn't want my next meeting with him to end with the same old, "Oh, Father, that's just not true." I needed his help because I was not going to confront father on my own. I might not live to tell about it.

It all came to a head pretty quickly, but not in the way that I had expected or would ever have imagined. My mind was half on my parish work and half planning my next step. I was thinking how to best handle the situation with the bishop and father when a good friend of mine from my early seminary days stopped by to visit me. He and Father Abdon also knew each other fairly well. It was just a casual visit. He stopped in at the parish office and we talked there for a little bit and then I walked with him over to the rectory.

We went into the rectory and Father Abdon was there, and I think all I said was, "I've got a visitor," and the change in father's demeanor was immediate. Don't ask me why—he just sort of went cuckoo. He suddenly became this angry, pouting little boy, as if he was jealous because I had a friend stop by and he didn't. He was radiating these pissed off, hostile vibes and all I had done was walk in with my friend. It was the most bizarre tableau—it made no sense at all—and I remember thinking that I was grateful that looks couldn't kill.

The next thing I know, he starts yelling at me. "You left the top off the jelly jar!" It took me a few seconds to register what he was saying.

I said, "Excuse me?"

He started yelling again, saying, "Look! The jelly jar was left open and now the jelly's ruined! Just look!" as he's waving the jelly jar around. He was on a roll, I mean this guy was screaming. He was ripping into me to beat the band and there was no stopping him.

A grown man, a priest no less, screaming at the top of his lungs, and waving around a jelly jar. I felt as if I had walked into a madhouse. I'd had it with him. I was done with his insane behavior—all of it—and finally, I blew my top right through the rectory roof. I shouted right back at him, "WHAT THE HELL IS WRONG WITH YOU? You're doing all this crazy shit! You won't put the heat on, you close up all the heating vents, it's freezing in here with icicles hanging off everything, you're in the house with your parka on, and now you're going off about the jelly jar? What-in-God's-name-is-wrong-with-you? I don't even eat jelly! I'm on a diet and I don't do jelly! And you know that! You're the one who's always scooping the peanut butter and jelly out of the jar with your fingers! You do that every day, all the time! So don't yell at me about the jelly jar because this is your own crazy shit, not mine!"

My friend is just standing there, kind of caught in the middle, and I hear him say, "Uh oh."

I turned to him and said, "My pastor's going crazy. That's all I can say."

I had to get out of there so I got my dog's leash and told my friend that I was going to walk my dog, and asked if he wanted to come with me. He shook his head no, and said that he would stay there and try to talk to father. So I went for a long walk with my dog and when I got back, he and father were sitting in the living room, deep in conversation, with serious looks on their faces. I went to bed and I guess my friend left shortly thereafter.

Later that night, I woke up at about three in the morning to use the bathroom, and when I got up the room tilted. I was dizzy, had a headache, felt kind of out of it, and a little confused. I thought, this is weird; what's happening? So I went over to the window—which I kept open a bit during the night—and I opened it all the way. I stood there for a minute, breathing in the cold night air, and then I checked on my dog who seemed to be okay.

As my eyes were scanning my room to see if anything was amiss, I noticed that my heating vent had dark smudges around it, like smoke marks. I thought, huh, I've never noticed that before, and wondered if something was wrong with the heating system. So I turned off the thermostat and decided that I needed to call the plumber first thing in the morning and get it checked out. I was feeling nervous about going back to sleep in case there really was a problem, so I left my window wide open, bundled up, and read a book until morning.

I called the plumber as soon as was decent, and then headed out with my dog in tow to see my doctor. I was still feeling a little off, so I thought it would be best to get myself checked out, and then I would take my dog to the vet just to be on the safe side (since he couldn't tell me if he was feeling dizzy too). The secretary was already at the office. She came to work each day right after the seven a.m. Mass, which Father Abdon had that morning. I stopped and told her what had happened, and said that the plumber was on the way and left.

I was able to get in to see my doc right away, which is one of the perks of living in a small town where everyone knows you. I explained to him what had happened, and after he examined me he said he thought I'd had some carbon monoxide poisoning. I asked him how something

Chapter 22

like that could happen, and he said that most probably there was something wrong with our heating system. He said that I needed to get it looked at right away, and not to use the heat again until I had. He told me that sleeping with the window open (and having a weak bladder) was probably why my dog and I hadn't died last night. Wow. That had me reeling. I told him that I had already called the plumber, and hopefully he could figure out what had happened and fix it. I took my dog to the vet where he got a clean bill of health, and then we headed back to the rectory.

I stopped at the parish office again and told the secretary what my doctor had said and then went to the rectory to talk to the plumber. I asked him if he had found anything, and he said, "Yeah, and it's the damnedest thing." I remember that he was scratching his head and looking perplexed as he was talking to me. He said, "I just don't understand it. Someone took the exhaust port hose and exchanged it with the fresh air hose. It's just the damnedest thing." He said that he had disassembled it, unscrewed all of the hoses, inspected them, then screwed them back on—correctly this time. I asked him when he had last checked the system, and he said that he did it yearly, and that the last time he had done an inspection, it was fine. He asked me if anyone else had been working on it, and I told him that I didn't think so, but that I would find out.

I told the secretary what the plumber had said and told her that I was going out, I was going to find the maintenance guys and talk to them. I tracked them both down and asked them if they had been working on the heating system at all, if they had to replace any parts, and maybe had to change the hoses. They both said no, they never worked on it, and they left that to the plumber. I asked them if they were sure and they both said yes, of course, they were sure; they didn't even have keys to get into the rectory. (Father Abdon had taken away their keys when he took over and hadn't given them new ones after he'd had the locks changed.)

I head back to the parish office and this time I went in through the side door because it was closest. As I'm coming in, Father Abdon and the secretary were walking up the hall from the convent side of the rectory and they were talking. They didn't know I was there, and I heard the secretary say, "My God, wasn't that terrible what happened to father (me) last night? The doctor said it was some kind of a carbon monoxide thing and he could've died!" She was really upset.

Then I heard father tell her very matter-of-factly, "Well, he deserved it. He was using the heat." When I heard what he said, the hair on the back of my neck stood up. He said it so nonchalantly, like he was telling her that he wanted a tuna fish sandwich for lunch or something.

I then heard the secretary say to him, "Father! That's a terrible thing to say!"

They walked to the secretary's office and I then heard father leave. I went up to the secretary and told her that I had heard their conversation. She got wide eyed and looked at me in alarm and said, "God, no, you don't think . . . ." I honestly didn't know what to think, but I told her that I thought I needed to call the bishop.

I didn't know what was going on, other than the indisputable fact that someone had switched the hoses in the heating system. And I was the only one using the heat, which everyone knew. And if it was some kind of bizarre accident, it could've been a deadly one. Had I pissed someone off, big time? I hadn't told father that I had found out what had really been going on behind those locked doors of his, hadn't told him that I was planning on meeting with the bishop about it, but maybe the fact that the kids were no longer coming around had him putting two and two together. Was that what this was about? I didn't know, but I had my suspicions. The only one who had the authority to do anything about this whole crazy mess was the bishop.

I had heard that the bishop wasn't at the diocesan office, but was visiting a parish in a different part of the state so I called the pastor of that parish. I identified myself and said that I had to talk to the bishop right now, and that it was an emergency. The pastor told me that the bishop was in the bathroom (I think his exact words were, "He's sitting on the pot"), but I told him that I didn't care and to either tell him to get off the pot or to pass the phone in to the bathroom because I needed to talk to him right now.

The bishop got on the phone and asked me what was wrong. Although I had spent a lot of time thinking about how to approach him with this so I could convince him that this wasn't my "personality" stuff, but a very real problem that the parishioners were facing with Father Abdon, all of my planning went right out the window. I was pretty agitated and just blurted it all out. I told him every crazy thing that Father Abdon had done since he got there, that I had still been seeing kids coming out of his back door late at night, and about what some of the kids had told me when I confronted them. I remember telling the bishop, "I think that Father Abdon is a pedophile and you've got a real problem here." I went on and on—it all came pouring out—and I ended it by telling him what had happened last night, and how I had almost died under suspicious circumstances.

A moment of silence, then the bishop said, "Oh, Father, that can't be true." (Well, thank you, bishop, I'm glad you were able to resolve all of this so quickly.)

Chapter 22

But I plowed on. I told him that yes, it was true—all of it—and that he had to do something about it. I told him that he had to move one of us out, and that I was willing to stay but not with father there. I flat out told him, "If I stay I don't think my life will be worth a wooden nickel. Get me out of here or get him out of here." I was practically shouting into the phone, but the bishop calmly insisted that, of course, none of it was true and that I was (as usual) misinterpreting things. He made a few more worthless comments, said he'd look into it, and hung up. That was it. It was as if nothing that I had said made an impression on him; as if he couldn't have cared less. I could almost imagine him smirking on the other end of the phone line.

The following week my transfer orders arrived in the mail.

Chapter 23

"It's Either Him or Me! Your Choice."

Less than a week after my phone call to the bishop, I got a letter from him notifying me that I was being transferred out of this parish to another parish in a different part of the state. He said that I had "personality" problems, and he felt that I would be "happier" in a different parish.

I was stunned by that letter. I picked up the phone and called the bishop and asked him why he was punishing me for what was going on here. I told him that I wasn't the one barricading the rectory and boarding up the heating vents, that I wasn't the one putting holes in the walls playing darts in my underwear with the parish kids at all hours of the night, and that I wasn't the one being complained about by the parents for inappropriate relationships with their children. And what about what some of the kids had told me?

His reply to me was just more of the same. I could hear the tsk, tsk in his voice as he said to me, "Oh, Father, none of that is true. You can't prove it."

Instead of just shutting my mouth about it like he expected, I asked him why he hadn't investigated, and why he hadn't talked to any of the kids. I could tell that he'd lost his patience with me because his tone got sharp. He said that things were just not done "that way," that *I* had the problem, and that's what he was addressing with my transfer.

Talk about a brick wall, and banging my head against it wasn't getting me anywhere. I had done all that I could, had taken it to the highest authority available to me, and it was now in the bishop's hands. He was the ultimate power and authority in the church, and any and all problems were brought to him and handled by him because his word was law—the buck stopped with him.

It's difficult for people in today's world—a world of instant access to each other via the internet—where the public is aware and involved not only in local but in global affairs, to understand the dynamics of the past.

Our society was a different place back then, and the people in power—whether it was religious groups or law enforcement or government officials—handled their problems in exactly the same way, by taking care of them on their own. When any person in an authority role got into trouble, it was handled discreetly, "in-house." You didn't go to anyone else for help; each group handled its own problems without interference from the other. Basically, you take care of your dirty laundry, and we'll take care of ours. Church matters, especially, stayed in the church because everyone knew that ecclesiastical authority trumped civil authority, and that civil authority had no place in the church.

Again, to be fair, it wasn't just the church that acted in this way. Back then abuses could be found across our societal landscape—in the law enforcement system among police and lawyers and judges, in the political system from mayors to congressmen to presidents—and in churches of every denomination, not just the Catholic Church. Not that abuses are a thing of the past because today's world still has its share of them, but what is different is how we handle them now as opposed to how we handled them back then.

Everyone went to great lengths to make sure that no whiff of impropriety was ever allowed to reach the public. The public was seen as being too naïve and too innocent to be exposed to scandal from its public officials. That would ruin our confidence in them and might even bring our society tumbling down. And this would play right into the hands of the communists who were lurking around every corner, lying in wait for just such a thing to happen. As long as the public persona was kept unblemished, any social awkwardness was avoided, and we avoided that at all costs. That's how it was done and it wasn't acknowledged, wasn't questioned, and was just accepted as being the way that it was. Because—that's the way that it was. It was as much a part of the fabric of our lives at that time as apple pie and the American flag.

This was the social climate when I entered the church, and it was the standard that was practiced in every aspect of our society. When something like this happens in today's world, we have options. We can go above the bishop's head or to the police or to the newspapers—and we do—because it produces results. But we are able to do that today only because we have grown in consciousness to that point. Back then, we didn't have those options because we weren't at that point in our development, and we could only live out of the point that we were at. So I took my concerns to the bishop, having to believe that ultimately he would do something about them.

Thankfully, in the seventies, things started to change. The first cracks in this system began appearing as people grew in consciousness. They did start acknowledging it, talking about it, and questioning the status quo. These were the first steps on that road to growth that we needed to take to be able to bring reform to the flawed system that governed the way our society's institutions handled these issues.

These are issues that we are still trying to right in today's world—things like the sexual exploitation of children, human trafficking, sexual harassment in the workplace, police brutality, the violation of basic human rights for people of color and the gay and lesbian population, to name just a few. We've come a long way since the seventies, but we still have a long way to go to erase these blights on the soul of humankind.

I had done what I felt was the right thing to do, and now I was being punished for it. So what did I do now? I felt that the only options open to me were either to accept the transfer or leave the priesthood. I still believed that I could make a difference, believed that I could affect some change in the institution of the church, that I could help stop the kind of dysfunction that I was witnessing, but I couldn't do that if I left. It had to come from the inside, and it had to start with one person influencing another, then another, then another—changing enough people's hearts on the inside to wrought wide-scale change on the outside. Maybe I was just being the ultimate fool, but this is what I thought it was possible to do, and that it was the only way to put a real stop to what was going on.

The thought of leaving my parishioners was crushing, but at least I knew that I would not be leaving them defenseless. Although I wouldn't be there, they would be able to take care of themselves. What had started out as a few phone calls to the bishop from a few parents concerned about father's relationship with their children had spread like wildfire through the parish grapevine, and everyone was aware of what was going on, even though father and the bishop might pretend otherwise. These parents would do what the bishop wouldn't. They would be keeping a close eye on their children, and a closer eye on father. In fact, they would do such a good job of keeping Father Abdon in his place that not long after I left, father left. He was saying Mass one Sunday when he suddenly just walked off the altar, out of the church, got into his car and drove off—never to return to that parish. And ultimately, it would be a group of parents just like these who would be the instrument of father's eventual downfall, and of his being kicked out of the priesthood in disgrace.

I remember feeling really depressed over all of it, and decided to just take it one day at a time. I let the parishioners know about my transfer, and a lot of them got depressed along with me. Not Father Abdon, though. He was as happy as a clam, but that wouldn't last.

I said my last Mass at the parish, and just about every parishioner showed up for it. After the Mass they held a farewell reception for me, and it was a somber affair. They expressed their dismay and sadness at my leaving, and I don't think there was a dry eye in the house. They did their best in wishing me luck in my new assignment, said that they felt blessed that I had been a part of their lives, and showered me with money and gifts. But the whole thing had a funereal air about it and left me feeling more depressed than ever. I felt raw, like I was being ripped from my family, from everything I knew and everyone that I loved, and tossed out into the wilderness. I said my final goodbyes to everyone, got into my already packed car, and with my doggie in tow, drove off.

I drove to my new assignment pretty much on automatic pilot. When I was about twenty miles from my destination, I noticed flashing red and blue lights behind me. I had been speeding again, which wasn't anything new for me, but this time I really hadn't been paying attention to my speedometer or anything else. I'm lucky that I hadn't gotten into an accident because my mind was back at the parish and not on the road. When I would start to think about what I was leaving behind and why, my anger would surge, my grief would well up, and I'd start to get teary eyed.

So this policeman pulls me over, walks over to my car, looks in the window at me and says, "Oh my God, what's wrong? I stopped you because you were speeding, but are you okay?"

My face was all blotchy and my eyes were red and swollen, and in a clogged voice I said, "No." (Real men can eat quiche, wear pink, and cry.) I told him that I was a priest and that I had been transferred out of my parish, that I was all torn up about it, and that I was heading to my new assignment. Here I was with a total stranger and my whole life story came pouring out.

He introduced himself, said he was sorry about what had happened, and said that we'd probably be seeing each other again because he belonged to the parish that I was now assigned to. He told me that his shift was over and he was heading back into the city and, if I wanted, he could escort me in. So I had a police escort to my new parish because the cop was worried about me and no doubt about the other drivers on the road, too.

I don't know what kind of first impression that made, but I guess it was an okay one because he and I got to be really close friends, stemming from his kindness towards me that day. (He didn't give me a ticket either.) We were about the same age and he was new to the area himself. I eventually performed the marriage ceremony for him and his wife, and also baptized their baby girl, so I became friends with his whole family.

We got to the rectory where we said our goodbyes, and then I hung around waiting for the pastor to show up, which he eventually did. Father was an older fellow, and as I was to find out, very conservative in his approach. He was not a fan of Vatican II and its reforms. We introduced ourselves, and one of the first things that he said was, "Oh, you've got a dog." (I don't know why pets were such an issue with most of these guys.) I told him that yes, I did, and where I went he went. I don't know if I sounded a little defensive because he said, "No, no, it's okay, it's just that your room is upstairs, so that might be a little problematic." (He had staked out the entire downstairs for himself, being the "king" of the castle, so to speak.) I assured him that it would be fine, that I walked my dog regularly, and would take him outside to do his business; problem solved.

I unloaded my car, locked my bike outside, and got everything else to my room. Then father gave me a set of keys and we went on a tour of the grounds. On our walk he was pretty talkative and threw out some theological-type things, which I was able to respond to knowledgably, and I think he was relieved that I at least seemed to know my stuff. After all, he hadn't asked to have me here; I was just dumped on him. He was a pretty successful one-man show at this parish, and I gathered from him that the bishop didn't ask him if he wanted an assistant, just told him that he was getting one. That could have caused some resentment on his part, but he seemed to take it in stride.

I felt comfortable talking with him, so I told him why I had been transferred. He said that when the bishop called him, he was told that he was getting a fairly new priest (me) who had personality issues, did a lot of complaining, couldn't get along with his pastors, and that I had developed a reputation as a "malcontent." He was very up front about it with me. I remember him telling me that although we had just met and that this was just a first impression, from what he had seen of me so far, he had a little trouble believing the bishop. He had been hearing "murmurs" about some of the priests in this diocese, the things that were going on, and how the bishop was not addressing them. I was really thankful that he at least believed me. I was at such a low point emotionally that this small kindness from a stranger—this fellow priest—was worth more to me than a chest full of pirate's gold.

We talked about my duties, which were a little complicated to work out because I wasn't assigned to him full time. I was going to work at his parish part time and also work part time at the Newman Center at the local university. At a non-Catholic university, the Newman Center (named after a famous cardinal) is kind of like a fraternity—a club that is a Catholic presence on campus. I would be saying Mass, hearing confessions, and holding Days of Recollection and retreats for Catholic students. My boss would be a nun, which I thought was great since I seemed to get along better with nuns than with my fellow priests.

I didn't know it at the time, but these kinds of part-time assignments were a set up for failure, which, I'm sure, is exactly what the bishop had in mind. As I was to find out, trying to serve two masters can become logistically impossible. You teeter with one foot in each camp so that you never have both feet planted securely in either camp. But I was going to give it my best shot.

After we had worked out my duties, I asked father if I could take a couple of days off before starting because I wanted to visit my family whom I hadn't seen in a while. He said sure. So the next morning I called sister, my other boss, to set up my meeting with her for when I returned, and headed home to my parents' house. I spent a couple of days visiting with them and my grandmother, and actually enjoyed being there. I was really close to my grandma and spent a lot of that time with her. Although it was good to be home, I couldn't quite seem to shake the depression that I had. I felt like I had been through the wringer and was still trying to iron myself out. I needed to frame that somehow, and put it away someplace so I could move on.

In my last parish, I was able to draw strength and comfort from my parishioners, but I didn't really know anyone yet at my new parish. I was able to find some solace in books. I love reading—read all kinds of books whenever I had the time—and found some books by a writer/poet/photographer that helped me a great deal. He had published a series of books about love and relationships, and his words were accompanied by photographs that he had taken.

All of his books were fantastic. Something that he said in one of them especially spoke to me—so much so that I tried to shape my whole life around it. He became one of the most influential writers in my personal development. He said—and this is the gist of it simply put—that it was sad that when we fall in love with that one special person that we are so consumed by that love that we don't need anyone else in our lives; that all of our love is given to this one person and that we focus only on that one person and exclude everyone else. And that by loving this one person with everything that is in us, we diminish our love for everyone else. He said to imagine what it would be like—how extraordinary it could be—if we loved everyone with the same intensity that we gave to our lover, to our one special person. Imagine what it could be like if we could bring every relationship that we had to that same level.

I can't begin to tell you how tremendously that impacted me. Ah, I thought, so I *can* fully love everyone—every single person that I come in contact with—from the teller at my bank to my best friend, and give each of them my "all," just express it differently in terms of whether it was a parent, an acquaintance, or a friend. Jesus tells us to "love one another," and this helped me to see how best I could do that. And that's what I tried to do from that moment on—to give every relationship I had that

Chapter 23

same level of total commitment. That became the model for my life, and I owe that author a huge debt of gratitude.

I headed back to my new assignments and got to work. I met with sister, who politely made it very clear to me that she, and not I, was the chaplain at the Newman Center, which was fine with me. The differences between my two bosses were hilarious, at least at first. Father, as I said, was ultra conservative. He was very strict about us always "looking" like priests, so I had to wear my cassock at all times in church and out. I could, however, take it off when I showered. Although I'm joking here, back in the day in some religious orders, priests actually had to wear swimming trunks when they bathed to avoid temptations of the flesh. I wondered what father thought when he looked at my long hair. He never made any comments about it, and never said that it looked "unpriestly." (Luckily for me, all of the pictures of Jesus circulating at that time showed Him with long hair, so I figured that gave me some credibility.) And father wanted nothing to do with any reforms and still preferred saying Mass in Latin, no matter what Vatican II said about offering the Mass in the vernacular of the people; in this case, English.

Sister, on the other hand, had burned her bra along with her veil and her Latin prayer book. Everything was cutting edge liturgy and she embraced every new practice that came along. At our Days of Recollection, our topics would be all of the current, controversial happenings of our day–Vietnam, the Farm Workers Movement, Communism, and the IRA, and what it all meant to us as Catholics, as people, as citizens. We talked about how we could get involved in righting the wrongs of our time. We discussed women being priests (a big no-no in the church), Liberation Theology (another no-no in the church), sexuality (you know how the church feels about that), and Humanae Vitae, the pope's encyclical on birth control.

Earlier, Pope John Paul II had sent those letters to all of the clergy saying that they could no longer hold public office or be involved in politics, and that he was the only one who should be speaking to the social issues of the day. Well, he had never met sister. When it came to social issues, she was right there in the forefront—leading the charge—and the pope could stand aside or get trampled underneath her size eight combat boots.

This was an exciting time in our country's history. We had just experienced love-ins, sit-ins, marches, and demonstrations. People were beginning to realize that we lived in a global society, and that what impacted one person impacted all of us. We were growing up as a society and these were our first steps towards that growth and reform.

With my two bosses being on opposite ends of the spectrum, life was never dull. At the parish with father I'd be dressed in my cassock and I'd follow his conservative program. When I went to the college, I'd take off my cassock and put on my bell-bottoms and follow sister's progressive platform. I was still being me, just expressing it in different ways. Though it was kind of funny in the beginning, reality always has a way of leveling things.

I soon began to feel pulled in two different directions—between sister and father. Each of them started complaining to me about the other, and I would tell them to talk to each other about it, rather than to me, which they never did. Then they got to arguing about my time, each thinking I should be with them more than the other. Individually they were both really nice people, but their temperaments and approaches were very different. They were constantly in competition with each other, each trying to prove that their own ways were the best, and both used me to vent their frustrations. Most days being in the middle of their squabbles made me feel like I was walking a tightrope over a minefield.

I made it work—barely. I'd finish up my duties at the parish, and then rush to the college to do my thing there. Then I would rush back to the parish for a late Mass or some other function, then rush back to the school to do the final invocation for some special program they were having. I was getting exhausted and my stress level was through the roof trying to get everything done. It was like this from the very first day, and I didn't know how long I could go on juggling things this way—being pulled in a dozen different directions at the same time. Logistics.

I wished that I had someone who I could talk things out with, about all of the stuff going on in my head and in my life. I was still reeling from what had happened at my last parish. I had done my best, given it my all, thought I had been doing a good job, and had thought I had been doing the right thing. Was I wrong about that and just couldn't see it? Did I have too much pride about it? Pride is one of the seven deadly sins, and what's that old saying—that pride goeth before the fall? This was still eating at me, and I couldn't figure out how it all went so wrong. I needed help.

I couldn't go to father or the bishop, since they were a part of the problem. My fellow priests, for the most part, treated me like a pariah, so that wasn't an option. I needed someone wiser than I, someone with objectivity who could give me the guidance that I needed because I wasn't doing so hot on my own. Then I met this woman who was a Professor of Social Work at the university. She was a Jewish lady who looked like Mother Teresa, had the mouth of a sailor, had a great sense of humor, and didn't stand for any bullshit from anybody.

Since our job paths crossed quite a bit, we spent a fair amount of time together and became friends, and she ended up becoming a mentor to me. I respected her opinion and found her easy to confide in, so I told

Chapter 23

her about what had happened. In the course of our friendship she helped me to see things more clearly. I remember her telling me that she felt that she knew me fairly well and that I was a levelheaded person. She felt that there was a lot of craziness going on but that it wasn't coming from me. She assured me that I wasn't going off the deep end and that my concerns were valid, and that I shouldn't doubt or second-guess myself. She didn't have a high opinion of the people that I worked for, and would ask me when I was going to wake up, get out of this gig, and go do something constructive with my life! (If only I had listened to her about that.) She helped me to do what I hadn't been able to do so far on my own, which was to sort things out and start putting them in their place so that I could move on.

In addition to his pastoral work, father was attending the college himself as a student. He decided that he wanted to get a degree in counseling because he felt that the priesthood hadn't adequately prepared him to address the types of issues that people were bringing to him. So whenever parishioners came to the office for counseling, father did all of that because he said he needed to practice his skills. He was pretty pumped about being an "old" guy going back to school, and would encourage me about going back myself. I did think about it, and I thought it was something that I probably would do, but this wasn't the time because I literally had no time to do it.

On my days off I would often drive home to spend time with my grandmother who had suffered a stroke and was in declining health. I would also frequently visit with my ex-parishioners—friends that I had made in my last parish. I might have lost my job there, but I hadn't lost them and we stayed in touch, and I was able to keep abreast of how things were going for them. Since I spent a lot of time on the road making these visits—and since I was a speed demon—I would often get stopped by the cops for speeding. I think every state cop, from one end of the state to the other, knew me by name. It got to be kind of funny because on a few occasions, I would get pulled over when I wasn't speeding. The policeman would come over to me, and I'd say, "Hey Joe, hi, but I know I wasn't speeding this time."

And Joe or whoever would say, "Yeah Father, I know, but it's my coffee break time so why don't we get off at the next exit and go have some coffee together?" I thought that was just the neatest thing.

The months passed, but my workload never got any easier. In fact, the more I got involved in my duties, the harder it got. I was giving it my best shot, doing the best that I could, but it didn't seem to be enough. It just wasn't working out. Father wasn't happy with the time that I was spending with sister, and sister wasn't happy about the time that I was spending with father. There was only so much of me to go around. They were always arguing with each other over my duties, and the tension at times seemed so thick that you could cut it with a knife. It seemed like all I did was rush from one thing to another, yet no one was happy, least of all myself. I was frazzled, I was stressed, and I was burning out. I thought that if the bishop had given me this assignment as a type of punishment, he had accomplished his goal.

I decided to call the bishop to ask him if he could reconfigure my assignment. Maybe he could have me work at the parish Saturday through Tuesday, and then work at the college Wednesday through Friday—something like that. Or maybe he could take one of these assignments away and just put me full time in either the parish or the college. I knew that he would see it as my complaining again, but I was "over" what he thought of me. Our relationship, which had never been good anyway, was never going to improve no matter what I did because I had done the unforgivable. Instead of turning a blind eye, I had spoken out about Father Abdon's behavior, and worse, I had dared to question the bishop's handling of it. (Basically, career suicide.) I didn't know it at the time, but I had helped to start a crack, one that eventually would widen enough to swallow the bishop. He would never forgive me for that.

So I made my call to the bishop and his response was predictable. He asked me why I was so ungrateful, why I couldn't be happy with my assignments, why I had to be such a thorn in his side, and he went on in that vein for several minutes. I apologized and told him that it was not my intention to upset him, but that I simply could not keep up this pace any longer. That physically, it couldn't be done; least of all, psychologically.

I wasn't surprised when he told me that he didn't have the authority to change my assignment (yeah, right). But he did present me with another option. He said that there was a small parish "out in the boondocks" whose pastor was in the hospital with a life threatening illness. The bishop said he needed to replace him, and offered me that position as pastor. You might be thinking—wow, pastor, that's a step up. Well, yes and no. Nothing the bishop did was ever straightforward.

Normally, a priest isn't considered suitable to hold a pastor's position until he's been a priest for five to seven years, preferably seven. I'd only been a priest for a little over two years, so I wondered what the bishop had up his sleeve, especially since he was offering the position of pastor, rather than administrator. There is a difference between the two positions that lay people aren't privy to. There have probably been times when parishioners think that the new priest they've gotten is their pastor when in reality he's not; he's the parish administrator.

So what is the difference? The title of "pastor" comes with prestige, autonomy, and the protection of his position by Canon (church) Law.

Chapter 23

Once a priest becomes a pastor, he can run the parish any way he wants. It's his show, and the bishop can't interfere unless the pastor is blatantly breaking Canon Law. If the bishop doesn't like the way the pastor is running the parish, he can't just yank him out on his own. He has to follow due process according to Canon Law.

An administrator's position, on the other hand, is not autonomous and not protected. The bishop can tell the priest/administrator what to do, how to run the parish, and can take him out of that position if he doesn't like the way things are going. Why appoint someone as an administrator rather than pastor? Sometimes the bishop will suddenly need someone to run a parish, perhaps because the previous pastor has unexpectedly retired, but no one suitable is available at that time. So he will ask a priest, someone who is available at the time but who perhaps doesn't have enough experience to be considered for the pastor's position, because someone has to do it. He doesn't want to make this guy a pastor and give him that much power or autonomy, so instead he makes him the administrator. And even a woman could be made an administrator of a parish; think of it as the general manager of a business.

And then there's the assistant priest who in the old days people would often call the assistant pastor. When you're the assistant priest, you're not there to help the parish. You're there to help the pastor. There is a big difference between the two, which is also something that lay people don't know. You are the pastor's assistant and you are there to serve him; the parish is secondary. You have absolutely no say in anything, and absolutely no power. Your only function is to do what the pastor tells you. Remember when I talked about some of my classmates who were assigned to internships where the pastor was king and they were treated like indentured serfs? Constantly being told what to do and how to do it, not having the authority to do anything on their own, being watched every minute, and living on the pastor's leftovers? That was the life of the assistant priest.

That isn't what parishioners see when they look at the priests in their parish. They see them united as "brothers" in Christ, that this is their relationship as they work together for the good of the parish. That's their perception and that's how we want them to see us. We don't want them to know that the pastor is king and the assistant pastor is his slave. That just doesn't sound very Christian, although that's the way it often was in reality.

So the bishop offers me the position of pastor, which brings us to another thing about assignments to small parishes "out in the boondocks." I don't mean to insult any Catholics who are reading this, but you would probably be justified if what I'm about to say does insult you. These are not parishes that priests want. These parishes tend to be poorer and more run down, have a larger than average population of older people, are out in the middle of nowhere with no social amenities, and exist on the periphery of church life.

It's common knowledge in the priesthood that these kinds of assignments are given to priests with problems—alcoholics, pedophiles, and malcontents. (The previous pastor of this parish, the one who was in the hospital, was a raging alcoholic who was suffering from liver failure.) Most priests want to go to bigger parishes, richer parishes, parishes in bigger towns and cities because they're more prestigious, and this prestige reflects well on the priest assigned there. Being assigned out in the boondocks is seen as a poor reflection of that priest's skills, as his being unable to handle anything better and being on that lowest rung of the priest ladder. Your fellow priests feel superior to you. I wish I could at least say that they felt sorry for you, but I can't say that I've seen much of that emotion in my fellow priests. I'll stick to superior because if you're the one on that bottom rung, then they are not. It's all about climbing that ladder, with no thought for who they have to climb over to get to that next rung.

So what would my choice be—the frying pan or the fire? This offer by the bishop was typical of his "modus operandi." He would present you with two impossible situations and ask you to choose one. When it didn't work out, as he knew it wouldn't, he would then be able to wash his hands of any responsibility for the failure. He'd say to you, "But Father, how can you complain? I gave you a choice and you took the assignment. I didn't force you. And now you're complaining about it? Honestly, there is just no pleasing you. I'm doing my best for you and this is the gratitude that I get?" Oh, he was good at that. He could manipulate with the best of them, absolving himself of any responsibility in the matter.

I told him that I would take the pastor's position. My current assignment wasn't working, and I couldn't do it anymore to anyone's satisfaction. Physically and emotionally I was spent. A thin thread was holding me together. If I didn't get out of there, that thread would snap and there would be nothing left of me. Pretty sad, but that's how I felt. I was still trying to come to terms with how badly things had turned out in my last assignment, hadn't yet finished processing that, and now this assignment was grinding me in to the ground. At least if I accepted the bishop's offer and took the pastor position, I would be able to do things my way, not his. I would have some protection from him due to the tenets of Canon Law. Maybe this would be a small parish, a poor one and a backward one, and out in the middle of nowhere. But it would be mine. Well, Jesus' and mine.

Chapter 23

The hard part was telling father of my decision. When I told him he was livid. He angrily wanted to know if I had called the bishop to complain about him, if I had been "telling tales" about him to the bishop, if he was the reason that I wanted to leave. I had to assure him repeatedly that this was not the case, but he didn't believe me and called the bishop himself. The bishop repeated what I had told father—that a pastor was needed immediately at this parish, absolutely no one else was available, and that's why I was being sent there. The bishop told him that it was absolutely no reflection on him or on anything that he had done. Reluctantly, father calmed down, but he still wasn't happy, which I could understand. I had taken over a lot of his burden, especially now with his being in school and having less time on his hands for parish work. It was kind of ironic because in the beginning, he hadn't especially wanted me there, yet now he didn't want to let me go.

Father was a nice man. He was intelligent and caring and we got along really well. I liked him and he liked me. So why did he have that angry reaction to my news? Most priests in this diocese lived in a climate of uncertainty. If climbing that ladder of success was the goal—and for many priests in this diocese it was—and who you step on in the process isn't important, then your position could be a tenuous thing.

When you're surrounded by a climate of intrigue—gossip, rumors, backstabbing, and secrecy—you're never sure of just how secure you are. So the goal was to get chummy with the bishop because only he could help you up that ladder. No one, other than the bishop's closest friends, ever felt totally secure in their positions, and this climate was fostered by the bishop's leadership style. You had to be careful of what you said, who you said it to, and especially of what you did because everything found its way back to the bishop. You didn't want to piss him off and find yourself being shipped out to the boondocks, or have one of his friends take over your position because they wanted it and the bishop had just been waiting for an excuse to remove you.

It was a stressful life and priests reacted to that stress in different ways. Father didn't know me from Adam before I got to his parish. Had I been spying on him for the bishop? Had I used him as a stepping-stone to get up that ladder? He was feeling insecure, and he lashed out at me. Even after he talked with the bishop, I still had to reassure him that I had not said anything derogatory about him to the bishop. If he knew how the bishop felt about anything that I had to say, he wouldn't have had to worry.

Because of the way the church system was set up, it nurtured priests' intellectual growth, but stunted their emotional development. This happened a lot to the older guys who went into the priesthood when they were really young. (In my sermons, I would often tell my parishioners that their teenage children probably had more emotional maturity than most priests.)

When you entered the priesthood at a really young age, like entering a "minor" seminary at the age of twelve—which was fairly common in the old days—your psychosexual development basically stopped at the age that you were when you entered the seminary. The church told you what was appropriate to feel, which responses were allowed, and which were not. This way you didn't have to learn by trial and error like you normally would. You were told what was right and wrong in every facet of your life, so your emotional/social/sexual self didn't have to grow with the rest of you. You were not exposed to the normal interactions between people that helped you develop those parts of yourself; you just parroted what the church told you to say and told you to feel. You had no way of assimilating your developing sexuality into your psyche. Your body was changing, your hormones were raging, and not only were you not given a healthy way of coping with these changes, you were taught that they were bad and that you needed to deny them. And now we all know what happens when those parts of the self are denied. They rear up in the most inappropriate circumstances and get us into real trouble.

So what does happen when you repress this part of your development? Well, you then have a fifty-year-old priest whose psychosexual development is that of a twelve or thirteen year old. What happens when you have him interact with twelve and thirteen year olds? He's basically the same age as they are in their emotional development, so he's found his comfort level. Father becomes like those children. And, like any prepubescent boy, he's curious about sex. As a priest, he doesn't have the same constraints as other men. He's been told that he is right up there next to God, that he can do no wrong. And who does he have close contact with on a regular basis? Altar boys, and in the more modern world, altar girls. A vulnerable population that is just as curious about their own emerging sexuality.

So father goes about his life and he's doing okay. He might realize that he really enjoys being around kids, and that emotionally he feels good when he's with them. But he's holding things together. Then things start piling up—just the problems of everyday life that we all experience—and he gets really stressed. We all get stressed, but we (hopefully) have developed more or less "normally," and we can turn to our families and friends and co-workers and even inward to our own resources to help us handle the stress. Father can't. He doesn't have most of those resources. He might be miles from his family. His friends and co-workers mainly are other priests who are in the same boat, developmentally, that he's in, and he doesn't have the inner emotional resources to rely on. And since the church doesn't believe in psychology, actually getting some real psychological help isn't going to happen. So he breaks down. And when the psyche breaks down, it does it through the weakest link in the chain that makes up our selves. For a lot of these guys their weakest link was their sexuality, and this is the area in which they started acting out.

If their weakest link was in a different area of their development, then you'd get priests who were alcoholics, drug addicts, or psychologically unbalanced. Others would have such overwhelming issues handling their anger and insecurities that they would end up living as oddball eccentrics, or be almost hermit-like in their existences, or get fanatically immersed in fringe groups like the Charismatic Movement.

This is how the church formed these men and it was a recipe for disaster, and disaster is what it produced.

I was able to make my peace with father, said goodbye to sister and all of my parishioners and friends, and headed out to my next assignment at the absolute fringe of the diocese.

Chapter 24

A New Beginning at The End of the World

I drove to my new parish and yes, it was definitely out in the middle of nowhere. It was pretty isolated, and I had this irrational feeling that if I drove just a little further down the road, I would fall off the edge of the earth! That feeling probably had more to do with my state of mind at the time than it did with geography, but it was close on both counts.

The End of the World

I arrived right around the time that the parish was celebrating its annual feast day. Catholic churches are named after Catholic saints, and each year on the day of that saint's death, the parish holds a celebration to honor them. It's a big event for the parishioners, and usually in the bigger parishes the bishop will make an appearance, but as far as I knew he had never attended this one. There will be a special Mass—often times with a procession—followed by a meal for everyone in the parish hall. The parishioners usually provide the meal so there's lots of good, homemade food and all kinds of other goodies. Many parishes have a mini-carnival type affair, with booths set up for cakewalks and other activities, especially things for the kids. They might have raffles and a special bingo, and the festivities will go on all day and well into the evening. This parish was named after a Franciscan saint, so I felt that this was a sign that I had come full circle from my Franciscan beginnings. I'm always looking for signs, although I seem to be oblivious to the ones that all but smack me right in the face.

I moved into the rectory and the next day met with the parish council. We met in the parish hall, which was attached to the rectory while the church was actually located about four blocks away. I remember that it was raining that day and as we were sitting there, rivulets of rain were trickling down the inside walls in various places. I introduced myself to the council members, told them that I was their new pastor, and gave each of them a copy of my letter of assignment. It was a rather formal introduction, but I respected them as the owners of this parish. They lived and worked here while I was just a transient in their lives. Priests would come and go; they stayed.

As we were talking, the rain outside started coming down harder. This one rivulet on the wall closest to me turned into a gushing waterfall of cold, dirty water and I was getting splashed big time. I told them, "Um, before we go on, what's with the water? Could I have an umbrella?" And I wasn't really joking–I was getting pretty soaked. I kept my eye on that wall during the entire meeting because it looked as if it was going to collapse at any moment. They apologized, saying that the building needed a new roof but that they didn't have the money. This parish was dirt poor and all of the church buildings were in terrible shape. Because all of the roofs were leaking, I found that the wooden floor in the church had warped over time and bowed upwards, so when you walked towards the altar, you literally had to walk uphill. The flooring was so uneven that you could get seasick just trying to get into your pew!

The physical aspect of all of the church buildings, including its mission churches, was one of total disarray. How sad, I thought, that these parishioners were routinely given priests who were church "throwaways," alcoholics, pedophiles, burn-outs, malcontents, priests who didn't care enough to take even minimal care of the place. They didn't deserve this. So we were going to do something about it. "Okay," I told them, "Our first priority will be new roofs, new floors where needed, and anything else that needs to be repaired or replaced is going to be repaired or replaced." I told them that together we would do a thorough inspection of all of the buildings and make a list of what needed to be done. They looked a little more hopeful, but again reminded me that there was no money. I told them not to worry about that part of it, that I would get the money. I already had a plan formulating in my mind. And I

Chapter 24

also had an example to follow. St. Francis began his ministry by repairing run down churches. I was going to follow in his footsteps.

As awful as the condition of the buildings was, it was still something that could be fixed. What concerned me more was the condition of the people themselves. As I began meeting the parishioners, I was struck by how dejected they all appeared. Many of them seemed to walk around with their heads hung low, and not quite meeting my eyes when I spoke to them. There was a palpable air of defeat about them, that as rejects of the diocese they didn't deserve any better. And that, more than the condition of the buildings, really pissed me off. That might be more difficult to fix, but I was going to try.

I recruited my team of volunteers made up of parishioners. We made our inspection of the main church and its buildings and also of the mission churches. We then drew up a list of things that needed to be done. I was also going through the parish books—looking at their accounts and overall financial situation. It looked as if this parish had difficulty paying its bills because I found numerous outstanding bills for electricians and plumbers and different businesses; some of them years overdue. We would deal with that, too.

The amount of work that needed to be done was extensive. Almost all of the buildings needed either major roof repairs or new roofs, most of them needed new floors or new carpets, and all of them needed to be repainted. The rectory was a disaster. The carpet was beyond salvaging. It was full of ground-in dirt, suspicious stains, and cigarette burns. Steam cleaning wasn't going to hack it. The walls were nicotine yellow, and most of the furniture was threadbare and rickety. I wasn't expecting anything fancy, but when I sit on a dining room chair, I prefer not to fall through it as the seat caves in. But that's just me.

Within a few days I had a plan worked out. This parish was a poor one, but it did have some money accumulated in its bank accounts dating from years past. The difficulty would be in getting access to it. More importantly, it sat smack dab in the middle of some of the biggest private ranches in the state, which were owned by well-to-do ranchers, some of whom were parishioners. Get my drift? I had no trouble approaching these ranchers and asking them for money. I told them my plans, said that I was setting up matching fund donations for the repair of their church, and appealed to their sense of pride and church fellowship. It worked. They were more than happy to see their parish church upgraded, and each and every one of them donated and I ended up getting quite a bit of money from them. Non-Catholics owned most of the largest ranches in the area, but I even approached them and they also donated to our fund. In fact, most of them were very generous in their donations.

I then made a call to the financial comptroller at the diocesan office. I told him that I was the new pastor at this parish and that it was falling down around our heads. I explained that the situation was intolerable, that it had to be fixed, and it had to be fixed now. I explained that I had studied the accounts, knew exactly how much money was in them, and that I wanted a check for the total amount. There was a long standing diocesan policy that a certain amount of money always had to be kept in a savings account in the name of the parish and it was to be used for investment purposes for the entire diocese. Yep, I wanted that money, too. So I made an appointment to see him the following Monday, first thing in the morning. Actually, I remember telling him, "You open at nine? Okay, I will be there at 9:01."

On that Monday morning I drove to the diocesan office for our meeting and I was dressed for battle–wore my black suit, had on my Roman collar, and had slicked back my hair. As I entered the office, word of why I was there had preceded me because a few of the secretaries popped their heads out of their cubicles, smiled at me and whispered, "Good luck!" I wasn't surprised since confidentiality seemed to be an unknown concept in this diocese.

One of the priests who worked there, a guy that I knew slightly, came up to me and laughingly told me that I certainly had balls demanding money the way that I had. That just wasn't done. You asked, you asked nicely, and a little groveling never hurt. And you just hoped that the comptroller was in a good mood that day. My problem, if it could be considered a problem—which of course they did—was that I didn't play their games. The fear that many priests had was that if they didn't play the game, if they pissed off those above them on the rungs of that ladder, that they would get passed over come promotion time. They might even get demoted or sent out to the boondocks. Well, I was already in the boondocks, so there wasn't much more that they could do to me, or so I naively thought.

I took a deep breath and knocked on the comptroller's door. I went in and shook hands with him, and reiterated why I was there. I told him that the state of the buildings was a disgrace and a poor reflection on the church, that our reputation was on the line, and that it would be to our benefit to take care of the problem now before things deteriorated even further. I outlined my plans, told him about the donations that I was receiving, let him know that I would forward copies of all of the bills and receipts to him, and asked for the money. He said, "Okay." Well, knock me over with a feather! The comptroller had a reputation as a tough guy—a not very nice tough guy— but he was financially savvy. I knew him and always had a cordial relationship with him, but relationships in the church can turn on a dime. But I guess he must've agreed with me, saw that I had a sensible plan, seemed to know what I was doing, and he gave me the check. Actually, it was already in an envelope waiting for me!

Although the comptroller really was a financial whiz and was in an enviable position of power, holding the purse strings of the diocese, he didn't stay in that position for very long. He had been using it as a stepping-stone himself, hoping to have his worth recognized so that he would be named bishop in a different diocese, one that currently had an opening. When he didn't get that appointment, he resigned in great anger and disappointment, and then retired from the priesthood shortly afterwards. Many times even if you played the game, it still didn't work out for you. That was the chance you took if you were ambitious.

So I returned to the parish and we got started. We hired contractors, carpenters, and workmen, and the parishioners and I rolled up our shirtsleeves and picked up hammers and saws and went at it. At the rectory I basically started at one end of the place, rolled up the rug and everything in it, and kept rolling until I hit the other end and then had the whole mess removed by dump trucks. I found caches of hard liquor hidden everywhere with an occasional bottle of altar wine thrown in, and I got rid of all of that too. It took a couple of months of hard work, but by the time we were finished the church buildings were all of sound structure, safe and comfortable to be in, and quite beautiful to look at. We were also in the process of paying off all of the parish's outstanding debts. And the parishioners now had a new air of pride about them; the pride of ownership. If they felt their church buildings were a reflection of them, it was now a good reflection—a worthy reflection. They were now walking around with their heads held higher.

Another thing that I did early on in my assignment there was to hire a secretary. The previous pastor had done it all by himself. He never left the main parish so he was always around when people called needing to talk to him, pay for Masses, or to set up funerals. He always brought in other priests to take care of the mission Masses, again so that he wouldn't have to leave the parish. I think he wanted to be by himself and didn't want any help so that he could drink in private without anyone seeing him. He had a reputation as a good man. He took care of the parish's needs and his parishioners liked him. But when he wasn't saying Mass or doing a funeral or otherwise engaged, he was drinking. The parishioners knew that he was an alcoholic, but you didn't tattle on your priest. Ever. That concept was ingrained in Catholics of that era.

The only one who was surprised when father ended up in the hospital dying from liver failure and cancer was the bishop. He didn't know about father's problems because he never came to this parish. Technically, the bishop is supposed to visit each parish in his diocese at least once a year, but in reality that didn't ever happen. The bishop spent all of his time at the bigger parishes, the ones that brought in more money for the diocese. The few times that the bishop had seen father was at mandatory meetings, and for those occasions father would sober up.

I had met a woman parishioner who had a reputation of being a curmudgeon (yes, that's actually what they called her!) but she was also an upfront, no nonsense kind of person who seemed to know every parishioner, every non-parishioner, all of their family members and friends, and always knew everything that was going on in town before anyone else did. So I hired her to be the parish secretary. I taught her the job from the ground up. She was a good learner, caught on quickly, and soon we had devised a system that worked tremendously well for the both of us.

She would give me my schedule first thing every morning and keep me informed all throughout the day, and I would do the same with her; always letting her know where I was going. This was before cell phones, so if I was at the hospital, forty-five miles away visiting sick parishioners, I would call her when I was finished. She then might tell me that a parishioner had just been brought to the emergency room and could I stop and see them before I left. Or, she might also ask if I could stop at so-and-so's house on the way back because they were having an emergency of some kind, needed counseling, or just wanted a visit.

Even on my days off, I would let her know where I was going. Before I left she might tell me, "Well, you'll be passing so-and-so's place on your way out, could you stop in for a few minutes because he's feeling poorly?" Or there would be other similar requests. And I would call her before I returned to the parish from my day off, and she'd let me know if I had to make any stops to visit parishioners on my way home. She was a real blessing to me, the glue that held the place together, and I couldn't have done it without her. She was still running the place years after I had left, and I kept in touch with her up until her untimely death from cancer several years ago.

Soon after I arrived at the parish, I gave a needs assessment form to every parishioner. I worked long and hard on that form and was pretty pleased with it. It was a fancy five-page questionnaire asking the parishioners what I could do for them. Did they want to know more about the latest theology on sin? Did we need to start any kind of study groups? Prayer groups? Anybody want to discuss Liberation theology? Oh, I had all kinds of things that I presented to them. This was my first pastorship and I was raring to go. As the forms started trickling back to me, they all said just about the same things. No, no, and no. The parishioners wrote—we just want you to be our priest. Say Mass for us, perform our baptisms and weddings (of which there were few), officiate at our funerals (of which there were a lot), and just be there for us. Just be with us. Share our lives with us. Just be our priest.

Okay. If that's what they wanted, that's what I would do. I found that after Mass on Sundays, many of the parishioners would be vying for my company. I'd find myself surrounded by a crowd of people asking me—usually all at the same time—to come to their homes for breakfast. Others would ask me to go with them to brunch at a local restaurant (well, the local bar that subbed as a restaurant on Sundays). I didn't want to seem as if I were playing favorites, so I worked out a system that tried to include everyone most of the time. We would all head out to one person's house for coffee, then we'd go over to a different person's house for breakfast, and then we'd head to yet another person's house for more coffee, to read the paper, or to just talk. Or the whole bunch of us would go to brunch together.

This became our Sunday routine and everyone got used to seeing father and, of course, his dog and a passel of parishioners making our "food rounds" after church. It was a lot of fun, especially in the summertime. Everyone seemed to enjoy doing it this way, and the little old ladies in particular were just "tickled pink" that father was sharing his time with them.

Oftentimes, as we were sitting in someone's kitchen having coffee and reading the Sunday paper, conversation would turn to things that were happening in our town or our state or in the world, and the parishioners or their kids or grandkids would ask, "Father, what do you think about that?" That was my opening, my chance to preach without preaching. I would talk to them about what was going on, what seemed right and what seemed wrong. How a moral person could view these happenings, what they meant to us as Christians, and what we could do about them.

Sometimes talk would turn to their families, and it would be a chance to discuss family values, and talk about the problems they might be having with their kids or grandkids. A whole range of issues would be brought up, and I don't know if they ever realized that they were getting a whole lot more than just bacon and eggs and conversation with father.

Again, I love to talk, and talk I did, but it was always with the purpose of enlightening and guiding and teaching. They didn't want anything fancy from me, they just wanted me to share their lives with them, and in this sharing I could show them how we were all connected, how it all related to the Divine Presence. Not preaching it from the pulpit but living it together with them.

One of the basketball coaches at the school asked me if I would come to basketball practices and help out by grabbing a ball and dribbling with the kids. I'd played some basketball in school and enjoyed it, so I said sure. Then the track coach asked if I would like to help him out too by coming to practices and running with the kids. I was really into jogging at the time, loved doing it, so I also did that. The kids all seemed to like me, and they knew I was a priest but I was "different." I was young, I had long hair, I was outgoing and talkative, and in a nutshell, I didn't act like any priests that they had ever known. So this was a way for me to hang out with my youngest parishioners and mentor them. Again, I was not preaching to them, but was just being with them, sharing in the commonality of life with them, and being a role model for them.

One day I was riding my bike down the street and I had my dog with me, settled in the bike basket. I was going kind of slow and just kind of meandering. As I passed one of the houses, the woman who lived there—a teacher at the local school—was out in her front yard and she waved me over. I rode up to her and said hello, and she laughed and asked me if I was the "Pied Piper." I asked her what she meant, and she told me to look behind me. I turned around, and behind me was this long line of kids. As they saw me go by on my bike, they all just started following me down the street, some on foot, some on their bikes. It had us both laughing.

When you're the only priest in town and it's time for Saturday confessions, you normally bring in another priest or two for the afternoon to help you out. Back then most Catholics went to confession every week without fail, and if you have a large crowd and just one priest, you'd be there half the night trying to get done. It also gave the parishioners an option. Some of them might feel a little funny, and a little embarrassed, confessing to someone that they knew. Familiarity might become a block for them to express some of their deepest problems, or, their sins, if you will. So you always bring in someone else so that people can feel comfortable sharing certain issues.

Inevitably, I would bring in other priests, yet the line to my confession box was always the longest. The other priests would ask me why I'd brought them in because it seemed like most everybody wanted to go to confession with me. So I'd come out of the confessional and ask a few people if they would like to go to the other priests for confession, that it would probably be faster for them, and they'd say, "Oh, but I'd rather talk to you; you know me."

I found that kind of funny because that's not how it usually works. Usually you hear people say, "Oh God, I can't go to confession with that priest, he knows me!" But it was the exact opposite with me–they knew me yet still wanted me to hear their confessions, and I felt very honored by that. Although they knew me and I knew them, they could still be able to say, "Look, this is me, Father, this is who I am, and I am comfortable enough with you to be able to bare my soul to you, to say that I have a problem with stealing, or with adultery, or with whatever the issue might be. And I trust you, that you will help me and not think less of me because of this, and that you will still want to be my friend despite my shortcomings." I felt privileged by this and honored to be their priest. God's love for people is unconditional. Mine should be no less.

And because I knew them, I really did have to work hard at maintaining objectivity. The pressure was on me because I had to be stern enough not to let them off the hook because of our friendship. I had to be able to tell them some hard things at times, like they might need professional counseling or therapy for their problems. I had to work to make sure that our friendship didn't get in the way of my helping them.

I tried to make confession a therapeutic process—a process that brought change and healing and growth. In the old days if you did something really bad, the priest might tell you that for your penance you had to pray the rosary every night for a week, pray for peace in the world and the conversion of Russia. I would think—what the hell does that have to do with the price of chickens in Toledo?

If the problem was say, one of stealing, I would tell the person, okay, you have a problem with stealing money from the petty cash fund at work. In order to address that, can you ask that you not have access to the petty cash at work anymore? You don't have to tell them why; just say it's too much pressure and you'd rather not. You're not lying to them, you're just not sharing with them that you have a tendency to pilfer the fund. And the money that you've taken, how much was it? They'd tell me, and usually I wouldn't give them the standard answer, which was to tell them to give that same amount to the church as a donation. Priests usually advised this, which is fine, but I thought we could do better and make it a little more personal. I also know of priests who asked that the money be given to them, which hopefully then went to someone who needed it.

Instead, I would ask the person what kind of business he or she worked in. If they said that they worked at say, a blood donor center, then I would ask them to send that same amount of money anonymously to the American Red Cross. I believed that you have to be truly sorry for what you've done, have to want to change, and have to make the penance personal for it to work.

Confession, like therapy, is a process. I don't think that one conversation can change a long-term problem. You have to keep working on it. But it seemed to work. I could see people responding, changing, growing, doing better, and that's what it's all about. And they kept coming back to me for confession, so I can only think that I must have been doing something right. Again, I felt privileged to participate in their lives this way, and privileged to help them.

For those of you who may not know this—although I'm sure that most everybody does—whatever a person tells a priest in confession is bound by what's called the Seal of Confession, which means that the priest can't tell anyone what's been confessed to him. People can confess murders and rapes and incest (and I've heard all of those), and the priest has to keep it confidential. We can't call a therapist or social services or the police. People have to be assured that they can talk about anything and everything to the priest without those kinds of repercussions. If they didn't have that guarantee, then they might be reluctant to discuss some of the things they've done that they feel they need help with.

In situations like the ones that I've mentioned, we can ask them to go to therapy or the police, but we can't force them to do that. It can be a moral dilemma at times and it can be really stressful for the priest, but he is bound by the Seal and can't waver from that. It's something he just has to live with. In the past, priests have actually been jailed or put to death for refusing to break the Seal of Confession.

I was in a job where I really didn't have a whole lot to do, had time to "be" and time to smell the roses, and it was good, although maybe a little boring at times. But I was young, full of energy and ideas, full of stuff that I wanted to do, still naïve enough to think that I could somehow change the church. Yet I also remember a thought creeping in—that if I couldn't effect any change, if I couldn't put up with the bullshit anymore—then what? What else could I do with my life?

I remember one evening when I had ridden my bike to the top of a little hill. As I sat there with my doggie watching the beautiful sunset, I thought long and hard about these things and decided to take my previous pastor's advice and go back to school.

I applied to the university to enter their master's program for counseling and got accepted. So besides my duties as pastor, I also became a student again. I didn't ask the bishop for permission since I would be paying for it myself, and would make sure that my role as pastor wasn't compromised. I worked my church duties around my school schedule, and it all worked out pretty well. I was busy once again, and I'm always the happiest when I'm the busiest!

I would take my dog with me when I went to classes because I didn't have anyone to watch him, and I didn't want to leave him locked up in the rectory for hours on end. I would keep him in the car, parked in a shady spot with the windows cracked open and a water bowl within reach. When we had a break during class, I would go out and walk him, let him do his duty if he needed to, give him a treat and refresh his water bowl, then hightail it back to class.

Chapter 24

After a week or two, one of my professors asked to speak to me. He said that my professors were concerned about my behavior. He said that instead of mingling with my fellow students during our breaks, being sociable, and forming bonds with them that could well extend into our professional lives, I would leave and do God knows what—and that concerned them. (Actually, the concern came from my fellow students who then went to the professors about it.) So I took him out to my car, showed him my dog, and told him what I had been doing. The professor said, "Oh, my gosh! You don't have to leave him out here—bring him in!" And from that moment on my dog joined me in class. The professors let him sit under my desk and he sat quietly through each class with me, never once making a fuss or being a distraction.

My fellow students thought it was great, and during our breaks I think my dog got more attention from them than I did! And when I finally graduated, the university actually presented him with a degree too, actually called his name from the stage, and said that of the two of us, he was the better behaved student!

I don't think I've mentioned paychecks yet, but as priests we did get paid for our work. I think it was once a month, and I think that as a new priest I was making about $225.00 a month. It doesn't sound like a whole lot, but back then it wasn't that bad. You have to remember that priests don't have a mortgage or rent to pay, and all of their utilities were paid for as well as medical insurance and medical bills. Food and liquor also came out of parish funds, and most priests got a monthly car allotment to help pay for maintenance and gas because they had to use their cars to do parish work. This was in the days before credit cards, so many parishes had standing charge accounts at all of the stores in town. So if father needed to buy material for say, a new altar cloth, he could go to the fabric store and buy the material and charge it. If father wanted to throw in some extra material for a new suit on occasion, no one would argue with him about it. And here and there you might find a few priests who had quite the collection of fine wine and liquor in their cabinets, caviar and steaks in their fridges, all of which were paid for by the parish.

This is why the seminarians called the priesthood the "good ship lollipop," because just about every expense was paid for. My paycheck was my "base" pay because priests also get money from other sources. One of these sources was the Mass itself. Catholics pay for "intentions" to be said at a Mass. Let's say that you have a family member who is ill or it's the anniversary of your mother's death. You ask father to include their names in the Mass to be read out loud so that the congregation can pray for them, and their names would also be printed in the parish bulletin. This was called an "announced intention." You had to pay a small fee for this—I think it might have been around five dollars. If there were a lot of people who wanted this done in any one Mass, father couldn't include them all or he'd be reading the list of names for most of the Mass. So you can pay a smaller fee—of about three dollars—for an "unannounced intention," which is an intention that's not read out loud or included in the bulletin, but is added in father's thoughts. After father has read the names of the "announced intentions" out loud, he will then add the other names, the "unannounced intentions," in a silent prayer.

All of the money from these intentions goes to the priest who is celebrating the Mass, so father could conceivably make an extra fifty to one hundred dollars at one Mass. I remember that at some point during my ministry, the bishop cracked down on this practice by putting a limit on how many intentions could be said at one Mass. Some priests were abusing it, piling on the intentions like there was no tomorrow, and collected up to five hundred dollars in intentions from just one Mass.

Priests also make money when they perform ceremonies for people. When you ask a priest to baptize your child or perform your marriage ceremony, you almost always give him a "little something" for his time.

So although your "base" pay might not have been all that much, when you add the other sources of income—coupled with the fact that you don't have very many expenses—you could do pretty well for yourself. Unscrupulous priests could do very, very well for themselves.

When I first came to the parish, collections at Mass were pretty dismal, and a portion of that money was used to pay my salary. The parish was having a hard time paying me so I got a job moonlighting at a local restaurant as a dishwasher. Wait, it's not as crazy as it sounds! One of my parishioners had opened up a restaurant that I frequented because the food was good. She needed a little help one day when her dishwasher had upped and quit. She was at her wits end so I volunteered to help her out and do the dishes for her. She was a fun person and we had a really nice relationship. We used to joke around a lot with each other, and I really enjoyed her company. She insisted on paying me and asked me if I could continue to help her out. I said sure, that most evenings my dance card was pretty empty, didn't have many commitments in the evenings, and so that's what I did. I also helped her to train her wait staff—since I knew that job inside and out—and had a great time teaching the kids how to take care of customers. It also gave me an opportunity to talk to them about things like workplace etiquette, cooperation, and responsibility.

The bishop eventually heard about my evening activities and referred to it saying that it wasn't "appropriate" for a pastor to be doing this, but he didn't tell me to stop. However, by that time the collections had picked up, so I didn't really need to do it for the money any longer, and with some regret did quit. I had really enjoyed it—the camaraderie and being back in the food service industry again—with all its good memories for me.

Soon after I had gotten to this parish, the chancellor called me from the diocesan office to discuss something with me, and while we were talking he kiddingly asked me if I was "happy" now. I asked him what he meant, and he said, "Well, you know why you're there, don't you? The bishop said he sent you to this parish to teach you humility and obedience because of the problems that you're having, because of the way you are." And I answered him by saying how sad I found that, and how unfair that these poor parishioners were given priests that the bishop hated and didn't know what else to do with. The chancellor didn't have a reply to that.

Something that the bishop liked to do at Easter time was to unexpectedly drop in at one of the parishes in his diocese on Good Friday. He would pick a parish at random, help out with the services, and spend a little time at that parish visiting with the pastor and the parishioners. I remember the first Easter that I was at this parish, and no, the bishop didn't visit me—no surprise there. But I do remember the fallout from a visit that year. He picked a parish, showed up unannounced, and couldn't find the pastor or any priests anywhere. The place was being run by the deacons and a few seminarians. The bishop had a fit over it, which we all heard about quite vociferously. It seems that the pastor had taken off for a little "fun" time, but hadn't informed the bishop about it. Again, that goes back to the poor communication in this diocese between the bishop and his priests.

Back then, many of the priests in this diocese each had their own little clique—guys they hung out with—and occasionally they would decide that it was time for all of them to get away for a little R&R. Priests vacationing together happens all the time, and for the majority of them it's just that, a nice vacation. But I remember this one clique that had about five older priests in it, all of whom I knew. They often went out of town together so that they could get drunk, smoke weed, and "screw around." This isn't gossip or hearsay; this is what one of the priests in that group told me. He said that they went out of town to do this because "a dog doesn't shit in its own backyard." (Those were his words, not mine.) I can't say that I approved of what he did, but at least he was honest about it. Most weren't.

I hadn't been pastor for more than a few weeks when the Vicar of Priests from the diocesan office paid me a visit. He was sent by the bishop to find out why I was such an "unhappy" priest, why I was always complaining, and what it was that I wanted.

I told him that like everyone else, I wanted to be happy. And what would make me happy would be to have some open and honest communication between the bishop and myself. I told him that whenever I took my concerns to the bishop, he didn't listen to me, just brushed me off, told me 'oh my, we do have some colorful characters in this diocese.' I told the vicar that I didn't think it was about colorful characters but about a lack of communication and leadership and some real problems within the church that needed to be addressed.

The vicar asked me about my concerns so I told him. I recounted my experiences with my pastors—of alcoholism, pedophilia, and downright craziness. As I was telling him my story, his jaw literally dropped open. He looked at me in shock and he said, "Really? That happened? Really?"

He didn't believe me.

The vicar was an older man, somewhere in his mid-sixties, and he was a very kind man. He was a born-again, Pentecostal Catholic, but not one of the crazy ones. He was one of the sincere, dedicated ones. He was a decent, innocent guy, not an ounce of guile in him; one of those guys who wouldn't even swat a fly. But I think he had led a fairly sheltered existence, and his experiences were very different from mine.

Not every priest ran into the situations that I had. There are many good priests in the ministry—good men, even some holy men—who are a good role model for other priests. I'd guess that a good percent of the priests in this diocese fell into that category. If you are lucky enough to only be exposed to that good percent, then you haven't had the misfortune of running into the other not so good percent like I had. You might have heard some vague rumors or innuendos, but they are outside of your experience; and if you didn't experience it, you couldn't speak to it.

I knew that I wasn't the only new priest to have those kinds of crazy experiences. There was a priest who was several years older than me—a generation up in age. I really liked and admired the kind of man and the kind of priest that he was, and he was a role model for me. When he was still fairly young, he was assigned to a parish as assistant to this crazy-mean, raging alcoholic of a pastor. This pastor was so awful that he ended up breaking my friend's spirit. My friend changed, became guarded and withdrawn and bitter, and got involved in the Charismatic Movement as an outlet for his rage. He stayed in the priesthood, but became a pale imitation of the man that he once was. I was not going to let that happen to me.

So I told the vicar of my experiences and he didn't believe me. He went back to the diocesan office, and in his report he said that I had told him some wild, unbelievable stories about my pastors, and it was obvious that I had some deep seated problems.

Did I hear anything from the bishop after the vicar gave his report? Maybe a phone call saying that we needed to talk? No.

Chapter 24

When I had previously talked to the bishop and told him that I suspected my pastor of pedophilia, I asked the questions "Why doesn't he believe me? Why doesn't he investigate? Why doesn't he do something about it?"

I didn't know the answers to those questions back then, but eventually I found out that it had nothing to do with belief. The bishop couldn't acknowledge that some of his priests were acting out sexually because if he did, he would then have to acknowledge his own sexual misconduct. And he didn't want to do that, so he just ignored the whole mess until it finally caught up with him and he could no longer ignore it, but that's for a later chapter.

I didn't blame the vicar for his report and honestly, I didn't get angry over it. My experiences were beyond his realm of experience, and beyond his belief system. This is similar to the way that I felt when my graduate school rector talked to me on our last day together—when he told me that I would probably have a hard time in the priesthood because the church was so backwards in its thinking and everyone was scrambling for power. I know that was a jaw dropping moment for me, and my first thought too was—really? That stuff really happens?

But it did make me sad, and caused me to engage in a little wishful thinking. What if . . . ? What if my pastors had belonged to that good percent? What if my role models had been good ones? What if none of these awful experiences had happened? But, they did happen and I couldn't change the past; I could only try to survive and make the future better.

Chapter 25

Here We Go Again

One of the complaints that the bishop had about me was that I couldn't get along with my fellow priests. So I should probably name this chapter "Here we go again."

I didn't know the pastor of the parish that adjoined ours, but I had heard from some of my parishioners that he was crazy—and I'm not judging—I'm just repeating what they told me. I had never met the man so I didn't have an opinion one way or the other. I'm not sure what was going on over there, but I'd heard various stories about his throwing people out of the parish because they weren't doing what he wanted, or had pissed him off, and that some parishioners were just fed up with him and left.

Whatever the reason, I suddenly found that a number of his parishioners were now coming to our church. So this pastor called the bishop and complained to him that I was "stealing" his parishioners, and that he wanted monetary compensation from me. He told the bishop that my parish was getting the money that "his" parishioners were tithing, and that I should give it back to him. Okay, at this point I did start forming my own opinion about him.

The bishop sent me a letter and asked me what was going on, and told me to take care of the problem by trying harder to "get along" with that pastor. In the meantime, that pastor had sent me a threatening letter and had also made some threatening phone calls to me. (I still have that letter and kept it in case they found me dead one day—I thought it would give them a clue as to where to look for the perpetrator.) The letter and phone calls were basically the same—who did I think I was, stealing his parishioners, and I'd better give him his money back or else.

So I wrote a letter back to the bishop and told him about the threats that the pastor had made to me, and I said that I was not going to tolerate his craziness. Period. I told him that I did not want to meet this pastor or talk to him, and if I ever saw him anywhere near my parish, I would call the police. I also told him that I had the threatening letter in hand, and if this guy bothered me, or any of my parishioners again, I would take his letter to the police and let them handle it. I knew the bishop's history of vacillating and not taking care of problems, so I felt that I needed to protect myself because the bishop certainly wasn't going to. He'd probably just tell me to celebrate how "colorful" that pastor's personality was.

Maybe it was the mention of the police, but I personally never heard anything more from that pastor. He did, however, continue to cause problems, and set into motion a chain of events that further alienated me from my fellow priests and the bishop. Big time, I might add.

A few months after the threatening letter incident, the bishop sends a letter to that very same pastor terminating his position there and transferring him out of that parish. He gave him a termination date and asked that he vacate the premises by that date. I'm not sure what the precipitating incident was nor do I know where he was being sent. All that we heard was that he was out and another priest, Father Ed, was going to be the new pastor. That was good news for me because we were friends. I really liked the guy, and thought it would be cool to have him so close by.

So Father Ed heads to his new assignment, gets to the parish, and no sooner does he go into the rectory when the old pastor jumps out of a closet where he had been hiding and starts screaming at Father Ed at the top of his lungs, "You can't take my parish! You can't take my parish!" and proceeds to beat the shit out of him. Father Ed then runs out of the rectory, screaming himself, finds a phone, and calls the police. The police show up and search the rectory, but the previous pastor had taken off and was nowhere to be found. Father Ed is really shaken up and doesn't want to go back into the rectory because he's fearful that the pastor might return, so the police escort him out of there and he goes back home. Not sure of what else to do, he goes on a retreat to recover from his ordeal.

When we all heard about what had happened, a big group of us—about twenty of his friends—went to visit him to see how he was doing and to see if there was anything that we could do to help. All of us, especially Father Ed, were upset by what had happened. A bunch of the guys were really angry about it, wanted some action taken, said that we should meet with the bishop and demand that this pastor be forcibly removed from the rectory, and that it wasn't right that any priest should be put in a dangerous situation the way that Father Ed had been. I agreed with them that we should meet with the bishop, but I advised that we talk it out amongst ourselves first and present it to the bishop in a cohesive manner.

Chapter 25

One of our group's concerns was the poor communication between the bishop and the priests in his diocese, which was one of the contributing factors in this incident. (Obviously, I wasn't the only one having communication problems with the bishop.) I told them that I was also concerned that there were more situations like this happening in the diocese that weren't being addressed (I was thinking of Father Abdon), and maybe we could contextualize our concerns in terms of the overall problem.

So we got together and brainstormed. Emotions ran high in our meetings with a lot of anger directed towards the bishop for the way he handled the problems we were having, or rather didn't handle them. There was a lot of complaining and a lot of criticism being voiced, but we were able to channel all of that negativity into a positive approach to present to the bishop, to let him know that we were all in this together, and were all willing to help in any way that we could to resolve these shared issues.

We called the bishop, told him that we were concerned about what had happened to Father Ed and wanted to meet with him. He agreed and invited us to have lunch with him before our meeting, which we did. We opened the meeting with a prayer and then the bishop read the list of concerns that we had prepared. After reading through them, he looked up at us and said, "It's too bad that that happened, but I've sent him (that pastor) a letter, and everything should be fine now."

That was it. He didn't discuss any of the specific problems that we had; didn't even mention them. We had met quite a number of times, had spent countless hours working on our list of concerns, and he dismissed them all with "it should be fine now." The group was stunned into silence, and everyone nervously glanced at each other like—what do we do now? Someone needed to speak up, to speak for us, and to make the bishop take us seriously, so I did.

"Well, Bishop," I said, "you already sent him that first letter transferring him out and that wasn't adhered to, so why do you think he's going to listen to a second letter? Shouldn't the first letter have sufficed?"

He replied, "Well, I am the Bishop."

I replied saying, "Well, we acknowledge that, but apparently this other priest doesn't. If you have to send a second letter, then he's not acknowledging that you have authority in this situation." Wrong thing to say. The bishop didn't like that comment.

He then told me, "I think you're being disrespectful with me."

I told him, "With all due respect, I apologize if that's how it sounded. I'm just saying that given the facts, it doesn't seem that it's just your authority that's at issue here. What's going on is that this man probably needs some kind of help. That's why law enforcement is involved. The civil authorities are involved and this could turn into something big—a scandal—and none of us wants to see that happen."

Silence. The bishop is visibly pissed, pissed that we haven't all said 'golly gee, Bishop, thank you so much for putting our minds at rest; we'll be on our way now.' At that point a couple of the guys, noticing how angry he was getting, stood up and said, "Bishop, we agree with you. Father (me) is being too aggressive with you. He needs to calm down."

Sometimes you only have a split second in which to make a life altering decision, to decide what's more important to you— your career or the truth. I made my decision. I stood up, faced the group, and said, "Excuse me? We all met with Father Ed. We met and we talked and we strategized. How many meetings did we have about how we could approach the bishop with this? This was our plan, we all agreed on it, and all I'm doing is presenting it and suddenly I'm being too aggressive?"

Things might still have been okay for me if at that point I had just shut up, but I didn't. I was angry and I was tired—tired of the bullshit, tired unto death of this sick dynamic that bound us all together—and I was going to do something unpardonable. I was going to bring it out in the open, and toss it out on the table for everyone to see. I said, "Bishop, let me tell you something. Do you realize what we think of you, we priests? We feel that you have absolutely no courage. The talk about you is that you vacillate, that the last person who speaks with you and gives you their viewpoint is what you do, whether they're right or wrong. You try to say yes to everybody so nothing ever gets done. And everyone here feels the same way."

I looked at my fellow priests, my so-called friends who by now were all cowering in their seats, and I said, "We strategized about how we were going to present our concerns to the bishop, I'm doing what we said we were going to do, and now I'm being too strong? Now you're all backing down? Now *I'm* being too strong with the bishop when I've heard every one of you say—and let me quote some of those remarks to you, bishop. "He's a coward. He doesn't have any balls. The only time that he has balls is when he hugs little girls."

I said, "Bishop, this is what we say about you when you're not present, and then we kiss your butt when you are present. This is the truth. This is the reality of the relationship between us. Now something needs to get done here. There are bigger issues at stake here. Should we not begin to address these? I may be out of line, but I'm speaking the truth. We can't address an issue if there's no truth behind it."

At that point pandemonium erupts. Every priest at that table jumped up in horror, saying as almost one voice, "No, no, no, we're

Chapter 25

sorry, Bishop. Oh no, no, he's not speaking on our behalf. We're so sorry."

The bishop looks at me smugly, confident in his power over us, and says, "You're being inappropriate."

I looked back at him and said, "Bishop, I don't believe I've been that disrespectful to you. I've cursed you out in front of my brother priests as much as the next guy because I believe that you're on a power trip and want to be charismatic and loved by everyone, so nothing ever gets done. I think you're the most ineffective bishop we've ever had, but that's just me. But I tell you these things to your face and you know that's the truth. We've met privately and I've told you how I felt about you, and you've told me how you felt about me. We've done that face-to-face. I won't speak badly about you behind your back if I cannot say it to you face-to-face, which I have, and you know I have."

I turned and looked at my fellow priests who obviously had all made their decisions, too, and said, "I can only speak for myself, but I can get up in the morning and look in the mirror and face myself because I'm doing what I feel is right. I can face myself with what I believe is the truth and no, sometimes it's not pretty, but it's the truth, and that's what I've got to work with. I don't have to hide my face because I'm a coward trying to protect my position in the church. From this moment on I will not attend any more of your stupid meetings on how to approach the bishop, and I don't want to hear about any more issues that we have regarding the bishop. Obviously, it's every man for himself now. You're on your own and I'm on my own."

I turned back to the bishop and said, "Bishop, I apologize if I came on too strong, and I also apologize to the group. But obviously nothing is ever going to get done because you all refuse to look at the reality of what really goes on. So fend for yourselves and don't include me anymore. Goodbye."

I was so angry that I couldn't even see straight. I blindly turned from the table and stalked out through the kitchen, jerked open the kitchen door—the crash it made as it hit the wall was magnified in the total silence behind me—stormed out and slammed the door behind me.

Did I get fired over the things that I had said? No. And for a long time that puzzled me that I didn't. (I finally did figure it out, which I'll tell you about later.) The bishop could have fired me on the spot, and could have fired every one of us at that meeting. He knew it and we all knew it, which is why the rest of my friends caved; they didn't want to lose their jobs. They made their decisions and cast their lots that their careers were the most important—albeit unspoken—topic at that meeting. Did I get reprimanded over it? Again, no. Everyone just pretended that it didn't happen and life went on.

That infamous pastor, however, was never found. The last I heard, he was a fugitive from justice—a "person of interest" in the unsolved killing of an altar boy.

Disastrous meeting over, I returned to my parish to get back to work. Did I think about quitting? Did I think that maybe I was the oddball here, that this was just another sign that I didn't belong in the priesthood? Well, I was definitely the oddball when it came to the bureaucratic part of the church, but the other part of my "priest" life helped to balance that out. The most important part of my life was still the same, and that was helping to "grow" my parishioners on their path to the Divine Presence. That never got old or stale and it's what helped to keep me sane.

And I was finding in my studies that I seemed to have a real knack for therapy. Everything that I was learning in psychology informed my spirituality, and all of the spiritual concepts that were a part of my life informed the psychology that I was learning. They seemed to fit together like a hand and a glove. It reminded me of that visiting professor that I had back in grad school—the one who said that everything that we learned should illumine our understanding of scripture. This seemed to be a natural progression of that, in that everything we learned and experienced could enhance our spirituality. For me it all came together in a psycho-spiritual way, which is the kind of therapy that I started practicing and continue to practice to this day.

I decided that what I wanted to do once I had my degree was to work with the clergy, with dysfunctional priests. When I had my oral exams for my master's degree, one of the questions they asked us was, "What do you plan to do with your degree?" And that's what popped out of my mouth—that I wanted to work with troubled clergy. Talk about job security! If church bureaucracy couldn't or wouldn't find a way to help these men with their problems, that's where I could channel my energies. Someone had to either help these guys or get them out of the priesthood, or both.

I went back to my parish and I never again went to any of their meetings. Of course, I was never again asked to, but I didn't feel like that was any great loss. (I also lost my position as dean and the title of Vicar Forane when I was transferred out of the parish that I had been in with Father Abdon.) We didn't talk about any spiritual matters at those meetings, about how we were doing in our effort to bring people to God. The main topics seemed to be how we could get people to do what we wanted and how we could get more money out of them.

When it came to money, it seems that the means justified the ends. I've heard a number of priests bragging about the older, wealthy parishioners they knew and were very close to, and how when these parishioners died, they had promised to leave their money or a portion of it to "father" to be used for the church. Sometimes it seemed like a "pissing contest" between the priests as they tried to one-up each other over the amounts of money that they would get. One priest would say, 'Oh, the widow so-and-so promised me that when she died I would get . . ." and then he'd name an amount.

His fellow priest in the conversation would then say, "Oh, that's nothing. The widow so-and-so that I'm friends with told me that when she died I would get . . ." and then he'd name a larger sum. And then a third priest would chime in and they'd all be laughing over their good fortune.

I had been privy to those kinds of conversations many a time, and each time I came away feeling disgusted.

So I didn't do very well at these meetings mainly because I could never keep my mouth shut. I was floored by the attitude of some of my fellow priests, talking about parishioners as sheep who needed to be led because they couldn't think for themselves. They were souls that were just a penny a dozen, there to serve the institution rather than to be served by it. (Unless, of course, they were wealthy.) Hearing about how we, due to the fact of our ordination, were in a different category than mere mortals—how we were practically divine—or at least the next best thing to it.

Did all priests subscribe to this view? Of course not. So how did they handle the bullshit? They listened and then they let it go. They recognized it for what it was, gave it no importance, and left it at the meeting. Then they went back to their parishes and did the right thing for their parishioners. They kept their mouths shut, and just did their own thing regardless of the prevailing opinions expressed in the meeting.

But I couldn't. It just wasn't in my nature. I had to call a spade a spade, and usually I had to do it as loudly as possible. There were times when I would hear some opinion expressed at a meeting, usually something derogatory about the parishioners, and I would stand up and challenge it and actually get shouted down by my fellow priests. With my own ears I've heard them say that we didn't want our parishioners to get too uppity, that we didn't want to tell them the truth, but just give them enough to hold them in their place. Yes, you can use a person's beliefs to hold them in their place, but you can also use a person's beliefs to set them free to be all that they can be.

When I made the comment at the meeting with the bishop that 'it was every man for himself and I was on my own,' truer words were never spoken. It got to be that when most other priests saw me coming, they would scatter. They were tired of me, of my bluntness, and my inability to compromise. I started living a parallel existence, still "in" the church but not really "of" it. I did my own thing and everyone left me alone to do it.

So I went back to work in my little far off corner of the world, and one day this woman approached me and asked for my help. She was Catholic and had gotten a divorce, and wanted my help in getting her marriage annulled. Back then divorce was more uncommon among Catholics than it is today, and divorced Catholics were penalized by the church.

If you were divorced, you were not allowed to partake of the Sacrament of Holy Communion, so you were no longer in full fellowship with your fellow Catholics or the church. Most Catholics found that embarrassing, that when communion time rolled around and just about everyone else was heading up to the altar, you stayed in your seat. That would usually cause some raised eyebrows among your fellow worshipers. You knew what they were thinking as they passed your pew—that you had some terrible sin staining your soul that you hadn't confessed, that you were probably in a state of mortal sin, and that wasn't a comfortable feeling. And if you ever wanted to remarry, you wouldn't be able to do it in the Catholic Church.

Marriage annulments were more common back then. An annulment was the dissolution of a marriage by the church when it could be reasonably proven that the marriage was not entered into as a sacrament, the Sacrament of Marriage. There were a number of things that could be used as a reason for an annulment. For instance, one of the reasons might be that after getting married the wife finds out that her husband does not want to have any children, which he didn't mention to her beforehand. If he had, she might not have wanted to marry him, so she married him under false pretenses. Since the Catholic Church believes that the procreation of children is the only valid reason for marriage, they would then grant the woman an annulment, dissolving the marriage as if it had never taken place, and she would then be back in full fellowship with the church.

To get an annulment you had to make an application to the Office of the Marriage Tribunal, and the process was similar to a civil court trial. The parties involved would present written documents explaining why an annulment was being requested. The Officialis, the priest in charge of the Marriage Tribunal, was the judge. One priest was assigned as a "lawyer" for the wife, and another priest was the "lawyer" for the husband. Using the written documentation, they would then argue the case in front of the Officialis. (The actual couple was not present at the "trial".) The Officialis would listen to the arguments being presented and would then render his decision as to whether the marriage was a sacramental union or not. If a decision was made not to grant the annulment, the matter was automatically sent to a different diocese to be "retried," like going to a Court of Appeals.

So this woman comes to talk to me. She was from the same city that I had been in my last assignment, but at a different parish so I didn't know her. She told me that she had a problem and didn't know what to do, that she had heard of me from my last assignment, and hoped that I could help her because she didn't know where else to turn.

I told her that I would be glad to help her if I could and she told me her story. She said that she had divorced her husband because he'd had an affair with the priest who was the pastor of their parish. (Wait—it gets better.) Because she was a devout Catholic, she wanted to get an annulment so that she could continue to participate fully in the church. The problem, however, was that their pastor was also the Officialis for the Marriage Tribunal in the diocese. Technically, that meant that the priest who'd had an adulterous affair with her husband and had broken up her marriage was the priest who would be deciding on her annulment.

Okay, I could see how that might be a problem. I told her that I could help her and asked her to write out her statement, which I then had notarized and placed in a sealed envelope. I called the bishop and told him that I was sending her request for an annulment to a different diocese for handling. He blew a cog over that, wanting to know why I wasn't handling it in the usual way. I explained the situation to him and told him that I was doing it because there was definitely a conflict of interest here. He wasn't happy about it since the priest in question was a good friend of his, but he couldn't interfere in the process. I never told anyone else the specifics of the case since it's not my role to judge or besmirch anyone's reputation. I was the facilitator of this process, not the judge or jury.

The woman got her annulment and that priest eventually was removed from ministry. He was charged with pedophilia, but he was an indiscriminate predator. When his activities came to light, among his victims were men, women, and children.

Every summer, a group of Capuchin Franciscans from out of state would come to our diocese and sponsor retreats as part of a vocation appeal. They would advertise the retreats for men who thought they might have a vocation to the priesthood or brotherhood, or who just wanted to find out more about the Franciscan way of life. They asked me if I would be a speaker at their retreat. Because of my young age and long hair, I was a "walking advertisement" for their stance that the priesthood or brotherhood had a place in it for all different kinds of people. (And I was definitely considered different!)

Because I had a spiritual connection to the Franciscans—they would always hold a special place in my heart—I agreed. That summer I went to the retreat, said Mass for them, and gave a talk to this big group of young men. I enjoyed meeting and talking with all of them, and I especially remembered these two young brothers who were identical twins. They were high school seniors, just the nicest guys, and seemed sincerely interested in finding out more about religious life. I spent a fair amount of time with them, answered their questions, and just enjoyed their company. Again, these were just really nice young men.

A week or so after the retreat, I had driven to a different part of the state on my day off to visit a friend of mine who was a priest. On my way back home, I pulled off the highway at a small town and stopped at a restaurant to get a soda to go.

As I'm going into the restaurant, who walks out but those twin brothers whom I had met at the retreat. We were surprised to see each other, and I remember that they said "Hi" and asked me if I remembered them. I said of course, and they each gave me a hug. I asked them what they were doing there, and they said that they were there with "father." I said, "What "father?" Can I meet him?" They said sure and walked me back into the restaurant where "father" was at the cash register paying their bill. I knew "father," knew that there were rumors of questionable behavior about him, although nothing but rumors at this time. He looked shocked to see me there. So I said hello to him and made it a point to tell him that these guys were friends of mine.

As we all walked out, I told the boys that it was good to see them again and, very loudly, so that "father" wouldn't miss it, told them that I wanted to give them my phone number and that I wanted them to call me—day or night—if they had any problems with anything. They looked at me kind of quizzically, but said sure, took my number, and then we hugged again. "Father" just glared at me as I wished them a safe journey home. They got home safely, and the few times that I ran into "father" after that he never acknowledged me; actually never spoke another word to me ever again.

Many years later, the rumors about "father" became substantiated, and he was charged with pedophilia and kicked out of the priesthood. (He was the "Officialis" of the Marriage Tribunal in the prior incident that I described in the annulment issue.)

Chapter 26

Parish Life, Okay, My Life Is Never Dull

I had complained that life out in the boondocks was a little bit boring at times, and that there was nothing very exciting going on. Someone very wise once said to be careful of what you wished for.

When I first arrived at this parish, the parishioners had been without a pastor for some time because he had gotten sick and was in the hospital, so no one had been living in the rectory before I got there. After I moved in, I remember several of the parishioners telling me that although the rectory had been empty while their previous pastor was in the hospital, a few times people had noticed that there were lights on inside. Lights would go on then later they would shut off, although the doors were locked and no one was inside the rectory. I heard this from several different people, but they also told me that this had been going on for years, that whenever the rectory was empty because the parish didn't have a priest in attendance, people would notice lights on in the rectory when they shouldn't have been.

A few of the parishioners told me that they thought the rectory might be haunted. I didn't give it much thought. This was a small, quiet town where nothing too exciting ever happened, and sometimes innocent things can be blown out of proportion or misunderstood—or sometimes embellished to make life seem more exciting.

But I did have some odd things happen—things that I couldn't explain—and it began not long after I moved into the rectory. The rectory was fairly large and heating it was expensive. So whenever I went out and the temperatures were going to be on the cool or cold side, I would close the inside doors to all of the rooms to conserve heat. There were several doors: between the living room and dining room, between the dining room and kitchen, and then the two bedroom doors and two bathroom doors. Anyway, if I was going to be gone for a while, I would turn down the heat and close the doors to help keep the rooms warm and to save money on the heating bills because this was a poor parish.

One of the first times that I closed all of those doors before going out, all of those inside doors were open again when I returned to the rectory. The first time that it happened I remember thinking—whoa, that's really weird—what's going on here? I knew that no one else had been in the rectory. So the next time that I left, I made double sure that when I closed the inside doors that I did it securely, making sure they latched so that they couldn't swing open if there was a breeze or something blowing through the house.

When I returned to the rectory, all of those doors were open again.

I didn't know why that was happening; I just didn't understand it. I never felt uncomfortable in the rectory, never felt nervous or scared, and never saw anything that scared me. I don't think I ever mentioned it to anyone. I just lived with it and figured it was just one of those things and just sort of ignored it.

One evening I had a friend over. He and I were sitting at the dining room table having coffee and talking, and the door from the dining room to the living room was closed. Suddenly, the door explodes inward, ripped right off its hinges, slammed down, and skidded to within a foot of the dining room table. My friend jumped up and said, "What the . . . ." It was as if someone had rammed it open from the living room side. Well, that certainly put a damper on our evening! I just looked at my friend, shrugged my shoulders, and we picked up the door and propped it against the wall. I told my friend that I didn't know what that was all about, but I remember thinking to myself that there was someone in this house who definitely had a thing against doors.

After my friend left, I sat back down at the table and I started talking to the empty room. I said, "Hey, I don't know who you are or what's wrong or what you want. I know that I'm just a visitor, but I have to live here right now and I would like to live in peace with you. I think we can do that, and I think we can share this place. Okay? Can we try?" Call me crazy if you want, but it seemed that after that conversation, things quieted down. At least there were no more flying doors.

A week or so after that, I was in my bedroom talking to my mom on the phone. It was my day off and I was going to take her out to lunch so we were talking about that. I had my bedroom door closed and locked. I wasn't scared to be in the rectory by myself, but I wasn't going to take any chances, either. So as I'm talking to my mom, I notice that the doorknob on my bedroom door starts to turn like someone's trying to open it, and I mentioned it to my mom. She got all excited and asked if she should hang up and call the police or if I should call the police, but I told her that I didn't think we needed to do that. As I'm telling her that, the lock pops up and the door slowly opens. It stays open for about a minute, during which time I walk over to the door and peer around it. I don't see anyone there, then the door closes and locks again. Okaaay. I remember thinking to myself, what is it about closed doors around here? I calmed my mom down, told her everything was fine, and we finished our conversation.

Then one evening I had some company at the rectory. Actually, I always had a lot of company at the rectory—people were always stopping by to visit or hang out. Really, always— everybody and their brother—so it was pretty rare for me to be home alone most evenings. But I especially remember this one evening because of what happened . . . .

I think there were about six of us sitting around the dining room table, just talking and drinking sodas. One was a young man, a parishioner around my age, along with his girlfriend, her two younger brothers, one of her girlfriends, and me. We were just relaxing, talking and laughing and telling jokes, and having a nice time when suddenly we see this kid looking in at us through the doorway, the one that separates the dining room from the living room. It all happened really quickly, but it looked as if this kid had been running, had started to run past the doorway, stopped for a moment when he saw us, looked in at us, and then he was gone again.

He looked to be about twelve years old and had dark blonde or very light brown hair. He was wearing a red plaid shirt and jeans with the cuffs rolled up, with black and white Keds sneakers on. I can still clearly recall the look of surprise on his face when he saw us.

So everyone at the table turns to me and says, "Oh, who's that? Do you have a friend or a relative visiting?"

No, I didn't have anyone visiting, other than my friends at the table. I didn't understand what had just happened, but I didn't want to make a fuss or scare anyone until we knew what was going on, so I think I said something like, "Oh, a friend . . . ."

I mean, it was possible that someone had come into the rectory—maybe I hadn't locked the front door (only I knew that I had). And then I thought about how the doors in this place were always opening, thinking, hmm . . . I didn't want to influence anyone one way or the other just yet, so when one of the girls jumped up from the table saying, "Oh, let's go get him and bring him into the dining room with us," I think I said something like, "Um, I think he might be really shy." But at that point everyone had gotten up and I just followed them out as they started searching for my "friend."

The other girl yelled something like, "Hey, come and join us." (You know, girls and their mothering instincts.)

I followed, not saying anything, as they all headed to the second bedroom, figuring that this would be where he was staying. As they were walking towards the second bedroom, the girls were again calling out to him, telling him to come out and join us. But when we got to the bedroom, it was empty, as was the bathroom. One of the girls looked under the bed and in the closet, wondering if maybe they had scared the little boy. But no one was there.

At that point they all stopped, turned and looked at me questioningly, and I finally confessed. I told them that I had never before in my life seen that kid, that I had no one visiting me, and that I didn't know what was going on. I then told them about the doors in the house opening after I had closed them, that I was beginning to think that maybe there was a "presence" in this house, and that maybe we had all just seen him.

I think they all said, "WHAT?" at about the same time and then said that we should search the rest of the house, which we did. We looked through all of the remaining rooms, the closets, anywhere someone could conceivably hide. I mean, we checked everywhere, and—nothing. All of the windows were closed and locked, just as they had been, and the front and back doors were both locked, not only locked but bolted on the inside. No one had left this house.

So we went back to the dining room, sat back down, grabbed our sodas and talked about what we had seen. No one seemed scared, and everyone seemed more excited about our encounter than anything else. We talked about it at length and decided that we must have seen a ghost—I mean, we couldn't come up with any other explanation. And if that's what it was, he seemed more scared of us than we were of him. And maybe he was the one turning on the lights that people were seeing because the dark scared him, and maybe he was the one opening the doors that I was closing because he didn't like to be shut in. No one felt that it was anything to be afraid of; everyone was calm and thought it was kind of cool.

I never saw that kid again, although the door thing still happened along with a few other weird things that some of my other friends witnessed. On the day of my departure when my assignment was over at this parish and it was time for me to leave, I sat in the living room for a little while and I talked to him, and said my goodbyes. I thanked him for letting me share the rectory with him, told him that I would pray for him, and pray that he find what he was looking for and get to wherever he needed to go.

What had we seen? To this day I don't have an explanation for what happened. I just know that we all saw what we saw.

The next thing that I want to tell you about didn't involve ghosts but real people, and it *was* scary.

I was going to take two days off from work to go out of town for some medical appointments, and I told the parish secretary that she could also take those days off. If there was an emergency in the parish and someone needed a priest, they could call the diocesan office and get instructions on what to do. Before I left, I first had to do the morning Mass and normally—if it was my day off and I was going out of town—I'd do the Mass and then go back to the rectory for my stuff, load my car, get my doggie, then take off.

On that morning, a couple of the older parish ladies had planned a special breakfast for me at one of their homes, and of course, I couldn't say no to a good home cooked meal! So before Mass, I packed up my car so that after breakfast I could just leave without having to go back to the rectory, and would make up a little lost time that way. I had my dog with me and he slept in the car while I said Mass. So I said Mass, had a delicious breakfast with the ladies, then my dog and I headed out.

Unbeknownst to any of us, the local bank was being robbed at gunpoint while we were having Mass. I heard about it when I called the secretary before I headed back from my trip. The secretary told me that the police had called her in the afternoon on the day that I had left asking her if she could let them into the rectory so that they could search it. There had been no sign of the bank robber, but he was armed and dangerous and the police didn't know if he had left town or was hiding out somewhere, so they were checking all of the abandoned and empty buildings in town. She used her key to let them in and they searched the place but didn't find anything.

So that evening as I get back to the rectory, I'm walking in with my bags and the first thing that I noticed was that a piece of furniture had been moved, a piece that no one would have any reason to move. There was a door in the main entrance room of the rectory that opened to a staircase leading up to the second floor. The stairs were old and rickety and the upstairs attic area was unfinished. We had kids come to the rectory for catechism classes and I didn't want any of them wandering up the stairs to the attic and falling through the rafters, so I had moved a large chest, like an armoire, in front of the doorway to block it off and keep everyone out. The chest was quite large and covered the entire doorframe so that you couldn't even tell that there was a door there.

I thought it was odd that the chest had been moved, but on second thought figured that the police must have moved it when they searched the rectory. But I still felt a little uneasy about it, and decided to check it out myself. So I moved it out of the way, opened the door, and went upstairs. I wasn't expecting to find anything amiss, so I was really surprised at what I did find. It looked as if someone had been up there, as the place was a mess with discarded food wrappers and empty soda cans strewn about. The last time I had been in the attic before closing off the doorway, there had been nothing up there but dust and mice.

So I went back downstairs to call the police, but first I took my bags to my room and I could immediately tell that someone had been in there too; it even looked like someone had slept in my bed. I called my friend who was a state policeman—the same guy who had stopped me for speeding on my way into town on my first day here. I told him that I had just gotten back into town and it looked to me as if someone had been in the rectory. He told me to stay put and that he would be there shortly.

He arrived pretty quickly accompanied by a fingerprint team. When he got there, he pushed me to one side and told me to stay put, got his flashlight out, drew his gun, and went upstairs. It was like something you saw happen in the movies! They searched the attic and the rest of the rectory and discovered that the back door had been cleverly jimmied, something that they hadn't noticed when they did their initial search. They dusted all over for fingerprints and surmised that the robber had holed up in the rectory after he had robbed the bank!

Thankfully, they caught the bank robber about two weeks later, and the story he told the police sent shivers down my spine. He was a guy from out of town who had been scoping out the town for a couple of days before the robbery. He said that he was planning on taking the priest as a hostage, so he had been watching me to see what my routine was. On the day of the bank robbery, he had figured that I would go back to the rectory after the morning Mass, after he had robbed the bank, and he would then break in, take me hostage, and I would be his ticket out of town in case anything went wrong.

I can never say no to food, which is why I've had a weight problem most of my life and have always considered that to be one of my shortcomings. This time, however, my love of eating very possibly saved my life.

The next incident that happened shortly after the previous one did not have a happy ending. In fact, it was quite tragic. This time, it wasn't my appetite but my tardiness that was the issue. And I'm alive today because of it.

It was a Friday night and the local school was holding a dance in the school gym. One of my parishioners invited me to her house for a drink before the dance. She said that four of her brothers would also be there, that we could visit and have a drink, and then we'd all head to the dance together. She said that they would need to get there a little early to help set up, and I said sure, that would be fine.

Anyone who knows me well knows that I have a tendency to be late. I think she told me that the dance was supposed to start at nine o'clock and had asked me to be at her house around eight. As usual I was running a little behind, but I think I was only late by a few minutes. When I got there, I knocked on the door but no one answered. I tried the

Chapter 26

doorknob and it wasn't locked, so I opened the door and stuck my head in, called out asking if anyone was home, but again there was no answer. So I walked in a little ways, called out again, but the house was empty. I figured that since I had been late, maybe they didn't want to wait for me and had all gone out for a drink, or maybe something had come up and they just went on ahead to the dance. I left and went back to the rectory for a little bit and then headed to the dance.

When I got to the dance, I noticed that she and her brothers weren't there. I asked a few of the other people there if they had seen them and they all said no, and that it was odd because they had volunteered to be there early to help set up and had never shown up. They never arrived that night and no one knew what to think, other than maybe some kind of emergency had popped up that they had to take care of.

The next morning we hear that the family is missing. The missing woman had a daughter, a little girl who was about seven years old, and sometime during the night the little girl turns up at her grandmother's house and tells her that she doesn't know where her mommy is. The grandmother calls the police, and the little girl tells them that she had been at home with her mom and uncles when a man came over and started arguing with her mom, and there was so much yelling and fighting going on that the little girl got scared and hid. And then suddenly it was quiet and everyone was gone. She also told them that a few minutes after the yelling stopped, father (me) had knocked on the door and come in but she was too scared to answer him so she just stayed hidden and he left. She waited for a while but her mom and uncles never came back, so she crawled out of her hiding place and ran to her grandmother's house.

The police treated it as a kidnapping and began their investigation. They talked to me, although I could tell them very little. Like everyone else, I was totally mystified. Something that did come to light during their inquiries was a feud that had developed between the missing woman and the dad of one of her daughter's classmates. It seems that the previous summer the woman had bought her daughter a new bike, which was then stolen. She believed that one of her daughter's classmates had stolen it, but she couldn't prove it. She got into a fight over it with the father of the boy that she believed had stolen her daughter's bike, and there had been "bad blood" between the two families ever since, and that they had been arguing over it almost constantly since then.

The police thought it was a little odd that the man that she was feuding with hadn't been seen around town since the night of the dance, so they got a search warrant for his home. The state police and a crime lab team went to the man's home and the man burst out shooting a rifle, wounding an officer, and the police shot and killed him. As the family's pastor, they called me to the scene to help comfort his mom and sister. His sister was a good friend of mine although I didn't know her brother, the man who was killed. And mercifully, the man's young son had not been home at the time of the incident. They had shot the guy in the chest at close range and the scene was gruesome—the whole front of his chest was gone, blood was splattered everywhere along with clumps of flesh and bone and God knows what else. I gave him the "Blessing of the Dead" and did my best to comfort his family in their shock and grief.

About two months after the shooting, five bodies were found buried in a shallow grave about five miles out of town. The missing family had been found. They had all been hogtied with barbed wire and shot in the back of the head. When the police processed the scene, they found fingerprints everywhere—fingerprints belonging to the man that they had shot and killed—evidence that that man had killed the family. All of that death and destruction—over a bike.

Afterwards, I remember one of the state policemen coming up to me and saying, "Father, you are one lucky son of a bitch. If you hadn't been late that night, we would've been pulling your body from that grave, too."

I conducted the funeral services for all of the victims. First we buried the woman and her brothers and the following week, the man who had killed them. He had been a Vietnam veteran suffering from post-traumatic stress disorder, heavily into alcohol and drugs, and apparently he had just "snapped." Since a lot of people in that town were related to each other by marriage, there were people from both sets of families at both funerals.

Before the first funeral, a friend of mine—actually the priest who had been my pastor in my last assignment—told me that he was concerned about me, saying that I needed to be careful about what I said at the services. Because there was a lot of anger and grief in the community, he didn't want me getting caught in the middle of it, making myself a target for some grief-stricken relative. He said that some of the feuds in these little towns could get really vicious and would put the Hatfield's and McCoy's to shame. He insisted on joining me and celebrating the funeral Masses with me so that I wouldn't be alone.

At the funeral of the woman and her brothers, her family members and friends sat on one side of the church while the family and friends of the man who had killed them sat on the other side. There was a huge "elephant" in the room with us, and I couldn't ignore it. This wasn't about them getting angry with me; this was about their trying to come to terms with what had happened so that they could begin the healing process. So in my homily I didn't skirt the issue but talked about it, about the feud and what had happened because of it, about the broken lives it had left behind for both families, and about the devastated children left behind. I spoke of how this had shattered the lives of not just a few people, but had broken the heart of the whole town. This was a community in pain.

I asked them if more pain was what they wanted for their future, if this tragedy was the legacy that they wanted to leave for their children, or if they would have the courage to use this tragic event as a catalyst to bring them together instead of driving them further apart. I remember pointing to almost each and every one of them on both sides of the aisle, pointing and saying, "You. And you. And you . . . and you . . . look at yourselves. Each and every one of you is broken up by this. The healing has to start, and it has to start now."

So for the Sign of Peace, which is the part of the Mass when people turn to their neighbors and shake their hands or hug and say, "Peace be with you," I told them that I knew how difficult it was for them, but that they needed to cross the aisle and at least shake hands with each other, that they had to start somewhere, and that somewhere was here and now. And they did it. They were drowning in grief, crying and sobbing, but they did it. And I did the same thing at the funeral of the man who had been killed, got rid of the elephant in the room. These were tiny baby steps, but steps that needed to be taken so that they could begin to heal and get on with their lives.

The town grieved for a long time, but there was no further violence.

They say that misfortune strikes in sets of three, and there was one more incident that was out of the ordinary. And by this time, boring was beginning to sound not half bad to me.

A few months after that tragic incident, I was asleep in my bed in the rectory. It was about two in the morning when suddenly there's a deafening explosion, and all of the windows in the rectory are blown out. I jumped out of bed and rushed outside to see what had happened, and I was met by this totally surreal sight. The whole block looked like a scene from war time London during the German blitzkrieg. All of the power lines were down, sparks were shooting up from multiple spots up and down the street, and smoke was billowing from several fires—the largest one from the abandoned building next door to the parish hall. The ground seemed to be sparkling in the moonlight, which was actually the moonlight reflecting off the broken glass from the dozens of windows that had been shattered. We had a volunteer fire department and their trucks were converging on the scene with sirens blaring and volunteer firemen rushing all over the place. One of the firemen stopped and asked me if I was okay, I told him yeah and asked if he knew what had happened.

He told me that it looked as if someone had blown up the abandoned building next to the parish hall. And then he said, "Um, Father, you might want to go back inside and put some clothes on." I realized then that I had run out wearing only my Fruit of the Looms, and had even stepped in my dog's food bowl in my rush so my feet were covered in dog food! I didn't even have my glasses on so everything was a blur, but I went back inside, found my glasses and searched for my dog who was cowering under the bed but was otherwise okay.

I found a flashlight and some candles, as it was pitch black in my room because the power was out, and started sweeping up the broken glass. I searched the rest of the rectory as best I could. Other than the broken windows, it seemed to be okay. I figured I would check out the parish hall in the morning, thinking that if there were any real problems there the firemen would let me know. I went outside a few more times during the night to see how things were looking and learned from the still busy firemen that while there had been a lot of property damage, no one had been hurt, and that the police had already arrested the culprits.

The next day we found out that two local guys, both of them hard core drug addicts, had decided to rob the bank (not again!) to get money to feed their habit. They had a half-baked plan. They were going to blow up the bank with TNT, which they must've figured that no one would notice, and sneak in and grab the money. The problem—other than it being a stupid plan to begin with—was that when they decided to do it they were both so stoned out of their minds that instead of wiring the TNT to the bank, they mistakenly wired it to the abandoned building right next to the bank. That building was next to the parish hall, which was attached to the rectory. So I was extremely grateful that in their drug induced haze, they hadn't mistaken the rectory for the bank and blown it up with me in it.

I was beginning to think that it was time for me to get out of Dodge while I was still in one piece and start the next chapter of my life.

Chapter 27

New Life Begins Yet Again:
My Counseling Degree

I graduated from school (magna cum laude) with my master's degree in counseling. I had been at this parish for about two-and-a-half years, and I felt good about the state of the parish and the state of the parishioners. All of the church buildings, including the missions, were in good shape and the parishioners were, too. This was their parish and they were the ones in charge with a little help from me, and they were doing just fine.

I felt that it was time for me to put my degree to use. I still had a hundred things that I wanted to do, and I couldn't do them from here. Here I was, after all that I'd been through, still thinking that I could somehow change the institution of the church because I sincerely believed that it needed to change. It needed to change to stay relevant, to stay viable, and to stay dynamic. Not only did I want it to change, I wanted it to blossom and to flower—to become all that it could be! Not for the institution, but for the people it could bring to the Divine Presence in a breathtaking, life-affirming experience. I know that is how a connection to God can feel, and the church had the power to do that. It had the power but it wasn't using it in that direction, or so I believed.

It seemed to me that what had happened over time was that the institutional aspect of the church was given all of the emphasis, ignoring all of its other aspects—the prophetic, the sacramental, the ministerial, and the pastoral. It was all about the rules and regulations and not about the service. I found that to be totally skewed because when you look at Jesus, you see an itinerant preacher who was pretty much anti-institution, anti-establishment (and pretty damn vocal about it), who went around preaching love and service to others. What happened to that? I honestly believe that if Jesus appeared amongst us at this moment, He would look around and say, "OMG, what have you guys done with my message? I don't even hear it from you anymore!" And then we'd have to tell Him, "Sorry, you need to make an appointment with the bishop (as we doubt that they'd let You in to see the pope on such short notice) to discuss your complaint. Since he's one of the authorities in this institution that has become Your church, you'd better have a darned good argument ready." Do I really believe that? Yes. Yes. Yes. But, that's just me.

Although there were frequently raised eyebrows from the establishment when I preached, they could never quite find anything wrong in what I said because in my preaching I went to the core message of Jesus' preaching—connecting from the heart. It wasn't anything new and it wasn't anything heretical. It was just something that was lost to us in the miles of bureaucratic red tape that ruled the modern church

If you live your life according to what Jesus said, and you do it correctly, and if you do it from the heart, what ends up happening is that suddenly you're no longer living it because Jesus said to, you're living it because *you* know it to be true. You develop your own authority, which is what I believe Jesus calls all of us to do. The pope has a relationship with God that is his alone, Mother Teresa had a relationship with God that was hers alone, and you have a relationship with God that is yours alone, because we are all unique and our relationships are unique to us. Then you use your own authority, your heart connection, as the standard upon which to measure your experience within the institution.

The church doesn't quite interpret it in the same way. They say that we, as individuals, don't have that authority (unless you're ordained), and that only the institution (made up of the ordained) has that authority. Only the institution can tell us how our relationship with God should be, because they know better than we, what God wants. Why? Again, because they are ordained. They have a "special" relationship with God that lay people can never have. And all I can say to that is—hogwash. We are all God's children, and God doesn't play favorites. It doesn't matter what your station is in this life; what matters is what is in your heart.

So I wasn't preaching an institutional message the way that other priests did because for me, the message of Jesus goes beyond the message of the institutional church—it can't be contained by any institution. So don't let yourself be limited by the institution. It should be there to help us, to guide us, and to say, "Here's the way–Go! Take off!" and then you grow beyond it. You grow through it and then beyond it so that you are still a part of the church, but you're not limited by any institutional parameters that it has set. The institution is the means to the end—not the end itself—which we seem to have lost sight of. It isn't the connection, but the vehicle to help you to make the connection.

But nowadays it seems that the institution, and not God, has become the "it" of our faith. It should merely be the beginning of our faith experience and not the end of it because our faith experience never ends. Relationships are a living thing, always growing, always evolving, but for some reason the church seems to find the concept of "growth" anathema.

That's what I preached to people—to do it "their" way. Not my way or the bishop's way or even the pope's way, but their own way—to develop their own personal spirituality—because it was about them and their relationship with God. Each of us has our own unique relationship with the Divine Presence, and that is what should be nurtured and honored. God made *each* of us in His image and likeness—not just the pope or the bishops or the priests. He calls all of us to a relationship with Him in our own unique way, and in our hearts is where Jesus speaks to each of us most profoundly.

Again, this isn't how it's seen by the institution of the church, which says that God only speaks to those who are ordained and are on the highest rungs of that ladder. (There have been a very few lay people in the history of the church who have said that God spoke to them, like Bernadette of Lourdes, but the church considers them an aberration.) So of course, Jesus speaks to the pope, that's understandable. But to Joe the plumber? No way! Why would He want to speak to someone like that? And if we even have to ask that question, I believe that we have absolutely no idea of what Jesus was really all about. Again, that's how it feels to me. And it feels right.

So what was I going to do now? I knew that I wanted to work with dysfunctional clergy, but that wasn't something that the diocese was set up for. There was no such position in this diocese. And I also knew that I wouldn't get anywhere talking to the bishop about it since he didn't believe that the clergy had any psychological problems. If they did, prayer, and not psychology, was the only answer for those problems. So one of the things that I wanted to do was to start my own private counseling practice and be available to any priest or minister who needed help. It would only be a small step, but at least it would be a step in the right direction. I knew that I would need to be in a bigger city for this to be viable because I would need to be where the majority of priests were. As for what else I might be doing, I would have to wait and see what the bishop said after I talked to him.

I called the bishop and told him that it was time for me to move on. Of course he didn't agree with me about that and said no. But I told him yes, that I was going, and actually gave him the date I was leaving the parish, which would be about two months in the future. He said that he didn't have anyone to replace me, but I told him that he had a couple of months to figure that out. Did he fire me for insubordination? No. He did seem a little flustered, though, and just sputtered that he'd get back to me about it.

So in the meantime, I set about preparing the parish for my departure. I let my parishioners know that I was leaving so that I could pursue being a therapist, and told them that I would make sure that their needs would be taken care of before I left. I wasn't going to just walk out on them as some pastors had been known to do. I hired two semi-retired priests that I personally knew, both of them were good, responsible guys who would take good care of the parishioners (and neither of them was an alcoholic or a pedophile). I met with both of them, outlined their duties, and had them sign contracts with me, which I then submitted to the diocesan office. Until the bishop named a new pastor, I would continue to be their boss and they would be responsible to me. I also set up a separate parish fund that would pay them for their services so there wouldn't be any confusion in that direction. I wasn't comfortable assuming that the bishop would take care of these details, and I wasn't going to leave my parishioners in the lurch, so I just went ahead and did it.

It all worked out really well. The parishioners were happy with their new part-time priests, took good care of them, and vice-versa. After I had left, I met with both of those priests on a regular basis so that they could let me know how things were going in the parish, and things were going well. They both told me that the parishioners were spoiling them rotten, constantly inviting them into their homes, cooking meals for them, and taking them out to dinner. I also stayed in touch with the parish secretary, and she too assured me that things were running smoothly.

I wasn't surprised because that's what happens when people become empowered, when they develop their own authority in their relationship with God. They act out of that authority, and don't need a priest breathing down their necks twenty-four seven telling them what to do. They are a reflection of Christ in this moment, and that reflection *is* the church. It's not a building, it's not the pope by himself or the bishops by themselves, but the people—all of us together—who are the church. This is just a comment from the whatever-it's-worth department, but I have always found it odd that we use the expression "Mother Church" when the institution is run only by men and in a very paternalistic way.

Although the bishop wasn't able to find a full-time replacement for me, he eventually made this parish a mission of one of the bigger parishes in a nearby city so the pastor of that city parish also became the pastor for this one. The two priests that I had hired stayed on to help because they enjoyed it so much.

Not yet knowing what the bishop had planned for me (or if he was planning anything at all), I decided that I'd better look for work. I applied for and got two jobs back in the city close to my home, which is where I wanted to be. The city was opening up a community college, and

Chapter 27

I was going to work part time for them to help set up their counseling program in addition to doing counseling for the faculty, staff, and students. I also got a contract job with the city to create an employee assistance referral counseling program for city employees.

Since I hadn't yet heard anything back from the bishop, I didn't know what I would be doing in the way of actual church ministry. I had told him, back when I talked to him about leaving the parish, that I would be glad to talk to him about my future in the church, whether he wanted me in or out, and that I would be glad to have that conversation with him anytime. He never took me up on it, but if he had known what the future was going to bring, he'd probably wish that he had.

I had all of my ducks in a row and it was time for me to move on. I said goodbye to my parishioners and it was bittersweet. When I first came to this parish, it was falling down around everyone's heads, and the parishioners were a sad bunch of souls because their parish had the reputation of being the last stop on the road to nowhere. But we had worked together to turn things around and now it was a nice place, a good place, with parishioners who held their heads up high and rightly so. I have a friend who laughingly tells me that in therapy I work magic in people's lives, but the real magic is in seeing people blossom as they come to recognize their own worth, and recognize their own authority. I was nothing more than the conduit for that process, and I felt blessed that they had allowed me to share in their lives and be that conduit for them.

I moved back home and was living in my parents' house. Since I hadn't heard from the bishop and hadn't yet gotten a new assignment, I didn't have a rectory to move in to. What did my parents think? They thought it was really, really weird that I was a priest living at home with my parents; they said that they'd never heard of such a thing. Well, I hadn't either, but here I was. I remember my mom frowning and shaking her head and asking me what she was supposed to tell people when they asked her about it. I was still a priest, wasn't I? (Yes folks, I'm still a priest. It is strange, but welcome to my life in the church. And tell them whatever you want.)

However, they quickly changed their tune when they realized that since I was home I would be able to help them to take care of my grandma and relieve them of some of their burden. She required a lot of care since her stroke and they were her main caregivers. I was glad to help out, and grateful to be able to spend time with her. While I was growing up, she had always been a constant, loving fixture in my life, and helping her now was a joy for me and not a burden.

I also wanted to be here at home, though not necessarily in my parents' house, so that I could be close to the rest of my family. Both my brother and sister had gotten married and had children, and I wanted to be involved in my nieces' and nephews' lives as they were growing up. They say that every man wants a son to carry on his name, and since I doubted that I would ever have any biological children of my own (despite what Father Abdon had told people to the contrary), they were the closest that I was going to get to in that regard.

I started my two new jobs, and at the college I think I was somewhat of an oddity. Occasionally, the college president would take important visitors on a tour of the facility. On the tour he would stop outside my office and in a hushed tone I would hear him tell the visitors, "This office belongs to a Roman Catholic priest in this diocese, but he works for us here at the college." That was unheard of at the time, and I think the president liked to throw that in to show people how "progressive" this college was. I never actually dressed like a priest when I was there, but wore a sports coat and tie.

My life settled into a routine. I was working my two secular jobs and starting up my private counseling practice. When I wasn't working, I would help take care of my grandma. After her stroke she had been housebound for quite a while, but now she was feeling better and was able to be up though not quite about because she really couldn't walk on her own any longer.

But she loved getting out of the house, loved going out, and she would look for just about any excuse to do that! I would take her out as often as I could, and it got to be a little joke between us. I'd start to ask her if she wanted to go somewhere with me, and before I could even get the question out of my mouth she'd say, "I'm ready, I'll go with you!" She didn't even know where we were going, but she was ready to go. So I would settle her comfortably in my car with her oxygen tank nestled next to her. My doggie would hop in, and the three of us would take off and go for a drive, or just go to get gas for my car, or run an errand for my mom. My grandma's favorite thing to do was to sneak out for some forbidden treats. She was a diabetic and my mom was very strict about what she let my grandma eat. But I would let her cheat a little bit, and take her out and let her have half of a doughnut or a small scoop of ice cream; it was our little secret.

Other times we would cook together. Growing up, I remember grandma always being in the kitchen. She loved cooking for us more than anything, and she made just the best stuff you'd ever eat. She couldn't really do any cooking or baking anymore, but she'd sit at the kitchen table supervising while I'd assemble all of the ingredients. She would tell me what to do as we made some of her favorite foods. And because of grandma I got to be a pretty good cook. (I still make a pretty mean low-carb carrot-zucchini cake with cream cheese frosting!)

Chapter 27

Sadly, about a year and a half after I had moved back home, my grandmother passed away. I ended up buying her house, which was just a stone's throw from my parents' house, moved out of my childhood home (much to my mother's relief), moved into my grandmother's house, and renovated it. I have many fond memories of the time that we spent together, was thankful that we had that time, and glad that I had made the decision to move back home when I did.

I was beginning to think that maybe the bishop had forgotten about me, but finally, after about three months, he called and asked to meet with me about my new assignment. We had a very cordial meeting, and he assigned me to a small parish just north of the city. The pastor there was a younger man who I knew and considered a friend. It seems that he was having a little difficulty getting his parishioners to warm up to him. The bishop felt that with my outgoing personality and history of getting along really well with parishioners, that I might serve as a buffer for him and maybe help him in his relationship with the people there.

However, the bishop gave me the assignment before speaking to the pastor about it. And when he did speak to him, the pastor said—absolutely not. He adamantly refused to have me there as his assistant. I was really surprised by that, couldn't understand what was wrong, and all that I could think of was that maybe my reputation was putting him off. I had already been a Vicar Forane and a pastor, had gotten my degree in counseling, and had a reputation of being loved by my parishioners. Maybe he felt threatened by that, felt that the parishioners would end up liking me more than they liked him, and perhaps he felt that this would undermine his authority. Whatever, he obviously didn't want my help with anything. Again, there was a lot of insecurity among priests in this diocese and that's what they acted out of. I don't know for sure, I just know that I was really surprised by it because in the past we had been friends and had always gotten along really well.

Time for "Plan B." The bishop then sends me a letter assigning me to a parish here in the city. Again, a pastor that I knew and was friends with, a much older guy, although this one was an alcoholic and there were rumors about pedophilia—a lot of rumors. Because we were friends, I had occasionally driven down to visit him from my last parish. I had heard the rumors, and although I never confronted him directly about them because you don't confront someone based on hearsay, I did talk to him a lot and during some of our conversations, I would talk about how the social climate was changing, about how secrets were being exposed, and about how the church and its priests were starting to be held accountable for their actions. I never pointed my finger, kept the conversation general, but let him know that help was available to priests who needed it.

So I show up at his parish with my letter of assignment from the bishop, and the first thing that he says to me is that he doesn't need me there. I think his exact words were, "This is a one man show." He said that the bishop had called him and told him about my assignment, but that he didn't agree with the bishop, and that he didn't need any help. However, being an older priest, he would never dream of saying no the bishop. Older priests came from the generation that would never, ever question anything they were told by an authority figure—they did what they were told, period. They were also a lot closer to retirement and their pensions, and they didn't want to do anything that might threaten that.

Instead, he said okay, but that I would have to follow his strict set of rules if I were going to work with him. He proceeded to give me this long list of rules that, honestly, I think he just made up on the spot. He said that I would be kept on a tight leash, that I wouldn't be able to come and go as I pleased, that I would have to ask his permission for everything, that I would have a curfew . . . I mean, it just went on and on. The one that really caught my attention, though, was when he said that he did NOT allow dogs in his rectory; no exceptions. He knew that I had a dog because I used to bring my dog with me when I came down to visit him. At that point I stopped him, told him that this was not going to work, and left.

I called the bishop, told him what the pastor had said, and went back home and continued on with my life. Let the guys in charge handle it; I was done with it. I knew that the pastor probably felt threatened to have me there. I was a therapist, I was treating priests who had all types of issues, and I had a reputation of calling a spade a spade. It was clear that although we had been friends for years, now he didn't want me anywhere near him—possibly learning about his "secret."

So I just continued doing my own thing and I stayed busy. My practice was getting off the ground, and I was counseling a number of Catholic priests and Protestant ministers who had come to me, and was finally getting these guys the help that they needed. It was an involved, complex situation with moral, ethical, and legal issues abounding, but at least I was using my degree for something that I saw as extremely worthwhile. It was just a small step because so much more needed to be done to right the wrongs of the institution, but at least it was a start. And, as it's said, the journey of a thousand miles begins with the first step. My contract job with the city had ended, but I got another contract job with the local court system doing pre-release counseling with first time juvenile offenders and their families, trying to keep them from becoming repeat offenders.

I felt as if counseling was exactly what I should be doing at this moment in time, but boy, I did miss my preaching! And then I got a call from a sister. She was part of an order that ran a local school, along with some Franciscan brothers. She heard that I was back in town and available so she asked me if I would say Masses for them on Holy Days, for special school events, and also for the upcoming Christmas season. So I put my collar back on for the first time in a long time, and helped them out. And got to preach again!

I finally got another letter of assignment from the bishop. In this one he said that he was assigning me part time to the community college, part time to the city, and also to help out if needed at the parish where the pastor didn't want me. Okaaay. The bishop had no authority to assign me to secular jobs as they had nothing to do with him or the church. This just told me that he had absolutely no idea what to do with me, but as long as he had given me some kind of assignment, the diocese would still cover my medical insurance even though I was no longer getting a paycheck from a parish. That was fine with me, and I just put the letter in a drawer and kept on doing my own thing.

Chapter 28

Saving the World One Soul at a Time

My dance card was pretty full these days. The community college had asked me to work for them full time, so I was doing that along with my private practice. I was also doing part-time contract work for the court system where I was working with the Children's Court and also doing that pre-release counseling at the state prison. I was also involved in some employer/ employee dispute resolution work for a community up north, and I did mental health workshops for different groups around town like teachers, the police department, and even the fire department. I also gave free talks to the community at large on different topics, things like parenting skills and sexual assault prevention for women. (Lately, there had been a rash of sexual assaults against women and rapes occurring in town.)

I was doing very little in the way of actual church ministry, just an occasional Mass for that group of religious teachers. I heard that people were calling me the "worker priest." Well, I was definitely working. If there was a pie available, I probably had my finger in it (right before I ate the whole thing!). I had said that I still had a hundred things that I wanted to do—I just didn't think I'd be doing them all at the same time!

For a bit of interesting history, there actually was something called the Worker Priest Movement that started in France in the 1930s. This was a group of French Roman Catholic priests who initiated a social experiment. They held secular jobs so that they could work among the people to try to determine why so many Catholics at that time were abandoning their faith, and why the church seemed to be alienated from the masses. What ended up happening was that those priests started advocating for better wages and working conditions for the people that they were working alongside, which caused a bit of an uproar so the pope eventually disbanded the group. However, their efforts weren't all in vain, because what they did influenced in part a future pope to initiate social justice reforms in the church (Vatican II).

Christmas was approaching and I heard through the grapevine that a couple of the mission churches outside of town—ones that belonged to the parish where I was supposed to be assigned but wasn't wanted at— were not going to be having Christmas services because there was no priest available to do them. (Hello, what was I, chopped liver?) I wasn't really surprised that the pastor hadn't asked for my help since we hadn't spoken a word to each other since that ill-fated day when I met with him about being his assistant. Very few of the priests in this diocese spoke to me these days, although, truth be told, our paths rarely crossed. I was out in the field working, and they were holed up in their rectories only to be seen on weekends for church services.

I was upset by the fact that those communities would be doing without Christmas Mass, so I called the pastor and volunteered to do those services at the missions and he said okay. That worked out well for him because I had also heard, again through the grapevine, that he didn't really care to spend any of his important time at those diddly little missions. This led to my finally getting more involved in the parish. The pastor then asked if I could start taking over some of the morning and evening weekday Masses at the main parish on a regular basis. That then led to my being assigned to regular weekend Masses along with weddings and funerals.

But anytime that I was at the parish, the pastor wasn't. Our paths never crossed, and his method of communication with me was really odd. He would communicate with me only by using notes. After finishing a Mass, I would go out to my car to leave and there would be a note from him on my windshield telling me my schedule for the next month or two. It was just so bizarre because he and I had been friends for so many years, and now he wouldn't talk to me, wouldn't even see me.

All I could come up with was just the fact that I was a therapist, and that fact was threatening to a lot of these priests. On top of that was the unorthodox situation that I was in— holding secular jobs and not living in a rectory (things that had never before been done in this diocese), so they just didn't know what to make of me. I guess I was neither fish nor fowl, as the saying goes. I know that I made many of them uncomfortable. On the whole, it seemed that mainly the younger priests steered clear of me, and maybe the ones who might have had something to be uncomfortable about.

I remember a number of little incidents involving some of the priests in this diocese that I found funny, but I guess weren't so funny for them. One time I went into a restaurant for dinner with a friend, and there was a priest that I knew who was having dinner with a woman. There's certainly nothing wrong with that, I've done it plenty of times myself, but when I caught father's eye and waved hello, he looked

Chapter 28

mortified and the next thing I knew, he and his dinner companion were rushing out the door. You don't have to be a therapist to know that this kind of a guilty reaction to something as simple as a wave isn't normal. Father was indulging in a little hanky-panky, but he wasn't very good at this cloak and dagger stuff because I would never have known that anything was amiss except for his reaction to my presence. Whenever I ran into him after that, he pretended that he didn't see me.

There were a number of restaurant incidents like that one, similar incidents but with different priests. There were also similar incidents when I ran into them at dances and cocktail lounges, things that my parishioners had invited me to go to with them. I'd be sitting and having a drink with my parishioners, we'd be talking and telling jokes and just having a good time, and I'd look over and see a priest that I knew sitting with a companion at a different table. I'd wave at the priest, mouth "hello," and the guy would turn his head as if he didn't see me and the next thing I knew, the table was empty.

Another time it was really early in the morning, around six a.m., and I don't remember why I was out—I might have been coming back from an emergency call—and I was driving by a little motel in town. As I'm passing it I see a priest that I knew come out of one of the units. He happened to look up just as I was passing, our eyes met, and I gave him a big smile and a wave. I thought he was going to have a heart attack right there on the spot because he looked so panicked. Well, there was nothing else that I could have done since I saw him and he saw me, so I just waved and drove on. (Well, at least I didn't stop and ask him, "Hey, what's up? You here by yourself?")

Seriously though, I don't know why I elicited such a strong reaction from these guys. I would never confront anyone over incidents like those, would never bring them up, and would never mention to anyone what I had seen because it was none of my business. I also didn't do gossip. Gossip may have been an art form in the priesthood, but it was an art form that I never indulged in. My reputation as a therapist hinged on my keeping things confidential, and confidentiality and gossip don't mix. I knew a lot of secrets, but they would go with me to my grave. And honestly, this is how I believed that all priests should be acting. Was I wrong in that?

I had made the statement that the social climate was changing, and it definitely was on several fronts. Pedophilia among priests was now an issue being talked about across the nation, and it seemed that every day there was something in the newspapers about it. There was nothing local yet, but I knew that it was just a matter of time. So I would talk about it in my sermons to my parishioners. I would tell them about priests who were very young when they went into the priesthood and who hadn't developed correctly, and about how and why pedophilia occurred. I would tell them the kinds of things to be aware of, behavior to be conscious of, and the kinds of things that they could do to protect themselves. And that, of course, not all priests had those problems, that it was just a few, but that everyone needed to be aware of and informed about what was happening.

To the parents in the congregation I would bring it down to a real practical level. I'd tell them that father might be a nice guy, they might like him, but if he suggested something like taking their young daughters on a camping trip with him, that this was not an appropriate thing to do, no matter how long they had known him or how nice he was. As parents, they needed to set those kinds of boundaries if father didn't.

To the kids in the pews, I would talk about "good" touch and "bad" touch. I would explain the difference, encourage them to trust their feelings in any situations that came up, and that if anything that father did made them uncomfortable, it was okay to say "stop" and to tell their parents.

My fellow priests were in horror that I was talking about it from the pulpit. I don't know, maybe they thought that if they just closed their eyes and pretended it would go away. I told them that people weren't stupid, that they read the newspaper before they came to church, that everyone was talking about it, and that we needed to be open and honest with them. I told them that there had been too much secrecy in the Catholic Church, that this was a part of the problem, that this is what it had brought us to, and that we had to do our part to stop it. Most of them didn't agree with me about it. The minute that Mass was over these guys would bolt from the altar, exit stage left, and rush to be gone before anyone could engage them in a conversation that they didn't want to have.

Another thing in the news was the AIDS epidemic, and I talked about that, too. I remember a sermon that I gave and started it off by saying that today we were going to talk about relationships, specifically the love that's shared between parent and child. I asked those of the parishioners who were here with their families to turn to each other—the parents to their kids and the kids to their parents—and to gently touch each other's faces. All faces turned towards me and looked at me like I was crazy, but then they turned towards each other and did what I asked.

Then I asked the kids to tell their parents that they loved them, and to do it loud enough so that I could hear them. Well, I think that every single kid there looked at me and rolled their eyes when I said that, but then I heard a chorus of "I love you's." Then I asked them to hug each other with a good heartfelt hug, which they all did.

Chapter 28

Then I said, "Okay now, parents, I want you to think of your teenaged son or daughter having pre-marital sex, which they might be doing. They are putting themselves at risk because the church says that we are not supposed to talk about condoms, and not supposed to use them. Kids are going to experiment, and they're going to do things that you may not approve of. Some of them are going to have sex. You parents—think back to when you were their age. Some of you did the same thing; some of you didn't. That was your generation. In this generation there is a disease out there that is killing kids who are having sex.

"Think of your kids. Think of how loving they are. Think of how good it feels to be here next to them, hugging them. Now, I want you to think of them dying. Think of how it feels as you're holding them in your arms as they're gasping for breath, their tongues so swollen with fungus that they can barely swallow, their emaciated bodies covered in sores, and looking like concentration camp victims. And I want you to think of them dying in your arms because it's a sin to use a condom. So hug your kids and talk to them about protecting themselves. Protect them as they are growing up just like your parents did when you were growing up. That's what love is all about." And I let everyone know that I had free condoms if they needed any, and I would dispense them after each and every Mass.

My parents were at that Mass and I watched them as I gave my sermon. At first they were sitting up straight and proud in their pew, smugly thinking—yep, that's our son up there, our son the priest. As I started my sermon, I could see them starting to slink lower and lower in their seats with horrified expressions on their faces, furtively glancing around to see if anyone was looking at them askance.

After that Mass, my mother had my father confront me with the question, "Are you homosexual, talking like that from the altar?" I was totally dumbfounded.

Well, that sermon got me reported to the bishop because the church does not believe in condoms. You can't use them before marriage because they promote illicit sexual intercourse (since then proven to be a false assumption), and you can't use them after marriage because they prevent conception, which is the only valid reason for marriage. So the bishop sent me a letter and told me that I shouldn't be talking about condoms because it went against church policy. I wrote back to him and told him that kids suffering and dying—when it could have been prevented—went against my policy, and that the church needed to work on that one. I also told him that, in the meantime, I was going to keep talking about it. I ended my letter with telling him that anytime that he wanted to have "that" conversation with me, the one about my future in the church, I was ready. I never heard back from him about it and continued talking about AIDS and dispensing condoms.

At the end of all of the services on the same day of the Mass I just spoke about, my pastor saw me at the dumpster outside the church as he was putting another note on my windshield. He asked me what I was doing, and I told him that I was disposing of the expired condoms that I had with me. He turned around and walked away from me without a word. (This pastor was later removed from ministry for pedophilia issues.)

How did I get away with it? Honestly, I don't know. The bishop at the very least could have suspended me over it, but he didn't. There were other instances where he could have called me on the carpet over things that I had said or done, but again, he never did. I think perhaps that he was following that age-old adage—the one that says to keep your friends close but to keep your enemies closer. As long as I was a part of the church, he still had some control over me. If he cut me loose, he didn't. Then I might go out and shoot my big mouth off to who knows who about who knows what. Because of the things that I had seen, the experiences that I'd had, and because I wasn't afraid to talk about the elephant in the room with us, I think that was his fear.

Remember after that Vicar of Priests had visited me and didn't believe my stories, that I felt kind of wistful, and was thinking about "what ifs?" Well, what if the bishop and I had a better relationship? What if he realized that the only thing that he had to "fear" from me was my always unbridled, often irritating, dogged enthusiasm for change? What if he knew that what I wanted with every fiber of my being was not to disparage the church but to make it better? What if he let me jump on that white horse and lead the charge to a renewal experience for the church that would knock people's socks off? I don't know if that makes me sound like a grandiose idiot or not, but that's how I felt about my role in the church. I was definitely a product of the seventies, believing that one person could make a difference. That was still my dream. A little battered by now, but still my dream.

In an attempt to try to better my relationship with the bishop, I decided to seek help. I made an appointment with a priest who I liked and respected, and who was a contemporary of the bishop's as well as a close friend of his. He held a respected position in the diocese, and I went to him in his official capacity because I wanted to ask for his counsel, get some guidance from him, and perhaps have him intercede for me with the bishop.

We met and I explained to him that the bishop and I couldn't communicate to save our lives and that I wanted— needed—to fix that, and that there were issues between us that we needed to address, but I couldn't seem to get through to him. I told him that I needed his help, asked for some advice, and said that perhaps he could mediate on my behalf because I knew that he had the bishop's ear.

He listened to me then said, "Oh, no, you can do this. The two of you can do it; you need to work it out. No, I can't get involved."

I was flabbergasted. I said, "Really?" I don't think that I said much more than that (which is pretty unusual for me) because I was so stunned. I had gone to this priest because he was a good guy, level headed, and respected by his parishioners and just about everyone else in the diocese. When you're having a problem in the institution, you go to someone in the institution, someone older and wiser who has the capabilities and the experience and the authority to help you, which this guy had. But he didn't want to get involved. Okay. I felt that this just reinforced the fact that I was pretty much on my own in this institution; damned no matter what I did.

Another sermon that I remember—and I remember it only because people complained to the bishop about me over it— was "Bring Your Flag to Church Sunday" in support of the war. The USA had just invaded another country and patriotism was running high in the wake of that first invasion. I had heard that to show support for the war and our troops everyone was supposed to bring their flag to church the following weekend.

So, after my sermons that weekend, I let people know that I would not tolerate any flags at my services, and to leave them at home or to leave them at the door. I let them know which services I would be doing the next weekend and told them that if they came to any of my services that it should be without their flags. I said that I was as patriotic as the next guy, but that one of the things that our soldiers had fought and died for was the concept of separation of church and state, and that we had to maintain that healthy separation. There were many ways in which we could show support for our troops, but this would not be one of them. Again, I didn't think too much about it, but quite a few of the more conservative parishioners fired off letters to the bishop about it (I guess complaining about my lack of patriotism), yet everyone complied with my request. My sermons that Sunday centered on the commandment, "Thou shalt not kill," and Jesus' interpretation of that for all of us.

In therapy I was working with damaged priests and that was a step, but again, there were many changes that needed to be made in the institution of the church. I could think of dozens of areas where we could improve or replace some of the systems that we were currently using.

One of them was a better assessment tool for the psychological testing of applicants before they entered the priesthood. We all had to do psychological testing before we entered the seminary, the basic MMPI

(Minnesota Multi-Phasic Personality Inventory), but that wasn't enough in this situation. That test would tell you if someone was obviously psychotic, a psychopath, or a schizophrenic. Of course, you needed to know those things, but it didn't look at the nuances that made up a person's sexuality, and that was something that also needed to be known. Basically, if the applicant took the MMPI and it said that he could be obedient, that he wouldn't steal the church blind, and that he wasn't a serial killer—he was in.

I approached the bishop about putting together something like that for our diocese, about brainstorming to come up with an innovative program that would help us to assess all of those areas, but he said no, he didn't feel that it was necessary.

So I was back to preaching again and I was preaching to beat the band. I've said before that the way to change an institution, according to Jesus, was one person at a time, and that enough hearts changed on the inside could eventually produce change on the outside. I didn't know if I could make that happen, but if it didn't it wouldn't be from lack of trying on my part. I had no idea how much of an impact just one person could make, but I was going to give it my all—one person at a time, one congregation at a time, and maybe even one diocese at a time.

This church belonged to the people sitting in the pews during Mass, and they needed to take a hold of it, which was a concept that over time had gotten lost. So in my sermons I tried to reconnect people with that idea. I wanted to bring the gospels to life for them so they weren't just some antiquated words that we followed because we were supposed to, but because they really did speak to each of us in the here and now.

I tried to bring my parishioners a very concrete experience that made sense to them, that resonated within their lives today, and to make the gospels as alive today as they were two thousand years ago. How many of us (and for you Catholics, be honest with yourself as you read this) as we're sitting there in church listening to father's sermon on the gospel, have had our thoughts start wandering just a bit, maybe start thinking about the nice lunch we're going to have after church, or the football game that we'll be watching later on? It's not that we're not listening to father, of course we are, but hey, we've heard it all before—many times—and there's nothing much there that's new. Yeah, it's good stuff, maybe a little dry, but nothing that makes us sit up and say, "Oh, Wow!" But that's exactly what it should make you say, and it can. Trust me on that one.

I would then discuss the church's perspective and how it interpreted the gospels, which was okay. But that if you looked at them from a slightly different perspective (like that cutting-edge theology that I keep talking about), it seemed to make a little more sense, seemed to challenge us more, make us think more, and make us grow more. I would tell people that I wasn't saying not to do what the church said, but to do it with their hearts, to make it real, and to make it theirs. Again, I would tell them to take it in, chew it, masticate it, and make sure that it feels right. And if it doesn't feel right, don't just stop there. Not to say, "Well, father says . . . ." Instead, challenge it. Challenge father. Ask, question, and talk about it. You all have the authority to do that. If something doesn't feel right, it's probably because it isn't right. Don't let them tell you 'no, you shouldn't do that, and you shouldn't question the church.' You are the church!"

In all fairness, I think that at some point the institution of the church tried to make our faith experience easier for us by telling us that all we had to do was follow this set of rules and we'd get to heaven. The initial intent was probably well meant. However, when you consistently do something for someone else because you want to make it easier for them, what happens then is that they don't have to think for themselves, don't have to connect for themselves, and don't have to grow themselves. They turn their authority over to someone else, so all they have to do is follow . . . like sheep. Ironic isn't it, that what the church accuses people of (behind closed doors) is the very thing that it set in place for them.

A church that is healthy, alive, vibrant, and pulsing with the Divine welcomes challenge, and welcomes discussion because that is a part of growth. A church that is stalled and stagnant does not. In my mind, yes, it is as simple as that.

I was trying to help people, one soul at a time, to find their connection to the Divine Presence, to grow that connection, to take back their authority, and then run with it. That is what it meant for me to "be" a priest.

This was my life for the next few years until a couple of things happened. I got a job offer that I couldn't refuse, and the day of reckoning arrived for the diocese and the shit finally hit the fan.

Chapter 29

The Shit Hits The Fan:
The Day of Reckoning Begins for the Diocese

I received a phone call from the director of a religious treatment facility in a neighboring city. This facility was a residential treatment center for Roman Catholic priests and brothers who had severe chronic psychological problems and addictions. These men had problems that were so severe that they could never return to ministry, could never even return to society, and would spend the rest of their lives either at this facility or in another one like it.

The director wanted to completely change the focus of the facility, changing it from a "warehouse" type situation to an acute care treatment center. It was the intention of this treatment center to return these priests and brothers to active ministry whenever possible.

I wondered if perhaps the governing board of this facility was becoming cognizant of the way the "wind was blowing" with regard to the issue of troubled priests that was sweeping the nation. Whatever their reason for their feeling that this type of treatment center was needed, it proved to be a golden opportunity for me.

The director had heard of my work in counseling clergymen with these kinds of issues, and I assumed that he was impressed with what he had heard. To be honest, I didn't have a whole lot of competition in the field, as I didn't know of any other Roman Catholic priests who were doing what I was doing. He asked if he could talk to me about redesigning his facility, and about my developing a program that would make it into a proactive, comprehensive therapeutic program.

We met and talked about his plans and he asked if I could design such a program. I said yes. He then offered me the position. Again, I said yes. How could I not? I had been helping priests and ministers one at a time, barely making a dent in the overall problem. This would give me the opportunity to serve a larger number of individuals, and perhaps make a bigger dent. So I accepted his offer and gave my notice at the community college, although I would still do consulting work for them.

As it currently operated, the facility basically did nothing more than "warehouse" these men. There was no therapy other than prayer. They had a psychiatrist on staff whose sole function was to medicate these men, to drug them to keep their behavior under control. They were all heavily medicated and just spent their days eating, sleeping, and walking around like zombies. Oh, and praying. It was a depressing sight. This handling of psychological issues in clergy hadn't advanced much from the Middle Ages. The standard treatment then was to banish men with these kinds of problems to monasteries in remote locations, lock them up behind the monastery's doors, and throw away the key. Or even, on occasion, to kill them.

So I got to work and developed a comprehensive program that was quite innovative for its time by the standards of the day (so innovative and successful that I eventually received a commendation from the Vatican—from Pope John Paul II—for my work there). I implemented a program that would take care of these men for the rest of their lives—from the moment they walked in our doors until the moment they died. I would design it so that we would do the initial evaluation on our clients, formulate an individualized therapeutic program for them, and treat them on-site or refer them to a different facility if that were more appropriate. After the completion of their therapy here, we would then make a multi-disciplined decision on what they needed to do next (or, as the church called it, their "final disposition"). I don't know about you, but I thought that those words sounded ominously similar to Adolph Hitler's "final solution," which might not be too far off the mark, as what I ran into from the church hierarchy, on multiple occasions, was their attitude of just wanting to get rid of these guys in any way that they could.

Their "final disposition" might be a return to active ministry, a limited return to ministry with certain restrictions in place, removal from the ministry to an appropriate secular job or to retirement, removal from ministry with placement in a monitored group home, or placement in a residential chronic care facility for the remainder of their lives.

I also established a follow-up program for all clients who were treated and released from our care, which was unheard of at the time. They would periodically return to us for re-evaluations so that we could monitor their progress and make sure everything was going according to plan. Many of these individuals would need lifelong support and we were going to provide it. We were not just going to "wash our hands" of them and throw them out into society without a backward glance, as more than a few church officials had suggested I do. (As you'll later read, this caused quite a few heated confrontations between myself and bishops,

Chapter 29

archbishops, and cardinals—in this country and abroad—all of which I won on behalf of my clients.)

My perspective was always about growth—whether it was from the pulpit to my parishioners or in the counseling arena to my clients, I always wanted the individual to grow to their fullest potential. For someone who is psychologically damaged, like the clients at our facility, maybe the amount of growth that they could realistically achieve would be limited, but I wanted them to be all that they could be within that framework. I found that good therapy is good spirituality, and good spirituality is good therapy, from any denominational perspective.

Something that stands out in my memory from that time was a visit the director asked me to make with him soon after I started working at the facility. The issue of priests accused of pedophilia first broke out on the east coast years earlier, and the priest who was implicated in the very first public case in this country was living here in this city. He was no longer a priest and had no connection to our facility, but the director had discovered that he was now living here and decided to pay (what you might call) a courtesy visit, just to see how he was doing. I didn't do much more than tag along, but I thought it was interesting that I got to meet this man, the first guy to fall and start the "domino" effect that was now toppling priest after priest in the Roman Catholic Church.

The same director who had hired me and was my immediate supervisor left shortly after I began working there. He quit or was fired; I never found out which. He'd had a long-standing, bitter personality conflict with a member of the religious society under whose auspices we operated, and who was now retired and living at the facility. One day this simmering conflict erupted in a fistfight between the two of them in a very public punch-up, drag down fight in the dining room (that I didn't see because it happened on my day off), which led to his departure. Both of these guys, of course, were priests.

A new director was appointed, and he was a priest who was already working at the facility as the spiritual director for the clients. He was quite well known in church circles as a renowned "Retreat Master." He was a very spiritual man, very church oriented, known nationwide for his retreat work, and had even published several books on the subject. But he didn't know the first thing about psychology, which he readily admitted. So, in the church's view, a man who knew absolutely nothing about psychology was obviously the best choice to be in charge of a psychological facility. (You're probably picking up here, as I did, that the ways of Mother Church are mysterious indeed.)

On one of his first days as the new director, he pulls me aside and tells me that "he doesn't know the first thing about anything here." Um, okay. He told me that he would make his decisions only after consulting with me, basically be the director in name only, and also told me that I was solely responsible for making the decisions when it came to any and all psychological matters. Um, okay. So he officially made me the clinical director, and he became the overall facility director. It didn't matter to me what they called me because it wouldn't change my priorities, which were the clients and their psychological health and well-being.

I got to work in implementing our new program. I was the program developer, the first therapist on staff, and now the clinical director—all in the space of a few months. I was having trouble keeping up with myself!

One of the first things I did was to hire additional therapists to join our team. I also asked the psychiatrist to start doing therapy with the clients, and to reevaluate his medication regimen because we were going to trade drugs for actual therapy. The only clients who would be on medication, in addition to their therapy, would be the ones who truly needed to be. Psychotropic medications definitely have a place in certain situations, and we did have a number of clients who wouldn't be able to function at all without some type of medication. But I didn't want it to be used indiscriminately across the board as a chemical restraint for church or staff convenience. So we definitely began to make a dent in the "zombie" population.

I also seemed to make a dent in that psychiatrist. He was in agreement with my program (or so he said) even though I found out that he still continued the same medication regimen with little or no therapy. To be fair, secular psychologists and psychiatrists did not accept spiritual practices and prayer as part of their psychological treatment. I, however, believed that incorporating traditional spirituality and prayer with psychology would be a more efficacious process in responding to individuals who also happened to be ministers.

This guy was a medical doctor (and never let any of us forget that), and wasn't happy that he was expected to take orders from a young whippersnapper like me who didn't even have a medical degree. He was so disgruntled by it that he eventually left and I was able to hire a different psychiatrist, someone who actually believed in therapy.

I hired the rest of my staff, which included several clinical psychologists, a social worker, and a new spiritual director. I remember that I caused a few raised eyebrows when I said that we were going to do "body therapy" and hired a massage therapist. Today we have all kinds of alternative and complementary therapies available to us, but back then it was considered a "woo-woo" kind of thing to do. Well, I knew "woo-woo" and this was good "woo-woo" because the clients seemed to love it and responded positively to it.

Chapter 29

In a very short time we had our facility up and running, and the desperate need for a program like ours quickly became apparent. No sooner had we opened our doors when we started getting calls from dioceses around the country, and from many different Catholic religious orders who asked us to evaluate priests for them. Then Protestant and Jewish religious officials began calling and consulting with me about our program and, like the ripple effect, the word spread even further afield. I made the decision to accept referrals from outside the US, and calls came pouring in from Canada, Europe, South America, and northern Africa. Obviously, there were a lot of troubled clergymen out there. This wasn't just an American problem, it wasn't just a Catholic Church problem—it was a worldwide institutional religion problem.

It was obvious to me that all of these religious institutions were experiencing the same kinds of problems. There was a core value that each institution was not addressing in the training of its clergy and religious brothers, and we needed to determine what that was and address it. I felt that this was the best way to fix the problems that we were seeing and to prevent them from occurring in the future. But since religious institutions don't really believe in psychology, the chance of that being recognized and addressed by anyone in power was remote, to say the least. Since it was such an obvious solution (to my way of thinking), it would be the last thing that the Catholic Church would ever consider. I knew my church well.

I had said that the issue of pedophilia among the clergy was sweeping across the nation, and a number of our clients were being treated for that problem. But that wasn't the only sexual issue that we were seeing and treating, as the problems that were presenting ran across the whole spectrum of sexuality. We were also treating clergymen who had been caught having sexual relationships with women. Technically, to be considered a pedophile, the victim, male or female, is under twelve years of age and prepubescent. If the victim is above the age of twelve but below the age of eighteen, the perpetrator is classified as a hebephile (although that term is rarely used anymore, everyone seems to prefer to use the term 'pedophile' when it comes to the abuse of a child of any age and gender). Although the majority of victims of abuse were young males (altar boys), young females (altar girls) were also being victimized.

Then there was the issue of male clergy who were having physical relationships with women who were age appropriate, which at least in society's view, seemed to be the least offensive behavior. These things can happen, right? Especially since most people seem to believe that the clergy, despite what the church might say, are not celibate. So they feel that it's not *that* bad.

However, for the Roman Catholic priest, it can still be *that* bad. A Roman Catholic priest's core identity as a priest is bound up with being celibate; bound by the serious and public vow that he made to the people, to the bishop, to the church and to God. Breaking that vow can crack that identity and lead to all kinds of psychological issues for that priest. I knew of several priests for whom our diocese had to pay monetary settlements to the women that they had been involved with. One or two of them had even fathered children with the women—children the church would have to support until they turned eighteen.

And what about women in the church—nuns and sisters with sexual issues? Can a woman be a pedophile? Yes. Have any nuns or sisters ever been accused of pedophilia? I think that in my entire counseling career to date, I've heard of only two or three cases. We don't often hear of women religious with these types of problems. For one, the Catholic Church is a male dominated entity, so statistically there are many more men in the limelight than women. Also, I believe that on the whole, women religious are more educated than the average priest, more "savvy" when it comes to recognizing the problems that they are having, and then attending to those problems. Many of them live in convents under the guidance of their mother superior, and their relationship with her is usually a closer and more personal one than that of priests and their bishops, so they have a more immediate resource available to them if they need help. So most often nuns and sisters with psychological issues tend to take care of them before they spiral out of control. I have counseled a few women religious with sexual dysfunctions in my private practice, but again, it's been only a very few.

While we're on the subject of women religious, it's my impression that in general the public sees priests and nuns/sisters as comrades in arms, working hand-in-hand for the good of Mother Church. I can only speak from my perspective as a priest at that time, but from what I've seen, that is more fantasy than fact. Most of the priests that I knew didn't care very much for their Sisters in Christ. As I've said, most women religious are more educated than the average priest, know more theology than their bishop does, are more up-to-date and involved in current issues, and they end up challenging father too damn much, trying to keep father "on his toes." I've frequently heard them called thorns in the sides of priests, and from the more eloquent of my brethren, pains in the ass. Not from all priests, but from most.

It might sound as if the only things we treated were sexual problems, but that certainly wasn't the case. We saw the whole range of psychological dysfunction in our clients, things like schizophrenia, obsessive-compulsive disorders, bipolar issues, and personality disorders. What happened for a number of these men, especially the ones who had entered the seminary at a very young age, was that their identities became totally bound up in their role as priests. The problem with that is that you can't limit the human experience to just one role. If you try to, you actually end up losing your identity altogether.

A man can be a priest, but he is also other things. He can also be a son, grandson, brother, uncle, cousin, nephew, neighbor, friend, teacher, lawyer, or a therapist. If all of those roles are completely subsumed by the priest role, you lose your connection to all of these other parts of the "self," and psychological dysfunction occurs. Your remaining role—that of being a priest—is also compromised because if you lose your connection to your "self," you lose connection to whatever the experience of the Divine is for you. If you don't have a good psychological structure and cannot handle your own growth and spirituality, how can you be expected to help your parishioners with those issues? Of course, you can't. So although sexual issues among clergy were the ones that had the spotlight on them at the time, they were only one among many issues that we saw and treated.

A new twist arrived on the scene and was added to the church's sexual dysfunction saga. It appeared that now we were going to blame homosexuals for all of our problems. It seems that parishioners were starting to report priests that they had seen at gay bars. Or in front of gay bars. Or near gay bars. (My initial response to that was—what was the parishioner doing at the gay bar? Or in front of it or near it?) So obviously, that must mean that the priest was gay. And if he was gay, then he must be a pedophile, and now that started to sweep across the country.

The church does not want homosexuals in the priesthood. Historically, attempts have always been made to weed them out, but again, the psychological testing that priests go through before admittance to a seminary falls short in that area. And, despite how people may have viewed it at the time, the number of gay priests was actually quite small when compared to the total population of the priesthood. I remember our bishop actually sending a letter around that time to all priests in the diocese telling us not to be seen in gay bars. If you're a celibate heterosexual priest, you should not be hanging out in a "straight" bar at two in the morning. If you are a celibate homosexual priest, you should not be hanging out in a "gay" bar at two in the morning. Period.

Our facility started getting numerous referrals from bishops all over the place asking us to evaluate priests for "suspected homosexuality." Are there homosexual pedophiles? Yes. Are there heterosexual pedophiles? Yes. It's not sexual orientation specific. It seemed to me there was a bit of a witch hunt going on, and I let the bishops know that I was not going to use psychology as an instrument of "inquisition" in any witch hunt. (Had they forgotten that the church had already been there, done that, in the past with disastrous results?)

We evaluated the men that were sent to us, and if the man was gay and a pedophile or a predator, then we would deal with that appropriately. If the man was gay but not a pedophile or a predator and never likely to become one based on psychological criteria, then we would deal with that appropriately. You can be heterosexual, celibate and mentally healthy; you can be homosexual, celibate and mentally healthy; and you can be bisexual, celibate and mentally healthy. It's not about your sexual orientation, but about keeping your vow of celibacy. If you're celibate, you can be attracted to someone and you probably will be many, many times during your lifetime. But as a celibate priest—heterosexual, homosexual or bisexual—you don't act on those attractions. Period.

The hysteria of homosexual priests on the prowl for children eventually ran its course and died down because what we were seeing wasn't a homosexual problem, it wasn't a priest or brother problem, it was ultimately a church denial problem. And this type of problem was not one that the church was in any way willing or able to respond to.

As busy as I was with my work at the facility, the court system, and my private practice, I was still involved in a number of other things in the community—probably way too many to list here without boring the pants off you. The reason that I want to mention a few of them is not to say, hey, look at what I did because what I did, any one of you could have done. Any one of you. But it's to say, hey, look at how great the needs of the community were at that time. There are so many services that we have today that we take for granted and depend on, but we didn't have those services back in the day although we desperately needed them.

I got involved on the ground floor of starting our city's first crisis telephone intervention program, a crisis hotline. I took my turn at manning the telephone lines, especially over the holidays when most people's issues seem to come to the boiling point. I also helped to start a DWI counseling program because that was a big problem in our state with no type of intervention other than jail time, which to me didn't seem to be much of a deterrent. And I was also part of the team that helped to create our city's first AIDS services program.

My life was crazy-hectic, but then something wonderful, and wonderfully helpful, arrived on the scene in the form of—cell phones! The first cell phones came on the market and they proved to be a godsend. They started out as these big, heavy, cumbersome things—kind of like smallish shoe boxes—and the reception was often "iffy." I remember that there were times when I would be driving on the interstate when I had to make or receive a call and I would have to pull over to the side of the road, hop onto the roof of my car, and wave the phone around in the air trying to get a connection. People driving by probably thought I was nuts, but thankfully no one ever called the highway patrol to report the lunatic they had just passed on the roadside. But if they had, I'm sure that it would've been a cop that I already knew and when he saw who it was, he would've just rolled his eyes and said, "I should have known it would be you!"

So that was my secular work, if you feel that there is a difference between secular work and priestly ministry, which I didn't. I was still doing church ministry at my parish, although amongst my peers it seems that I wasn't considered to be a "real" priest.

Chapter 30

God Is Love and Service

Comments were swirling about, coming from my fellow priests who were expressing doubts about how much of a "priest" I actually was because of all of the "secular" jobs that I was involved in. Because I didn't live in a rectory, didn't wear my collar or cassock twenty-four seven, and didn't spend every hour of the day at my parish, they said that I wasn't a "real" priest like they were. (Thank God I wasn't still living at home with my parents because that would have been the icing on the cake for them!)

We seemed to be on different planets when it came to understanding what made a priest a priest, and what it was that priests were supposed to be doing. Really, that was nothing new. I don't know why it still surprised me so much when I heard this stuff, but it did. I felt that being a priest wasn't defined by what you wore or where you lived. Instead, it's something that comes from within you, a response that is a part of you like the tears that well up in your eyes when you're feeling sadness or joy. It just *is*. No matter where I was, be it in the courtroom or the counseling room or on the altar of the church, I was a priest at my core and that's where I worked from. Everything I did, I did from there. Everything that I was, I was from there.

They saw being a priest as being set apart, being set above the people around them. I didn't, never had, and never would. I didn't feel that there was any difference between myself and anyone else, and that it didn't matter if you were a plumber or a priest or the president or the pope. What mattered was that you lived out of your connection to the Divine Presence and that you consciously lived and shared that connection with each other on this wondrous journey called life.

For me, finding fulfillment in our human experience—not priest or layman but human experience—is always, always, always by growth. It is by each of us growing on our journey to that experience of "self." It is where and when we find ourselves being fully alive, fully aware, fully present, fully engaged, fully committed, fully connected with ourselves—and with each and every other person with whom we share this life. It is the connection with all of the wonders of the world around us and with the Divine. I believe that the journey to the self is the journey to the Divine, and that the journey to the Divine is the journey to the self. It is an intimate, intertwined relationship. When you find one, you find the other; you become "whole" and the "whole" becomes you. For me, that's what it's all about. It's the bedrock of the life that I live and the therapy that I practice. For them, well, I can't answer for them. I just know that they didn't seem to "get it" in the same way I did.

And I guess I didn't "get it" like they did either. It seemed to me that most of the other priests that I knew stayed comfortably cocooned (and isolated) in their rectories, only coming out to say Mass and do baptisms, weddings, and funerals. (For some reason, the image of a cuckoo clock comes to mind—you know how the cuckoo briefly pops out every hour on the hour, makes some noise and then goes back in.)

I felt that they could and should be doing so much more, like getting out into the community with the people they're supposed to be serving, sharing life with them on a personal level, and becoming a part of their lives. The needs of people go beyond having Mass said for them or having their children baptized or their dead buried. There were so many needs in our community that we could be addressing, like the ones I previously mentioned, and so many lives that we could be touching. But we weren't, and I felt that that was a sin of omission being committed by the priesthood; one of many.

So I just kept plugging along, my primary goal still that of growing people in their connection to the Divine. That was the objective of every sermon that I gave at Mass, of every word that I spoke to my parishioners and to everyone else with whom I came into contact. Why did I believe that this was the most important thing that I could do for people? Because I believed that if you can help people to ignite that spark, to make that initial connection, to recognize that "Presence," then you've at least given them the opportunity to grow into "wholeness." I believe that "wholeness," whether looked at from the psychological perspective or the spiritual perspective, equals "holiness." And a person who is "holy" has their own power—no one has to give it to them. Unlike most priests who I feel have power only because others, like their parishioners, give it to them.

One of my parishioners at the time (a woman who had the most beautiful singing voice) used to make me laugh. She would tell everyone within hearing distance that all I had to do was open my mouth and five hundred years of church doctrine went flying out the window! I don't know if that was true, but I knew that if I could at least get people to stop and think about what they were doing and also to deeply feel it (instead of just doing it because the church "said so"), then I was on the right track.

Again, I wanted people to make the connection between what they were doing, why they were doing it, what it all meant to them on a "feeling" level, and how all of that was woven together into an experience of growth. That's how you make "church" an experience that speaks to you and has meaning for you. If people go to church only because that's what Catholics are supposed to do, that means that they are doing it mechanically, mindlessly, and without feeling. And that makes for a pretty empty experience.

Take for instance, the Sacrament of Communion. Many people feel that communion is the most important part of the Catholic Mass, and everybody wants to receive the Body and Blood of Christ. So everyone gets in line for communion with heads bowed and hands clasped reverently in prayer. Then after Mass they go out to their cars and try to get out of the crowded church parking lot and someone in another car cuts them off, and you hear this torrent of four-letter words spewing from their mouths as they're screaming at the people in the other car.

And they just went to communion, incorporating Jesus into their daily lives. Oh, really? Do they see any connection between what they just did at Mass and what they're doing in the parking lot? It didn't seem so to me.

For me, that's where the real power of being a priest lies—in helping people to see that connection, and more importantly, to live that connection on a "feeling" level that is beyond emotion. Since the Catholic Mass is a commemoration of the Last Supper that Jesus shared with His apostles, we emulate Jesus during the service by "breaking bread" together as a community. (From the "whatever it's worth" department: To the Jewish people of that era, bread symbolized nourishment and renewal; wine represented an uplifting of the soul from the banality of their daily lives.)

At Mass it's all of us together as a community who give meaning to the act of consecration of the bread and the wine. In that act we consecrate our shared daily lives with each other and with the Divine. The actual consecration is the incarnating of Jesus in ourselves and in one another, and that is what is meant by the doxology of the consecratory prayer. It starts with the priest saying, "Through Him, with Him, in Him . . . ." By this act, we're saying in effect that we are consciously making Christ present in our lives, and how we live our lives will be a living reflection of Him. We are also saying that we have connected with Christ on an interior, personal level and that we will live out of that level—out of that connection with Him and with each other—whether it's in our pew in church or in our car in the parking lot.

When we partake of communion, we receive and incorporate the Divine into our selves. As the priest gives the person communion, he says simply, "The Body of Christ."

The person's reply to that is, "Amen" (so be it). So we have acknowledged the act that we just took part in and have just said yes to it. As we walk away from that altar, it should be with a renewed purpose and a renewed commitment to go forth and "walk our talk." That's what communion should mean to Catholics, but I think that for many people it's become more of a routine, a rote activity.

What did I say earlier, that they come to Mass just to "eat Jesus" and run? I was surprised to find out that some people actually believed that the more times they took communion, the more hosts (consecrated communion wafers) that they ate, the more like Jesus they would automatically become. That just the very act of putting the host on their tongues would somehow magically make them better and make them holier. Sorry, but I really don't believe that it works that way. It's about connection on the inside to what you're doing on the outside, about your understanding and commitment to the depth and beauty of meaning in the act, for therein lays the real magic.

I didn't intentionally set out to rattle anyone's cage (well, okay, maybe on occasion I did), but I will admit that some of my sermons were a bit out of the ordinary. That's because I wanted people not just to hear the words of the sermon but to "feel" them and to connect to them on an emotional level instead of a solely intellectual one. Jesus speaks to each of us in our hearts, and our hearts are what we need to share, as this is how we make our faith a heartfelt experience.

I remember a sermon that my parishioners dubbed the "Divine Santa Claus Sermon." I was doing the Christmas Eve Mass at one of the mission churches, and I started out by asking everyone if they had sent their letters to Santa Claus and if they were excited about all of the presents that Santa was going to bring them. I talked about how it was fun to get presents, and I think I mentioned that I'd sent my letter, too, and that I hoped that I would get a new rosary, maybe a new crucifix, and a brand new Mercedes (well, a guy can always hope!)

I talked a bit about how there was nothing wrong with material possessions, that they had their place in the scheme of things, but that they weren't the be-all and end-all of our lives. I said that you weren't going to find true happiness—trust me on this one—by filling your life with things, no matter how beautiful they were, if you also didn't find meaning in your life (as Mother Teresa had said of us). There were other things that we could get during this Christmas season, non-material things, that could be just as wonderful—maybe even better—than the material ones.

Chapter 30

Sadly, we seem to have lost the connection between the gift of Jesus' life and the giving of gifts to one another at Christmas. All of those presents underneath the Christmas tree should be a representation, a symbol, of the gift of Jesus being in our lives through one another.

I don't believe we've lost Jesus, but our conscious connection to Him. We seem to get caught up in all of the things that we have to do to get ready for the Christmas season. We moan and complain about all of the cleaning and shopping and baking and cooking–without realizing that Jesus is there with us, through all of those things, too. He's not just present to us when we see the wonder on our children's faces as they open up their Christmas presents, or when we see the sparkle in grandma's eyes as her family at the dinner table surrounds her.

He is present to us in our hustle and bustle and rush, in our complaining and griping and sacrifice. That is his gift to us, that He is present to us ALWAYS. The Divine Santa Claus.

Anyway, at that point in the service I picked up the little statue of Baby Jesus that was lying in the crèche and wrapped it up in a small altar cloth and swaddled it like you would a real baby. For this part of my sermon, I got down from the pulpit and walked around gently rocking the "baby" in my arms and talking to it instead of the parishioners. I talked to the statue as if it were the real Baby Jesus, saying how happy we all were that He was going to be born this night. I talked about the meaning of Christmas and of everything that was now made available to us because of this night. I talked about the life that He was going to live, the things that He was going to do, and the wonderful things that He was now going to make possible for us. I said that people would be asking Him for things too—just like they asked Santa Claus—but that the things that He could give us were different from the things that Santa brought us, but were just as real as the presents sitting under our Christmas trees.

After my conversation with "Baby Jesus," I then focused my sermon on the things that Jesus would bring us, non-material things like love and connection. I talked about the wonders of life and the feelings of love and belonging that we could experience in those wonders. I spoke about the joys of love shared between family and friends, and about how love could make us feel so alive, so in touch with everything around us, and just so darned good! I even brought up sexual love, saying that when it's in the right circumstances and the result of two people connecting from the heart, it can be a beautiful, life-enhancing experience. Or at least that's what I'd heard! And that since I'd heard such good things about it from so many people that I thought that maybe someday I might even like to have some of that good stuff for myself! Everyone laughed at that.

(Looking back on it, maybe what they really found funny was that there actually was a priest left in this diocese who wasn't having sex!)

I then asked everyone to turn for a moment to their family members and friends to express their love by giving everyone else a Christmas kiss on the cheek. So for a few moments everyone was busy kissing and giggling and laughing. I talked about how love made us feel, about how it connected us to each other, to the wonders of life, and to the Divine.

Of course, everyone has heard the expression that "God is love." If you follow that statement to the next logical step, then it means that every expression of love in our human lives is an expression of the Divine. Holding the hand of that little old lady to help her across the street—that is God. Giving up your seat on the bus for that pregnant woman—that is God. Letting someone who is in a desperate hurry get in front of you in line—that is God. Kissing the cheek of your friend in joy—that is God. And God is present especially when you give another person an expression of love not out of your need, want, or desire, but simply because they are here, right now, present to you as God is present.

I remember the feeling in the church that Christmas Eve. The only way I can describe it is by saying that it felt so "right." It was alive with warmth and goodness, with sharing and connection, with fellowship and life. It was the Divine being made manifest. That is God.

Afterwards I heard that some of my fellow priests made the comment that I was nothing more than a charlatan, an actor who knew how to play an audience. How sad for them, I thought, and sadder still for the people who looked to them for spiritual guidance. I wondered how some of these guys thought that they could help people to find a God that they hadn't yet seemed to find themselves. But that was just my opinion, from the "whatever it's worth" department.

From the pulpit at my Masses I still talked about pedophilia and AIDS, still continued to dispense condoms, with nary a peep about any of it from the bishop. I think that might have been because he had bigger things to worry about. A couple of cases of pedophilia had been reported in our diocese, although they were cases that were reported by victims who were now over the age of eighteen, and were reporting incidents that had happened years before. These incidents were handled quietly and settled (monetarily) by the diocese and didn't make the newspapers. (The priests involved in these incidents were sent to our facility for evaluations.) But everyone, especially the bishop, seemed to be waiting with bated breath for the axe to fall, knowing that the time was coming, and that it was in fact almost here.

I said, "Especially the bishop" because I think that it wasn't only the pedophilia issue that he was dreading having to face. From the very beginning of his career, since the time of his ordination as a priest,

Chapter 30

rumors were always circulating about him among the priests in the diocese. I don't know if these rumors ever reached the ears of the parishioners, but with the bishop being so beloved by them, I doubt that they would have given them much credence. His priests, however, had no such qualms. The rumors were that he liked the women—young women—and that he liked them a lot. As far back as I can remember, there was always talk about him being involved with "young" women and that adjective never changed. Even as he grew older, the involvement was still with "young" women.

I remember attending a meeting years ago at the diocesan office. All of the priests were gathered and waiting for the bishop to arrive and begin the meeting. We were all sitting around and talking, and there was this one priest who at the time was really angry at the bishop over something, I don't know what, and he was very vocal about how he felt. As we were all sitting there, he began making disparaging remarks about the bishop. One of the things that he said in that very public place in front of everyone was that everyone knew that the only time that the bishop had any "balls" was when he was hugging a little girl. Everyone, including the bishop, heard him and he was required to formally apologize to the bishop for his remark—or else. He apologized.

One day I was approached by a couple who asked if they could speak to me about a serious matter. They told me that they were concerned about the relationship between the bishop and their daughter, felt that what was going on between them was inappropriate, and asked me if I would speak to the bishop about it for them. They wanted me to tell the bishop to leave their daughter alone (oh, boy). They also wanted to know if I could also counsel them and their daughter about it in my role as a therapist.

I told them that since they had sought me out and brought this to my attention, I would pass on their concerns to the bishop with their written permission. But professionally, that was all that I could do in this situation. Yes, I was a therapist, but I was also a priest. The bishop was my boss and my superior, and ethically this presented a conflict of interest. Although it couldn't be me, I urged them to find another therapist (a neutral party) to handle the situation from here on in, to which they agreed.

They gave me a written release to present their concerns to the bishop, and I called him and set up a meeting. I remember that it was very late in the afternoon when we met and that it was dark and stormy—an accurate portent of things to come. A huge thunderstorm was raging at the time with blackened skies and non-stop thunder and lightning, pelting hail, and a driving rain that was lashing us up, down, and sideways. I think the reason that I've remembered all of these little details is because the meeting did not go well, as you may be guessing. The skies were about evenly matched with the bishop's rage.

When I got to the diocesan office, the place was dark, and everyone was gone for the day except for the bishop. When I went into his office, he asked me why I was there and what this was about. I started out by saying, "First of all, I would like to ask that you not respond to anything that I tell you. In my role as a therapist, I was released to present this information to you, so I'm going to present it to you. I don't want any kind of comment from you other than to acknowledge that you received it, and then you can do whatever you have to do about it." I then handed him a copy of the written release.

He seemed really surprised and taken aback by my little speech, and looked at me curiously. I have to tell you, I was really, really, nervous. I mean—this was my boss. So I took a deep breath and asked that we take a moment and pray, which we did. I then told him what had happened and that the parents of a young woman (I gave him the woman's name as I had been released to do) had come to me and said that they were concerned about the relationship that he had with her, and that they wanted him to leave her alone.

I then told him that the only other comments I would make were to tell him what action I had taken—that I had told the family that they needed to find another therapist, and that I wanted him to know that they might take legal action. I also advised him to take care of the situation immediately to avoid a public scandal because the public and the media would no longer tolerate these kinds of situations in silence. I gave him some recommendations as to what he should do, thanked him for his time, and started to leave.

Before I could get up from my chair, he said to me, "Oh, how can you think this of your bishop?"

I told him, "Don't respond. I don't want to hear any response. I gave you the information and some recommendations out of courtesy because I am your priest. That's it. I need to leave."

In a heartbeat his demeanor changed from poor, misunderstood bishop to Screaming Mimi. He was enraged, his red, flushed face contorted as he shouted at me, "How can you think this of your bishop! How? That's terrible! I can't believe this, I can't believe what I'm hearing, that you believe this, that you believe what they're saying about their bishop!" (I got the feeling that he thought that I was making it up.)

I told him, "It's not my place to believe you or not believe you—this is your issue, not mine. I simply brought this information to your attention as I was asked to. You need to know that this is out of the church's hands now; it's now in the public forum with secular therapists and possibly lawyers involved who will now be advising these people. So please take care of it, whether it's true or not, or you may end up like that other bishop who was removed from his position and made national headlines. The same thing will happen to you if you don't take care of this issue now."

He shot up from behind his desk, beyond angry, stalked to the back door in his office, flung it open (buckets of rain started pouring in), gave me a flinty look and screamed, "LEAVE! GET OUT! GET OUT! IMMEDIATELY!"

Quite unnerved, I thanked him for his time and skedaddled out the back door. I had to climb down the slippery fire escape in the dark, thunder booming, and the rain coming down so hard that I couldn't see a thing except for brief moments when the skies were lit up by lightning. By the time that I got to my car I was soaking wet from head to toe, but at least I was still in one piece.

Just about a year to the day after that encounter, the bishop resigned. One of the women that he'd had an affair with came forward and made an accusation, and then several more followed suit. It quickly became public knowledge and was splashed across the news throughout the country. The bishop quietly resigned from his position and in absolute secrecy left the state. A few months after he left, the chancellor of the diocese told me that as the bishop was getting on the plane to leave, he turned to the chancellor and yelled, "That Father So-and-So (me), SUSPEND HIM! EXCOMMUNICATE HIM!" Sorry, bishop, but that didn't happen. Canon Law doesn't list "intense personal dislike" as a valid reason for suspension or excommunication.

Meanwhile, back at the facility, I and the other therapists on staff discovered something that took us all by surprise. (Consider the next few paragraphs "Pedophilia 101," the super-condensed version.) Pedophilia has been around for as long as humankind has been around, for as long as people have suffered from mental illness and psychological problems, so it's not something that had suddenly just "popped" up on the scene. The treatment modality we used to treat it was based on pedophilia exhibited by married heterosexual men because clinically that is the group from which the majority of pedophiles presented. However, what we were discovering was that the recommended standard treatment wasn't working for clergy members who were pedophiles—neither the heterosexual nor the homosexual clients.

What we were finding was that the root of the problem stemmed from different places in the psyche of the clergymen as opposed to laymen (non-religious men). The pedophilia that is expressed by heterosexual men is a psycho-sexual development issue stemming from seriously dysfunctional early childhood relationships with their parents. When these men become adults, these problems are always expressed in relationship issues, as out of balance power and control dynamics in their dysfunctional relationships with their girlfriends or wives.

When a man is a pedophile and he cannot balance the power and control in his intimate relationships, he acts out sexually, most often with a daughter or stepdaughter. The relationship that he's in with his girlfriend or wife is already dysfunctional, and then a stressor occurs—perhaps a big fight with his significant other—which ends up with her belittling him or being angry with him and refusing him sex. So he turns to what he sees in his mind as an available substitute for his needs (his daughter), and coerces his child into "standing in" for mommy. As disturbing as that is, he can usually function more or less "normally" in all of the other areas of his life.

I think many of us have read or heard of cases of pedophilia making the news where the initial response on the part of the public was stunned disbelief. This happens oftentimes because the man being accused is a respected member of society, someone prominent in the community with a sterling reputation, and a "church going" family man. (A favorite high school sports coach, for example, or the kindly local judge). People are shocked because they can't believe that someone who seemed so good, so "normal," could do something so heinous.

The treatment for pedophilia that we had at that time was based on that scenario, on that kind of presentation. However, the pedophilia that we were seeing in the clergy did not spring from that scenario. In fact, it had no connection to it whatsoever. We felt that in these cases we weren't seeing classic pedophilia, the one that was "in the books," but something that seemed entirely different.

What we were seeing in the clergy were men who were psychologically "disconnected" at a much more basic level. It was still a psycho-sexual development issue, but it was compounded by dysfunctional development in other very basic psychological areas. I had talked about the psyche as being made up of links in a chain. These men had multiple links that were dysfunctional, especially the men who had entered the seminary at a very young age. The structure of the church took over for all of their psychological growth and development. Although we were treating men who chronologically were in their forties, fifties, and sixties, emotionally they were all at a prepubescent or early pubescent age, close to the age of their victims—almost exactly their same age as a matter of fact.

What we saw were men who were not any more emotionally mature than their victims; something that we didn't see in most cases of classic pedophilia. They couldn't function normally in society, and couldn't function normally in any sense of the word if they were taken out of the church structure. Again, this was something not often seen in classic pedophilia. In classic pedophilia, the actual physical, sexual act with the victim is usually the desired outcome for the perpetrator, while with the clerical pedophile, actual intercourse seemed to be secondary—or even absent—with "exploring" (touching, feeling, fondling, kissing) being the more important activity. And many of these clergymen also exhibited other mental health issues, like schizophrenia, obsessive-compulsive disorders, and manias, unlike their "lay" counterparts.

What I just described is a simple overview of the "typical" pedophile (insofar as such a term exists) in both the religious and secular worlds, but it doesn't address more specific kinds of predators like rapists. The issues that these men have, whether in the clerical or secular world, come from a different, very violent place within the individual, and was something that we rarely saw at our facility.

Since the standard treatment for classic pedophilia didn't work for our clerical clients, we had to develop different techniques for treating these individuals. Pedophilia is normally very difficult to treat and most often the only thing you can do is to make sure that the offender never again has access to children. The client may be truly contrite, and he may vow that he will never again engage in that kind of behavior. When he makes that statement he sincerely means it, but this condition is beyond the realm of any kind of choice. No matter how sincere he is, if he is a pedophile and there is a child around, he will engage in that behavior. There's no way that he could not.

I still get Christmas cards from some of my ex-clients from that facility. These guys are now in their late seventies and eighties—one is even in his nineties—and they still keep in touch with me to let me know that they are doing okay and that they have never reoffended. These are clients who, after treatment, were placed in supervised positions where they would never again have contact with children. Remove the source of temptation, give them a structured environment and ongoing outpatient therapy, and they can lead productive lives and never hurt anyone again.

One of the major problems that I faced in treating these clients came from the church hierarchy, both in this country and abroad. What the guys in charge wanted to do was to get rid of these men, wash their hands of them by laicizing them (stripping them of their religious title, kicking them out of the priesthood, and making them "lay" people again), and throwing them back into society and letting it become society's problem, not the church's. I fought against this tooth and nail and had no trouble confronting bishops, archbishops, and cardinals over this issue. I told them that the church had helped to form these men into what they had become, and now had to take responsibility for what they had done by taking care of them for the rest of their lives. (I could easily imagine some of these guys in administration still wishing it were the

Middle Ages so the only decision they would have to make would be of where to dispose of the bodies!)

Also, I could not accept putting these men out into society without any emotional support, where they would reoffend and continue to victimize. I told everyone in the church hierarchy that I felt that this would be the greater sin.

The church owed these men support, support that would be needed to ensure that their treatment plan worked and would continue working. In therapy, when you're trying to restructure someone's life in a healthy direction, you have to base it on honesty. I remember a cardinal in a different state who sent one of his priests to us for pedophile issues. This cardinal was quite well known and was very powerful—sort of the leader of the pack in the cardinal hierarchy in this country at the time. He didn't ask me to lie to my client (his priest); he ordered me to.

He told me to get the guy through therapy by telling him whatever he needed to hear, to tell him that his cardinal and his diocese would support him through this, and would be behind him all the way. Then the cardinal said that once this priest's therapy was finished, they were going to "kick his ass" out of the priesthood and out of their lives. I told that cardinal no, that he was not going to do that; and no, that I didn't lie to my clients. My clients' therapy had to be based on truth and honesty for it to be effective.

I also told him that I didn't know about him, but I had been taught that lying was a sin, unless I misunderstood what they had taught us in the seminary. Maybe I had slept through that class? Needless to say, after that conversation that cardinal was not a fan of mine because "no" was not a word that he was used to hearing. I didn't care if he liked me or not, all I cared about was that he did what was right for my client. (I was told later that he was so angry with me that he put pressure on my supervisor to have me removed from my position, which didn't happen.)

I was always up front and honest with my clients about their situations. Many of them were facing the ends of their careers, ostracism from the church and society, and lawsuits and legal proceedings that could and would land some of them in jail after their treatment. I even had lawyers regularly come in to give workshops to our clients on matters of justice and legal issues because many of them were so emotionally immature that they had no idea of the real life consequences of their actions. They had to know exactly what they were facing. Whatever they had done, they had to know that they weren't going to be thrown to the wolves, and that we were there to help them and would support them through this. Again, without the church's support, some of these guys might end up on the streets—free to victimize again—and I was not about to let that happen. This was a fact that I had to keep repeating, again and again and again to those in the church hierarchy.

The church didn't want to hear that. Instead of just dumping these guys and saying "good riddance," they would have to pay for their legal proceedings, or retire them and pay them their pensions, or foot the bill for them to spend the rest of their lives in a supervised setting or a psychological chronic care facility. It was costing the church money, which it wasn't happy about, but I felt that morally there was no alternative.

I butted heads on many occasions with church officials over these issues, but I always won the arguments each and every time (even with that cardinal). And believe me, there were a lot of arguments. But I always got each client the support that he needed from the church. This ensured that we were doing our best for each individual—in the present and in the future—because these guys were our responsibility and we needed to take care of them, like it or not.

Oh, and I got another promotion at the facility. The overall facility director decided that he couldn't handle the stress of the job and quit. Before he did so, he recommended me to the board of directors as his replacement. So they asked me if I would also take over that position, to which I said yes. I think that I was now involved in every role in that facility except for the one of being an actual client there! The upside of that was if I ever had a breakdown from my overloaded work schedule, at least I knew of a good treatment facility that I could get into!

So that was my crazy-busy life for several years until life changed irrevocably for all of us. The day of reckoning finally arrived and the dark secrets of this diocese were secret no longer.

Chapter 31

The Real Truth Will Set You Free

I will always remember that the end of life as we knew it in this diocese began over a beautiful weekend in autumn. I woke up to a normal Monday morning, and my waking up was the last normal thing that happened that day. I went to work at the facility, and when I walked in the staff was buzzing about the "news." I asked them what had happened. They told me that it was all over the radio and the television this morning that over the weekend five cases of suspected pedophilia, naming priests in our diocese, were reported to the diocesan office and had also been reported to the media.

I immediately called the chancellor at the diocesan office to see if the facility or I could help in any way. He told me what he thought he should do was to immediately set up a meeting with the accusers and the accused priests and have all of them get together in the same room and "hash it out." Very bad idea. I told him no, that he absolutely could not do that, and that was not the way that these things were handled. Even though pedophilia among the clergy had been in the news for years—and we'd had those few cases ourselves—evidently no one in authority thought that it might have been a good idea to take a look at what was happening and formulate and put into place a contingency plan just in case. And now they were all clueless. Well, that was nothing new.

I told the chancellor that he did need to set up an immediate meeting, but that it should be attended only by him and the bishop, the diocesan lawyers, the director of the religious order that operated the psychological facility (that I directed) along with their lawyers, and the lawyers of the families making the accusations. I asked him if the diocese had a sexual abuse policy in place, to which he said no; no surprise there.

Right then and there I asked the chancellor to grab a pen and paper and write down everything that I told him, and gave him a step-by-step sexual abuse policy—basically off the top of my head. I then told him that he needed to get it to the bishop and the lawyers immediately so that they could look at it, make any necessary changes, and then pull it all together into an official Diocesan Sexual Abuse Policy. I stressed to him that it was imperative to get it officially implemented as quickly as possible (like that day), have it sent to every parish and school in the diocese, and have all diocesan employees read and sign it.

The atmosphere at the facility was charged. No one there could seem to stop talking about what had happened, and neither it seemed could anyone else. It was on the television and in the papers every day for months, and it was the number one topic of conversation among the locals. What I found surprising was that there actually were priests in this diocese who were stunned when the news first broke. Maybe if some of these guys had come out of their rectories a little more often, they wouldn't have been quite so surprised.

I remember that the atmosphere in the diocese seemed to have changed overnight and had become oppressively somber, as if a dark pall had fallen over the priesthood. Many of my fellow priests seemed shamed by what had happened, and responded by altering their behavior towards their parishioners and especially towards children. Instead of engaging in their usual lighthearted conversations with parishioners after Mass, many of them would leave quickly and with mumbled goodbyes as soon as Mass was over. It was obvious that they didn't know what to say to people and didn't want to face them.

Not me. I told my fellow priests that we had to talk about it to our parishioners, that we couldn't hide our heads in the sand and ignore what was going on, and that this time the elephant in the room with us was too big to ignore. I remember telling them that I too was embarrassed and shamed by what had happened, but that I wasn't going to hide in shame because of it. And if I did, I might as well be as guilty as those pedophile priests were. I told them how important it was that we assured people that not all priests were like that, and that we should share with them how we felt about what was going on. It was crucial for us to finally be open and honest with them. Of course, they all looked at me like I was crazy, but by now I was pretty used to that.

At my sermons I not only acknowledged the elephant in the room, I shone the spotlight on it. There had been too much secrecy in the church, and we needed to demystify the experience so that what people saw was reality and not smoke and mirrors. I told my parishioners that priests were human beings just like everyone else, and that they had the same problems and struggles that everyone else did. I also told them that we needed their support during this time just as much, and maybe even more, than they needed ours.

I continued to talk about pedophilia, to bring it out in the open as much as I could. Many of the parishioners were dazed by the situation—confused and fearful—and they didn't need us hiding from them in embarrassment. We had lost their trust, and I felt that we needed to face that fact head on, to "lay our cards on the table," so to speak, and to show them that we weren't hiding anything else from them. The atmosphere was now thick with paranoia on the parts of both the priests and the parishioners, and it was going to last for a long time.

I urged the parishioners to talk to us and to invite us out for coffee or to have dinner together so that we could talk about what was going on. It was important to let them know that the majority of priests they knew didn't have these kinds of problems, and not to ostracize all of us for the sins of a few. I emphasized that we were family, and families supported each other in times of crisis.

I don't know about my fellow priests, but I got dozens of invitations to meet and talk to people. They wanted and needed to know what was happening, why it was happening, what they could do, and what it all meant for us as people and as a church. A lot of times at coffee or dinner they would start out by giving me a hug and telling me that they knew that I wasn't "like that," that they knew that most priests weren't, but nonetheless their faith in us and in the church had been badly shaken.

The church had put its priests and itself on a pedestal. Now that the pedestal had tipped and fallen—and as awful as this whole situation was—I felt that maybe it could be the impetus that the church needed to begin the process of reform. We needed to start that process by talking to people about what was going on, by being open and honest with them, and by letting go of the secrecy.

I remember that at some point a letter was sent to all of the priests in the diocese telling us to be "circumspect" in our dealings with children. Whenever we were with children—in the classroom or the church or at a basketball game—we had to be conscious of our behavior. We were told that we should never be alone with a child. If we needed to speak to any children, there should always be another adult with us, a sister or a parent, but not another priest.

For confession, the doors to the confessional box were to be kept open so that people could see that father was where he was supposed to be. The same rule applied if we were doing face-to-face confessions—the door to the room we were in had to be kept open at all times. The paranoia was so great that they advised us that it might be best if we no longer even touched children in any way so that our actions wouldn't be mistaken for something sinister.

I had said Mass one Sunday at our church and my parents happened to be there. After Mass was over, I was talking to some of the parishioners when two young children, a little boy of about six and his little sister who was about four, came running up to me and were all happy and excited about saying "hello" to father (me). The little boy extended his arms and launched himself up at me, so I scooped him up and held him as he talked to me. I remember him telling me that he wanted to say hello to me because I was a nice priest and that he liked me. His little sister, not to be outdone, grabbed onto my cassock and wrapped her arms around my legs, insisting that I pick her up too. So I scooped her up and talked to them while the children's parents looked on, all smiles at their squirming little bundles in my arms.

Afterwards, my mother came up to me with a scowl on her face. She told me that I shouldn't have picked up those kids. I asked her why not, and she said that if I acted like that, people would wonder about me and think that I was a pedophile.

I rolled my eyes at her and told her that this was how I always acted, and that I wasn't going to change my behavior because my behavior wasn't wrong. I was not going to give in to the paranoia that had everyone in its grip. I wasn't going to stop doing what was good and right because of fear. I was not going to let fear dictate my life, and that if I did, I would be allowing even more damage from the actions of those few who were truly guilty. I also told her that I hadn't dragged the kids off to some dark corner to hug them, that I did it in front of their parents, the parishioners, and God, and that a hug did not a pedophile make.

She walked away from me with a bigger scowl, muttering that I never listened to her anyway so why start now.

Most priests did stop touching children; no more spontaneous hugs, no pats on the back—no touching, period. Some even refused to do confessions for children or even to give them communion at Mass. Many of them just suddenly stopped interacting with kids at all unless it was absolutely necessary. I found that to be really sad that we had let the actions of the guilty stop us from doing what was good by turning it into something suspect.

Around that time I got a call from the corporate director of the group that owned the facility that I ran. He said that he had gotten a call from the media, and that they wanted to interview him about a priest who had undergone treatment at our facility years ago. It was a priest whose name was infamous across the country as being among the first and most notorious pedophile priests to date. He had been convicted and defrocked (kicked out of the priesthood) and was doing time in prison. The media got wind of the fact that a decade earlier he had been sent to our facility for pedophilia issues, had been declared "cured," and sent out into the ministry again.

They obviously wanted to know why the facility had felt that it was safe for him to continue being a priest and having contact with children because after leaving the facility, he continued to perpetrate his crimes on dozens of children. Back when he was at the facility, the state-of-the-

Chapter 31

art treatment for pedophile priests was telling them to keep their pants zipped, to fast, and to pray really, really hard. Since the church didn't believe in psychology and didn't believe that pedophilia was a psychological problem, it only occurred because the priest wasn't sufficiently "devout." The church believed that only God could help him, and that all he needed to do was pray it away.

So the corporate director calls to inform me what's happening, to warn me about it, and to let me know that they were going to try to "nail him to the wall" so he was taking off. He thought that I might want to take off too in case they came looking for me as the facility's current director. He said that he had already called the bishop, who was also taking off.

Well, I thought to myself, it looks like the big boys are running for cover. Okay. I told him that I wasn't going anywhere, and that I would be glad to talk to the media and anyone else about it. I remember him telling me okay, if that's what I wanted to do, I certainly had more "balls" than he did (those were his words), and that he trusted me to talk to them. He didn't give me any other instructions other than to make sure that I didn't tell anybody where he was.

The news people (every one of the big national stations) let me know when they were arriving, and I let the staff know about it and set up one of the facility's meeting rooms for the interview. When they arrived, I had coffee and tea set up along with doughnuts and cookies for everybody, which they were all munching on as they set up their cameras and equipment.

With lights on and cameras ready, they shoved the microphone in front of my face.

They started out by asking me, "So what do you have to say about father who spent time in your facility for pedophilia, and has now been charged with all of these crimes because he continued to perpetrate?"

I answered by telling them that it was really sad that this happened, but at the time that father so-and-so had attended our facility—along with the other similar facilities across the US that he had attended—we didn't have the information about treating pedophilia that we now had. Back when father so-and-so was here, there really was no treatment on the books other than abstinence, and that simply putting the priest back in ministry with the order to abstain obviously didn't work, which we knew now but didn't know back then. I told them that our program, just like every other program available at the time that father so-and-so attended, was based on a twelve step/abstinence treatment model, which was state-of-the-art for its time, but which we now realized doesn't work with a severe psychological issue like pedophilia.

They turned off the cameras and said that they didn't want to hear about that. I told them okay, and to ask me any other questions they wanted. They turned the cameras back on.

They asked, "Why was the church complicit in this?"

So I went on to explain that the church, like every other institution in the sixties—such as the police and the judicial system and even the media—all followed the same protocol when it came to handling any authority figure in the community who was caught in a pedophile situation. It was handled quietly and in-house whether it was a minister, rabbi or priest, or a police chief, judge, or any other elected official. And it was kept quiet by the media, so the media was as complicit as everyone else in perpetrating this societal problem.

They turned off the cameras again and said that they didn't want to talk about that either. I said okay, and told them to ask me another question. They turned the cameras back on.

They asked, "Don't you think that the church should pay for its sins?"

I said, "Yes, the church should pay for its sins just like your news organizations should pay for theirs in being complicit in the same way back then. And at times the media also perpetrates information that is not true so that the story can sound more titillating and your ratings can shoot up."

I went on saying, "Let me tell you the truth about pedophilia, about why it happens, and about how institutions today are really struggling to catch up on . . . ." But at that point, they shut the cameras off again and told me that they didn't want to talk to me anymore.

I said, "It seems to me that you don't want to talk to me anymore because I'm not telling you what you want to hear. You don't want to hear that the responsibility that the church bears in this situation should be borne by all of society's institutions—including your own—and I think that by ignoring this, you are doing a real disservice to the public."

They packed up their equipment and left. I guess I wasn't "titillating" enough.

They didn't air any of the interview. What was on the news that night was a shot of the facility and of me getting into my car after work with the sound bite saying, "Father so-and-so spent time in this facility and was allowed to go free." That was aired on every major news network.

The next day I got another call from the corporate director of the facility telling me that he had seen me on the television, and was wanting to know what I told them because they had suddenly quit calling him.

I told him that I just tried to tell them the truth but they didn't want to hear it. He said, "God, I don't know how you do it. I couldn't have

Chapter 31

done it; I would've frozen on camera and made a fool of myself." I told him that it was just a matter of telling the truth and that when you did that, it wouldn't go wrong. His reply was, "Well, thanks, you saved our ass again."

So that was my fifteen minutes of fame, only no one ever got to see it.

Chapter 32

I'm Free

Divine Messenger

There was no one thing that I could point to and say 'that's the reason that I left the priesthood.' Rather, it was the culmination of a lot of the things that had happened and also of the things that hadn't happened.

I had started out on my journey as a very idealistic, very young man. I was a lot older now. Had I lost my idealism? No, but maybe it had gotten tempered just a little bit. I would always be a child of the seventies, with a spark of that "hippie" still in my soul.

I believed then and still believe today that one person can make a difference. We see it happening in today's world—sometimes on a small scale and sometimes on a big one—but it does happen. But it wasn't meant to be for me; not at that time or in that place. I honestly believed right up until the very end that I could make a difference in the church. You might laugh at this or consider me a delusional megalomaniac, but I even believed that I could bring the institution of the church to the Divine Presence in a way that it simply did not seem to be, at least to me.

I thought of Mother Teresa and about how she was just one woman, one sister, who went to the poor, dirty streets in the slums of Calcutta and started her ministry by helping the sick and the dying—one person at a time. Her actions grew into a movement that was now helping thousands of people all around the world. She was my inspiration, that perhaps I could start out in one small diocese and start a trickle of reform that would turn into a river of change. But I knew now that it wasn't going to happen.

Once those accusations of pedophilia were made in our diocese, life became very different for all of us in the priesthood. It seemed as if the blind trust and faith that people had in us were gone. I found that to be a good thing, although I'm sure that I was the only priest in the diocese who did. For me, that meant that people could now see us as we really were—as people just like themselves who were struggling to live our lives in connection to the Divine Presence with the same joys and sorrows as everyone else; no better, no worse, and certainly no holier, than anyone else.

This was our chance to demystify the experience of "priest." This was our opportunity to show the reality of the person underneath the myth so that people would have the information they needed to form real, balanced, and healthy relationships with us. I thought that maybe now we could rebuild our relationships with our parishioners with openness and honesty, and get another chance to do it right.

But, of course, that didn't happen. The Roman Catholic Church learning from its mistakes? Mother Church growing in a positive, healthier direction? Sadly, not in my lifetime. It was just more of the same old (albeit with a more cautious atmosphere), less trusting parishioners, and thankfully, with fewer impaired priests around.

I thought of the bishop who could have confronted the issue of pedophilia back when I first brought my suspicions to him, although I probably wasn't the first of his priests to approach him about it. To acknowledge that some of his priests had sexual problems with boys and young men would have meant that he would have had to acknowledge that he was doing the same thing with girls and young women. Psychologically, he couldn't do that because his psyche wouldn't have been able to handle it. Because he couldn't face his own issues, he chose—either consciously or unconsciously—not to deal with the pedophilia issues. So it was ignored until we ended up with more lives ruined—including his own.

I see my poor relationship with the bishop as one of the failures of my life. I took some pride in knowing that I had a gift, that I could ignite that spark for people, and that I could help them to connect to God. But if I was so good at it, why hadn't I been able to help the bishop? Why couldn't I have been the one to show him that there was a better way, maybe have made a difference in his life and a difference in the way that things eventually turned out? I seemed able to help everyone else, but not him. Never him. That's a question that still bothers me today. Although I have recently arrived to an answer for that, it's a topic for another time.

I got to the point where I was physically spent with all of the work I was doing. Still "doing" rather than "being"—God, I still needed to work on that, but I was beginning to think it might be hopeless! I believed that I was doing a lot of good things. But no matter what I did, the church wasn't changing and I was just getting tired. I was pretty much on my own, just doing my own thing, as the majority of my fellow priests ignored me. They would all get together and have dinner or go to the movies or go on little jaunts and trips, but I was never invited. The priests who were around my age didn't want to hang out with the guy that the bishop hated, and didn't want an association with me to "tarnish" them in the bishop's eyes and possibly impede their climb up that ladder of success.

I remember a funeral that I had attended around that time for a local politician. At the reception in the parish hall afterwards, I saw a priest that I knew. He was a local guy who was a few years older than me whom I had known almost my entire life. I hadn't seen him in quite a while and wanted to say hello to him before I left. I noticed that he was heading towards the front door, so, being closer to the side door, I went out that way to catch up with him. When I found him, he was standing next to this long row of rosebushes with his back to me. I called his name and when he turned and saw me, he took off—right through the rosebushes. That was not an easy thing to do because those bushes were huge, thick and dense, and in full flower with lots of thorns.

I called his name again saying that I just wanted to say hello, but he didn't acknowledge me and just kept tearing through those bushes trying to get away. You could see his vestments catching on the thorns and ripping, but he didn't stop. It was kind of funny, but mostly it was kind of sad.

At least the older priests still talked to me. Either they were secure enough in their positions or they didn't care what the bishop thought. But for the most part, I was still the round peg trying to fit into all of the skewed holes of the church. It was time for me to acknowledge that I wasn't really a part of this institution and never would be, and that it was beyond time to make some changes in my life.

I think it finally came to a head for me when I started having health issues. Whenever I was saying Mass and was at the point of consecrating the bread and the wine, without fail I would start having heart palpitations and feeling weak. (It was probably a sign from above saying hey, buddy, I tried to tell you a long time ago that this wasn't going to work.) I felt like I couldn't catch my breath, like I was gasping for air, and my voice would get all weak and wobbly as darkness enfolded me and made me feel faint.

The parishioners probably thought that I was just really "getting into it," going into "ecstasy." There was this one priest in the diocese who would occasionally do that at Mass. He'd just suddenly stop in the middle of Mass with his arms outspread and his entire body would go rigid. He'd stand there with this silly grin on his face, and the parishioners would whisper, "Oh, look at Father! He's gone into 'ecstasy'," meaning that he was so caught up in the spirituality of the moment that he was "touched by God," that God had transported him momentarily to a heavenly state. In reality, the guy was actually suffering from catatonic schizophrenia—but since the church doesn't believe in psychology, let's just call it "ecstasy." There were occasions when he didn't snap out of his catatonic state and a few of the parishioners would have to carry him off the altar, rigid arms and all.

Anyway, my health issues on top of everything else finally made me stop and reassess my life. I was never going to fit in with the rest of these guys, which I think I unconsciously realized during that first week I was at the seminary. But I had wanted to give it a try, and I believe that I gave it my best shot—twenty-one years of my life.

I made an appointment to meet with the bishop. As I sat down with him, I told him that I was going on a leave of absence (which in church circles means that everyone knows that what you really mean is that you're leaving the priesthood, but you have to follow the protocol). I told him that I had come to the realization that I was not like the other priests, and that I was just too different. And although I had tried, I just could not be like the rest of them. I didn't fit into the priesthood and it was time to acknowledge that fact.

He gave me a big smile and said, "Oh, I'm so glad! *So* glad!" He was practically levitating with joy! I looked at him with this blank stare thinking, why is he so freakin' happy? He said, "I'm just so glad and so happy that you've come to this decision!" Well, okay. I don't know exactly what I was expecting, I mean I didn't think there would be a choir of angels breaking into sobs at my news, but I thought that maybe he would say that he was at least a little sorry to see me go or something. Listening to him babble on in delight about my leaving was just another validation that I was doing the right thing. I obviously had made his day (had probably made his whole ministry), and I figured that he was just waiting for me to leave so that he could jump for joy and maybe do a few cartwheels.

Chapter 32

We talked about a few practical matters like my insurance coverage and benefits for the year that I would be on leave. All I had to do now was to write an official letter stating that I would be going on leave. I wrote the letter and in it I bared my soul in honesty. I said that I could no longer act as a priest on behalf of this sinful institution, that I could no longer represent people to God through this sinful institution, nor could I represent God to people through this sinful institution. (And I actually said those very same words out loud to the bishop at our meeting, which didn't seem to faze him or do a thing to temper his joy.) I don't know if anyone at the diocesan office ever actually bothered to read it, but it was cathartic for me to write it down and I assume it's still there somewhere in my personnel file.

That was the last time I saw the bishop. When he was later interviewed by the media about the pedophilia cases in our diocese, he said at first that he hadn't known what was going on (yeah, right). Then he said that he didn't know that it was a criminal matter to have sex with children (uh-huh). But he did know that you could be excommunicated for slapping a priest. Only priests could slap each other silly without being excommunicated. There are rules, you know.

While I was on leave, the bishop's sexual scandal broke and he resigned and fled the state.

So I spent the next month saying goodbye to my parishioners, which wasn't as difficult to do as I had thought it would be. Surprisingly, they all seemed pretty matter of fact about it. They told me that they loved my preaching, and that I had made a real difference in their lives. They said they would miss me a lot, and that I was like "family" to them. But it was obvious to everyone that I didn't fit into the priesthood, so I think that my leaving might have been a bigger surprise to me than it was to them.

Many of them said that they considered me to be "one of them," one of the people, and not "one of those guys," meaning the other priests. And that is probably why most of them called me by my first name, and not "Father." That would really tick off some of my fellow priests who would insist that when parishioners didn't call you "Father," they lost respect for you. I don't think that many of my fellow priests understood what real respect was about—that it was something that a person garnered from their inside, from their "being," and not from a title that someone else gave them.

There was one thing that some of the parishioners told me that did surprise me. It was a comment that I heard mainly from the older women in the parish, the grandmas and great-grandmas (women are very wise). They asked me why it had taken me so long to leave! They said that it was obvious to them from the get-go that I didn't belong in the priesthood. They said that I was a "good" priest because I listened to them, that I was friends with them, and again that I was family to them. But that I was just too different from the other priests, and that it was so obvious that I didn't fit in with the others.

I found that remark to be rather telling—since I was a "good" priest I didn't fit in with the others? What a sad commentary on the priesthood. They went on to say that they never before had a priest like me, and that they were pretty sure that they never would again; I was one of a kind. They said, "We hate to see you go, but we understand."

They had let me share intimately in their lives, had given me their friendship, their love, and memories that I would cherish for the rest of my life.

I officially went on my one year leave of absence. There was so much going on in the diocese at the time with the pedophile priests' cases, new cases surfacing, and then the bishop's scandal—that my leaving barely caused a ripple in the pond. I still continued doing all of the other work that I had been involved in—my private practice, the facility, the court system, the community college and more; just no more parish work.

After my leave of absence was over, I formally left the Catholic priesthood behind. I remember that I was invited to a local bar with some of my friends. At a minute after midnight when my year's leave was officially over, I raised my glass of rum and Diet Coke in a toast and said, "That's it, I'm officially out!" It was kind of anticlimactic, but the rum was good! It remains one of my more memorable New Year's Eves.

Over the years I've been contacted by the diocese a few times asking if I wanted to be "laicized," to be officially and canonically stripped of the title of "priest" and become a "lay" person again. Each time I said no. "Being" a priest is not the same as "functioning" as a priest. I *am* a priest whether I function as one in the church or not. Canon Law itself says that the mark of priesthood is indelible, and that once a man is ordained a priest he will be a priest forever. I am still a priest, I still try to be representative of the Divine Presence, but I no longer do it as a member of the Roman Catholic Church; only on behalf of God and the people.

A year or so after I left, I ran into the chancellor of the diocese at a restaurant. We said hello and stopped to talk. He asked me the usual things like how are you doing, what have you been up to—those kinds of things. I remember that before we parted, he put his hand on my shoulder, laughed, and called me by my childhood nickname and said, "I hope you never decide to write a book about all of this. With everything you know about us, we could be in a lot of trouble!"

But he was wrong about that. They were already in trouble long before I arrived on the scene. I believe that they will continue to be, long after I'm gone, until the church breaks the constrictive, man-made shackles that hold it inert and decides to embrace growth, as every living

Chapter 32

thing must grow to survive. I could be wrong, but that's my opinion—for whatever it's worth.

Chapter 33

"Bless Me Father, For They Have Sinned"

Since leaving the church those years ago over all that I lived through, I am reminded of the admonition of Jesus wherein He said, "It would be better for you that a large millstone be tied around your neck and you be cast into the sea and drown, rather than you lead one of these my little ones astray." Matthew 18:6.

And like Jesus, with my head hung low and so sadly, I find myself so sincerely praying for the little ones like myself (albeit without the same youthful urgency and enthusiasm in expecting a response from the church), "Bless me Father for they have sinned. Bless me Father, for they have sinned.

But there's more to that prayer: What then wells up inside of me is a deep gratitude and joy for the answer to that once-desperate prayer of mine when the Heavens seemed to say: "I don't need you to *do* anything for me. I need you to *be* Someone for me." As we live in His resurrection by sharing our daily lives with one another, Catholic and non-Catholic alike, our deep connection to the Divine Presence is always: "*Be* Someone for me." And that is the blessing.

Acknowledgments

It all began when Sandy Milsen came to me and asked if I would be willing to teach her, one on one, all about the Bible. As time went on she would say I had great anecdotes and stories that illustrated and expanded for her the meaning contained in the books of Holy Scripture. The material mushroomed and she said I should write a book. And she repeated and repeated that until it became a mantra.

After much cajoling, she said she would help me and now we have a book! It is to her that I owe a debt of thanks for her tireless undertaking in uncovering the many layers of material that she says comes out all at once when I open my mouth to speak and invariably gives her a headache!

My thanks also to Matt Ryan for offering his computer skills and invaluable advice in birthing this project.

A heartfelt thanks to Ondrea Levine who encouraged us and shared her expertise during the writing and then introduced us to Sacred Life Publishers, and Sharon Lund.

Sharon's constant inspirational message and wise direction has been the key to bring forth the heart for all to see in shaping this work into its present form. Our gratitude to her is immeasurable.

And to Mary and Elaine whose deft skills in editing this work has helped in making my story understandable and readable for Catholics and non-Catholics alike, along with Miko whose artistic eye made this book aesthetically pleasing.

A special heartfelt Thank You, to those who took the time to read my manuscript and offer your endorsements. Your kind and thoughtful words have given me support and encouragement in sharing my journey with all.

A special Thank You to my canine companions over the years whose loyalty and unconditional love I have always been able to rely on, especially in my darkest moments.

And finally, to those in my life who have acted as my mentors, whether they knew it or not, teaching me how to be open, how to be honest, how to Love from my heart, how to laugh, and how to recognize and approach the Divine by taking the risk to live life to the fullest.

Thank you!

About the Author

Father Paul Roberts is a man of diversity: minister, psychotherapist, educator, pilot, bicyclist, artist, actor, singer, stargazer, and avid animal lover. He spends his time with his faithful canine companion—experiencing, interacting with and reflecting upon the wonders of creation.

He makes his home in the picturesque and enchanting foothills of the mountains with his Princess of nine years, writing of their fascinating adventures together. Grateful for the opportunity.

www.ingramcontent.com/pod-product-compliance
Lightning Source LLC
Chambersburg PA
CBHW050611300426
44112CB00012B/1459